YOUR FAVORITE... CRAB CAKES!

YOUR FAVORITE... CRAB CAKES!

A **CRANKSHAFT** COLLECTION • BY TOM BATIUK & CHUCK AYERS

Andrews McMeel
Publishing

Kansas City

Crankshaft is distributed internationally by Universal Press Syndicate.

Your Favorite...Crab Cakes! copyright © 2002 by Media Graphics, Inc. All rights reserved. Printed in the United States of America. No part of this book may be used or reproduced in any manner whatsoever without written permission except in the case of reprints in the context of reviews. For information, write Andrews McMeel Publishing, an Andrews McMeel Universal company, 4520 Main Street, Kansas City, Missouri 64111.

02 03 04 05 06 BAH 10 9 8 7 6 5 4 3 2 1

ISBN: 0-7407-2666-8

Library of Congress Catalog Control Number: 2002103771

www.uComics.com

To our families, for their support and inspiration.

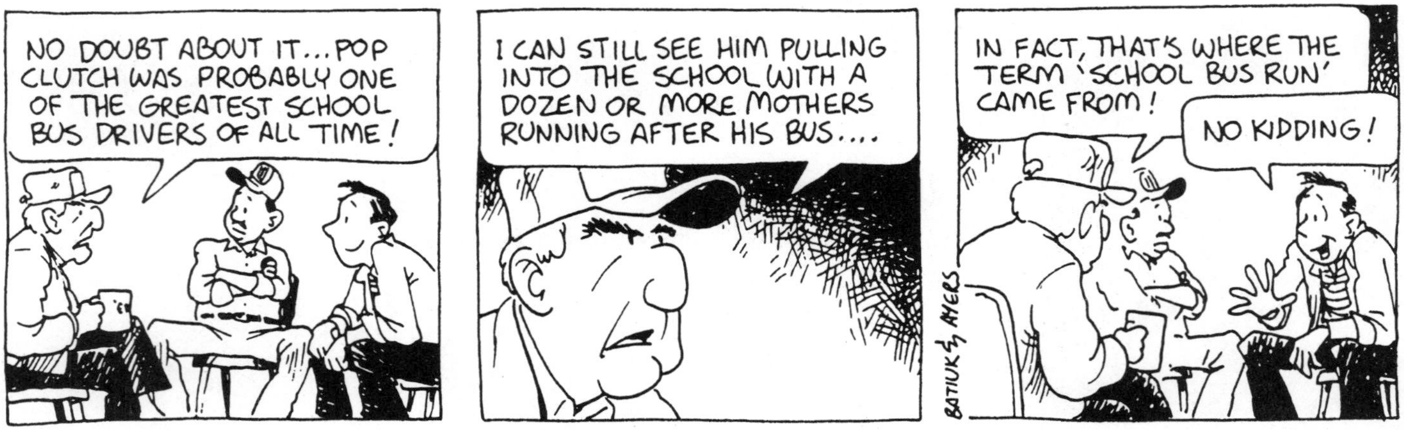
NO DOUBT ABOUT IT... POP CLUTCH WAS PROBABLY ONE OF THE GREATEST SCHOOL BUS DRIVERS OF ALL TIME!
I CAN STILL SEE HIM PULLING INTO THE SCHOOL WITH A DOZEN OR MORE MOTHERS RUNNING AFTER HIS BUS....
IN FACT, THAT'S WHERE THE TERM 'SCHOOL BUS RUN' CAME FROM!
NO KIDDING!
BATIUK & AYERS

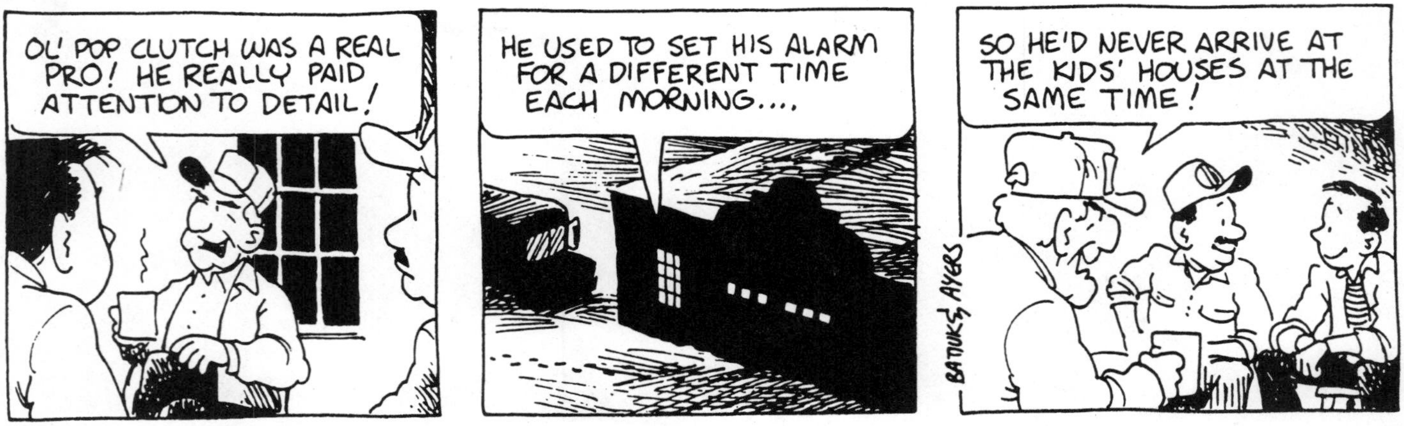
OL' POP CLUTCH WAS A REAL PRO! HE REALLY PAID ATTENTION TO DETAIL!
HE USED TO SET HIS ALARM FOR A DIFFERENT TIME EACH MORNING....
SO HE'D NEVER ARRIVE AT THE KIDS' HOUSES AT THE SAME TIME!
BATIUK & AYERS

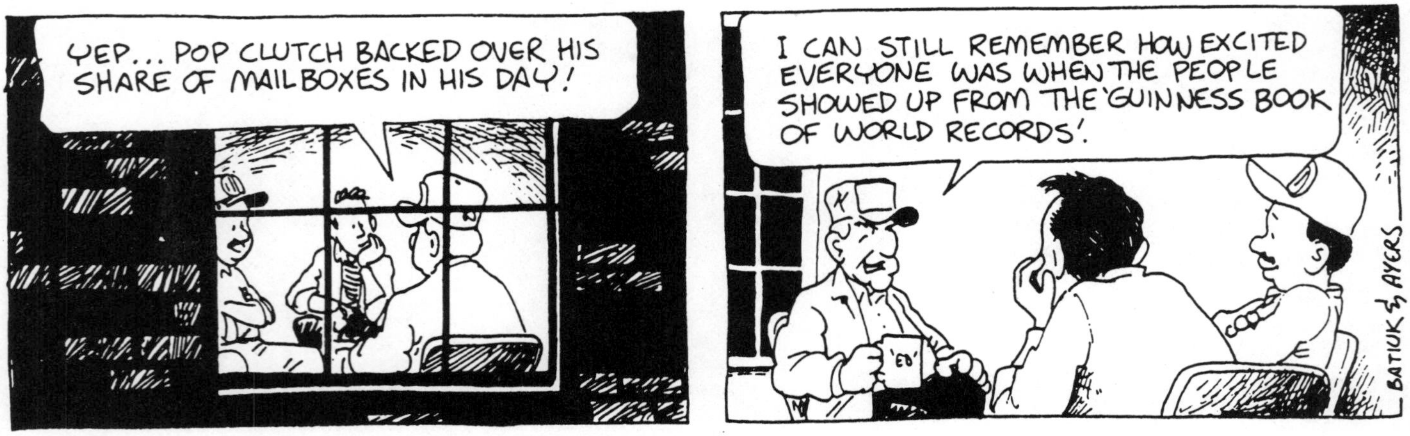
YEP... POP CLUTCH BACKED OVER HIS SHARE OF MAILBOXES IN HIS DAY!
I CAN STILL REMEMBER HOW EXCITED EVERYONE WAS WHEN THE PEOPLE SHOWED UP FROM THE 'GUINNESS BOOK OF WORLD RECORDS'.
'ED'
BATIUK & AYERS

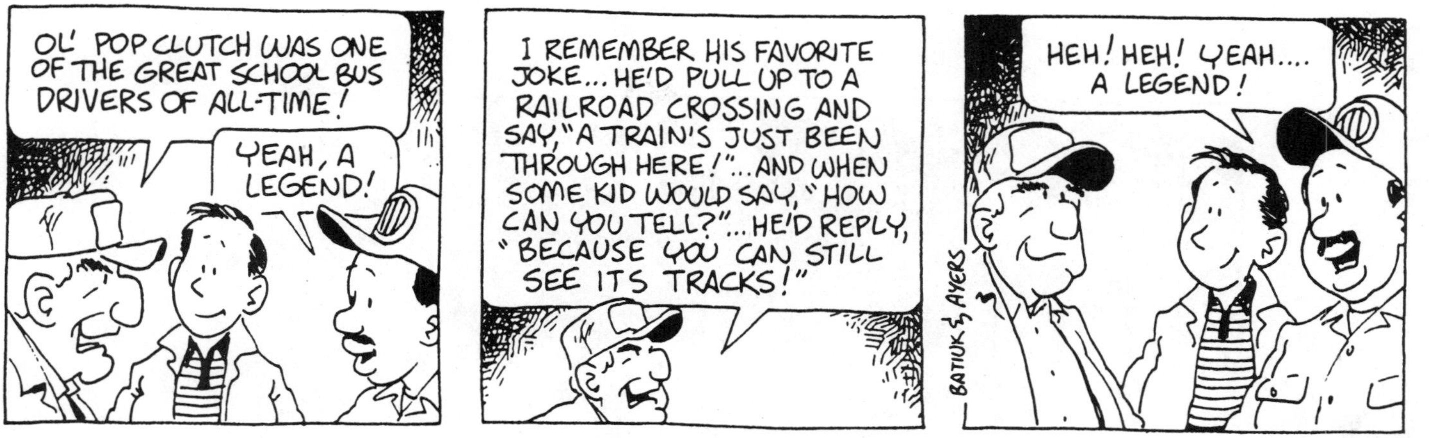
OL' POP CLUTCH WAS ONE OF THE GREAT SCHOOL BUS DRIVERS OF ALL-TIME!
YEAH, A LEGEND!
I REMEMBER HIS FAVORITE JOKE... HE'D PULL UP TO A RAILROAD CROSSING AND SAY, "A TRAIN'S JUST BEEN THROUGH HERE!"... AND WHEN SOME KID WOULD SAY, "HOW CAN YOU TELL?"... HE'D REPLY, "BECAUSE YOU CAN STILL SEE ITS TRACKS!"
BATIUK & AYERS
HEH! HEH! YEAH.... A LEGEND!

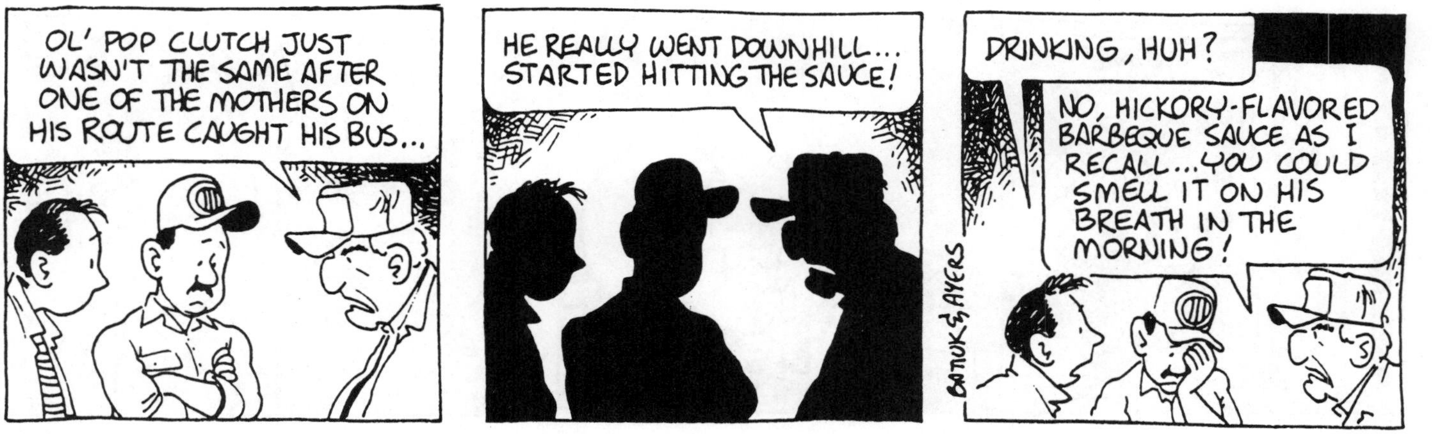
OL' POP CLUTCH JUST WASN'T THE SAME AFTER ONE OF THE MOTHERS ON HIS ROUTE CAUGHT HIS BUS...
HE REALLY WENT DOWNHILL... STARTED HITTING THE SAUCE!
BATIUK & AYERS
DRINKING, HUH?
NO, HICKORY-FLAVORED BARBEQUE SAUCE AS I RECALL... YOU COULD SMELL IT ON HIS BREATH IN THE MORNING!

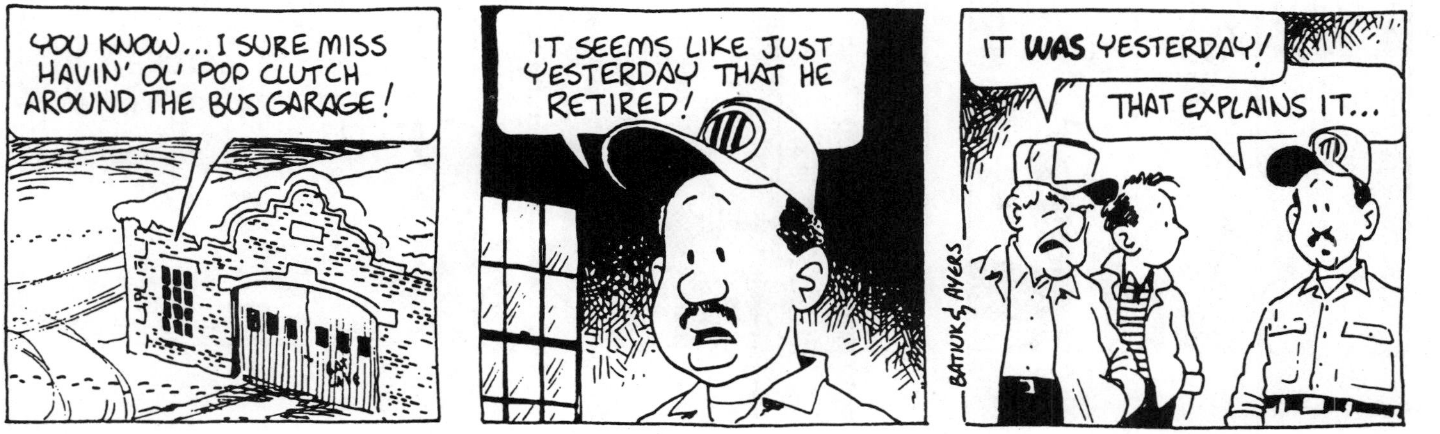
YOU KNOW... I SURE MISS HAVIN' OL' POP CLUTCH AROUND THE BUS GARAGE!
IT SEEMS LIKE JUST YESTERDAY THAT HE RETIRED!
BATIUK & AYERS
IT WAS YESTERDAY!
THAT EXPLAINS IT...

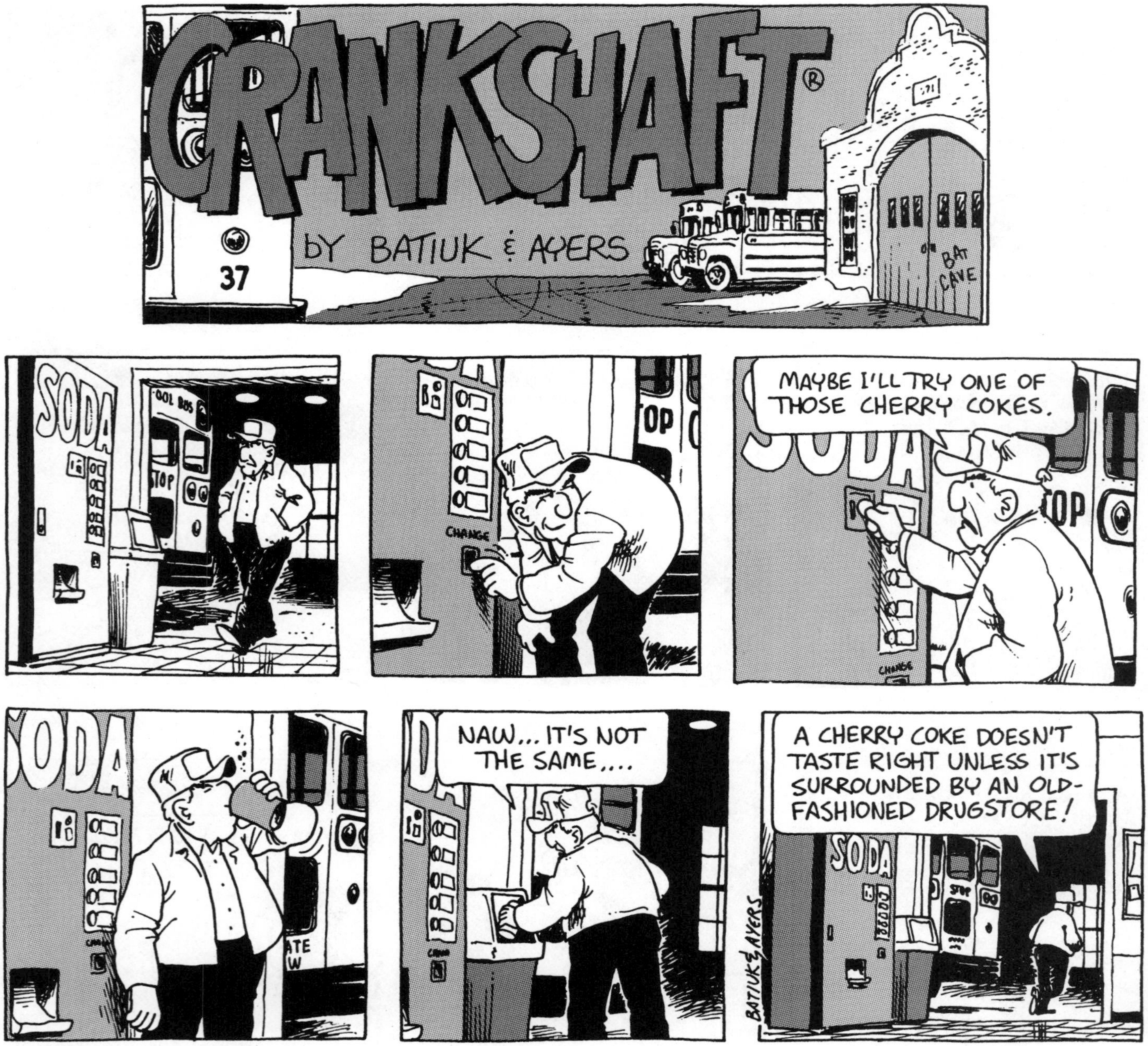
CRANKSHAFT®
BY BATIUK & AYERS
37
MAYBE I'LL TRY ONE OF THOSE CHERRY COKES.
NAW... IT'S NOT THE SAME....
A CHERRY COKE DOESN'T TASTE RIGHT UNLESS IT'S SURROUNDED BY AN OLD-FASHIONED DRUGSTORE!
BATIUK & AYERS

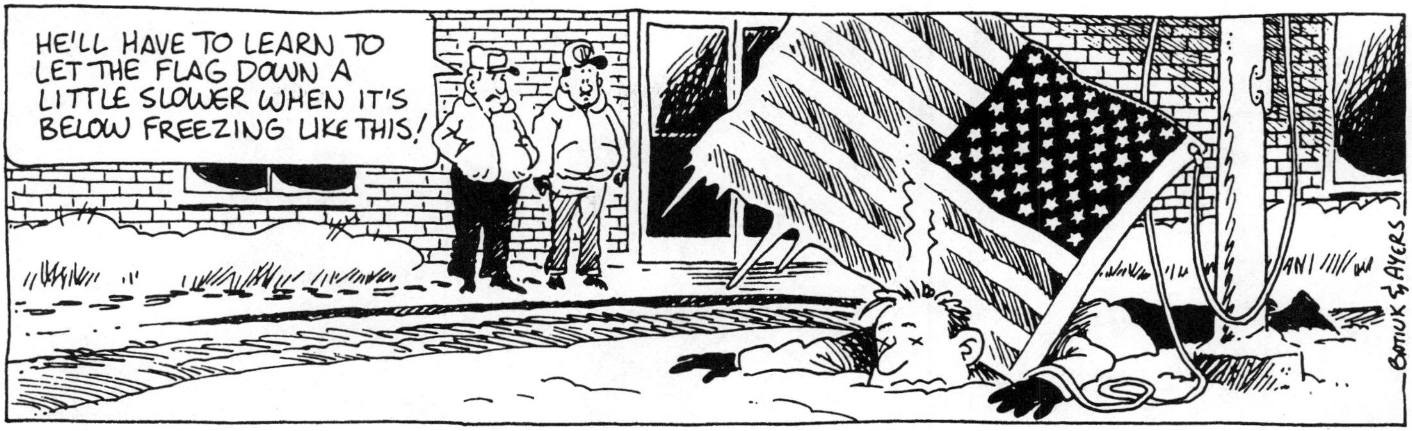
HE'LL HAVE TO LEARN TO LET THE FLAG DOWN A LITTLE SLOWER WHEN IT'S BELOW FREEZING LIKE THIS!
BATIUK & AYERS

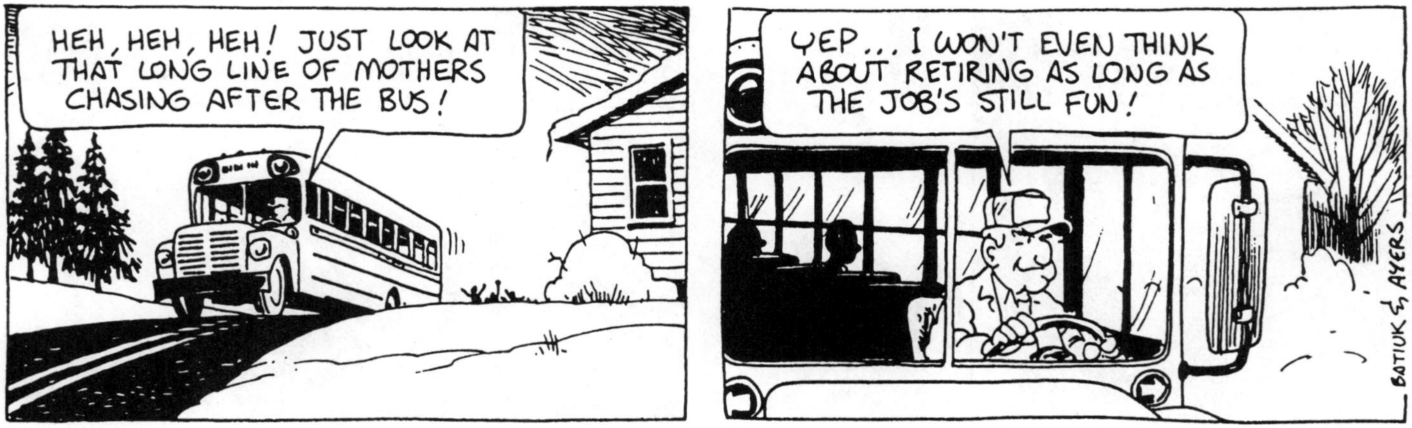
HEH, HEH, HEH! JUST LOOK AT THAT LONG LINE OF MOTHERS CHASING AFTER THE BUS!
YEP... I WON'T EVEN THINK ABOUT RETIRING AS LONG AS THE JOB'S STILL FUN!
BATIUK & AYERS

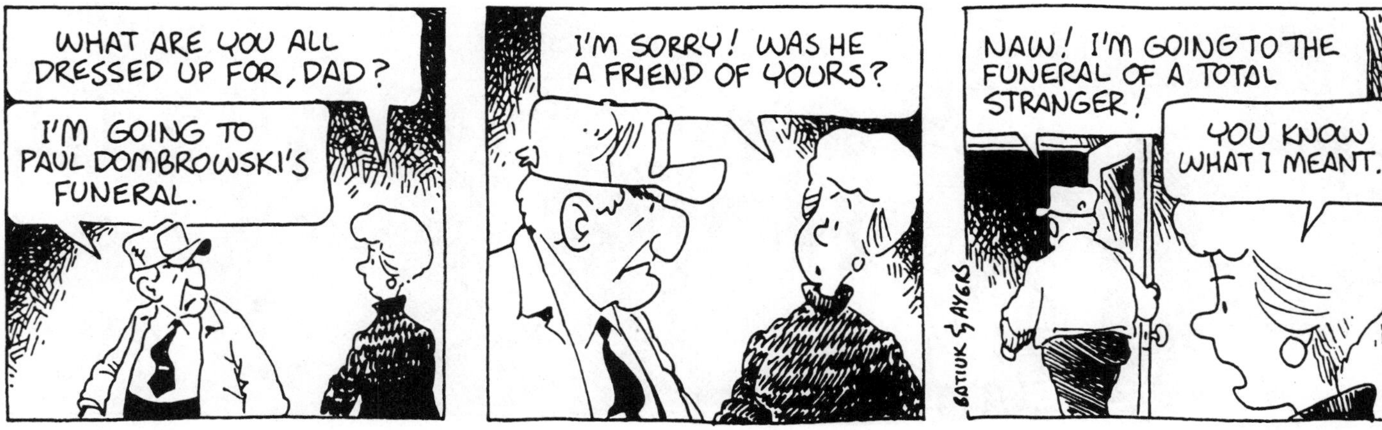
WHAT ARE YOU ALL DRESSED UP FOR, DAD?
I'M GOING TO PAUL DOMBROWSKI'S FUNERAL.
I'M SORRY! WAS HE A FRIEND OF YOURS?
BATIUK & AYERS
NAW! I'M GOING TO THE FUNERAL OF A TOTAL STRANGER!
YOU KNOW WHAT I MEANT...

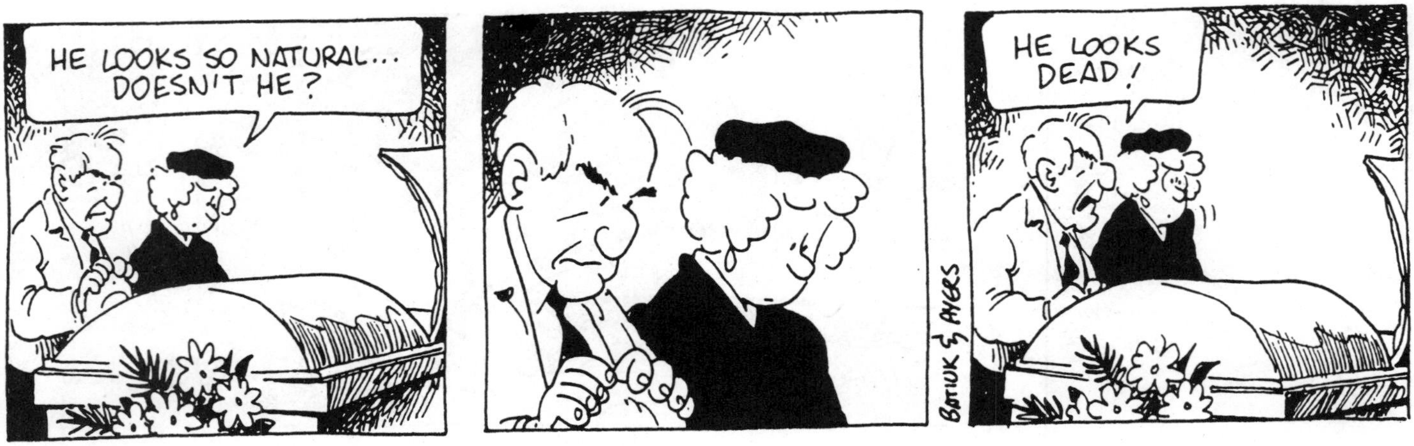
HE LOOKS SO NATURAL... DOESN'T HE?
HE LOOKS DEAD!
BATIUK & AYERS

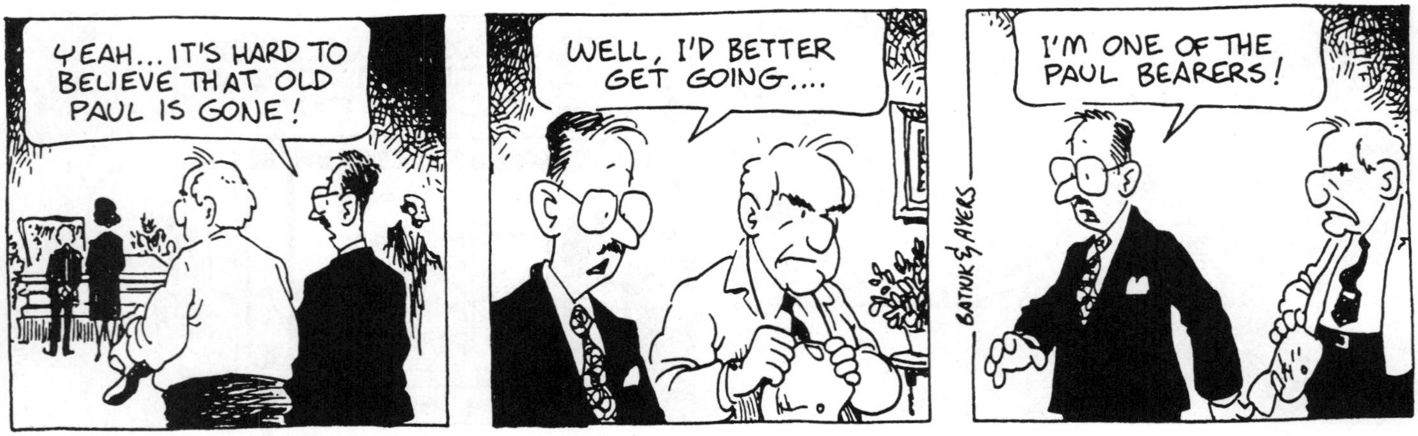
YEAH... IT'S HARD TO BELIEVE THAT OLD PAUL IS GONE!
WELL, I'D BETTER GET GOING....
BATIUK & AYERS
I'M ONE OF THE PAUL BEARERS!

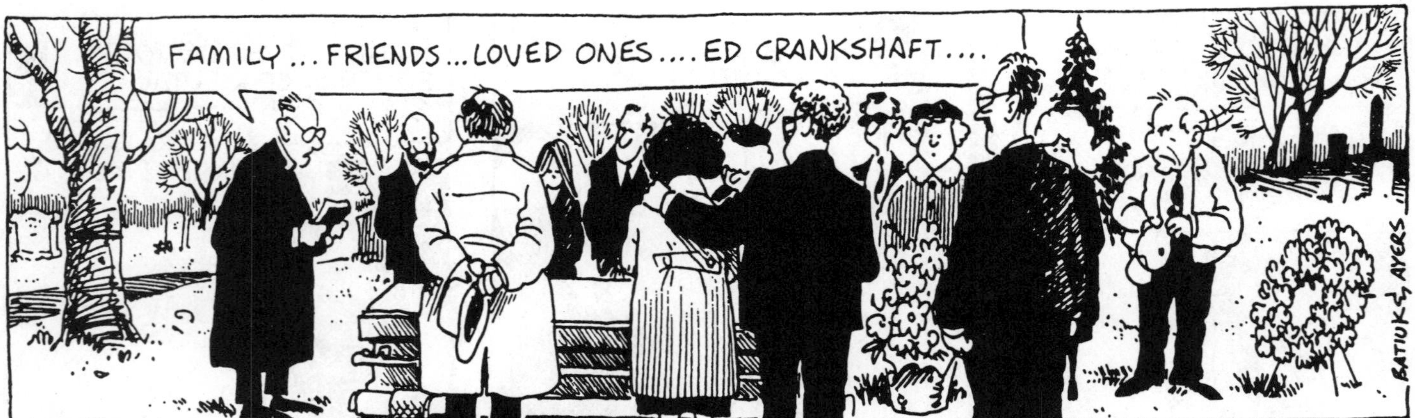
FAMILY ... FRIENDS ... LOVED ONES .... ED CRANKSHAFT ....
BATIUK & AYERS

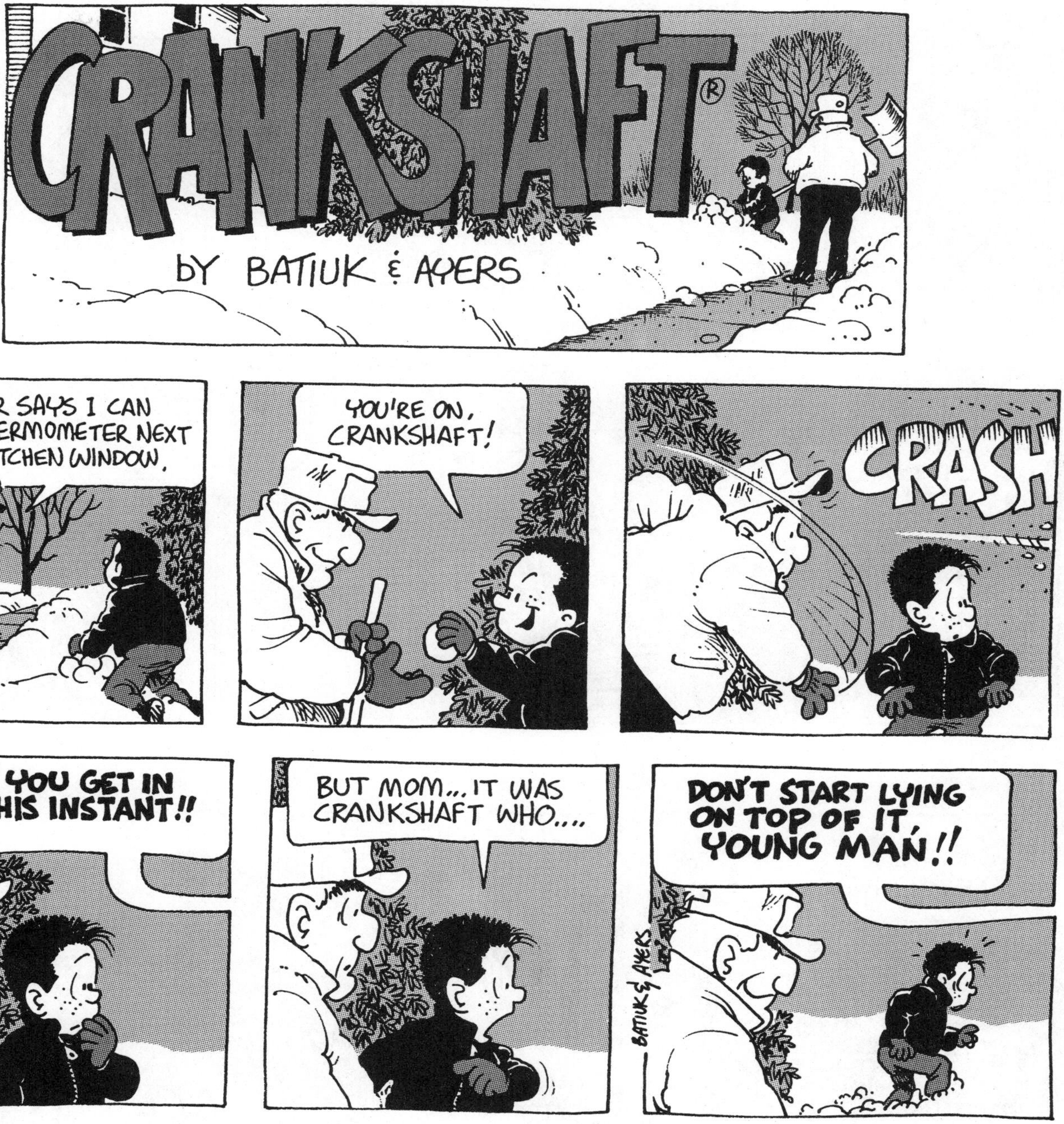
CRANKSHAFT®
by BATIUK & AYERS
A QUARTER SAYS I CAN HIT THE THERMOMETER NEXT TO YOUR KITCHEN WINDOW.
YOU'RE ON, CRANKSHAFT!
CRASH
OZZIE! YOU GET IN HERE THIS INSTANT!!
BUT MOM... IT WAS CRANKSHAFT WHO....
DON'T START LYING ON TOP OF IT, YOUNG MAN!!
BATIUK & AYERS

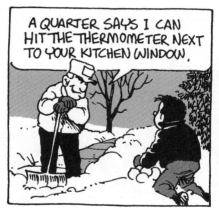

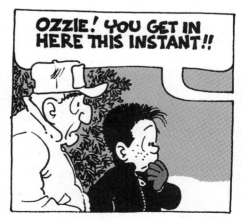

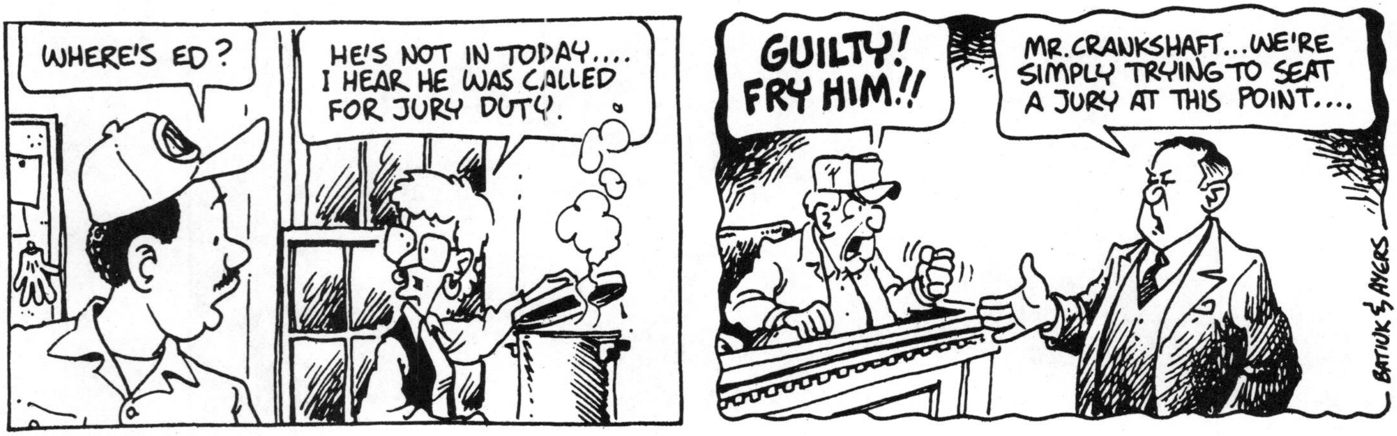
WHERE'S ED?
HE'S NOT IN TODAY.... I HEAR HE WAS CALLED FOR JURY DUTY.
GUILTY! FRY HIM!!
MR. CRANKSHAFT...WE'RE SIMPLY TRYING TO SEAT A JURY AT THIS POINT....
BATIUK & AYERS

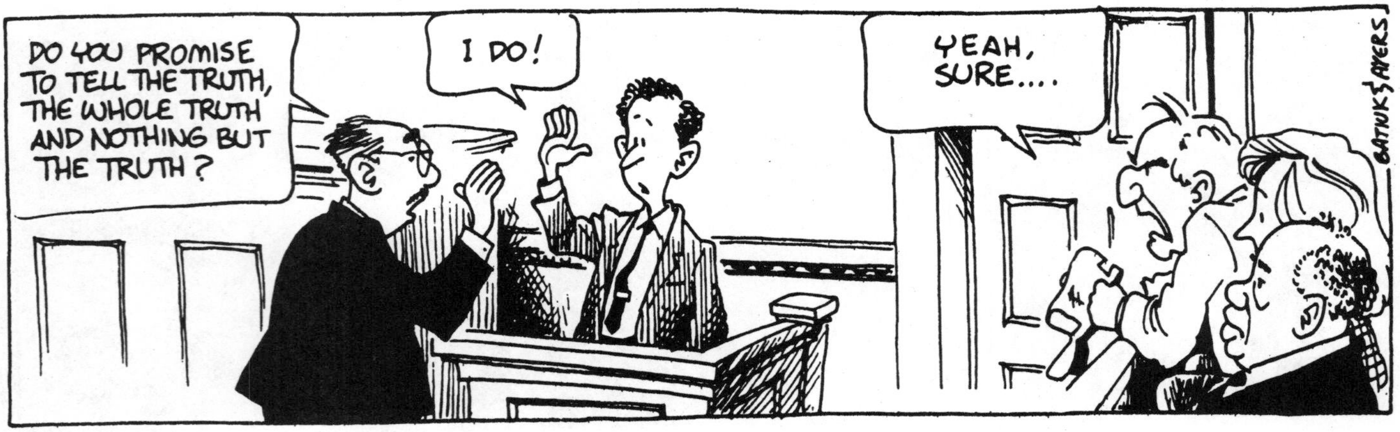
DO YOU PROMISE TO TELL THE TRUTH, THE WHOLE TRUTH AND NOTHING BUT THE TRUTH?
I DO!
YEAH, SURE....
BATIUK & AYERS

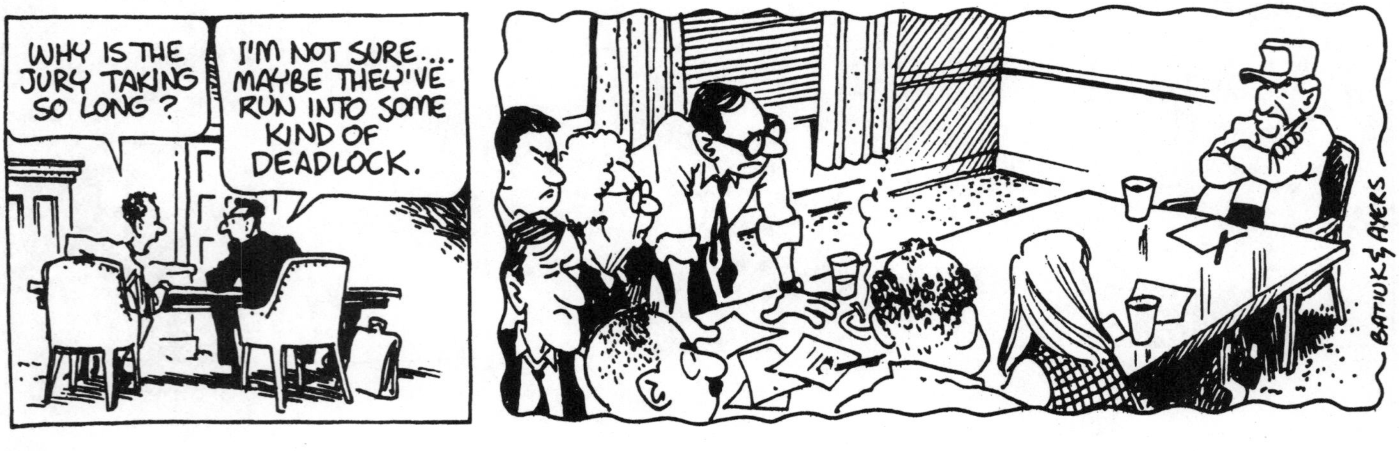
WHY IS THE JURY TAKING SO LONG?
I'M NOT SURE.... MAYBE THEY'VE RUN INTO SOME KIND OF DEADLOCK.
BATIUK & AYERS

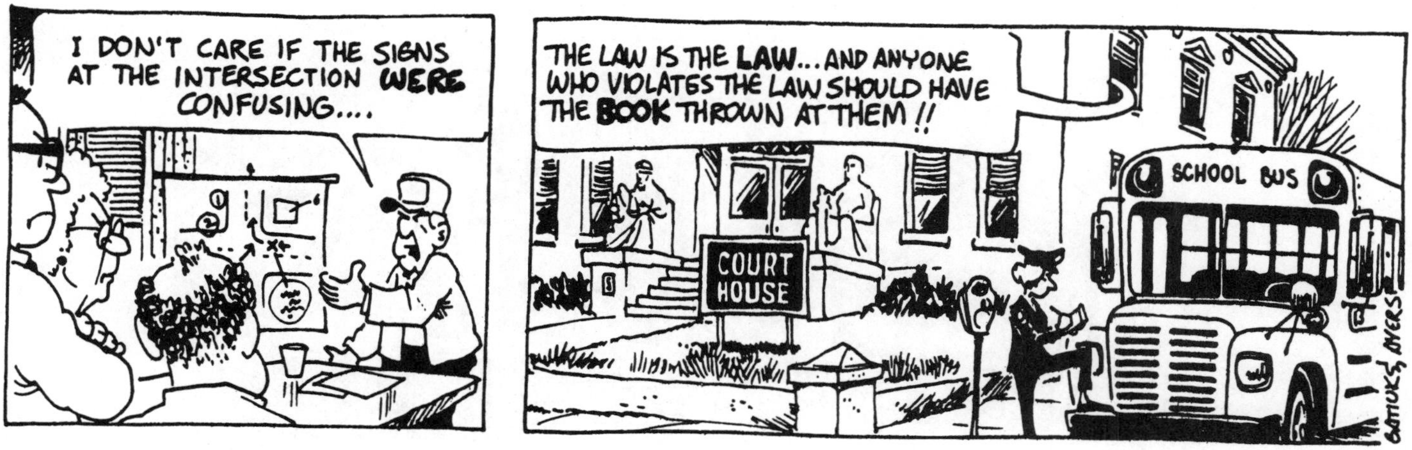
I DON'T CARE IF THE SIGNS AT THE INTERSECTION **WERE** CONFUSING....
THE LAW IS THE **LAW**... AND ANYONE WHO VIOLATES THE LAW SHOULD HAVE THE **BOOK** THROWN AT THEM!!
COURT HOUSE
SCHOOL BUS
BATIUK & AYERS

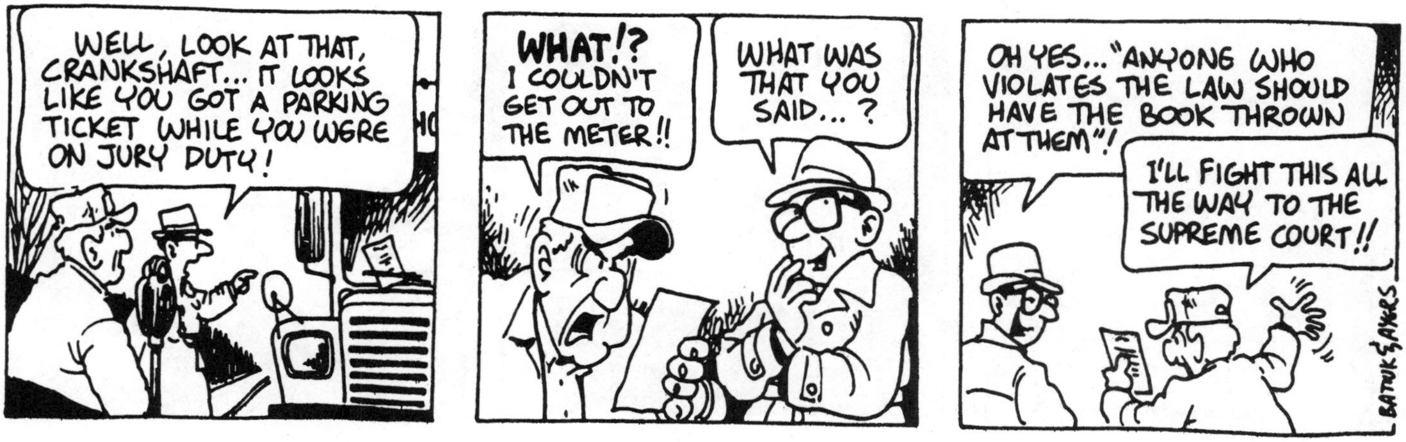
WELL, LOOK AT THAT, CRANKSHAFT... IT LOOKS LIKE YOU GOT A PARKING TICKET WHILE YOU WERE ON JURY DUTY!
WHAT!? I COULDN'T GET OUT TO THE METER!!
WHAT WAS THAT YOU SAID... ?
OH YES... "ANYONE WHO VIOLATES THE LAW SHOULD HAVE THE BOOK THROWN AT THEM"!
I'LL FIGHT THIS ALL THE WAY TO THE SUPREME COURT!!
BATIUK & AYERS

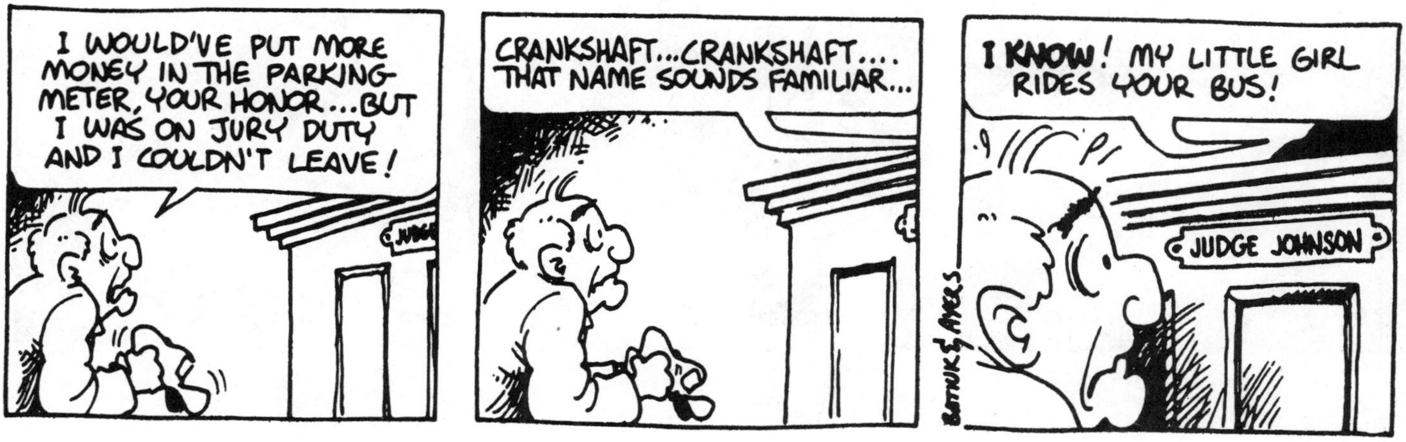
I WOULD'VE PUT MORE MONEY IN THE PARKING-METER, YOUR HONOR... BUT I WAS ON JURY DUTY AND I COULDN'T LEAVE!
CRANKSHAFT... CRANKSHAFT.... THAT NAME SOUNDS FAMILIAR...
BATIUK & AYERS
I KNOW! MY LITTLE GIRL RIDES YOUR BUS!
JUDGE JOHNSON

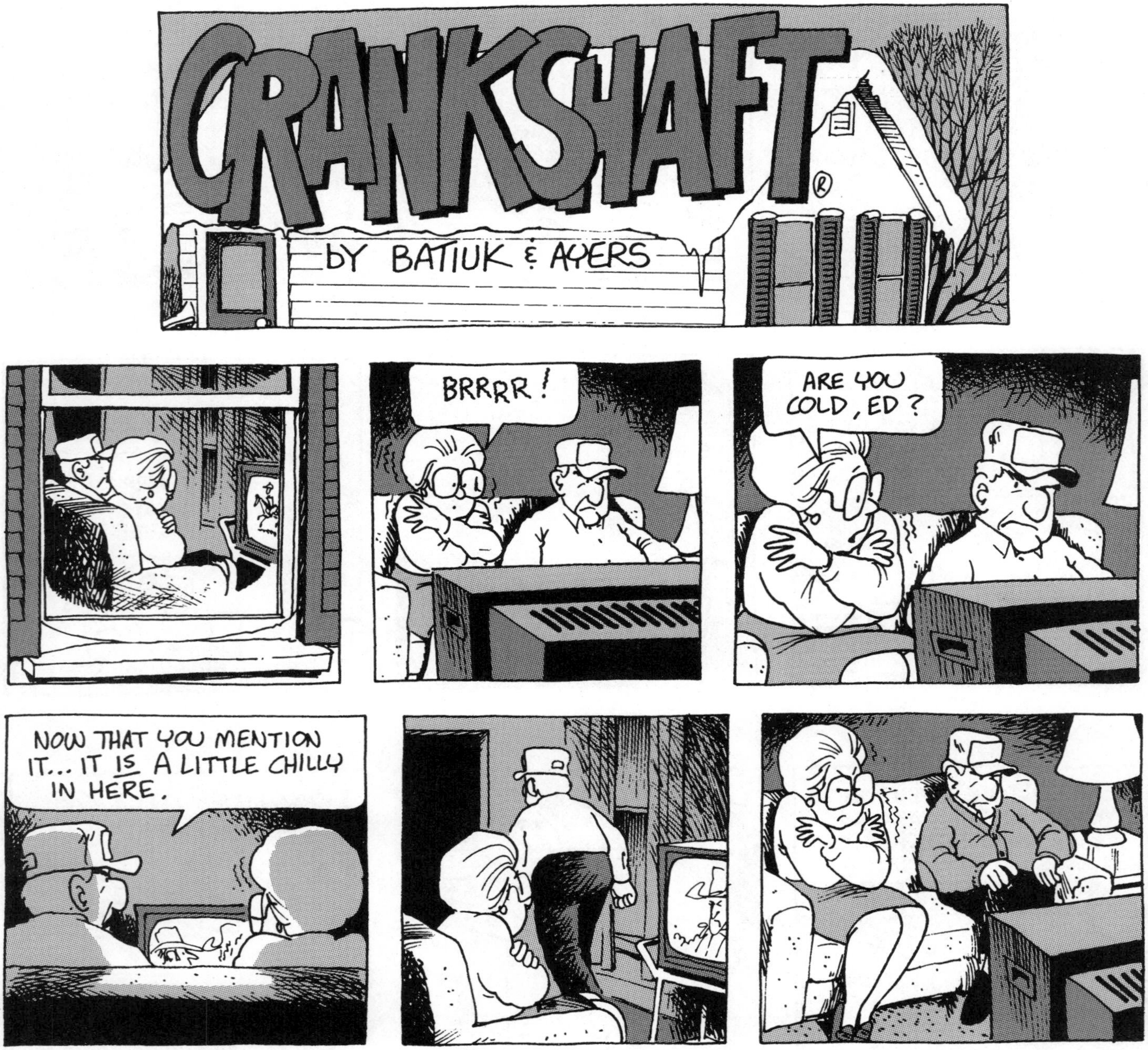
CRANKSHAFT®
BY BATIUK & AYERS
BRRRR!
ARE YOU COLD, ED?
NOW THAT YOU MENTION IT... IT IS A LITTLE CHILLY IN HERE.

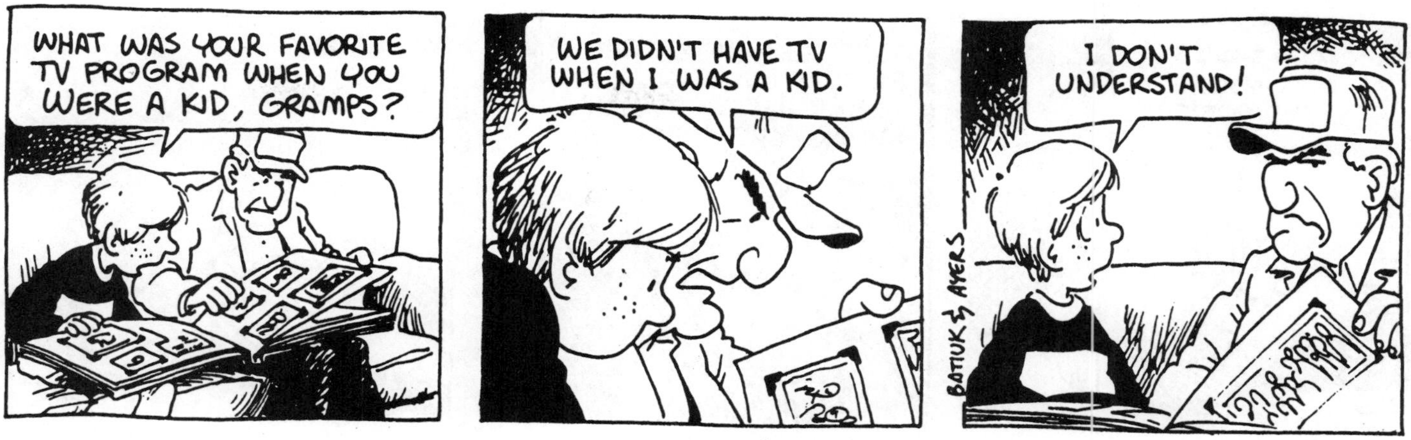
WHAT WAS YOUR FAVORITE TV PROGRAM WHEN YOU WERE A KID, GRAMPS?
WE DIDN'T HAVE TV WHEN I WAS A KID.
I DON'T UNDERSTAND!
BATIUK & AYERS

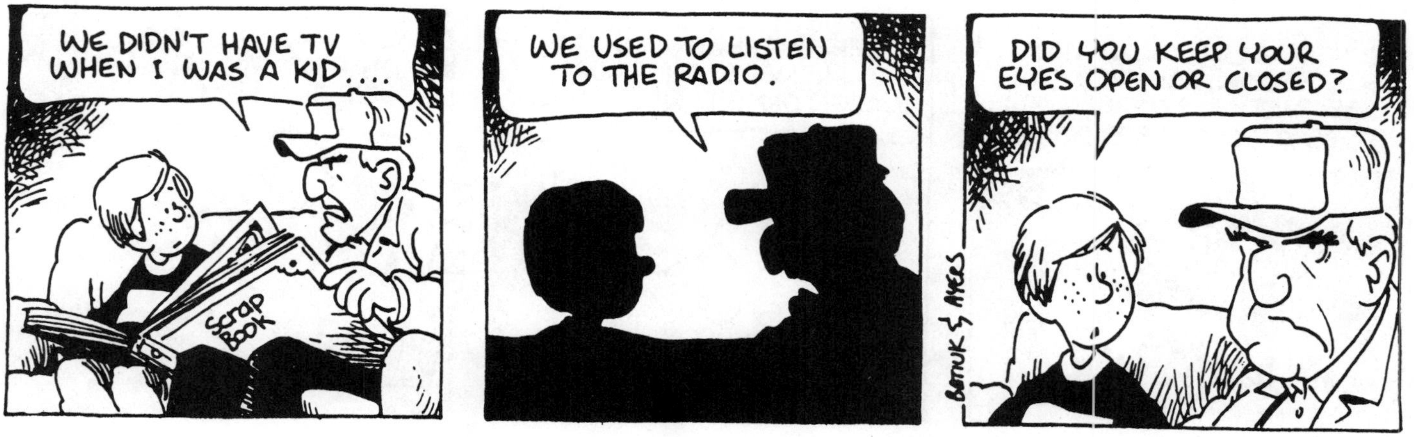
WE DIDN'T HAVE TV WHEN I WAS A KID....
Scrap Book
WE USED TO LISTEN TO THE RADIO.
DID YOU KEEP YOUR EYES OPEN OR CLOSED?
BATIUK & AYERS

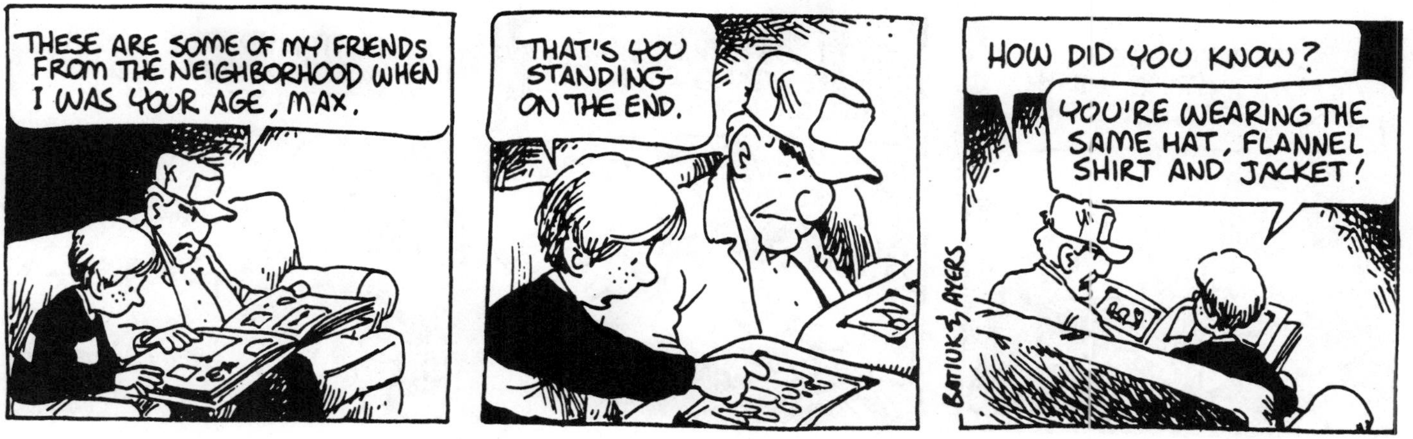
THESE ARE SOME OF MY FRIENDS FROM THE NEIGHBORHOOD WHEN I WAS YOUR AGE, MAX.
THAT'S YOU STANDING ON THE END.
HOW DID YOU KNOW?
YOU'RE WEARING THE SAME HAT, FLANNEL SHIRT AND JACKET!
BATIUK & AYERS

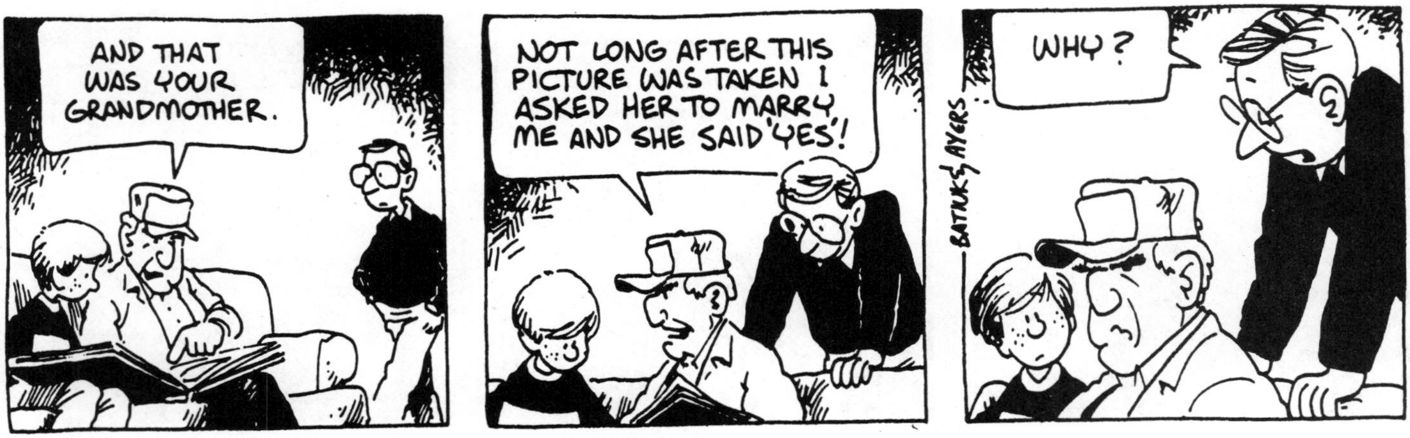
AND THAT WAS YOUR GRANDMOTHER.
NOT LONG AFTER THIS PICTURE WAS TAKEN I ASKED HER TO MARRY ME AND SHE SAID 'YES'!
BATIUK & AYERS
WHY?

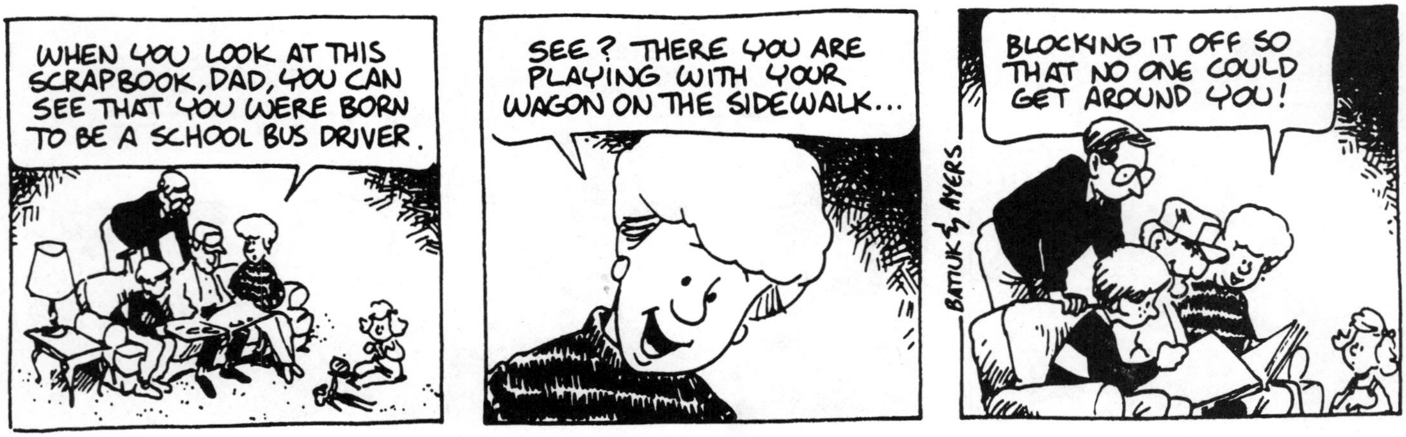
WHEN YOU LOOK AT THIS SCRAPBOOK, DAD, YOU CAN SEE THAT YOU WERE BORN TO BE A SCHOOL BUS DRIVER.
SEE? THERE YOU ARE PLAYING WITH YOUR WAGON ON THE SIDEWALK...
BATIUK & AYERS
BLOCKING IT OFF SO THAT NO ONE COULD GET AROUND YOU!

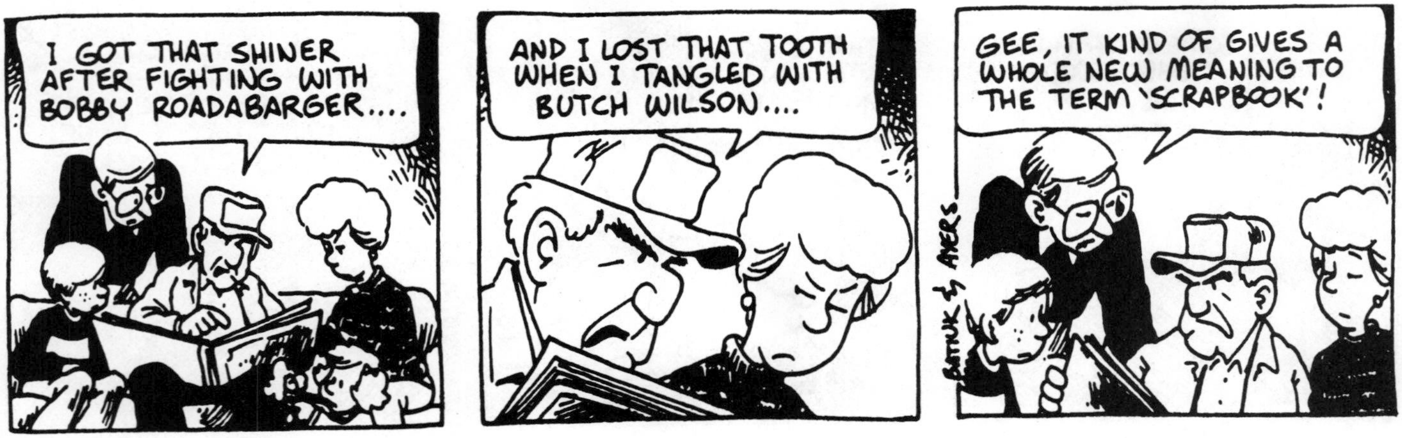
I GOT THAT SHINER AFTER FIGHTING WITH BOBBY ROADABARGER....
AND I LOST THAT TOOTH WHEN I TANGLED WITH BUTCH WILSON....
BATIUK & AYERS
GEE, IT KIND OF GIVES A WHOLE NEW MEANING TO THE TERM 'SCRAPBOOK'!

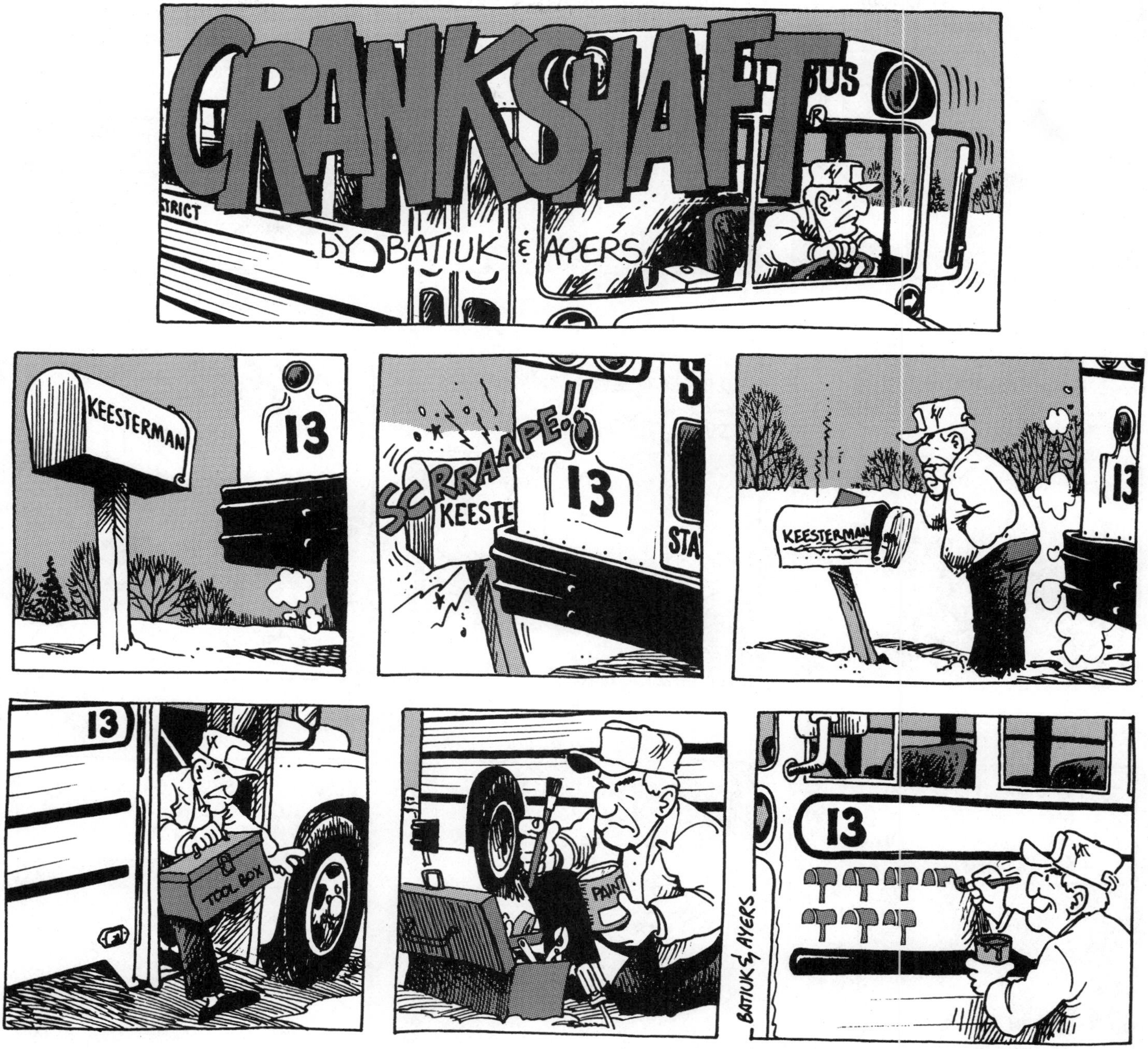
CRANKSHAFT
BY BATIUK & AYERS
BUS
KEESTERMAN
13
SCRRAAAPE!!
KEESTE
13
KEESTERMAN
13
TOOL BOX
PAINT
BATIUK & AYERS
13

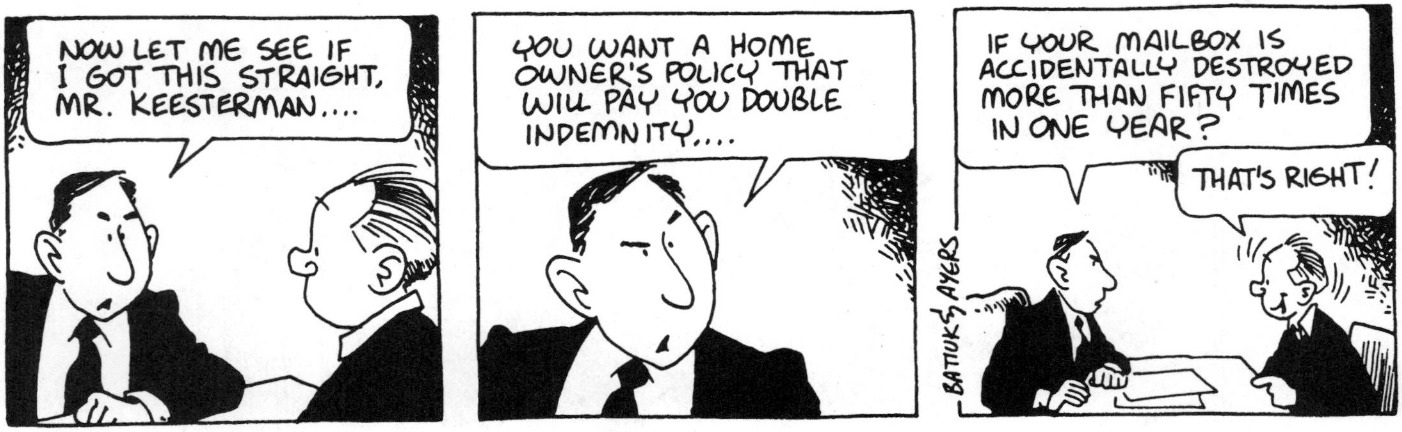
NOW LET ME SEE IF I GOT THIS STRAIGHT, MR. KEESTERMAN....
YOU WANT A HOME OWNER'S POLICY THAT WILL PAY YOU DOUBLE INDEMNITY....
IF YOUR MAILBOX IS ACCIDENTALLY DESTROYED MORE THAN FIFTY TIMES IN ONE YEAR?
THAT'S RIGHT!
BATIUK & AYERS

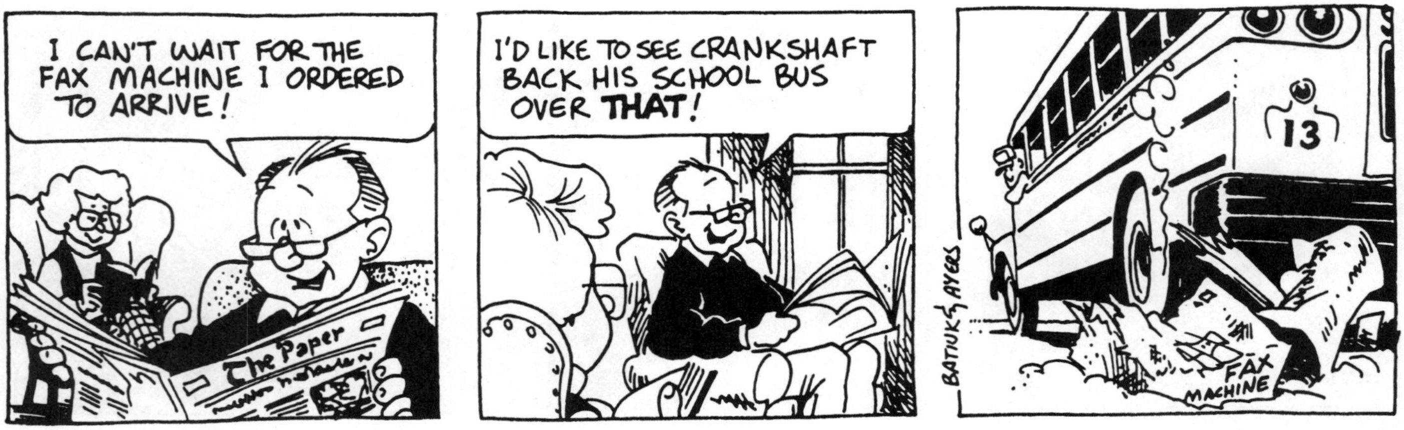
I CAN'T WAIT FOR THE FAX MACHINE I ORDERED TO ARRIVE!
The Paper
I'D LIKE TO SEE CRANKSHAFT BACK HIS SCHOOL BUS OVER THAT!
13
FAX MACHINE
BATIUK & AYERS

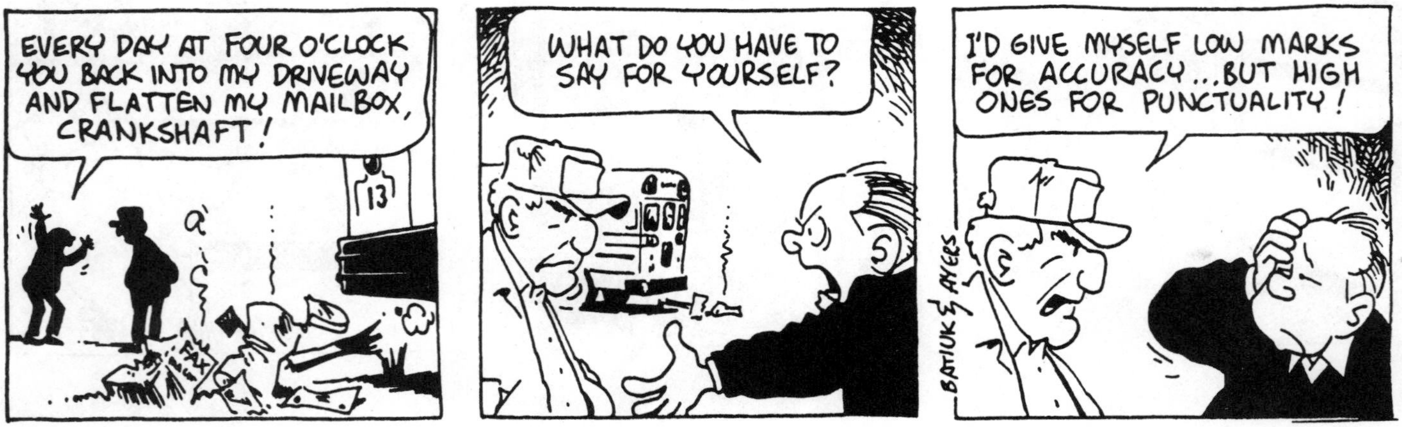
EVERY DAY AT FOUR O'CLOCK YOU BACK INTO MY DRIVEWAY AND FLATTEN MY MAILBOX, CRANKSHAFT!
13
WHAT DO YOU HAVE TO SAY FOR YOURSELF?
I'D GIVE MYSELF LOW MARKS FOR ACCURACY...BUT HIGH ONES FOR PUNCTUALITY!
BATIUK & AYERS

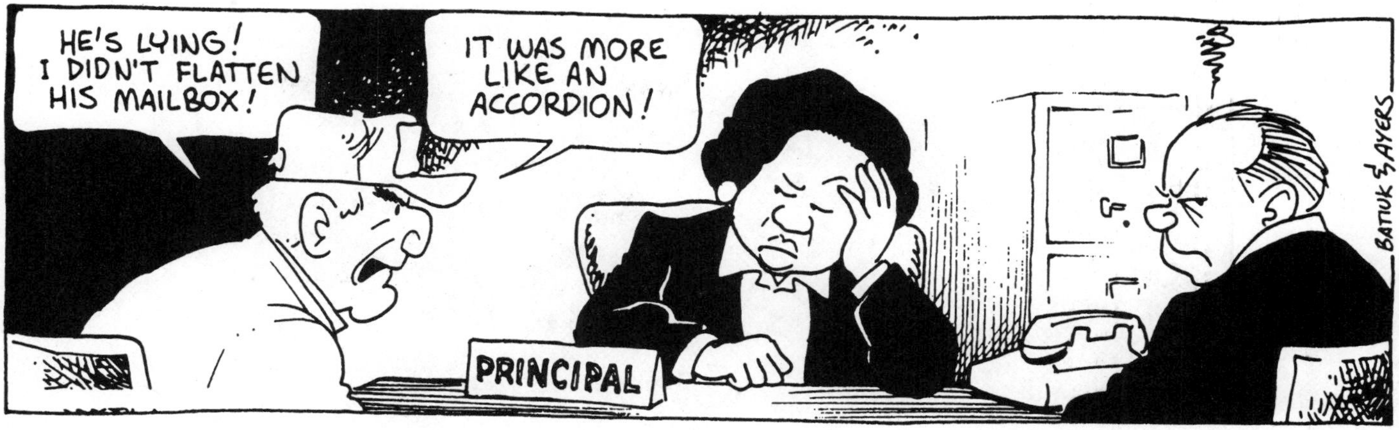
HE'S LYING! I DIDN'T FLATTEN HIS MAILBOX!
IT WAS MORE LIKE AN ACCORDION!
PRINCIPAL
BATIUK & AYERS

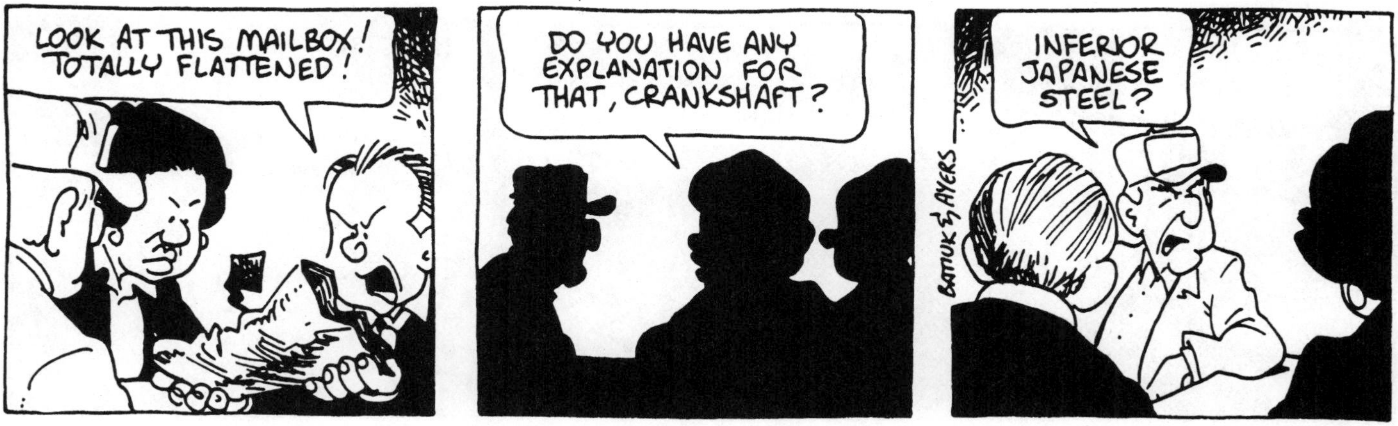
LOOK AT THIS MAILBOX! TOTALLY FLATTENED!
DO YOU HAVE ANY EXPLANATION FOR THAT, CRANKSHAFT?
BATIUK & AYERS
INFERIOR JAPANESE STEEL?

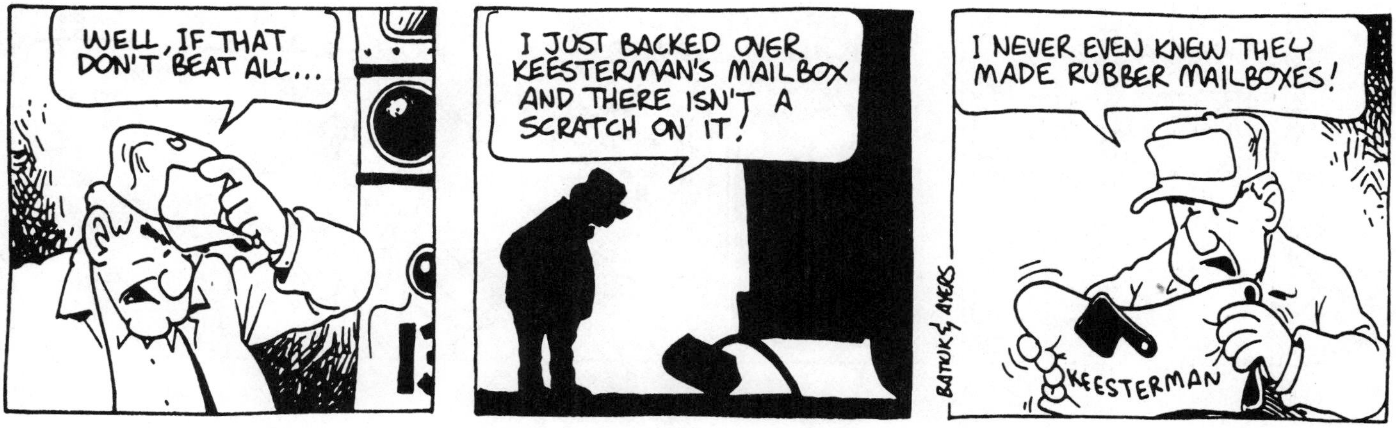
WELL, IF THAT DON'T BEAT ALL...
I JUST BACKED OVER KEESTERMAN'S MAILBOX AND THERE ISN'T A SCRATCH ON IT!
BATIUK & AYERS
I NEVER EVEN KNEW THEY MADE RUBBER MAILBOXES!
KEESTERMAN

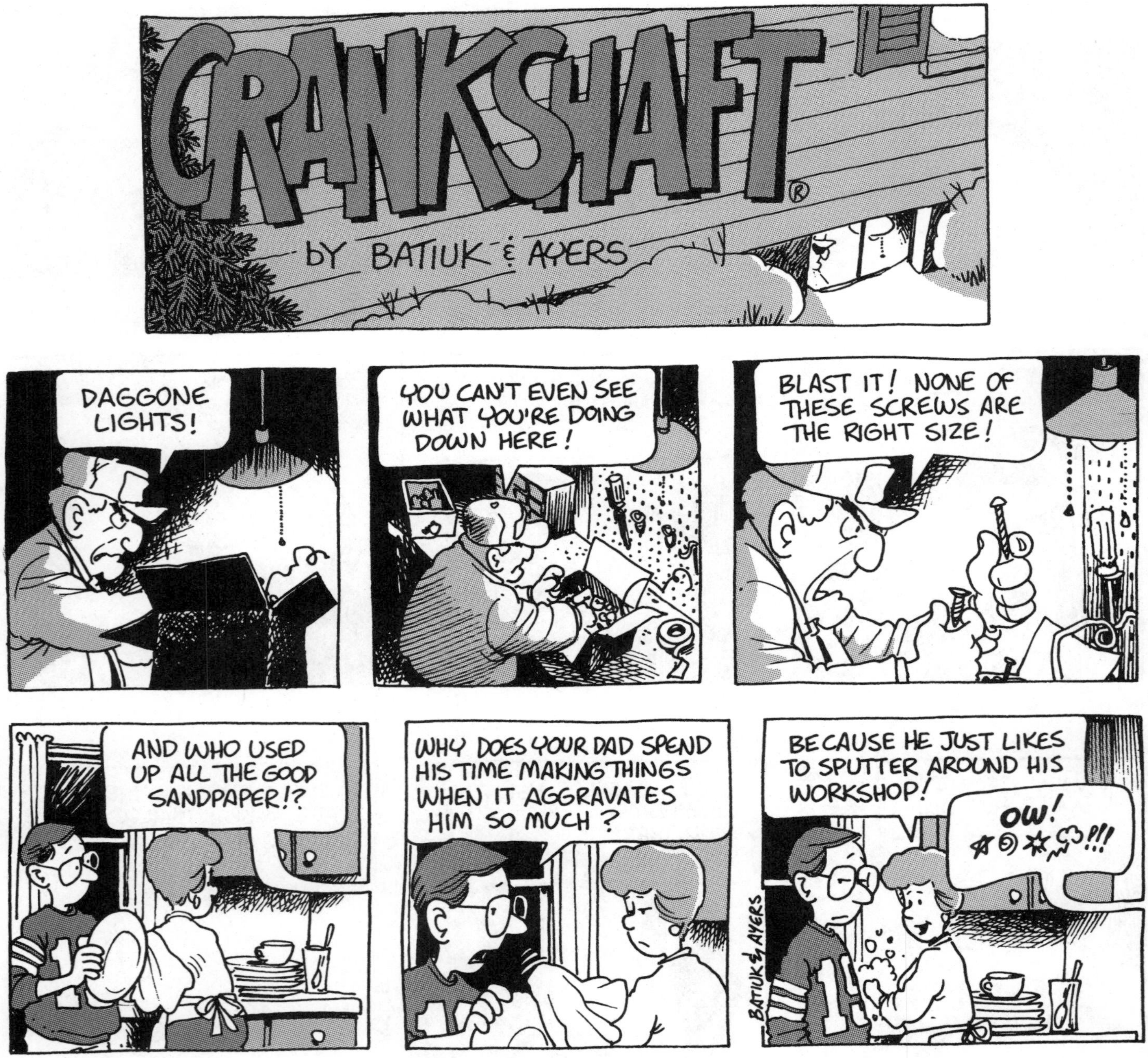
CRANKSHAFT®
BY BATIUK & AYERS
DAGGONE LIGHTS!
YOU CAN'T EVEN SEE WHAT YOU'RE DOING DOWN HERE!
BLAST IT! NONE OF THESE SCREWS ARE THE RIGHT SIZE!
AND WHO USED UP ALL THE GOOD SANDPAPER!?
WHY DOES YOUR DAD SPEND HIS TIME MAKING THINGS WHEN IT AGGRAVATES HIM SO MUCH?
BECAUSE HE JUST LIKES TO SPUTTER AROUND HIS WORKSHOP!
OW!
BATIUK & AYERS

DO YOU WANT TO GET A VALENTINE FOR YOUR SCHOOL BUS DRIVER MR. CRANKSHAFT?
Valentines
alentine
NO!
YEAH... WHAT AM I THINKING?
Vale
BATIUK & AYERS

OH, NO! ALL MY VALENTINES!
TOO BAD!
OF COURSE, YOU KNOW THAT MEANS YOU'LL NEVER HAVE ANY BOYFRIENDS!
BATIUK & AYERS

A VALENTINE CARD!? OH, ED... HOW THOUGHTFUL!
Grace
WHY IS THIS OTHER NAME CROSSED OFF HERE?
I DIDN'T FIND THE CARD ON MY BUS IF THAT'S WHAT YOU'RE TRYING TO SAY....
BATIUK & AYERS

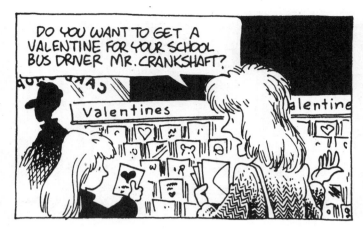

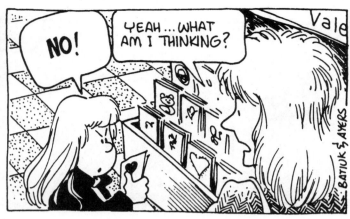

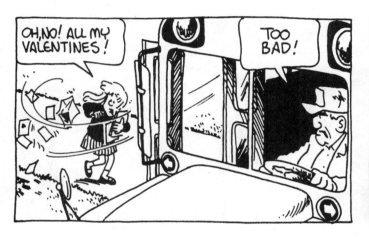

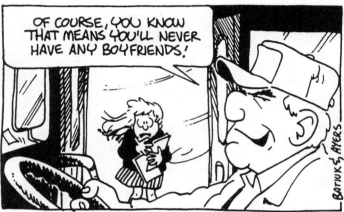

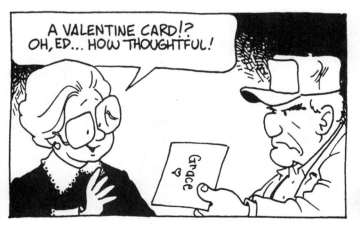

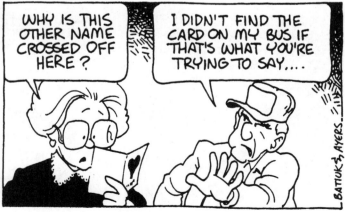

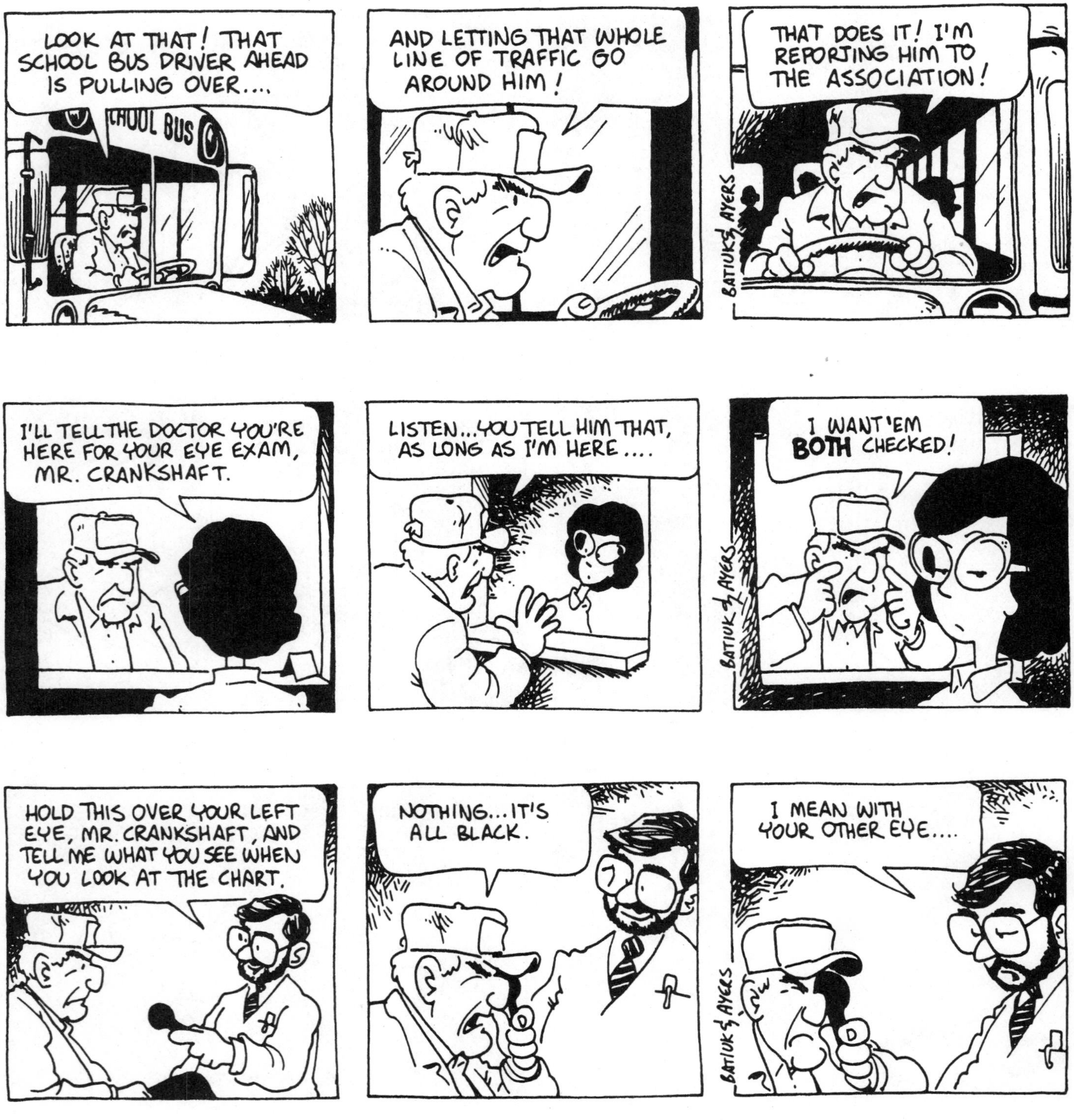
LOOK AT THAT! THAT SCHOOL BUS DRIVER AHEAD IS PULLING OVER....
SCHOOL BUS
AND LETTING THAT WHOLE LINE OF TRAFFIC GO AROUND HIM!
THAT DOES IT! I'M REPORTING HIM TO THE ASSOCIATION!
BATIUK & AYERS
I'LL TELL THE DOCTOR YOU'RE HERE FOR YOUR EYE EXAM, MR. CRANKSHAFT.
LISTEN...YOU TELL HIM THAT, AS LONG AS I'M HERE....
I WANT 'EM **BOTH** CHECKED!
BATIUK & AYERS
HOLD THIS OVER YOUR LEFT EYE, MR. CRANKSHAFT, AND TELL ME WHAT YOU SEE WHEN YOU LOOK AT THE CHART.
NOTHING...IT'S ALL BLACK.
I MEAN WITH YOUR OTHER EYE....
BATIUK & AYERS

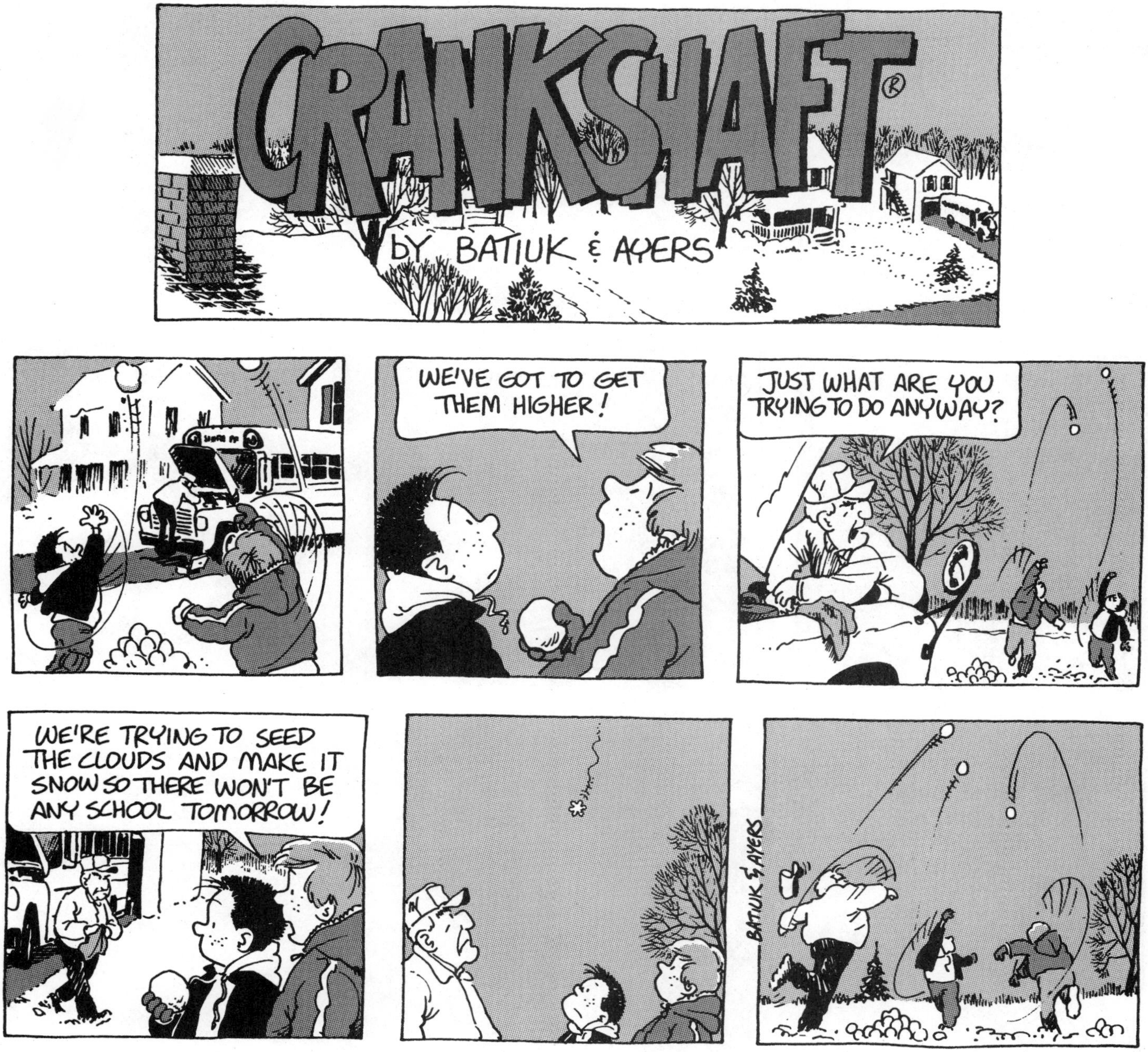
CRANKSHAFT®
BY BATIUK & AYERS
WE'VE GOT TO GET THEM HIGHER!
JUST WHAT ARE YOU TRYING TO DO ANYWAY?
WE'RE TRYING TO SEED THE CLOUDS AND MAKE IT SNOW SO THERE WON'T BE ANY SCHOOL TOMORROW!
BATIUK & AYERS

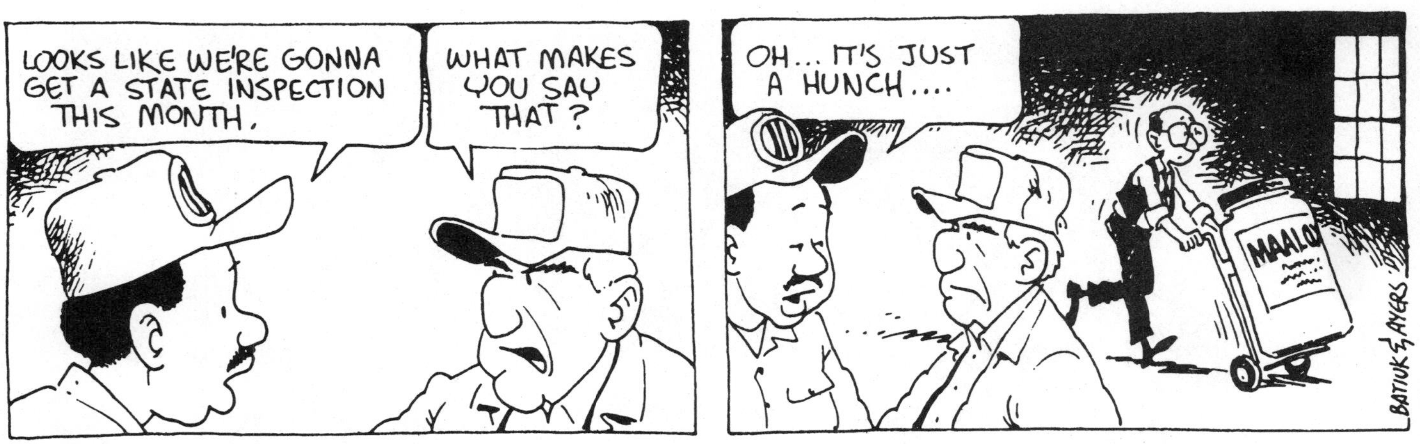
LOOKS LIKE WE'RE GONNA GET A STATE INSPECTION THIS MONTH.
WHAT MAKES YOU SAY THAT?
OH... IT'S JUST A HUNCH....
MAALOX
BATIUK & AYERS

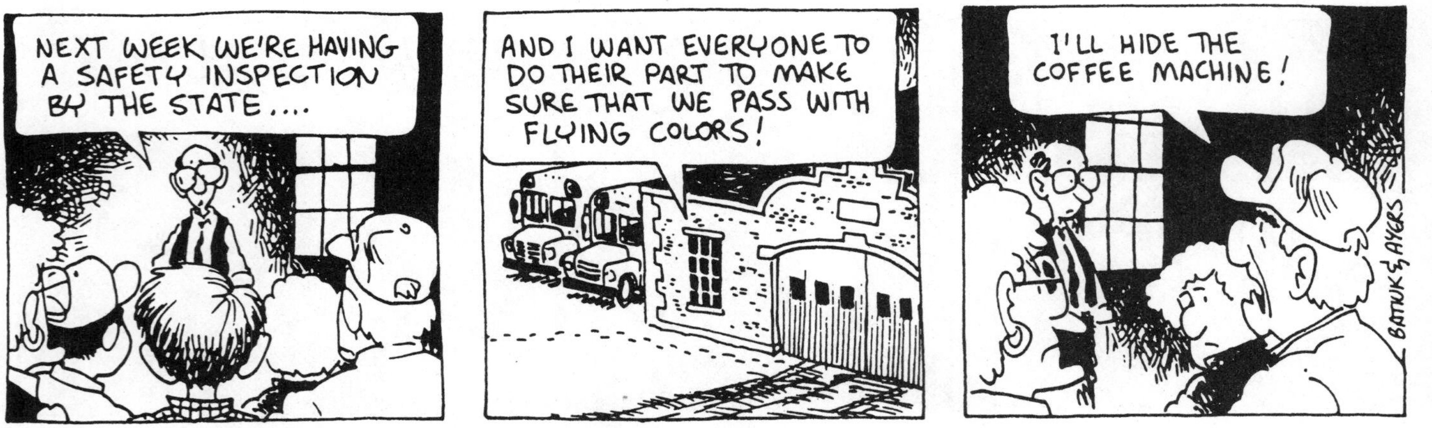
NEXT WEEK WE'RE HAVING A SAFETY INSPECTION BY THE STATE....
AND I WANT EVERYONE TO DO THEIR PART TO MAKE SURE THAT WE PASS WITH FLYING COLORS!
I'LL HIDE THE COFFEE MACHINE!
BATIUK & AYERS

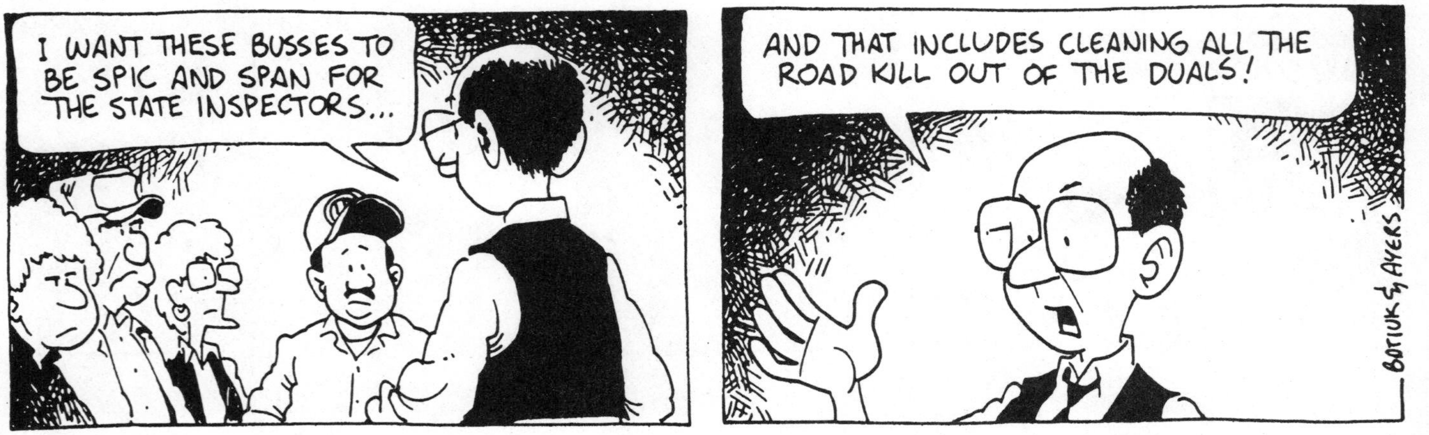
I WANT THESE BUSSES TO BE SPIC AND SPAN FOR THE STATE INSPECTORS...
AND THAT INCLUDES CLEANING ALL THE ROAD KILL OUT OF THE DUALS!
BATIUK & AYERS

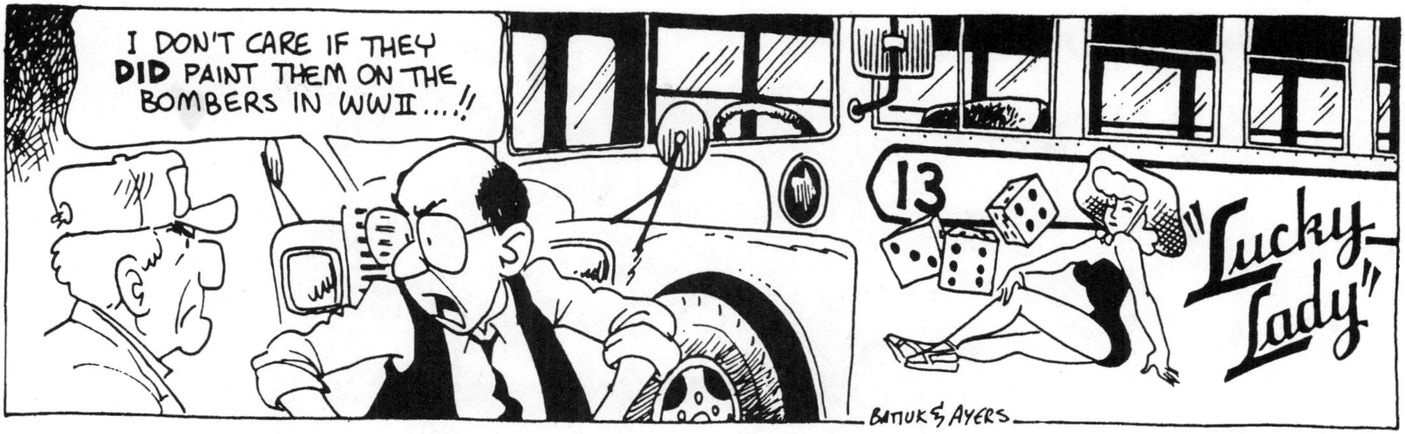
I DON'T CARE IF THEY **DID** PAINT THEM ON THE BOMBERS IN WWII....!!
13
"Lucky Lady"
BATIUK & AYERS

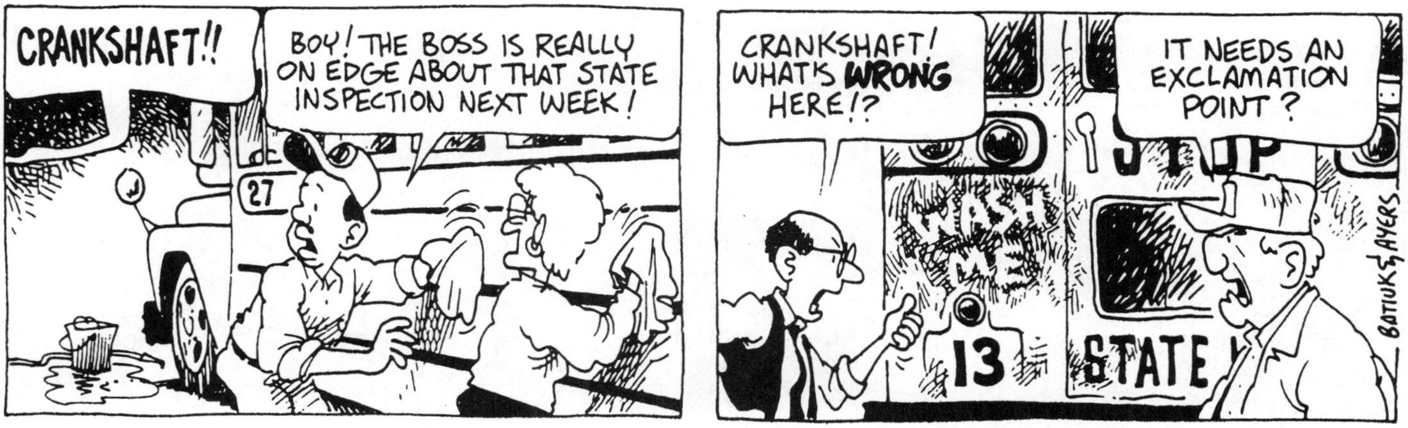
CRANKSHAFT!!
BOY! THE BOSS IS REALLY ON EDGE ABOUT THAT STATE INSPECTION NEXT WEEK!
27
CRANKSHAFT! WHAT'S **WRONG** HERE!?
IT NEEDS AN EXCLAMATION POINT?
WASH ME
13
STATE
BATIUK & AYERS

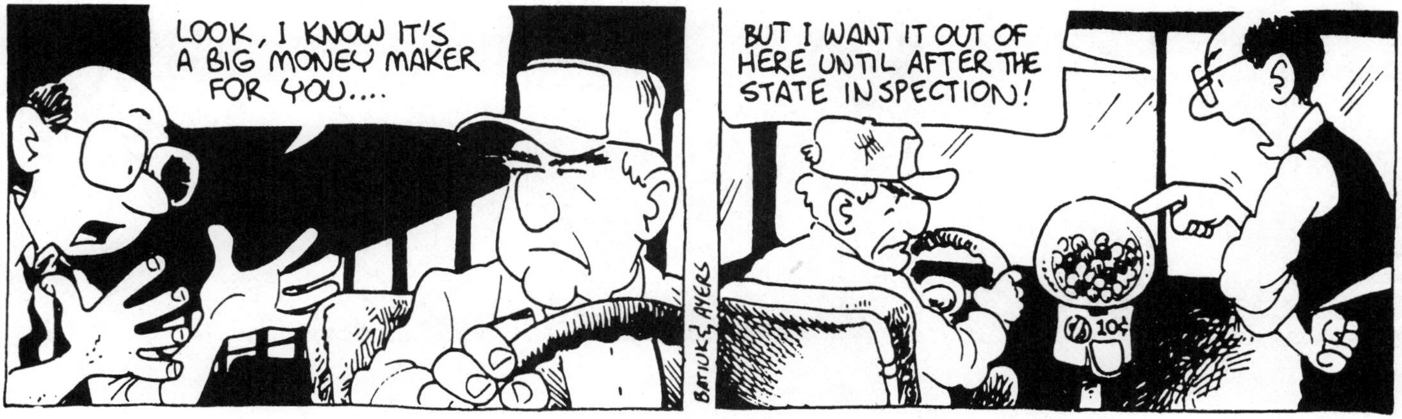
LOOK, I KNOW IT'S A BIG MONEY MAKER FOR YOU....
BATIUK & AYERS
BUT I WANT IT OUT OF HERE UNTIL AFTER THE STATE INSPECTION!
10¢

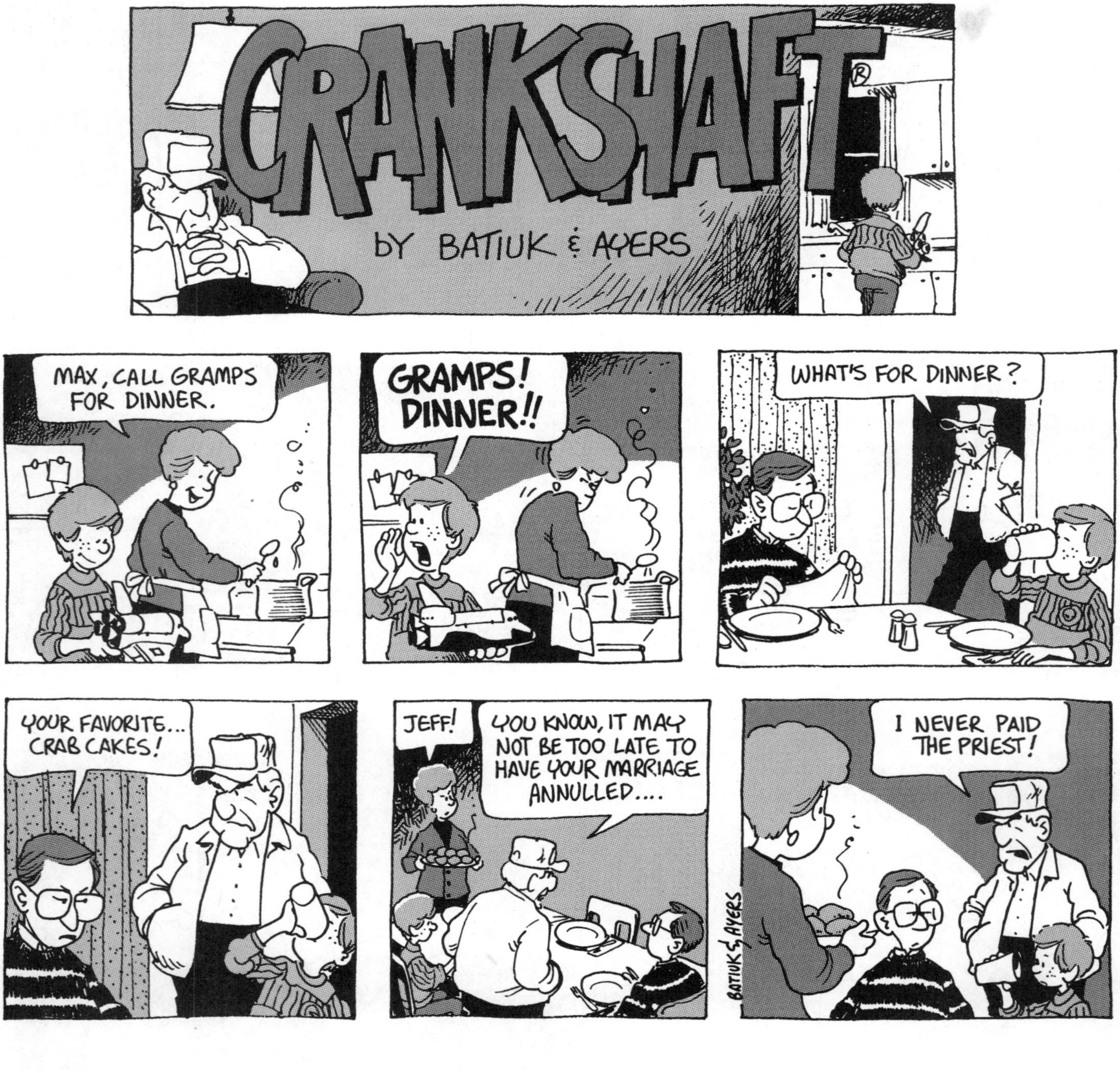
CRANKSHAFT®
BY BATIUK & AYERS
MAX, CALL GRAMPS FOR DINNER.
GRAMPS! DINNER!!
WHAT'S FOR DINNER?
YOUR FAVORITE... CRAB CAKES!
JEFF!
YOU KNOW, IT MAY NOT BE TOO LATE TO HAVE YOUR MARRIAGE ANNULLED....
I NEVER PAID THE PRIEST!
BATIUK & AYERS

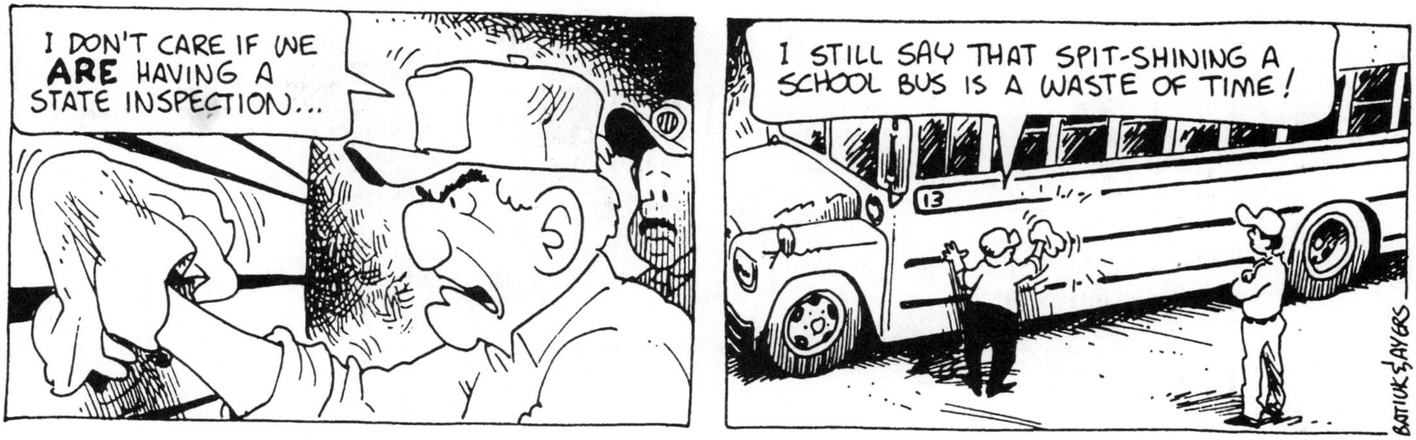
I DON'T CARE IF WE **ARE** HAVING A STATE INSPECTION...
I STILL SAY THAT SPIT-SHINING A SCHOOL BUS IS A WASTE OF TIME!
13
BATIUK & AYERS

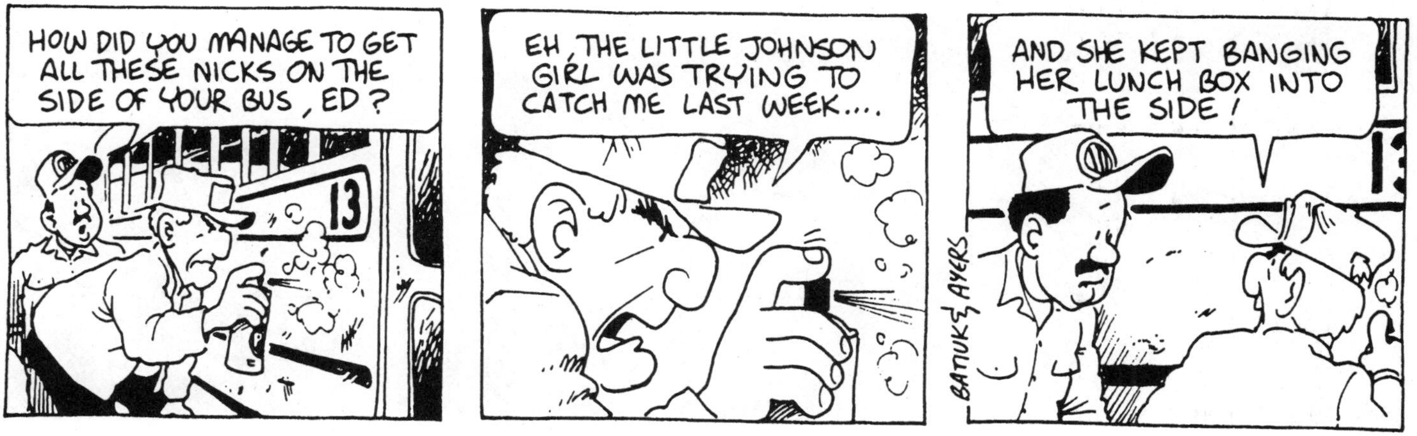
HOW DID YOU MANAGE TO GET ALL THESE NICKS ON THE SIDE OF YOUR BUS, ED?
13
EH, THE LITTLE JOHNSON GIRL WAS TRYING TO CATCH ME LAST WEEK....
AND SHE KEPT BANGING HER LUNCH BOX INTO THE SIDE!
BATIUK & AYERS

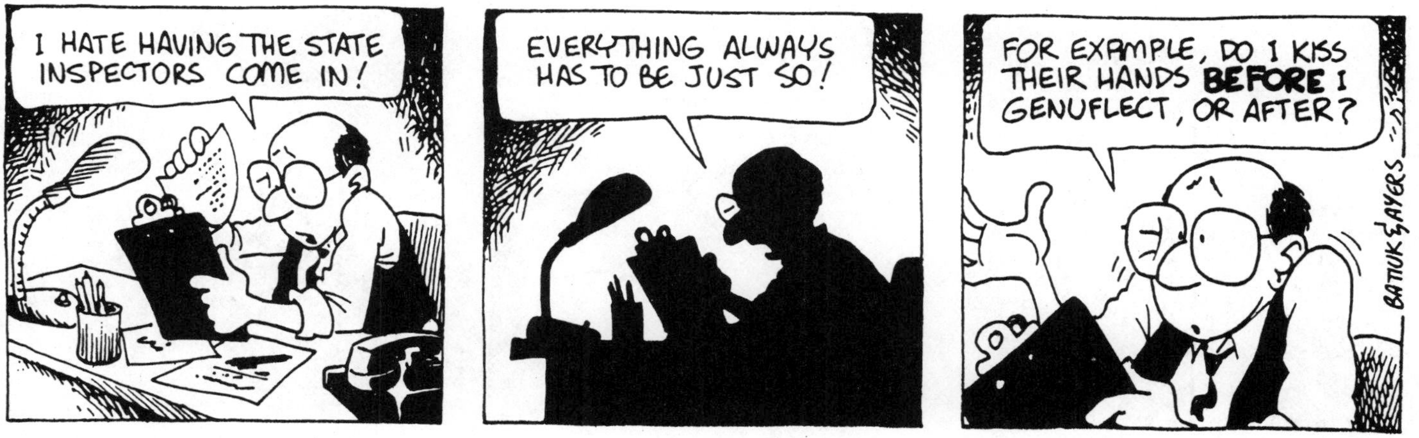
I HATE HAVING THE STATE INSPECTORS COME IN!
EVERYTHING ALWAYS HAS TO BE JUST SO!
FOR EXAMPLE, DO I KISS THEIR HANDS **BEFORE** I GENUFLECT, OR AFTER?
BATIUK & AYERS

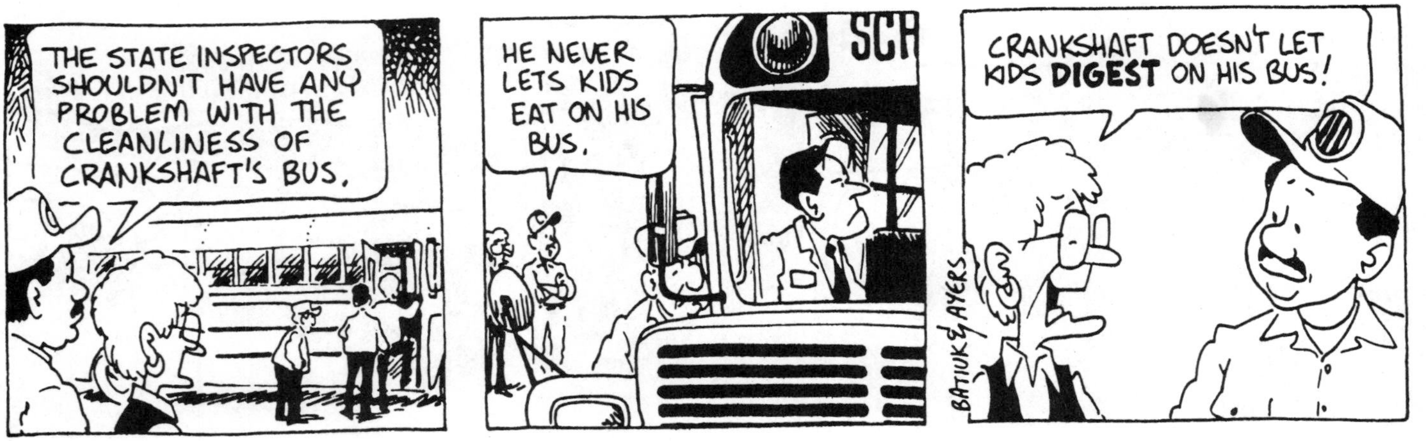
THE STATE INSPECTORS SHOULDN'T HAVE ANY PROBLEM WITH THE CLEANLINESS OF CRANKSHAFT'S BUS.
HE NEVER LETS KIDS EAT ON HIS BUS.
SCH
CRANKSHAFT DOESN'T LET KIDS **DIGEST** ON HIS BUS!
BATIUK & AYERS

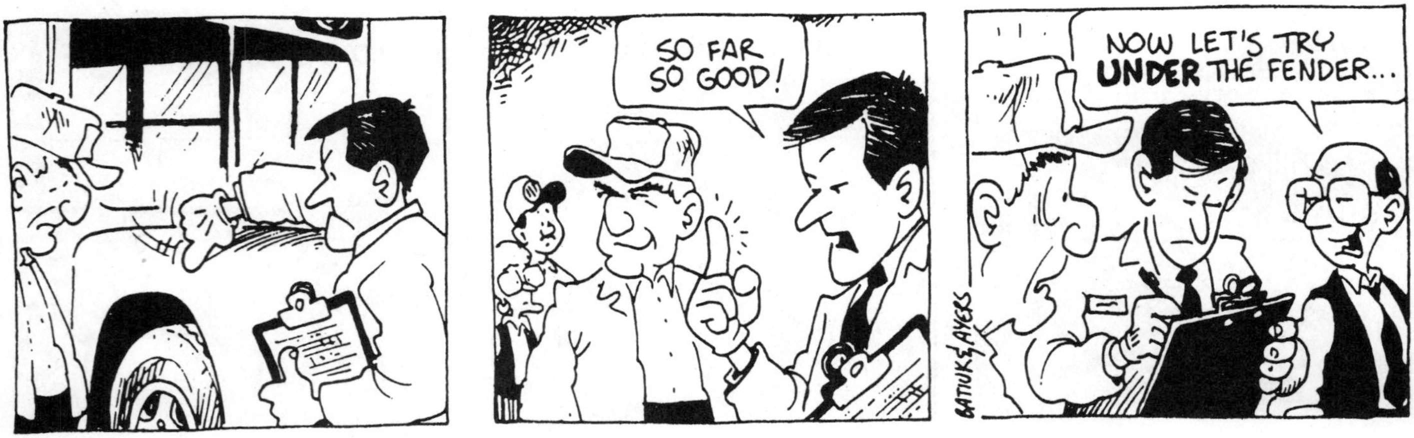
SO FAR SO GOOD!
NOW LET'S TRY **UNDER** THE FENDER...
BATIUK & AYERS

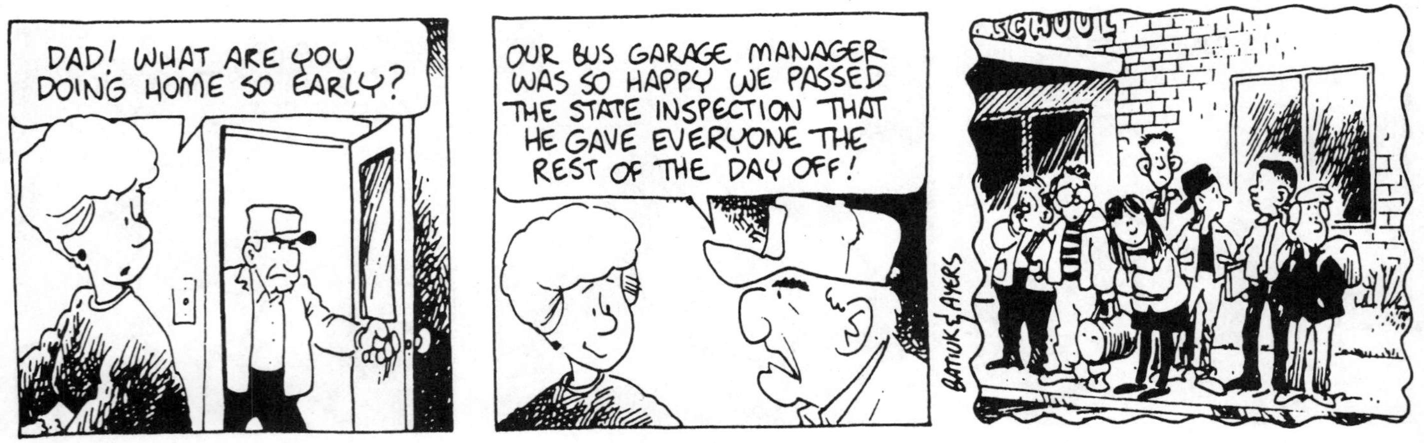
DAD! WHAT ARE YOU DOING HOME SO EARLY?
OUR BUS GARAGE MANAGER WAS SO HAPPY WE PASSED THE STATE INSPECTION THAT HE GAVE EVERYONE THE REST OF THE DAY OFF!
SCHOOL
BATIUK & AYERS

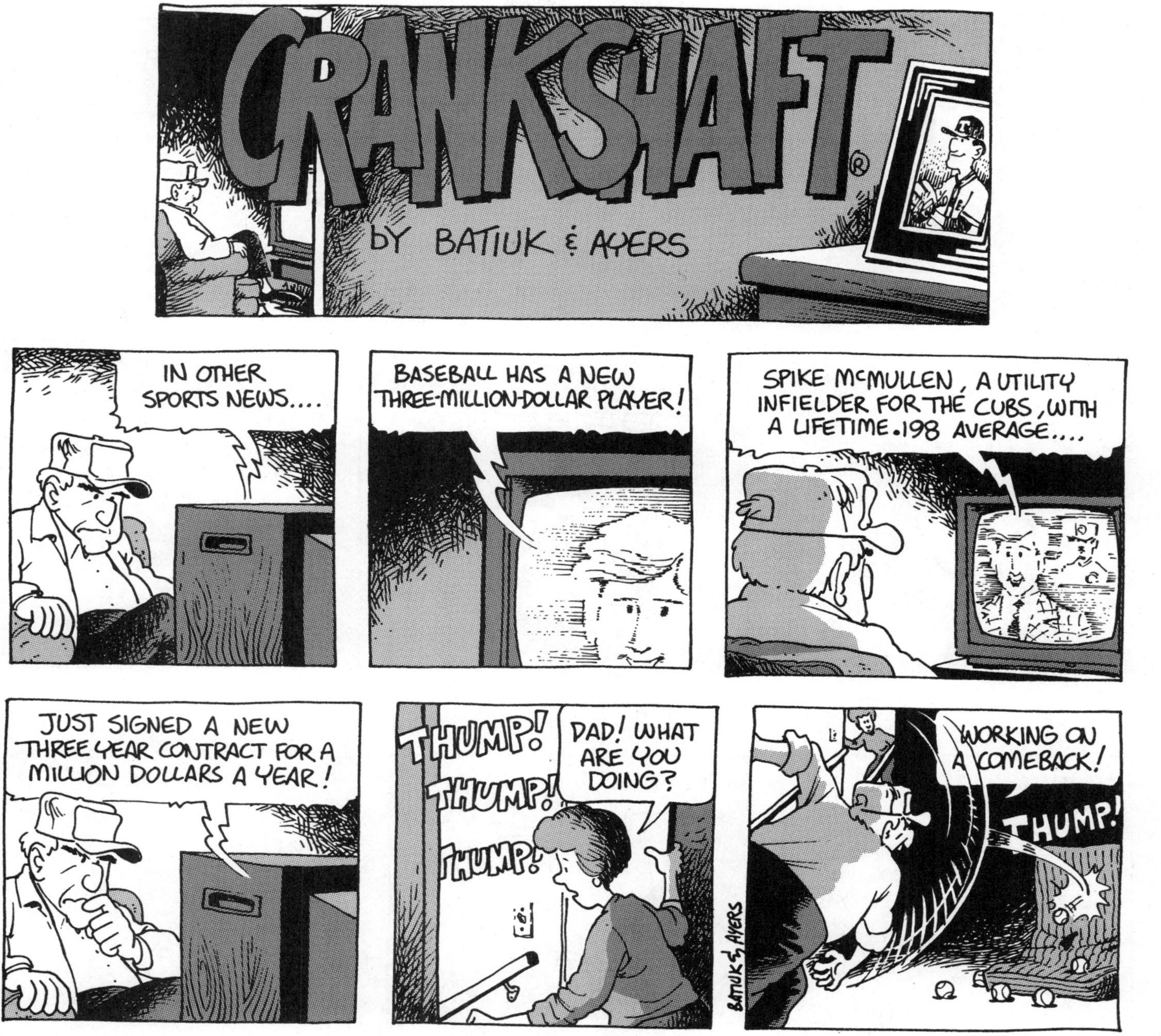
CRANKSHAFT®
BY BATIUK & AYERS
IN OTHER SPORTS NEWS....
BASEBALL HAS A NEW THREE-MILLION-DOLLAR PLAYER!
SPIKE McMULLEN, A UTILITY INFIELDER FOR THE CUBS, WITH A LIFETIME .198 AVERAGE....
JUST SIGNED A NEW THREE YEAR CONTRACT FOR A MILLION DOLLARS A YEAR!
THUMP!
THUMP!
THUMP!
DAD! WHAT ARE YOU DOING?
BATIUK & AYERS
WORKING ON A COMEBACK!
THUMP!

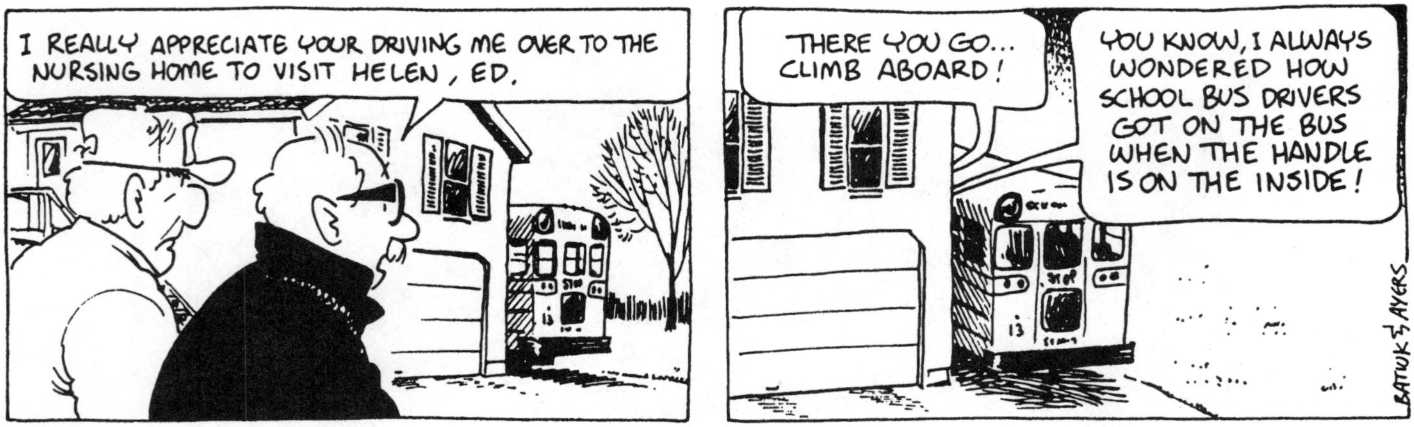
I REALLY APPRECIATE YOUR DRIVING ME OVER TO THE NURSING HOME TO VISIT HELEN, ED.
THERE YOU GO... CLIMB ABOARD!
YOU KNOW, I ALWAYS WONDERED HOW SCHOOL BUS DRIVERS GOT ON THE BUS WHEN THE HANDLE IS ON THE INSIDE!
BATIUK & AYERS

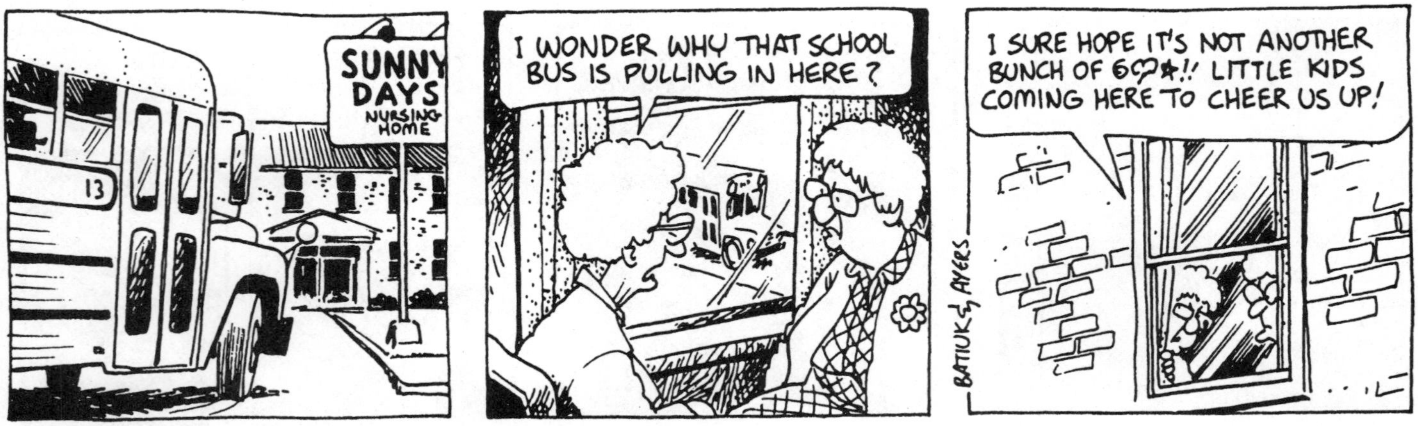
SUNNY DAYS NURSING HOME
I WONDER WHY THAT SCHOOL BUS IS PULLING IN HERE?
I SURE HOPE IT'S NOT ANOTHER BUNCH OF 6♡★!! LITTLE KIDS COMING HERE TO CHEER US UP!
BATIUK & AYERS

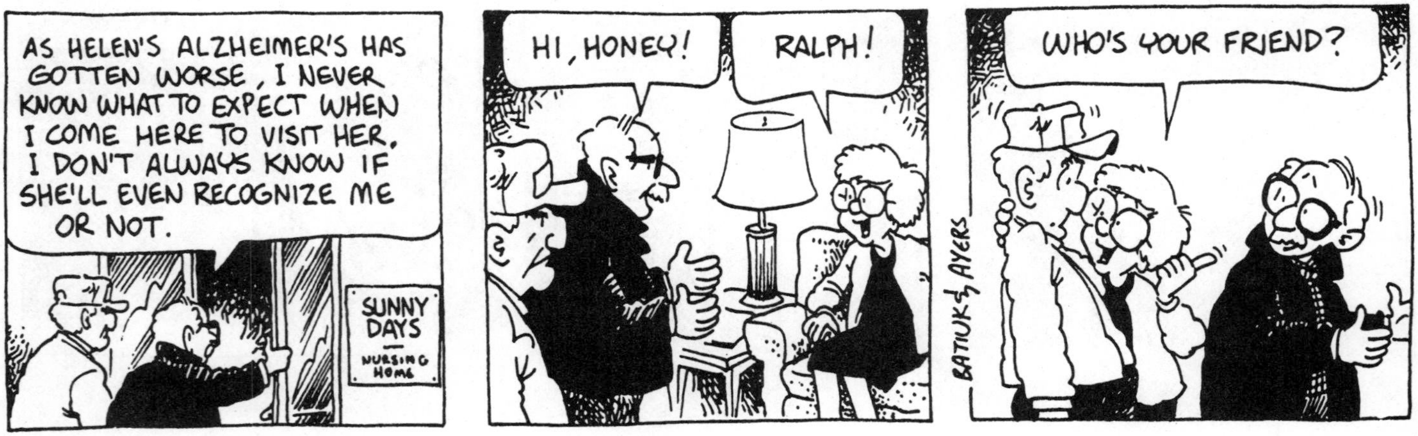
AS HELEN'S ALZHEIMER'S HAS GOTTEN WORSE, I NEVER KNOW WHAT TO EXPECT WHEN I COME HERE TO VISIT HER. I DON'T ALWAYS KNOW IF SHE'LL EVEN RECOGNIZE ME OR NOT.
SUNNY DAYS NURSING HOME
HI, HONEY!
RALPH!
WHO'S YOUR FRIEND?
BATIUK & AYERS

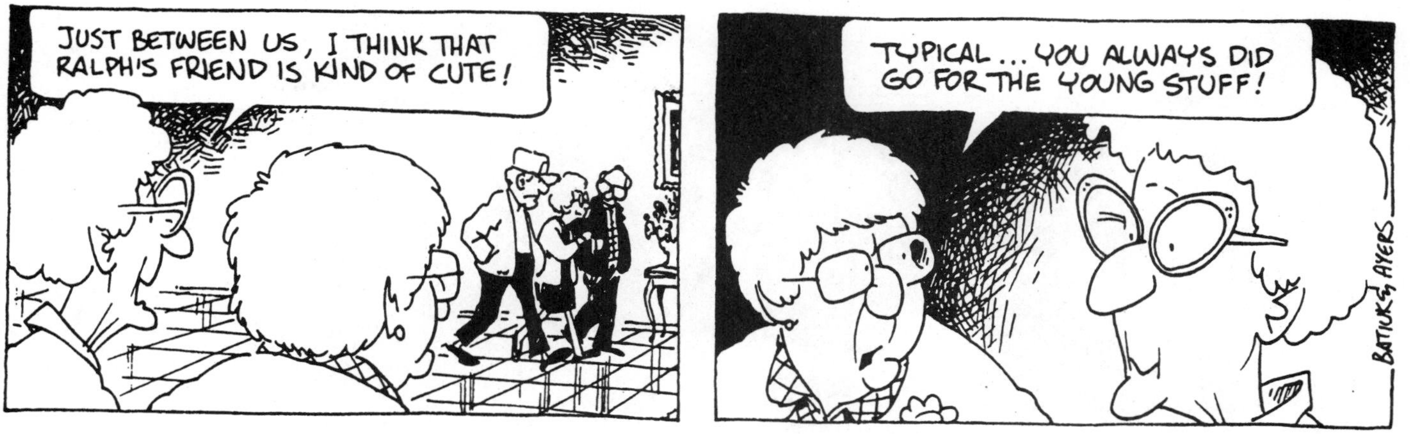
JUST BETWEEN US, I THINK THAT RALPH'S FRIEND IS KIND OF CUTE!
TYPICAL... YOU ALWAYS DID GO FOR THE YOUNG STUFF!
BATIUK & AYERS

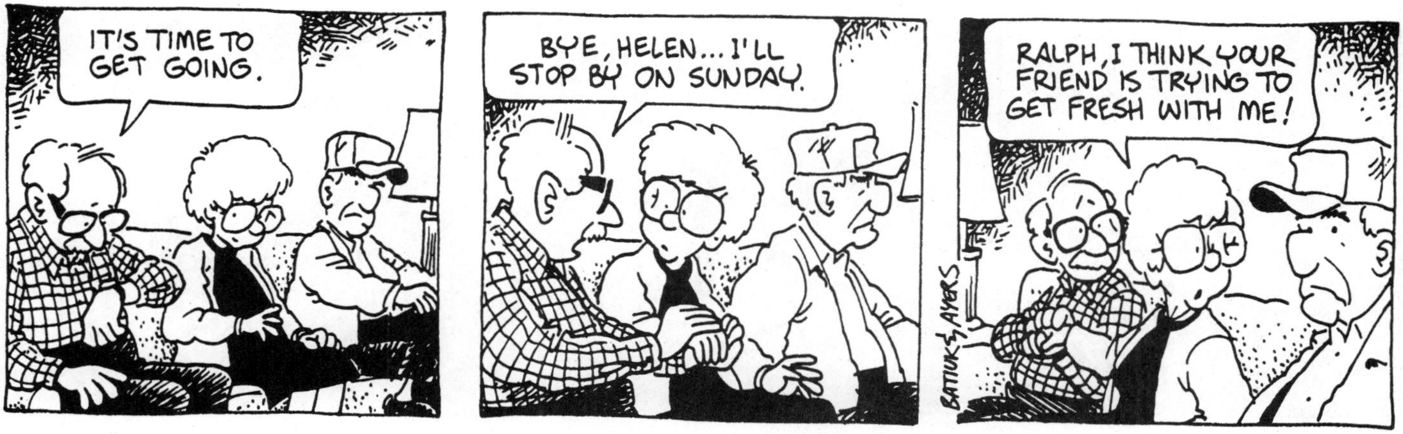
IT'S TIME TO GET GOING.
BYE, HELEN... I'LL STOP BY ON SUNDAY.
BATIUK & AYERS
RALPH, I THINK YOUR FRIEND IS TRYING TO GET FRESH WITH ME!

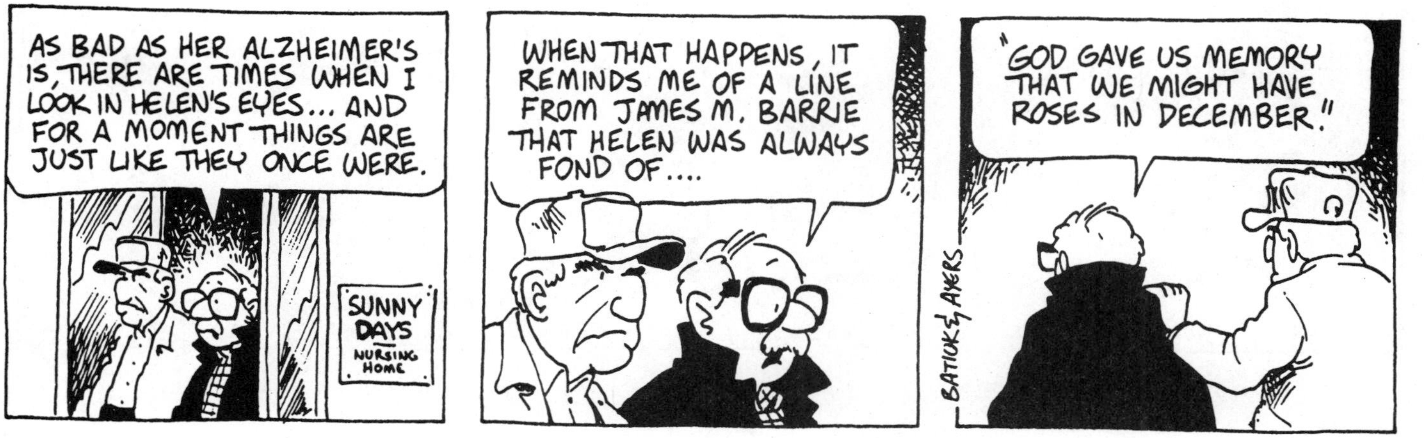
AS BAD AS HER ALZHEIMER'S IS, THERE ARE TIMES WHEN I LOOK IN HELEN'S EYES... AND FOR A MOMENT THINGS ARE JUST LIKE THEY ONCE WERE.
SUNNY DAYS NURSING HOME
WHEN THAT HAPPENS, IT REMINDS ME OF A LINE FROM JAMES M. BARRIE THAT HELEN WAS ALWAYS FOND OF....
BATIUK & AYERS
"GOD GAVE US MEMORY THAT WE MIGHT HAVE ROSES IN DECEMBER."

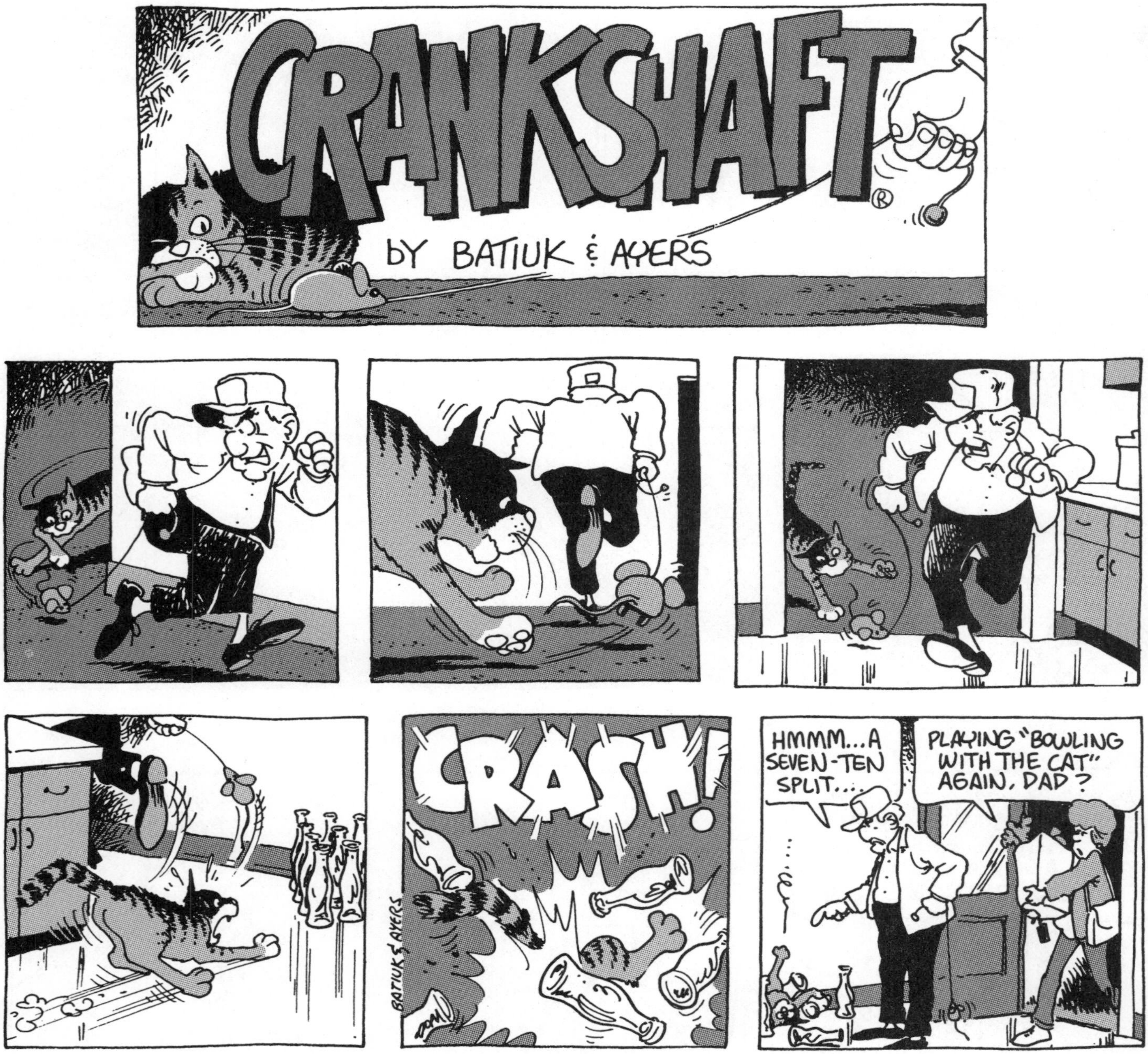
CRANKSHAFT
BY BATIUK & AYERS
CRASH!
HMMM...A SEVEN-TEN SPLIT....
PLAYING "BOWLING WITH THE CAT" AGAIN, DAD?
BATIUK & AYERS

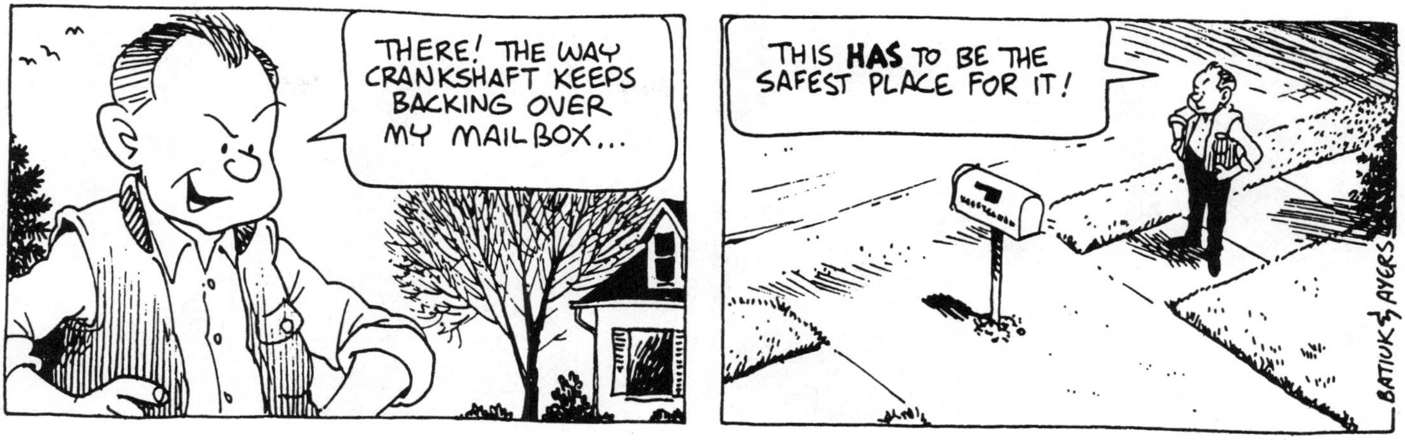
THERE! THE WAY CRANKSHAFT KEEPS BACKING OVER MY MAILBOX...
THIS **HAS** TO BE THE SAFEST PLACE FOR IT!
BATIUK & AYERS

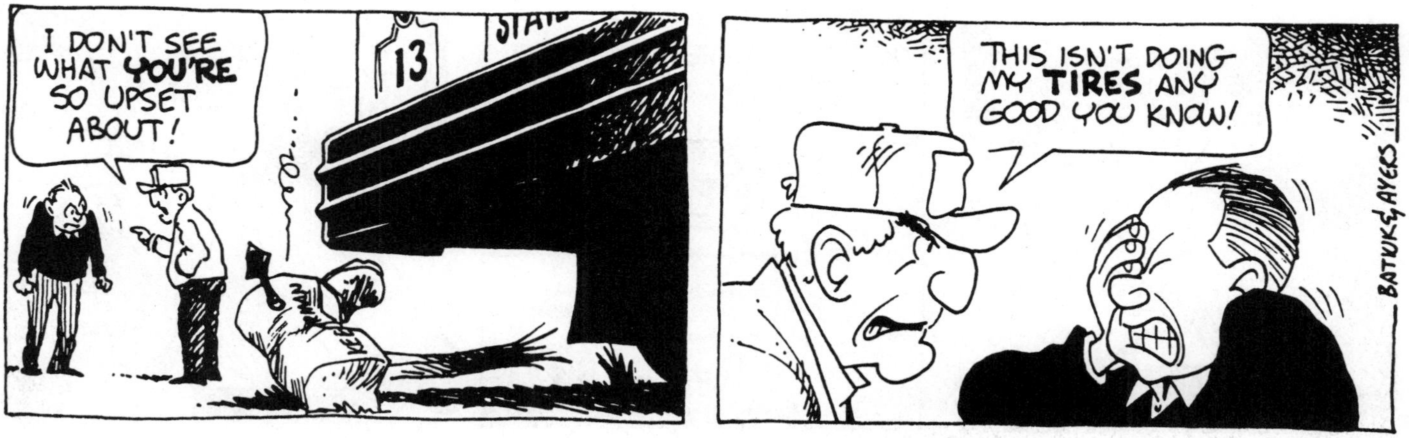
I DON'T SEE WHAT **YOU'RE** SO UPSET ABOUT!
13
THIS ISN'T DOING MY **TIRES** ANY GOOD YOU KNOW!
BATIUK & AYERS

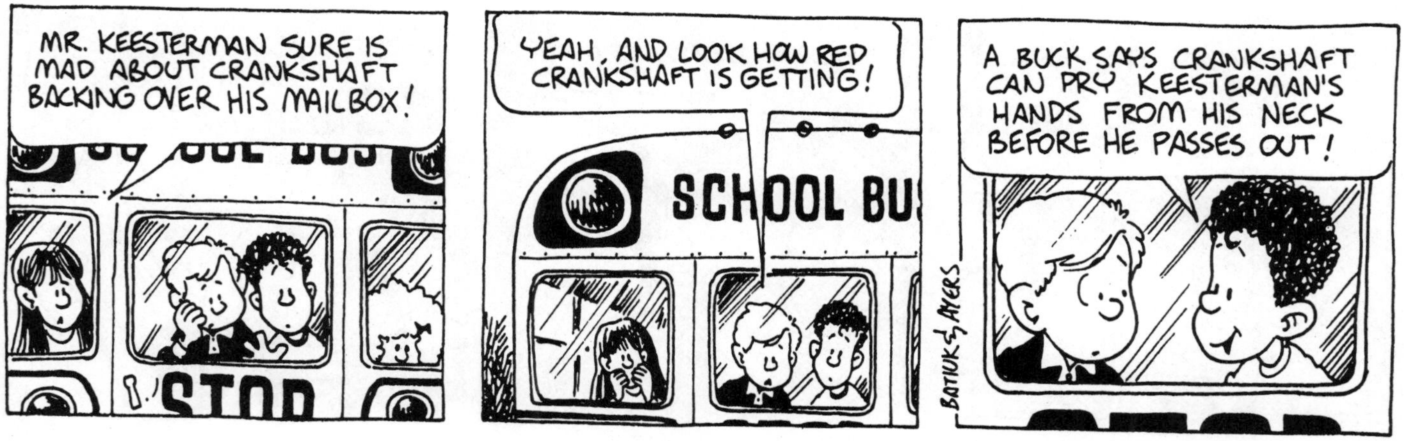
MR. KEESTERMAN SURE IS MAD ABOUT CRANKSHAFT BACKING OVER HIS MAILBOX!
YEAH, AND LOOK HOW RED CRANKSHAFT IS GETTING!
SCHOOL BUS
A BUCK SAYS CRANKSHAFT CAN PRY KEESTERMAN'S HANDS FROM HIS NECK BEFORE HE PASSES OUT!
BATIUK & AYERS

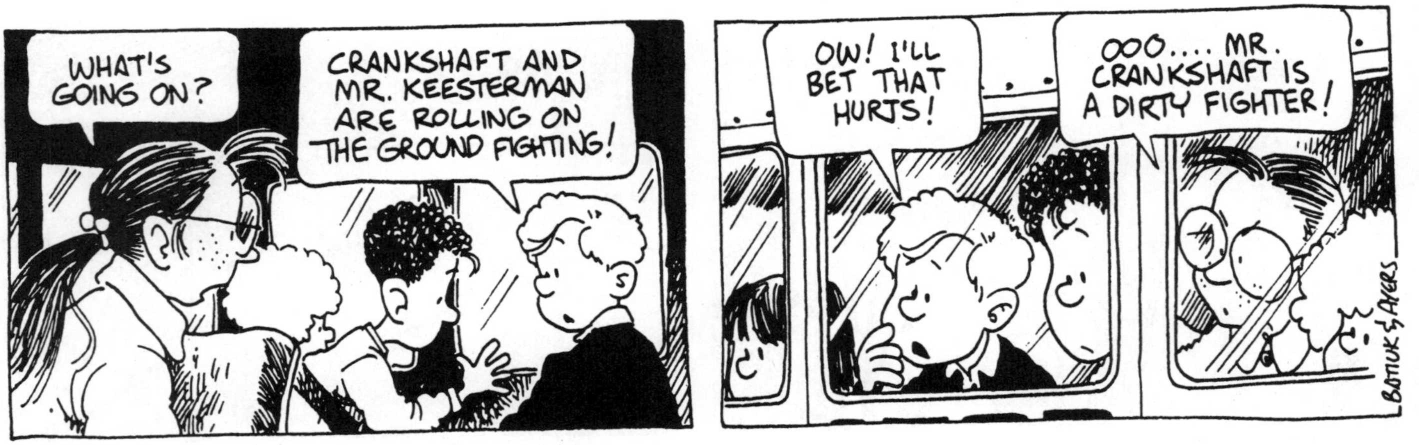
WHAT'S GOING ON?
CRANKSHAFT AND MR. KEESTERMAN ARE ROLLING ON THE GROUND FIGHTING!
OW! I'LL BET THAT HURTS!
OOO.... MR. CRANKSHAFT IS A DIRTY FIGHTER!
BATIUK & AYERS

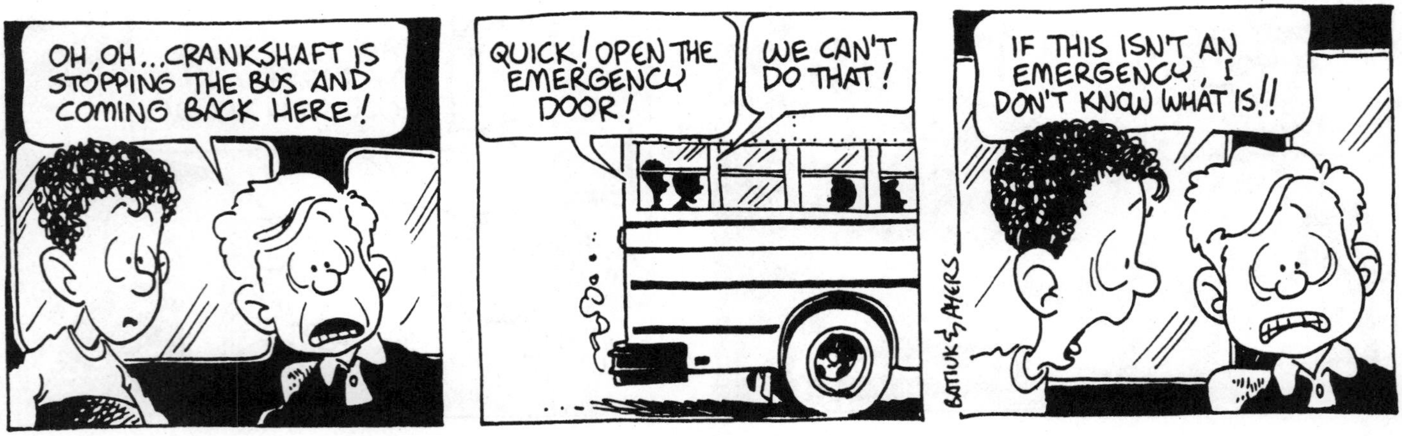
OH, OH...CRANKSHAFT IS STOPPING THE BUS AND COMING BACK HERE!
QUICK! OPEN THE EMERGENCY DOOR!
WE CAN'T DO THAT!
BATIUK & AYERS
IF THIS ISN'T AN EMERGENCY, I DON'T KNOW WHAT IS!!

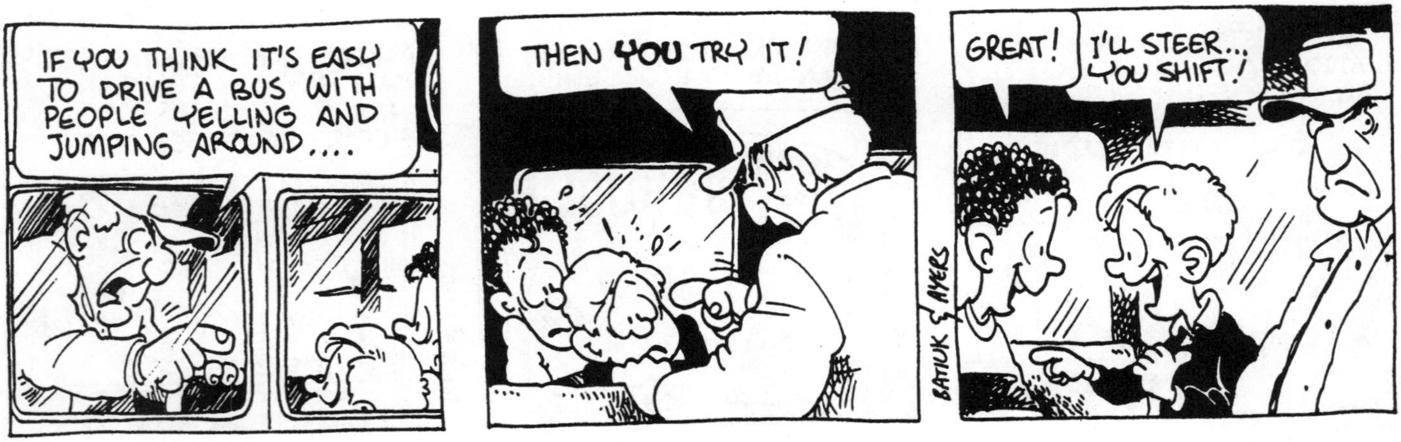
IF YOU THINK IT'S EASY TO DRIVE A BUS WITH PEOPLE YELLING AND JUMPING AROUND....
THEN **YOU** TRY IT!
BATIUK & AYERS
GREAT!
I'LL STEER... YOU SHIFT!

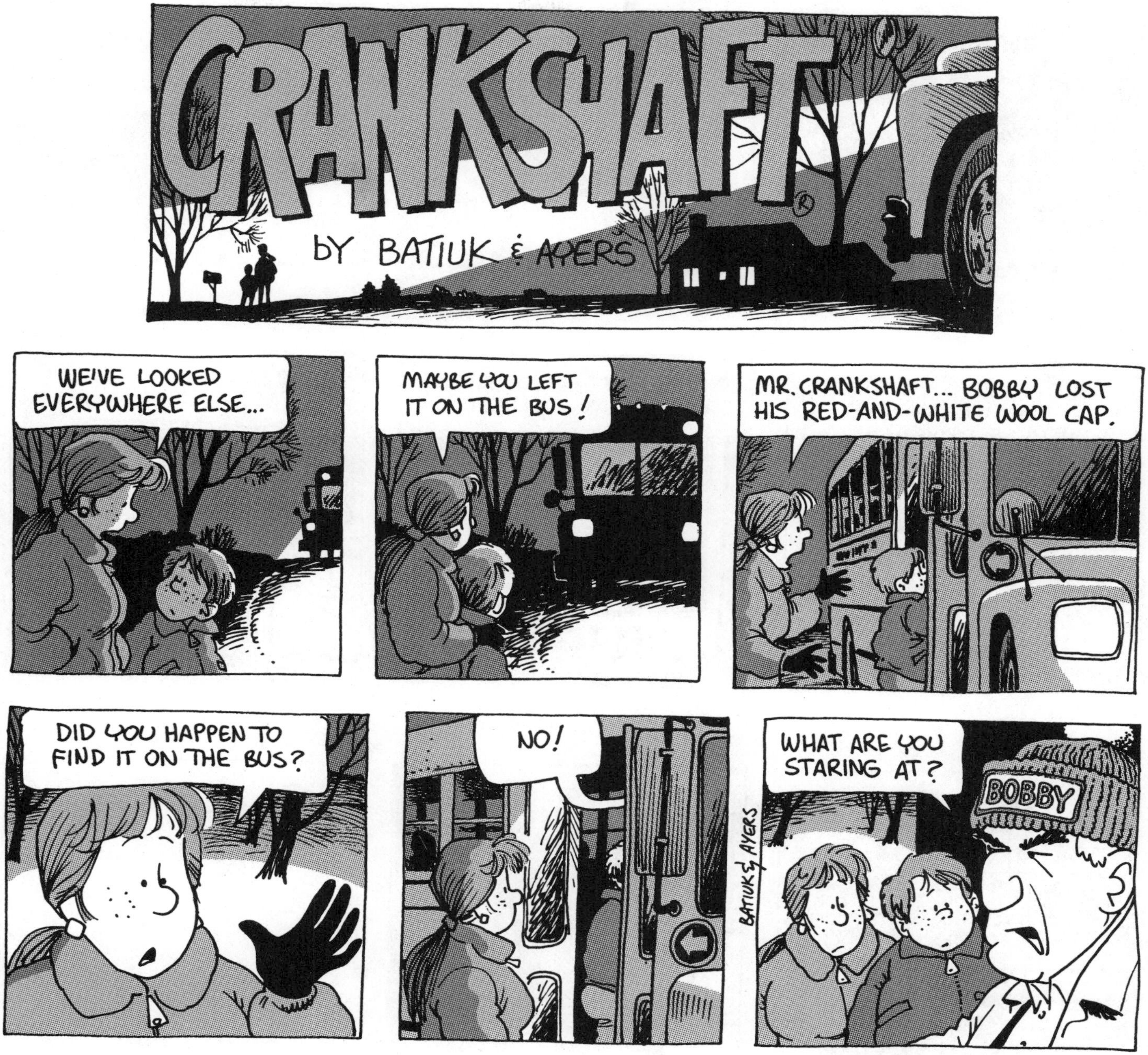
CRANKSHAFT
BY BATIUK & AYERS
WE'VE LOOKED EVERYWHERE ELSE...
MAYBE YOU LEFT IT ON THE BUS!
MR. CRANKSHAFT... BOBBY LOST HIS RED-AND-WHITE WOOL CAP.
DID YOU HAPPEN TO FIND IT ON THE BUS?
NO!
BATIUK & AYERS
WHAT ARE YOU STARING AT?
BOBBY

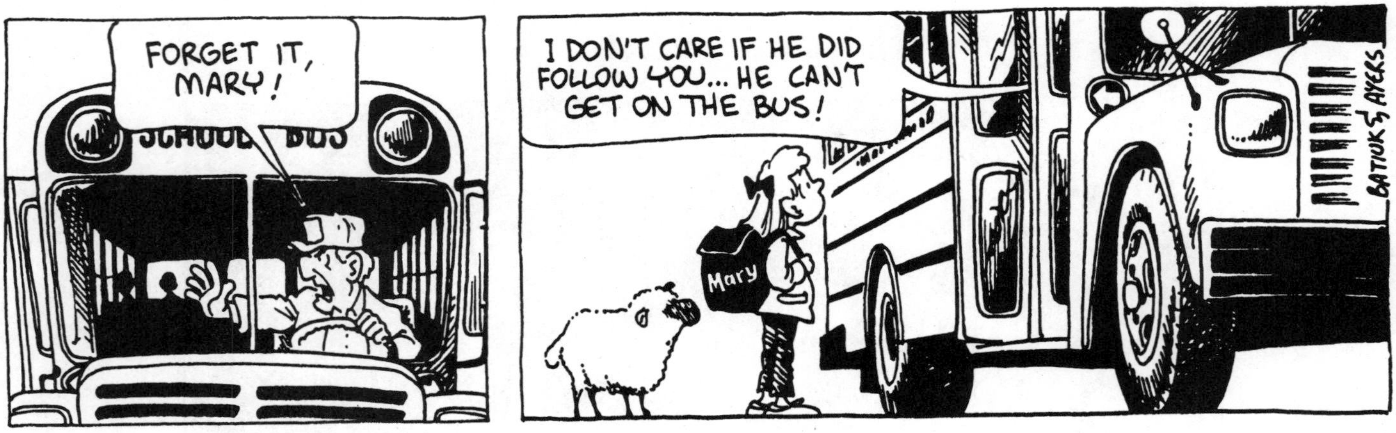
FORGET IT, MARY!
I DON'T CARE IF HE DID FOLLOW YOU... HE CAN'T GET ON THE BUS!
Mary
BATIUK & AYERS

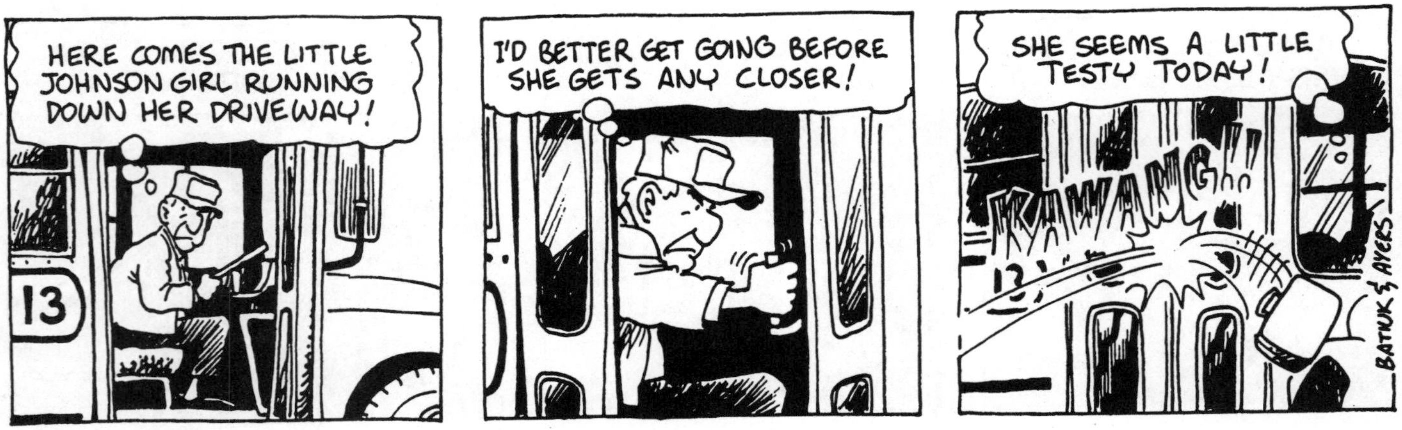
HERE COMES THE LITTLE JOHNSON GIRL RUNNING DOWN HER DRIVEWAY!
13
I'D BETTER GET GOING BEFORE SHE GETS ANY CLOSER!
SHE SEEMS A LITTLE TESTY TODAY!
KAWANG!!
BATIUK & AYERS

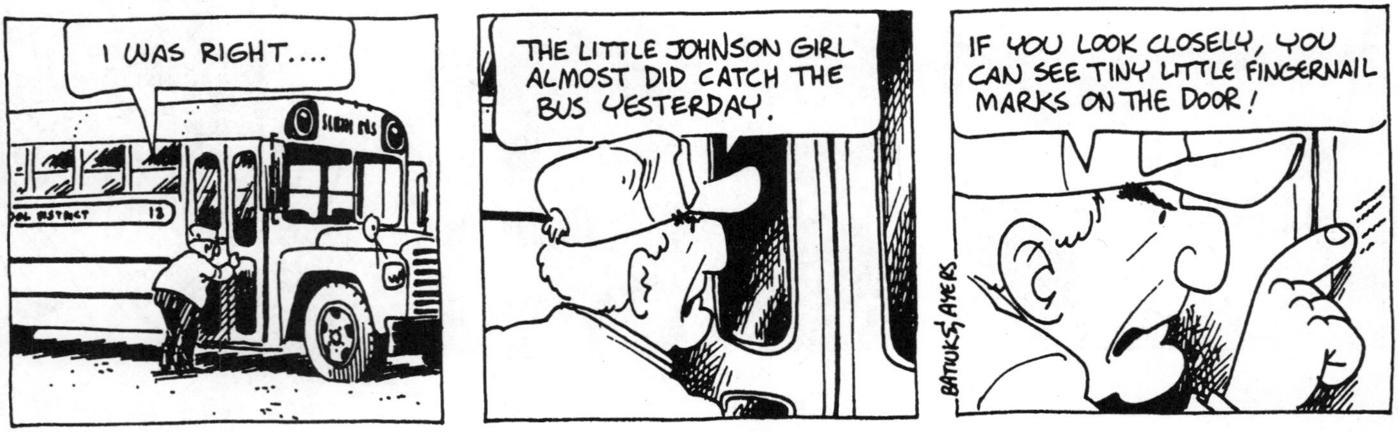
I WAS RIGHT....
THE LITTLE JOHNSON GIRL ALMOST DID CATCH THE BUS YESTERDAY.
IF YOU LOOK CLOSELY, YOU CAN SEE TINY LITTLE FINGERNAIL MARKS ON THE DOOR!
BATIUK & AYERS

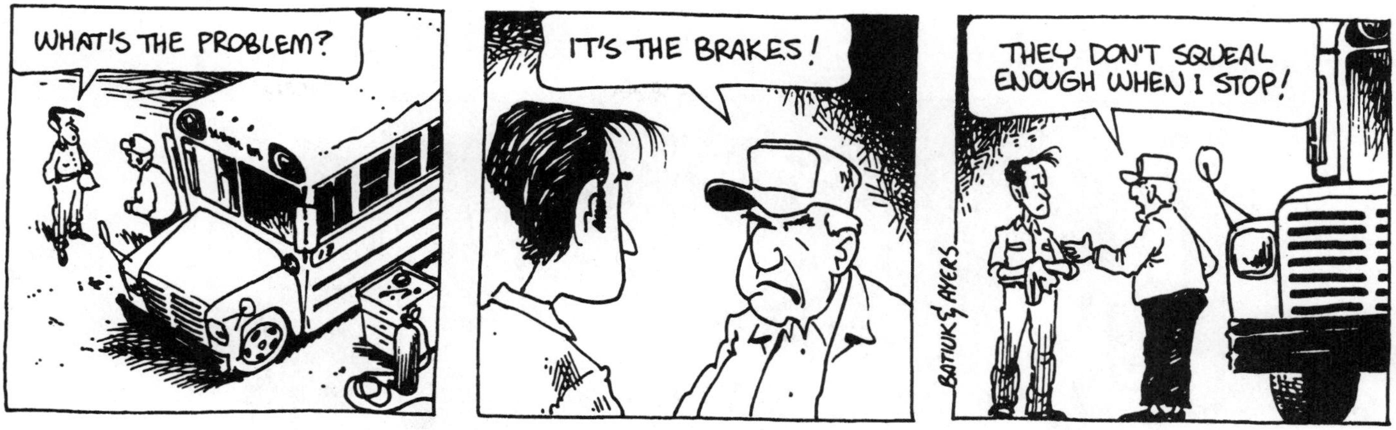
WHAT'S THE PROBLEM?
IT'S THE BRAKES!
THEY DON'T SQUEAL ENOUGH WHEN I STOP!
BATIUK & AYERS

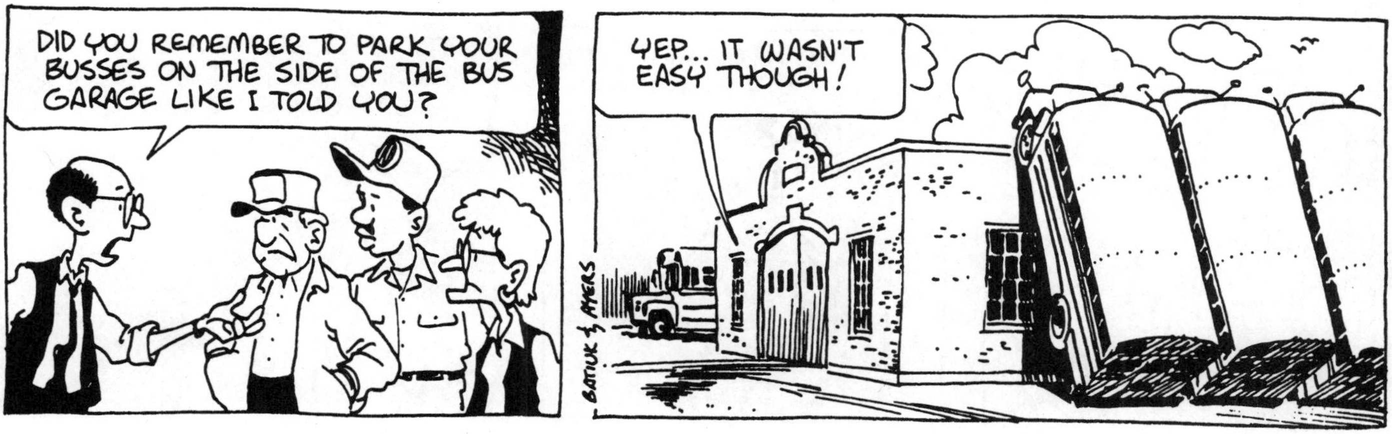
DID YOU REMEMBER TO PARK YOUR BUSSES ON THE SIDE OF THE BUS GARAGE LIKE I TOLD YOU?
YEP... IT WASN'T EASY THOUGH!
BATIUK & AYERS

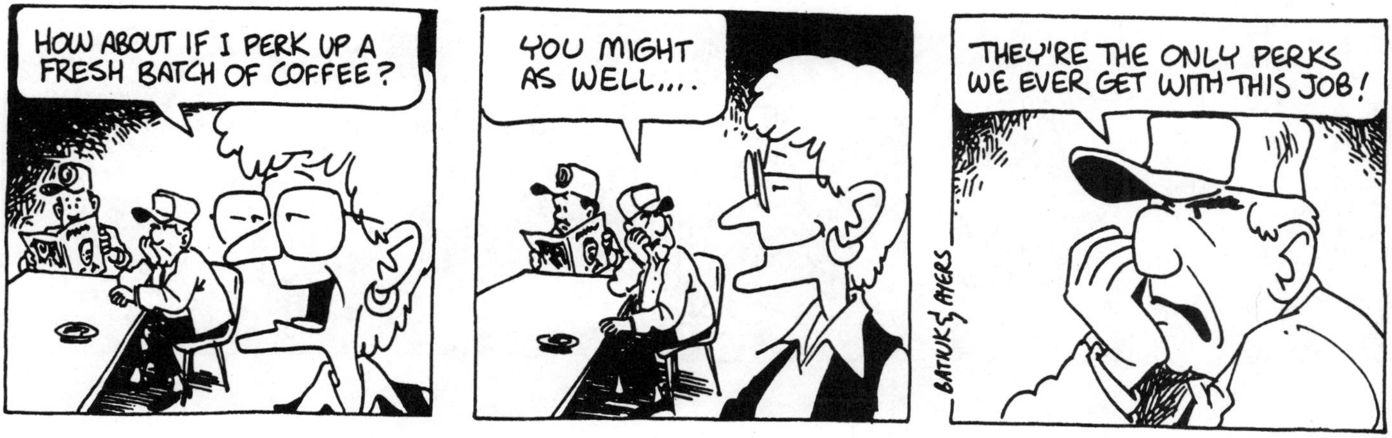
HOW ABOUT IF I PERK UP A FRESH BATCH OF COFFEE?
YOU MIGHT AS WELL....
THEY'RE THE ONLY PERKS WE EVER GET WITH THIS JOB!
BATIUK & AYERS

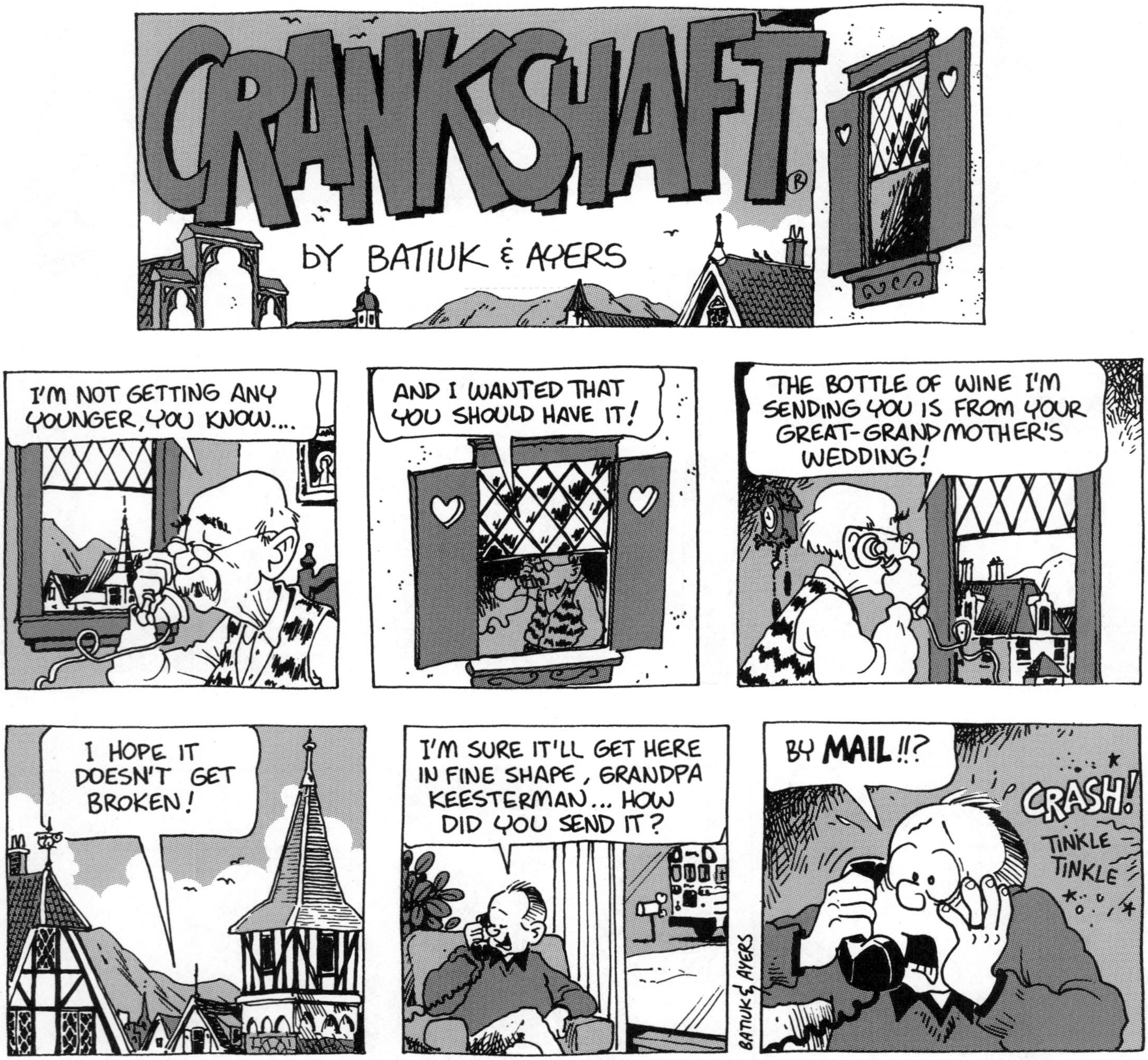
CRANKSHAFT®
BY BATIUK & AYERS
I'M NOT GETTING ANY YOUNGER, YOU KNOW....
AND I WANTED THAT YOU SHOULD HAVE IT!
THE BOTTLE OF WINE I'M SENDING YOU IS FROM YOUR GREAT-GRANDMOTHER'S WEDDING!
I HOPE IT DOESN'T GET BROKEN!
I'M SURE IT'LL GET HERE IN FINE SHAPE, GRANDPA KEESTERMAN... HOW DID YOU SEND IT?
BATIUK & AYERS
BY MAIL!!?
CRASH!
TINKLE TINKLE

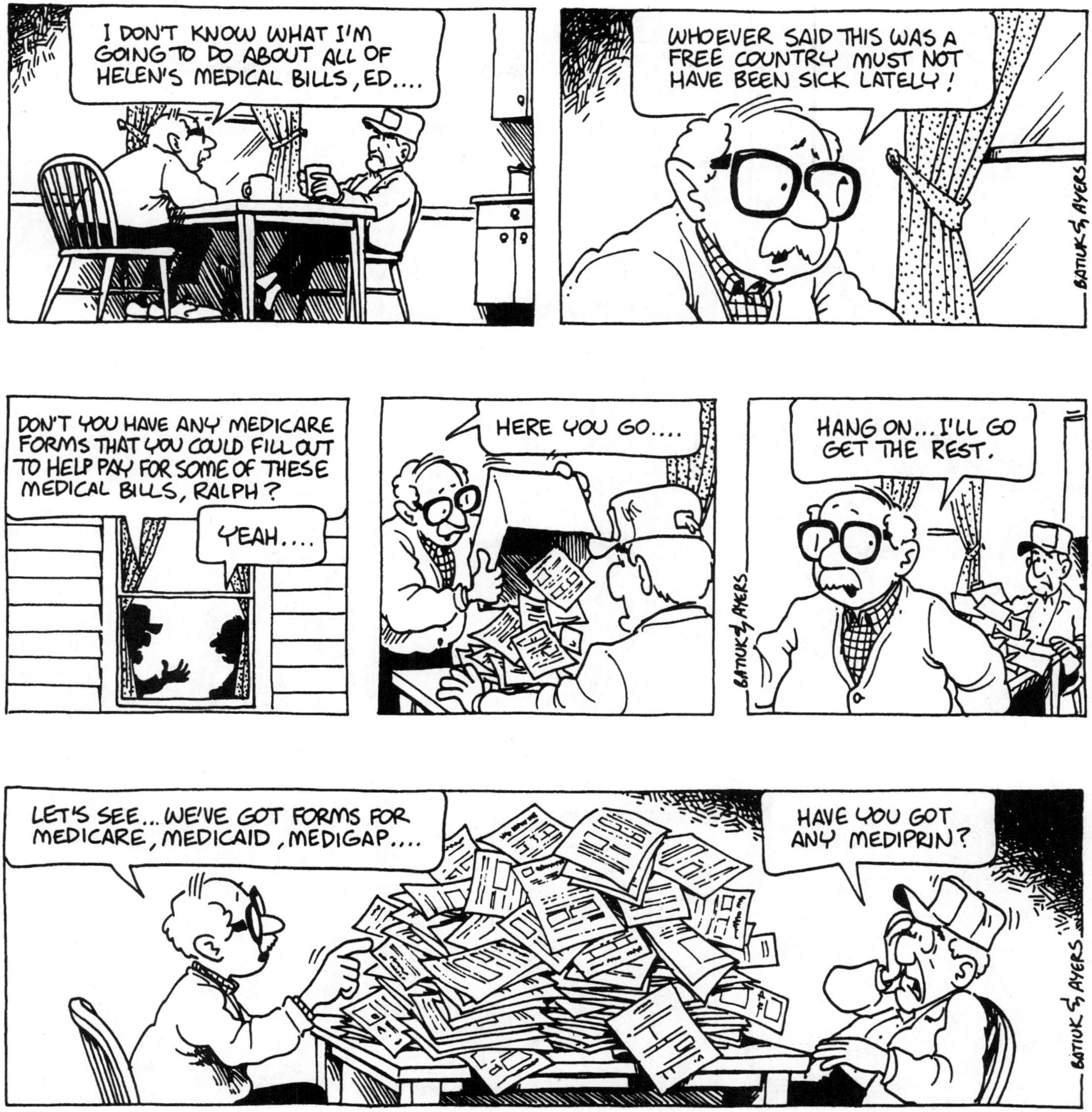
I DON'T KNOW WHAT I'M GOING TO DO ABOUT ALL OF HELEN'S MEDICAL BILLS, ED....
WHOEVER SAID THIS WAS A FREE COUNTRY MUST NOT HAVE BEEN SICK LATELY!
BATIUK & AYERS
DON'T YOU HAVE ANY MEDICARE FORMS THAT YOU COULD FILL OUT TO HELP PAY FOR SOME OF THESE MEDICAL BILLS, RALPH?
YEAH....
HERE YOU GO....
BATIUK & AYERS
HANG ON... I'LL GO GET THE REST.
LET'S SEE... WE'VE GOT FORMS FOR MEDICARE, MEDICAID, MEDIGAP....
HAVE YOU GOT ANY MEDIPRIN?
BATIUK & AYERS

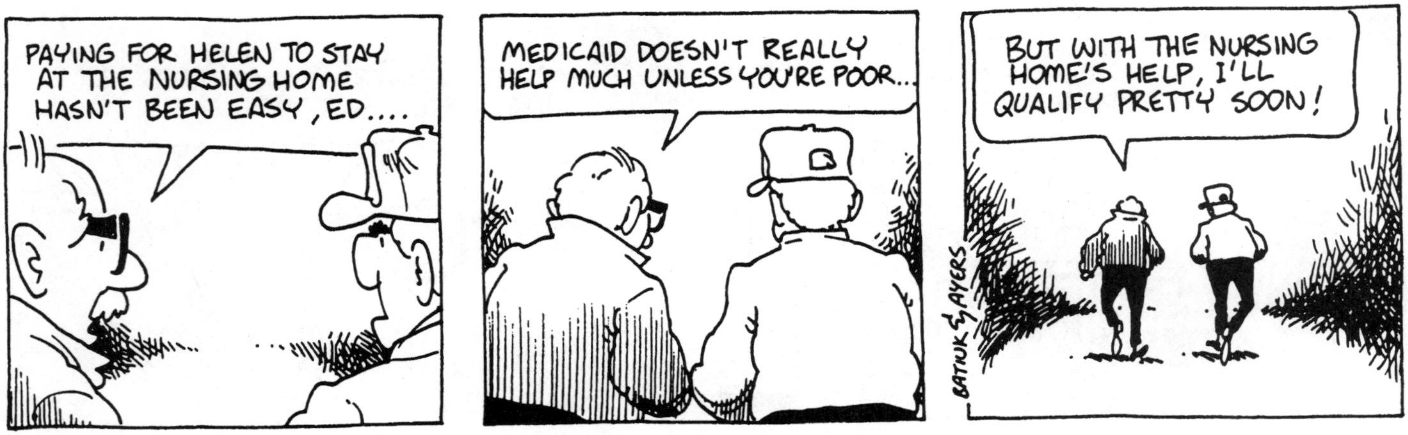
PAYING FOR HELEN TO STAY AT THE NURSING HOME HASN'T BEEN EASY, ED....
MEDICAID DOESN'T REALLY HELP MUCH UNLESS YOU'RE POOR...
BUT WITH THE NURSING HOME'S HELP, I'LL QUALIFY PRETTY SOON!
BATIUK & AYERS

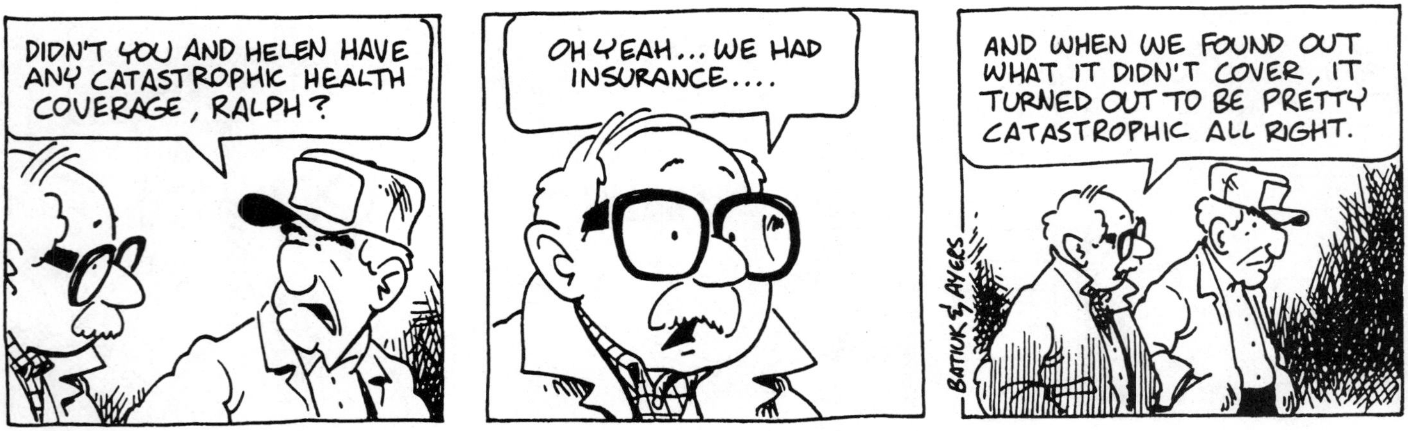
DIDN'T YOU AND HELEN HAVE ANY CATASTROPHIC HEALTH COVERAGE, RALPH?
OH YEAH... WE HAD INSURANCE....
AND WHEN WE FOUND OUT WHAT IT DIDN'T COVER, IT TURNED OUT TO BE PRETTY CATASTROPHIC ALL RIGHT.
BATIUK & AYERS

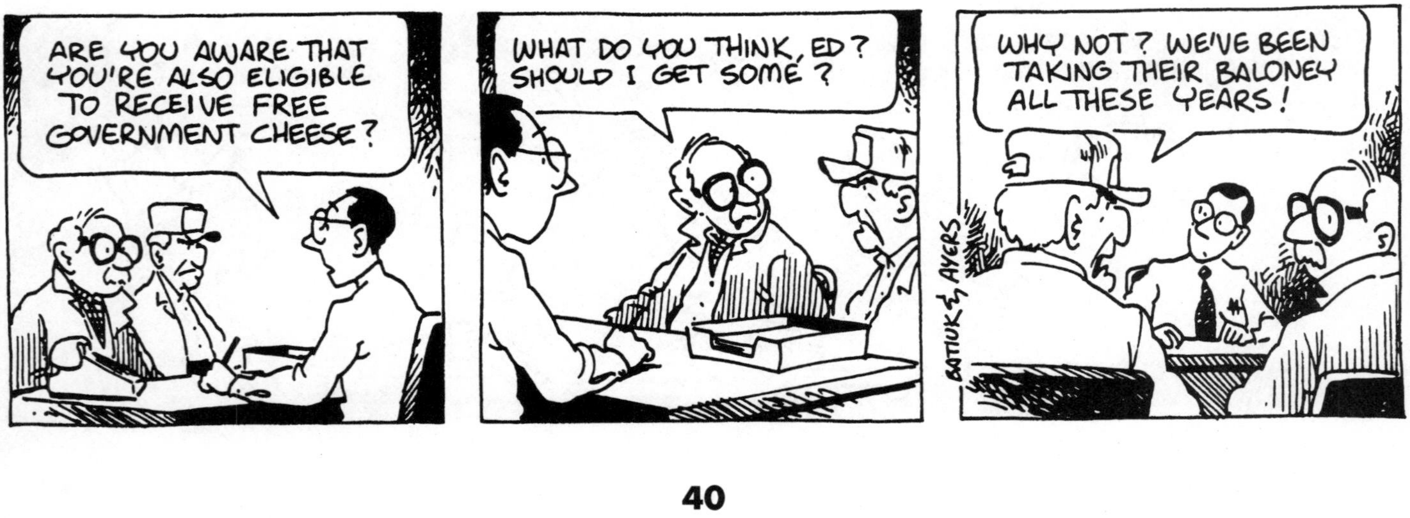
ARE YOU AWARE THAT YOU'RE ALSO ELIGIBLE TO RECEIVE FREE GOVERNMENT CHEESE?
WHAT DO YOU THINK, ED? SHOULD I GET SOME?
WHY NOT? WE'VE BEEN TAKING THEIR BALONEY ALL THESE YEARS!
BATIUK & AYERS

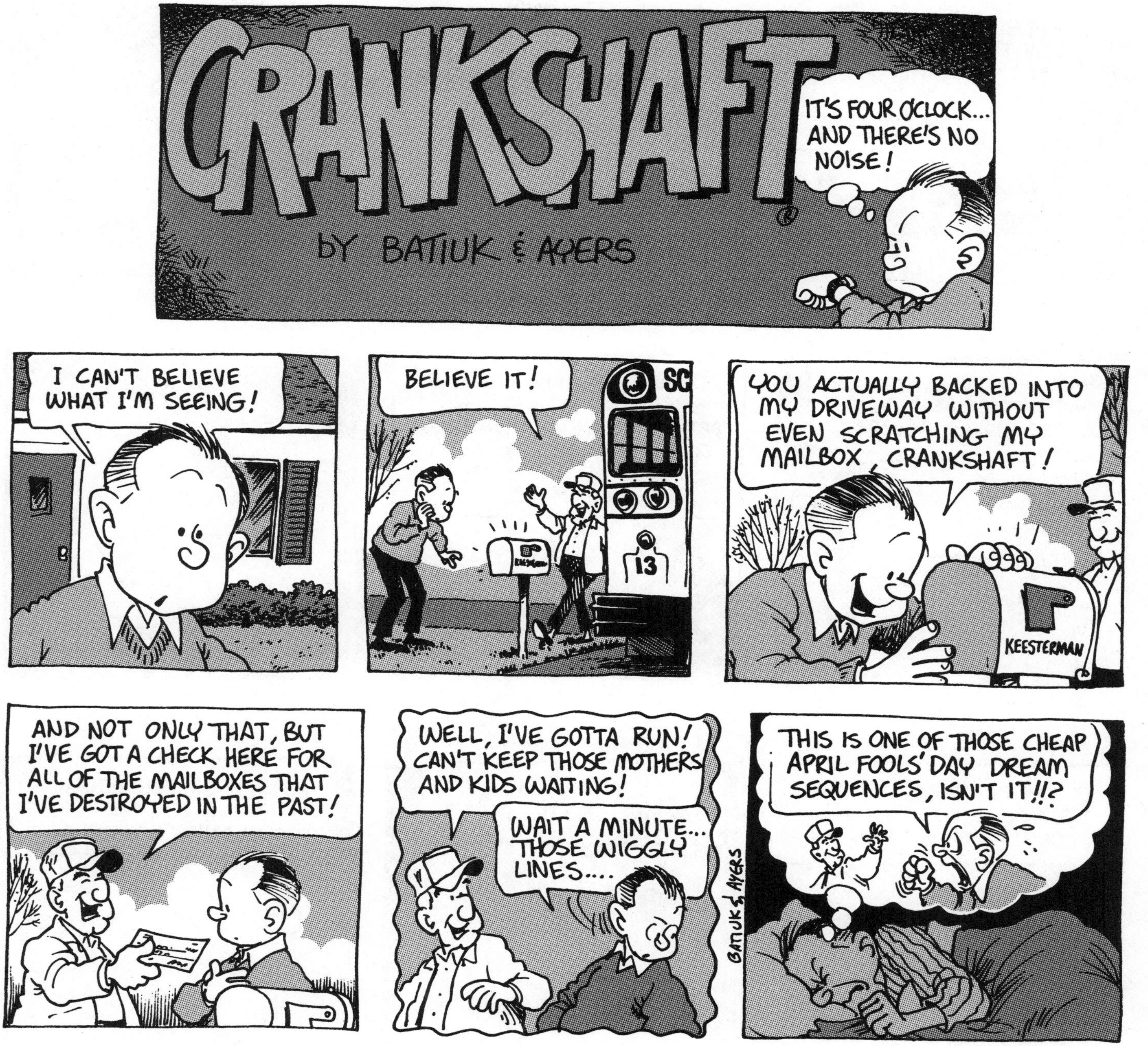
CRANKSHAFT
BY BATIUK & AYERS
IT'S FOUR O'CLOCK... AND THERE'S NO NOISE!
I CAN'T BELIEVE WHAT I'M SEEING!
BELIEVE IT!
13
YOU ACTUALLY BACKED INTO MY DRIVEWAY WITHOUT EVEN SCRATCHING MY MAILBOX, CRANKSHAFT!
KEESTERMAN
AND NOT ONLY THAT, BUT I'VE GOT A CHECK HERE FOR ALL OF THE MAILBOXES THAT I'VE DESTROYED IN THE PAST!
WELL, I'VE GOTTA RUN! CAN'T KEEP THOSE MOTHERS AND KIDS WAITING!
WAIT A MINUTE... THOSE WIGGLY LINES....
BATIUK & AYERS
THIS IS ONE OF THOSE CHEAP APRIL FOOLS' DAY DREAM SEQUENCES, ISN'T IT!!?

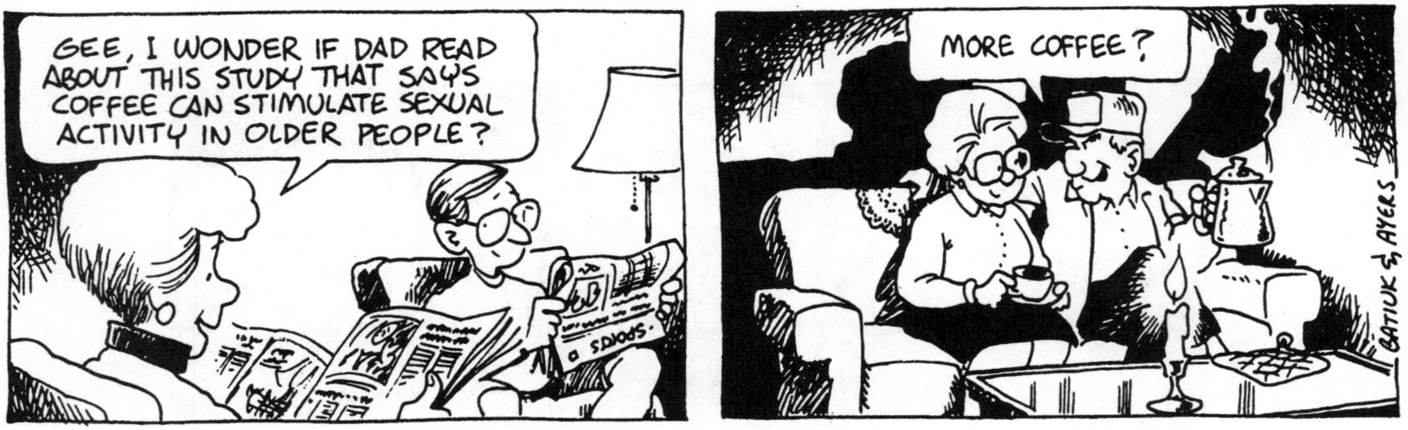
GEE, I WONDER IF DAD READ ABOUT THIS STUDY THAT SAYS COFFEE CAN STIMULATE SEXUAL ACTIVITY IN OLDER PEOPLE?
MORE COFFEE?
BATIUK & AYERS

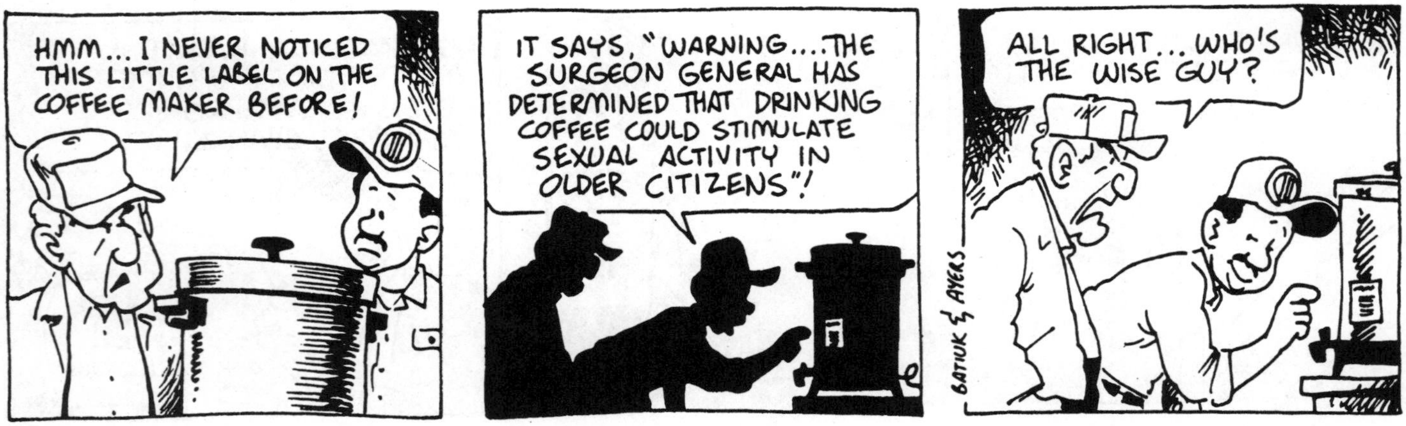
HMM... I NEVER NOTICED THIS LITTLE LABEL ON THE COFFEE MAKER BEFORE!
IT SAYS, "WARNING.... THE SURGEON GENERAL HAS DETERMINED THAT DRINKING COFFEE COULD STIMULATE SEXUAL ACTIVITY IN OLDER CITIZENS"!
BATIUK & AYERS
ALL RIGHT... WHO'S THE WISE GUY?

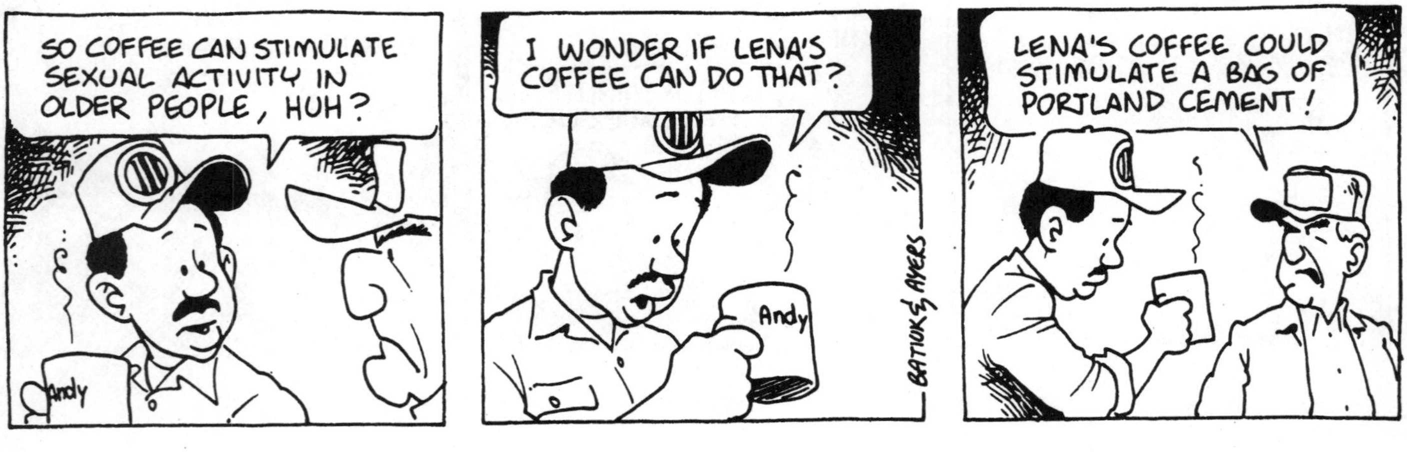
SO COFFEE CAN STIMULATE SEXUAL ACTIVITY IN OLDER PEOPLE, HUH?
Andy
I WONDER IF LENA'S COFFEE CAN DO THAT?
Andy
BATIUK & AYERS
LENA'S COFFEE COULD STIMULATE A BAG OF PORTLAND CEMENT!

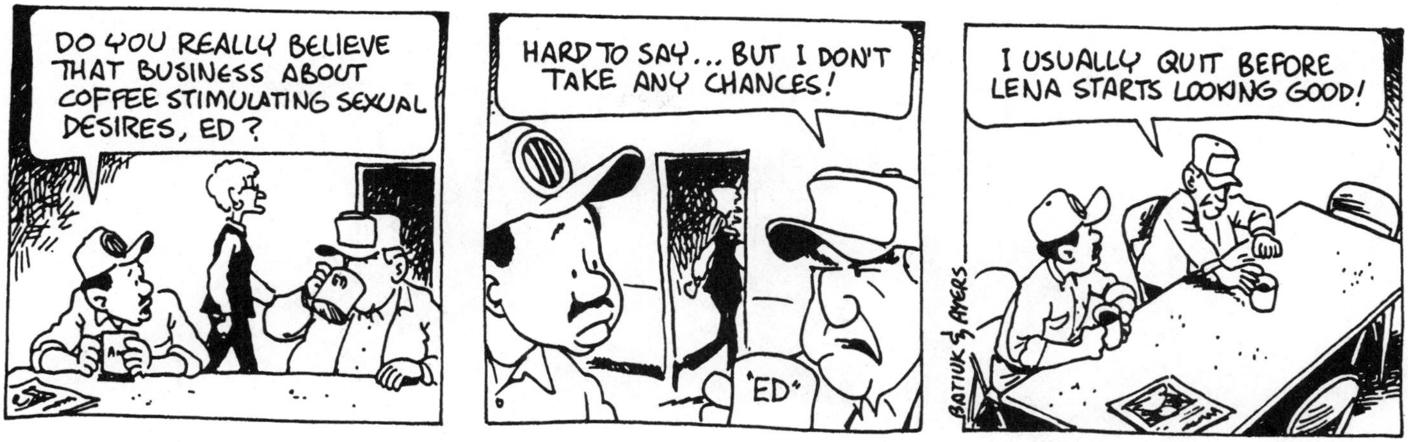
DO YOU REALLY BELIEVE THAT BUSINESS ABOUT COFFEE STIMULATING SEXUAL DESIRES, ED?
HARD TO SAY... BUT I DON'T TAKE ANY CHANCES!
"ED"
I USUALLY QUIT BEFORE LENA STARTS LOOKING GOOD!
BATIUK & AYERS

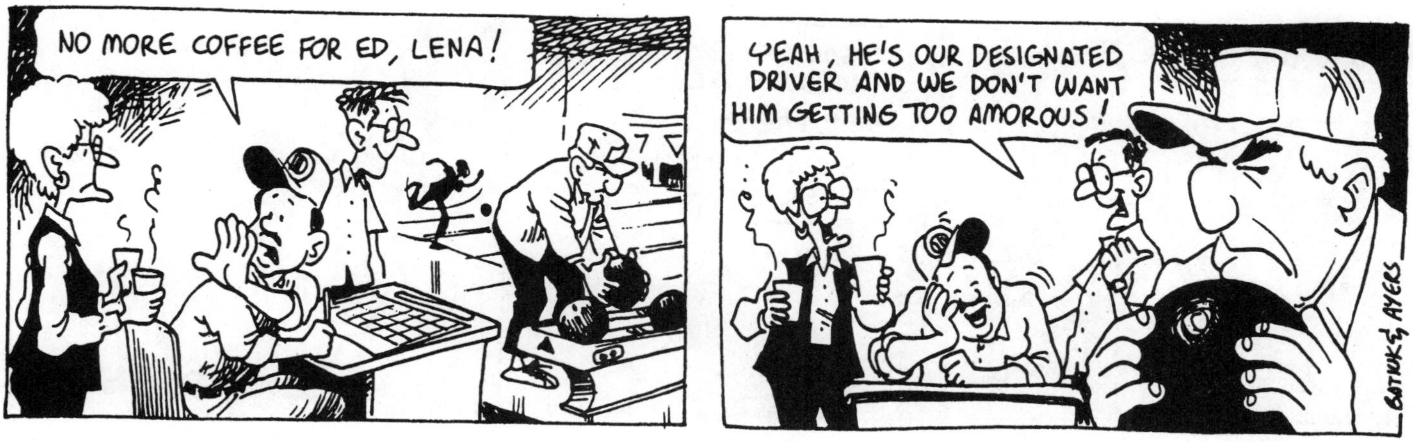
NO MORE COFFEE FOR ED, LENA!
YEAH, HE'S OUR DESIGNATED DRIVER AND WE DON'T WANT HIM GETTING TOO AMOROUS!
BATIUK & AYERS

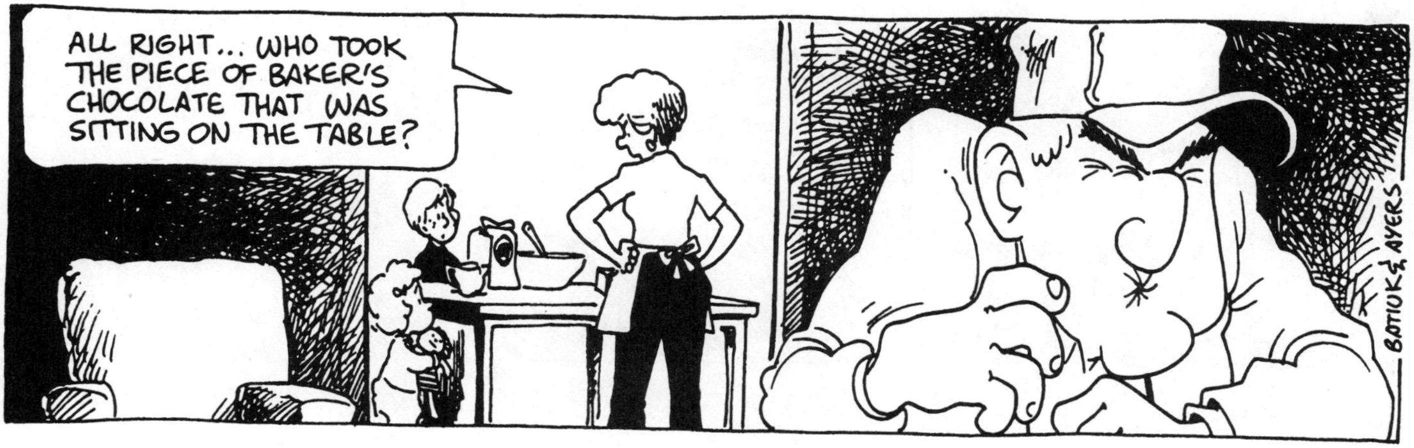
ALL RIGHT... WHO TOOK THE PIECE OF BAKER'S CHOCOLATE THAT WAS SITTING ON THE TABLE?
BATIUK & AYERS

CRANKSHAFT®
BY BATIUK & AYERS
WORLD'S BEST DAD
1989 TAX
MAX... DON'T BOTHER YOUR FATHER!
HE'S WORKING ON HIS INCOME TAXES.
WATCHA DOIN', DAD? WORKING ON STUFF FOR THE ETERNAL REVENUE?
NO, MAX... THAT'S....
BATIUK & AYERS
YOU GOT IT RIGHT ON THE MONEY, MAX!

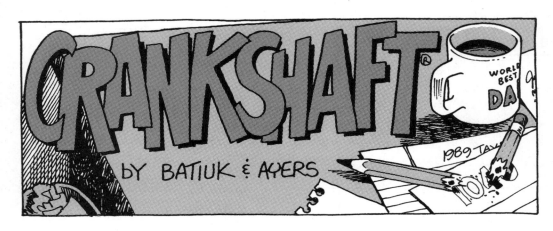

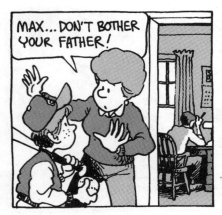

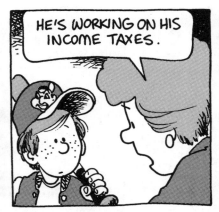

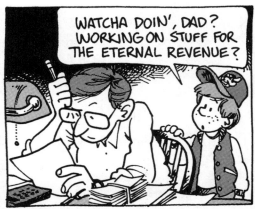

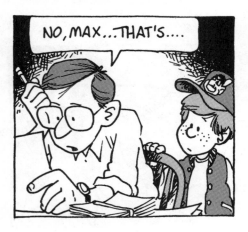

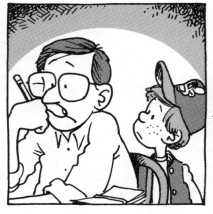

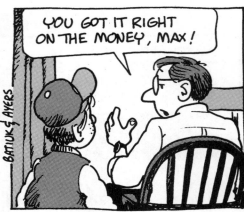

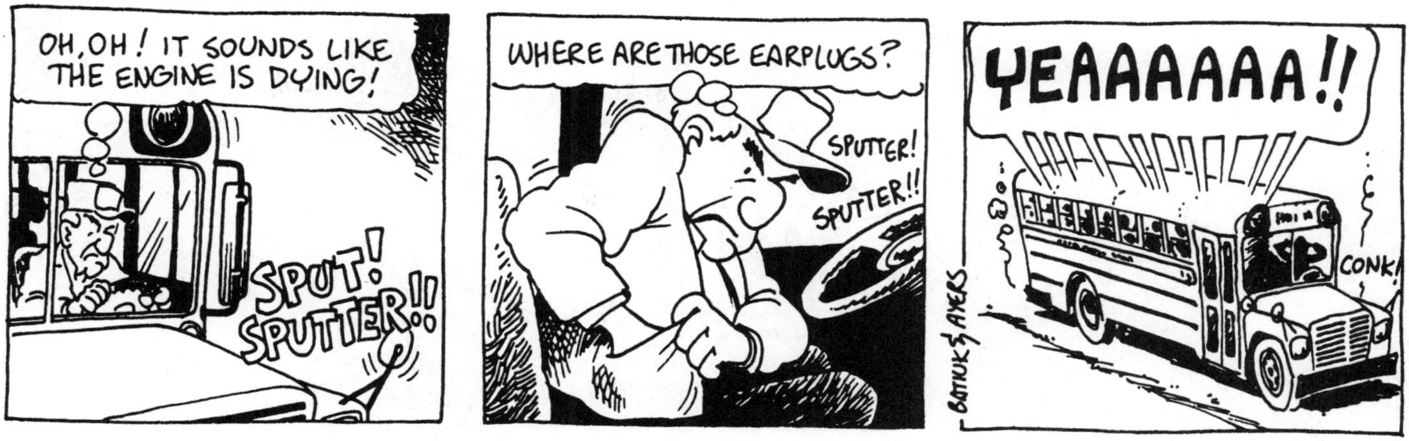
OH, OH! IT SOUNDS LIKE THE ENGINE IS DYING!
SPUT! SPUTTER!!
WHERE ARE THOSE EARPLUGS?
SPUTTER!
SPUTTER!!
YEAAAAAAA!!
CONK!
BATIUK & AYERS

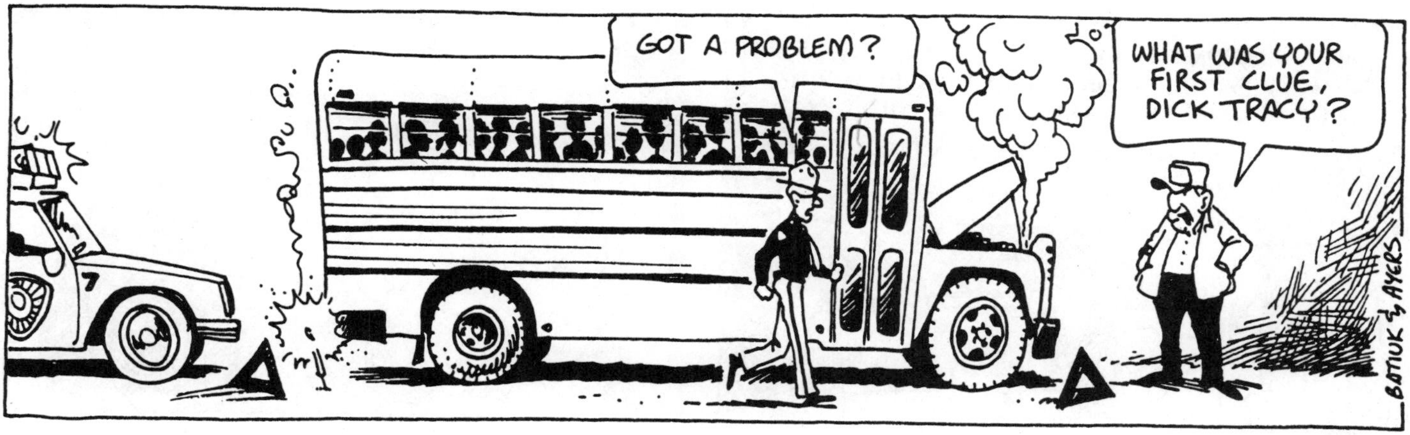
GOT A PROBLEM?
WHAT WAS YOUR FIRST CLUE, DICK TRACY?
7
BATIUK & AYERS

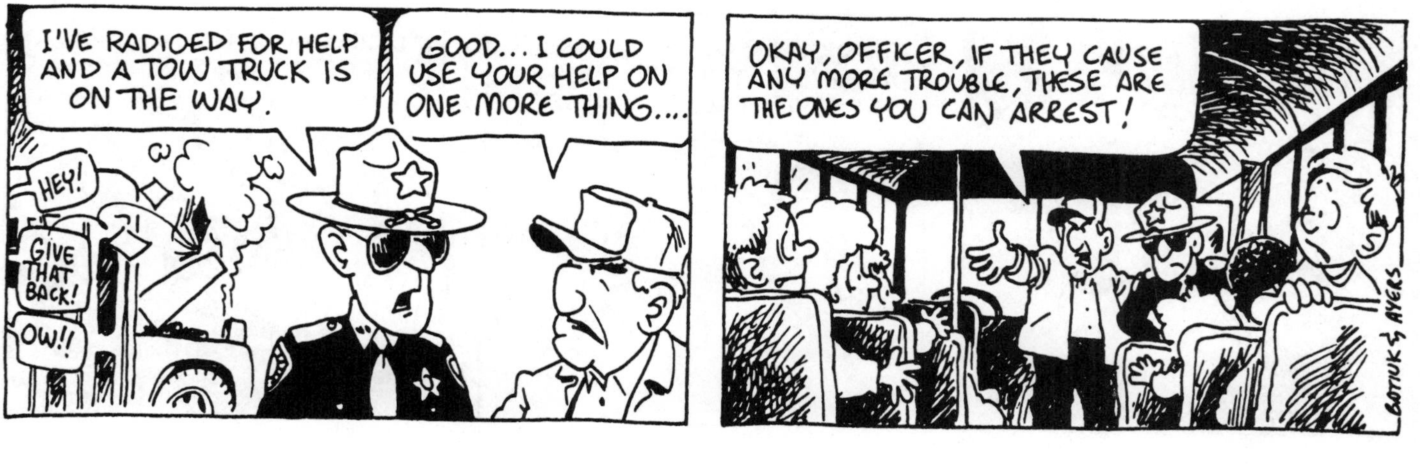
I'VE RADIOED FOR HELP AND A TOW TRUCK IS ON THE WAY.
GOOD... I COULD USE YOUR HELP ON ONE MORE THING....
HEY!
GIVE THAT BACK!
OW!!
OKAY, OFFICER, IF THEY CAUSE ANY MORE TROUBLE, THESE ARE THE ONES YOU CAN ARREST!
BATIUK & AYERS

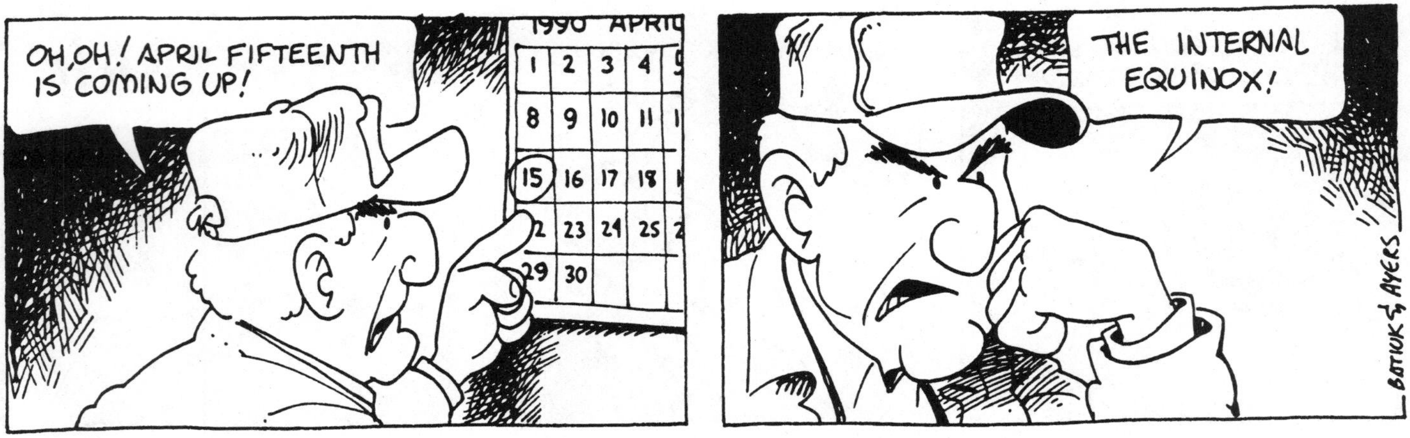
OH, OH! APRIL FIFTEENTH IS COMING UP!
THE INTERNAL EQUINOX!

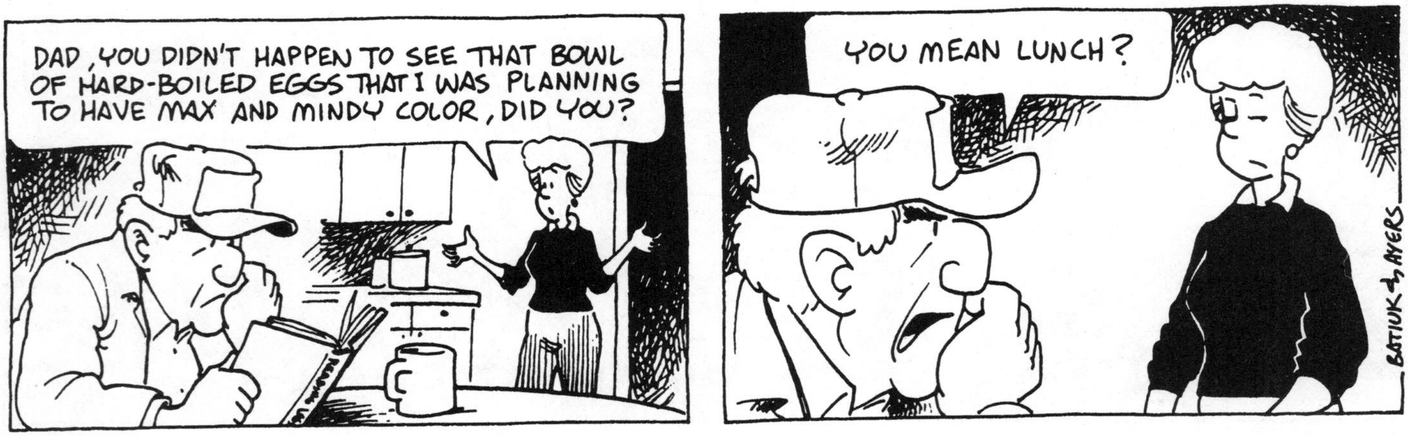
DAD, YOU DIDN'T HAPPEN TO SEE THAT BOWL OF HARD-BOILED EGGS THAT I WAS PLANNING TO HAVE MAX AND MINDY COLOR, DID YOU?
YOU MEAN LUNCH?

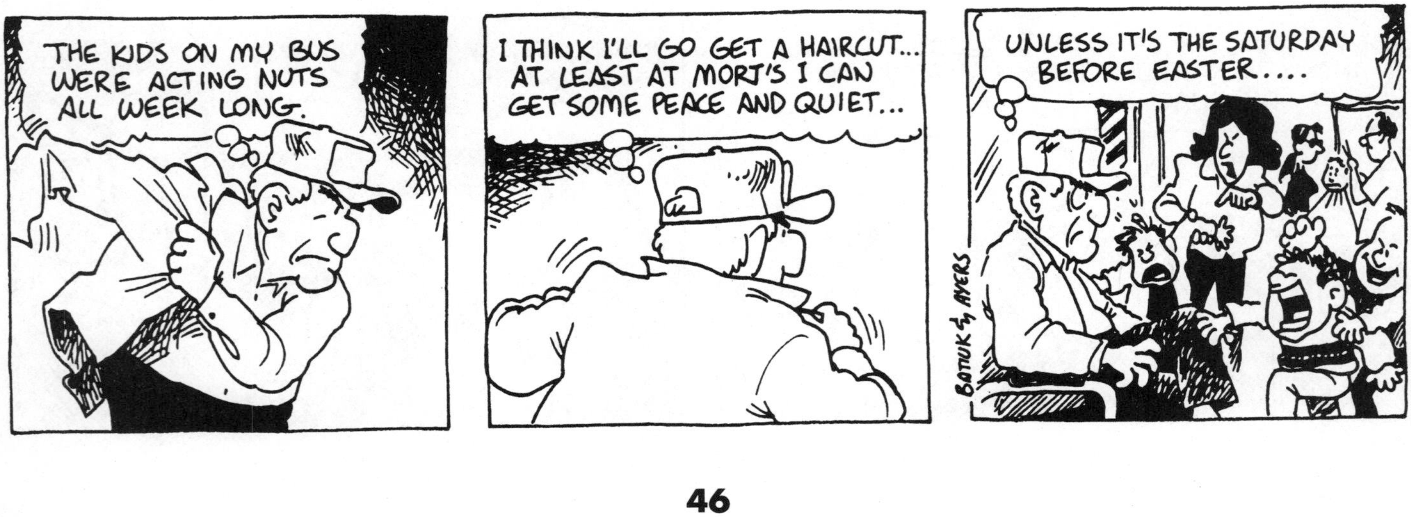
THE KIDS ON MY BUS WERE ACTING NUTS ALL WEEK LONG.
I THINK I'LL GO GET A HAIRCUT... AT LEAST AT MORT'S I CAN GET SOME PEACE AND QUIET...
UNLESS IT'S THE SATURDAY BEFORE EASTER....

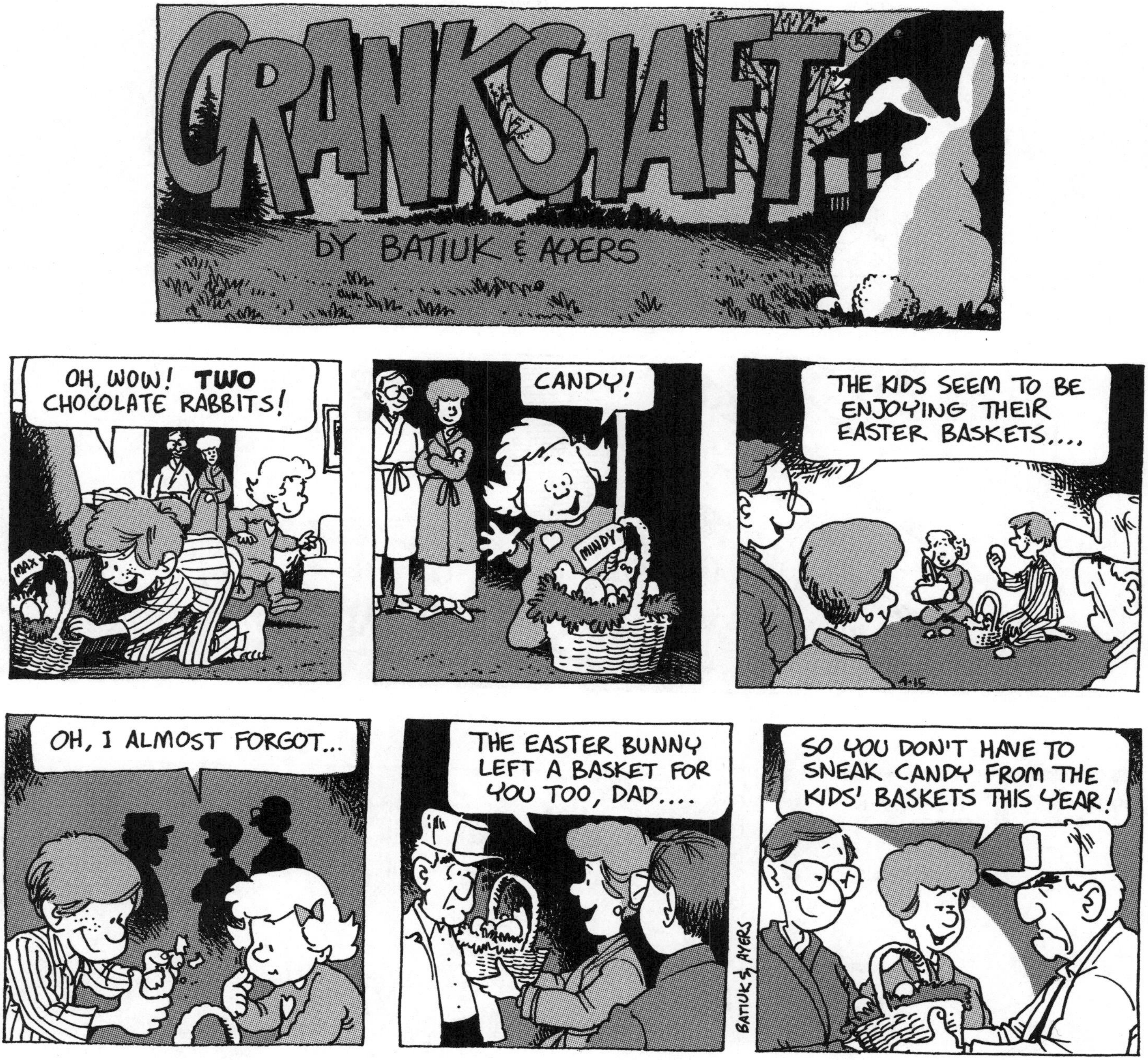
CRANKSHAFT®
BY BATIUK & AYERS
OH, WOW! TWO CHOCOLATE RABBITS!
MAX
CANDY!
MINDY
THE KIDS SEEM TO BE ENJOYING THEIR EASTER BASKETS....
4-15
OH, I ALMOST FORGOT...
THE EASTER BUNNY LEFT A BASKET FOR YOU TOO, DAD....
BATIUK & AYERS
SO YOU DON'T HAVE TO SNEAK CANDY FROM THE KIDS' BASKETS THIS YEAR!

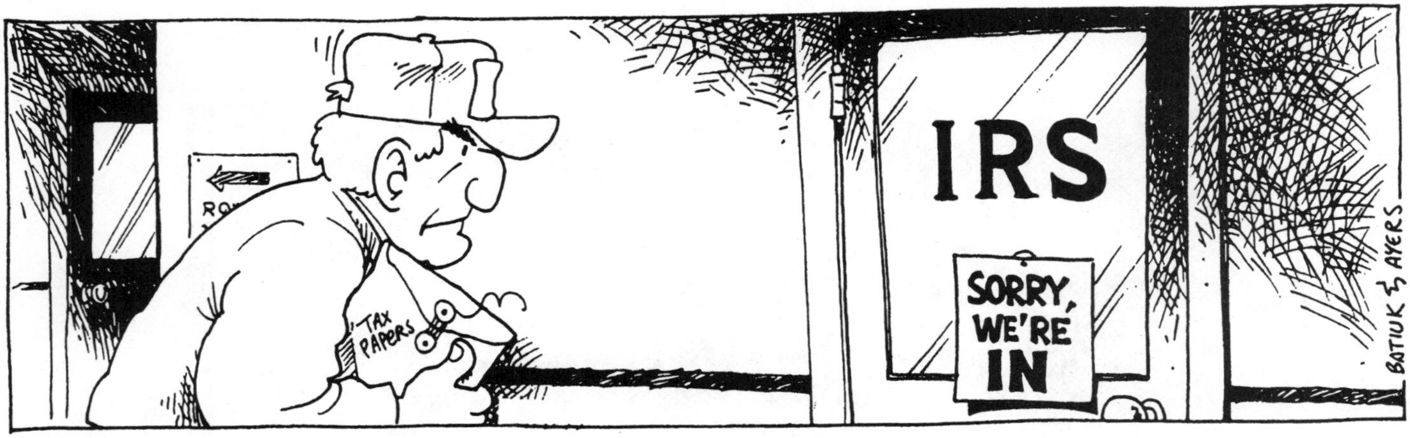
TAX PAPERS
IRS
SORRY, WE'RE IN
BATIUK & AYERS

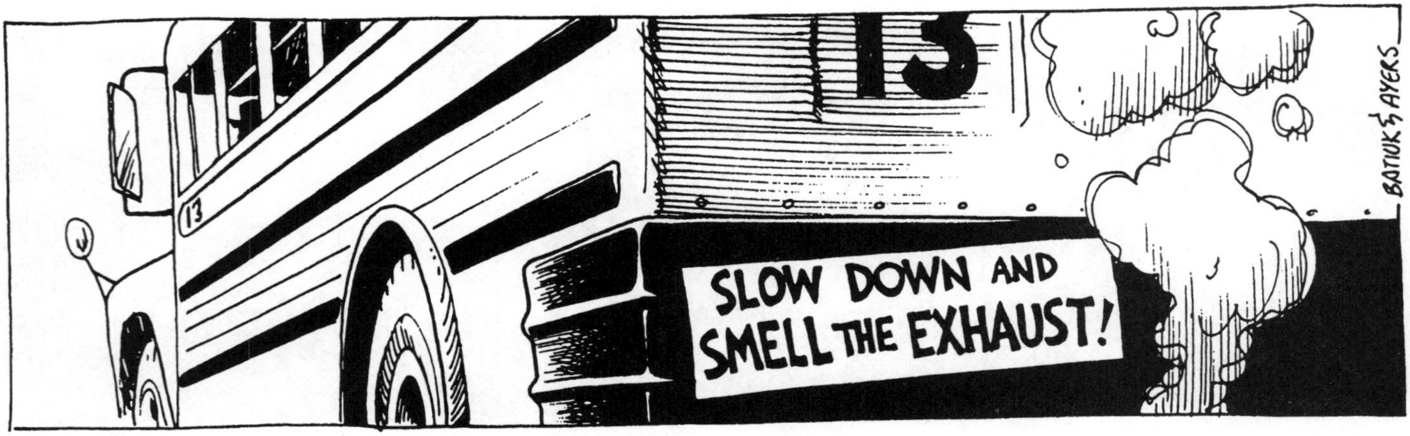
13
SLOW DOWN AND SMELL THE EXHAUST!
BATIUK & AYERS

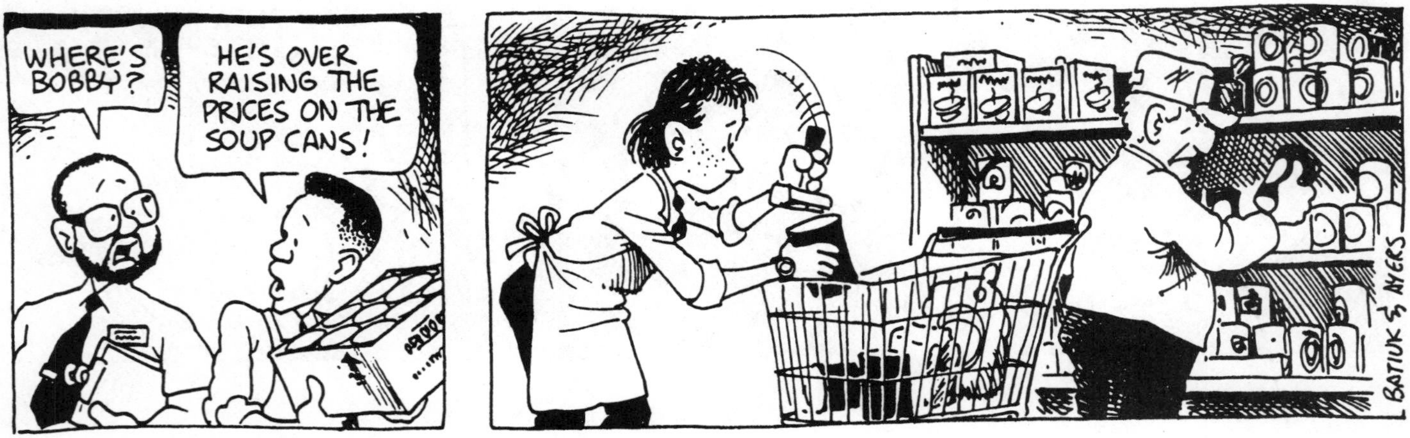
WHERE'S BOBBY?
HE'S OVER RAISING THE PRICES ON THE SOUP CANS!
BATIUK & AYERS

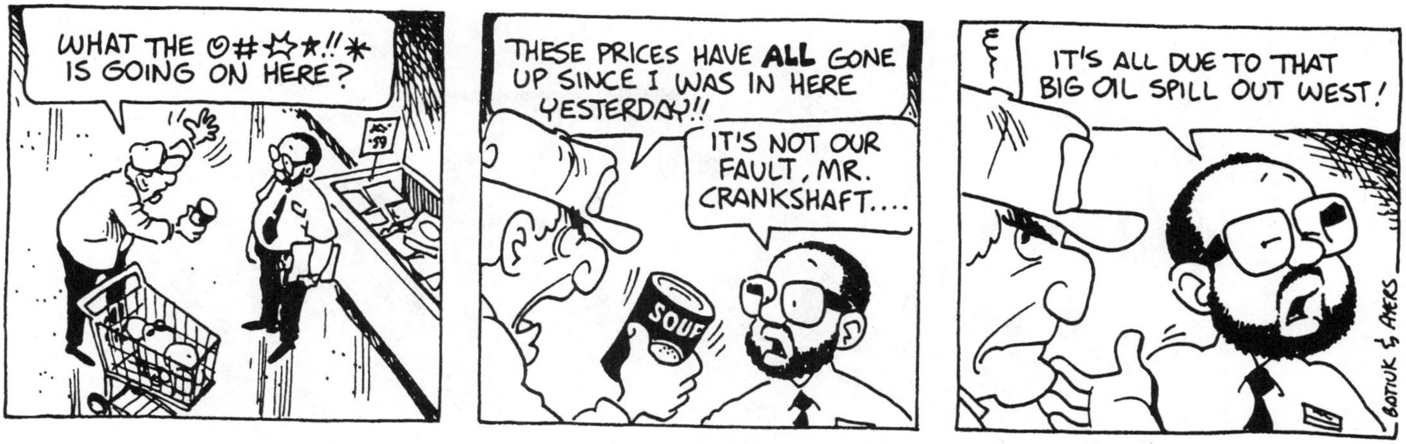
WHAT THE ☺#☆★!!* IS GOING ON HERE?
THESE PRICES HAVE **ALL** GONE UP SINCE I WAS IN HERE YESTERDAY!!
SOUP
IT'S NOT OUR FAULT, MR. CRANKSHAFT....
IT'S ALL DUE TO THAT BIG OIL SPILL OUT WEST!
BATIUK & AYERS

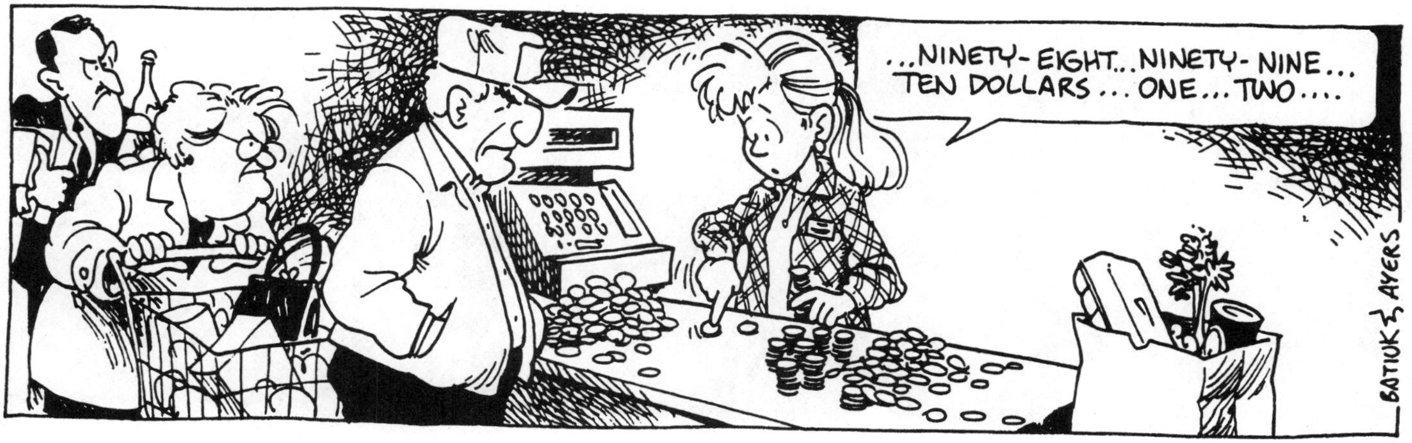
...NINETY-EIGHT...NINETY-NINE...
TEN DOLLARS...ONE...TWO....
BATIUK & AYERS

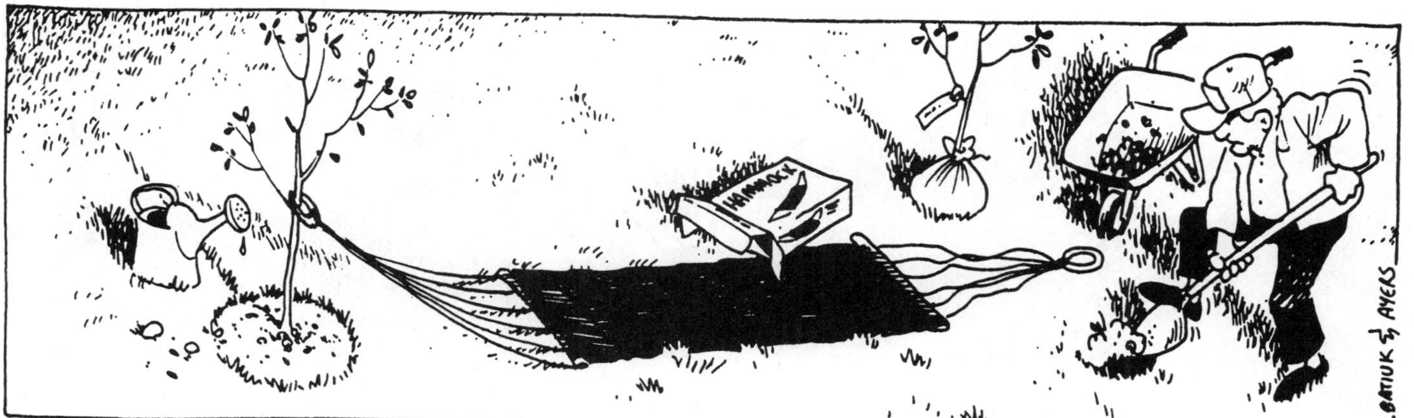
HAMMOCK
BATIUK & AYERS

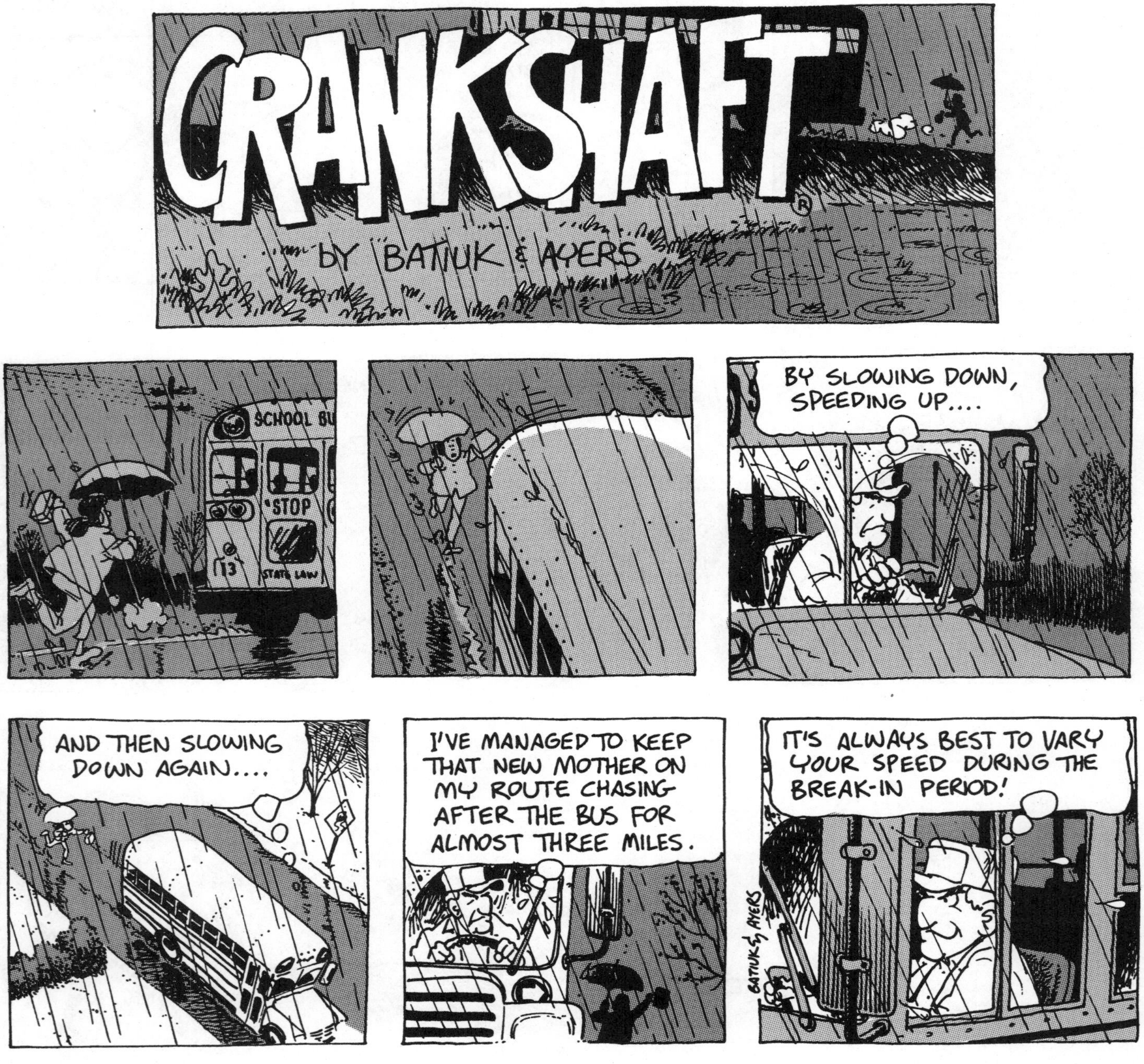
CRANKSHAFT
BY BATIUK & AYERS
SCHOOL BU
STOP
13
STATE LAW
BY SLOWING DOWN, SPEEDING UP....
AND THEN SLOWING DOWN AGAIN....
I'VE MANAGED TO KEEP THAT NEW MOTHER ON MY ROUTE CHASING AFTER THE BUS FOR ALMOST THREE MILES.
IT'S ALWAYS BEST TO VARY YOUR SPEED DURING THE BREAK-IN PERIOD!
BATIUK & AYERS

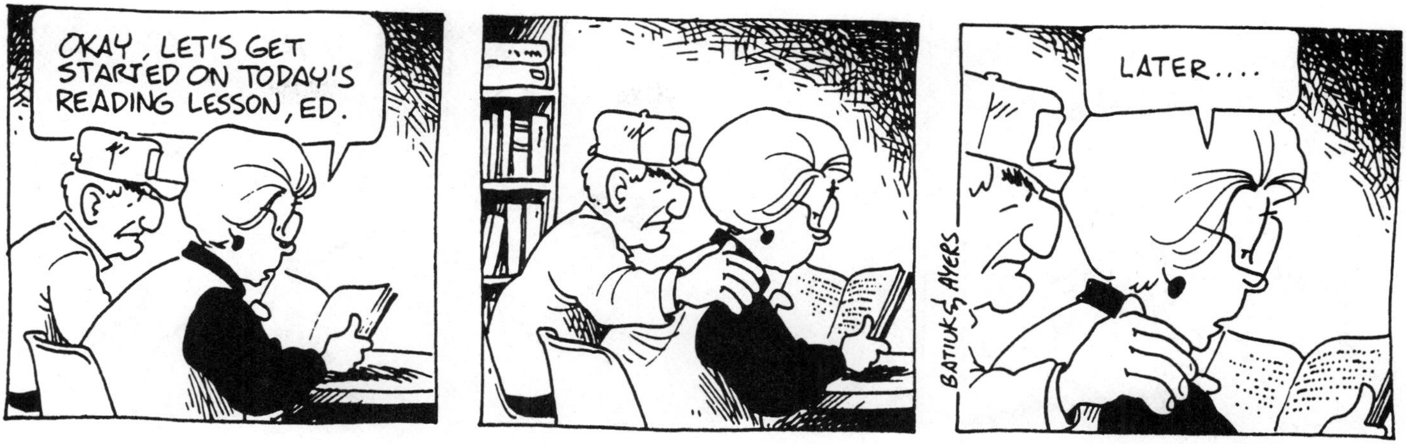
OKAY, LET'S GET STARTED ON TODAY'S READING LESSON, ED.
LATER....
BATIUK & AYERS

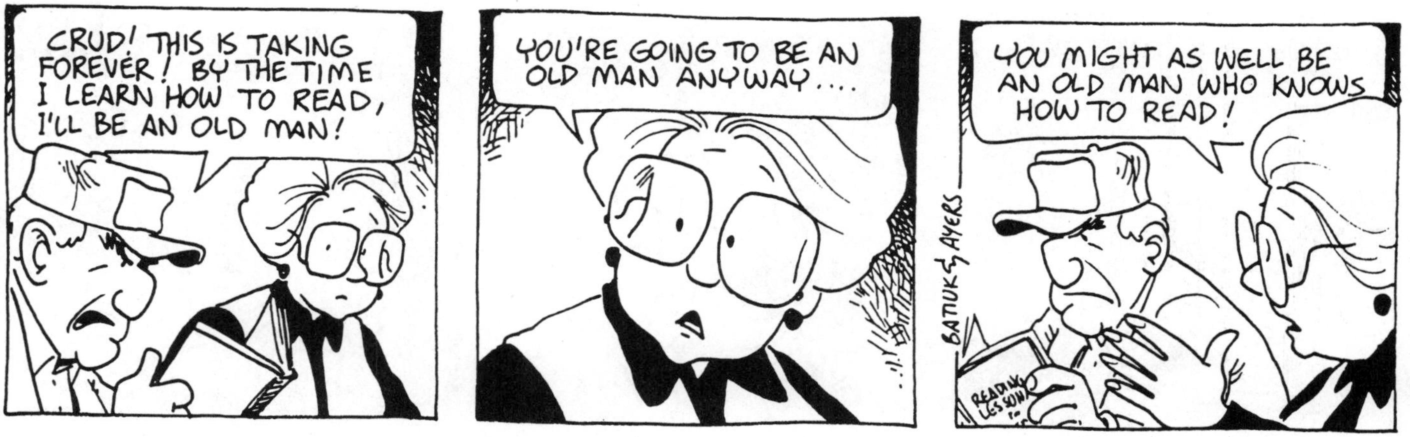
CRUD! THIS IS TAKING FOREVER! BY THE TIME I LEARN HOW TO READ, I'LL BE AN OLD MAN!
YOU'RE GOING TO BE AN OLD MAN ANYWAY....
YOU MIGHT AS WELL BE AN OLD MAN WHO KNOWS HOW TO READ!
BATIUK & AYERS

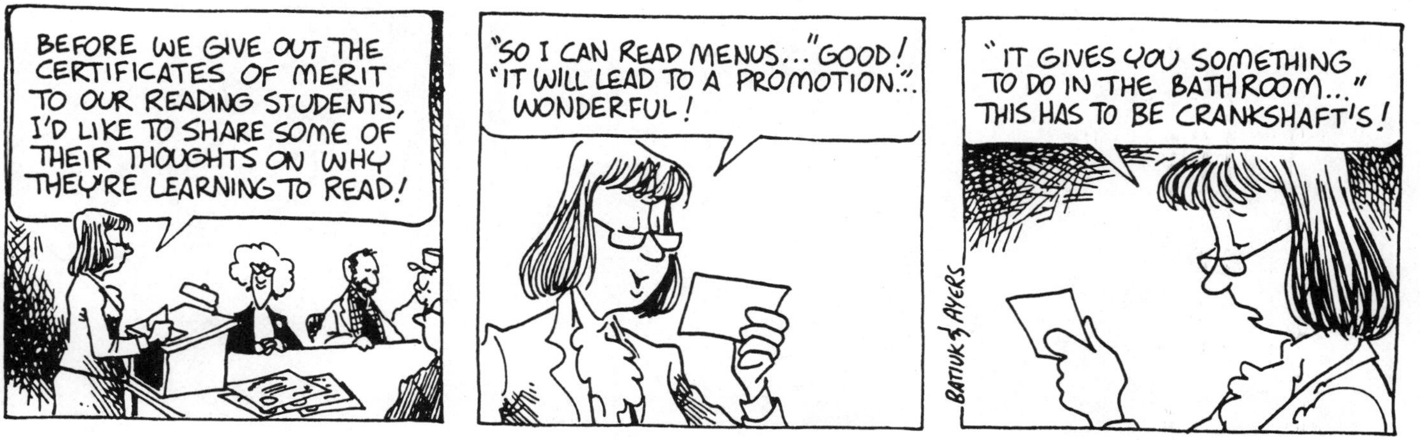
BEFORE WE GIVE OUT THE CERTIFICATES OF MERIT TO OUR READING STUDENTS, I'D LIKE TO SHARE SOME OF THEIR THOUGHTS ON WHY THEY'RE LEARNING TO READ!
"SO I CAN READ MENUS..." GOOD! "IT WILL LEAD TO A PROMOTION..." WONDERFUL!
"IT GIVES YOU SOMETHING TO DO IN THE BATHROOM..." THIS HAS TO BE CRANKSHAFT'S!
BATIUK & AYERS

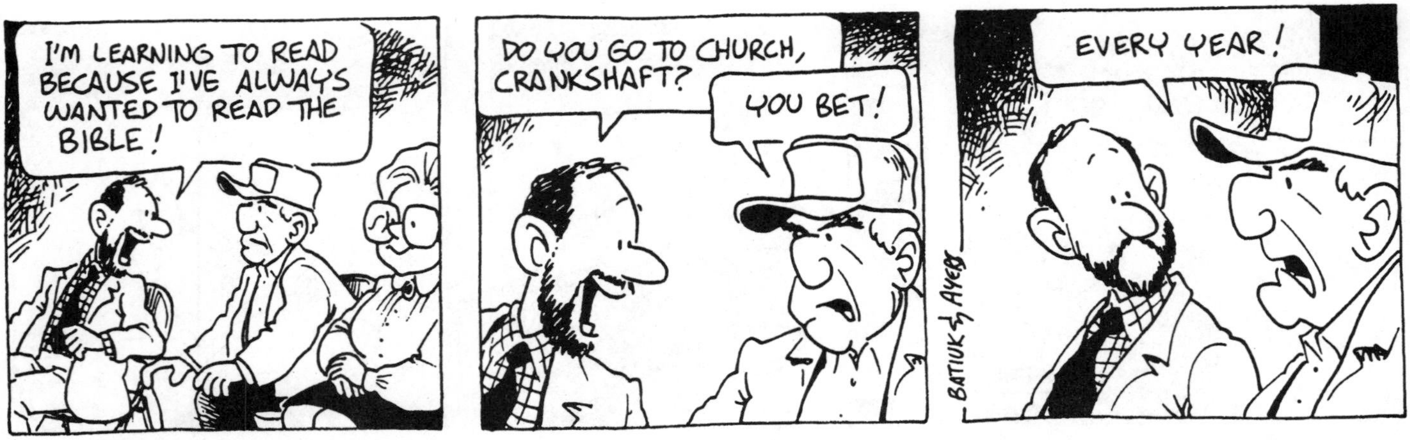
I'M LEARNING TO READ BECAUSE I'VE ALWAYS WANTED TO READ THE BIBLE!
DO YOU GO TO CHURCH, CRANKSHAFT?
YOU BET!
EVERY YEAR!
BATIUK & AYERS

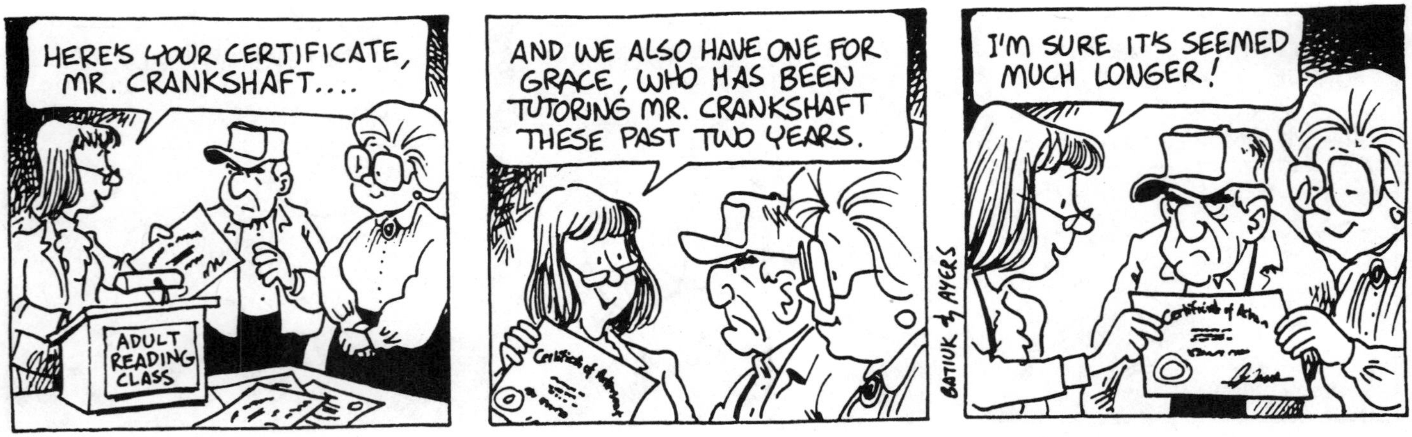
HERE'S YOUR CERTIFICATE, MR. CRANKSHAFT....
ADULT READING CLASS
AND WE ALSO HAVE ONE FOR GRACE, WHO HAS BEEN TUTORING MR. CRANKSHAFT THESE PAST TWO YEARS.
I'M SURE IT'S SEEMED MUCH LONGER!
BATIUK & AYERS

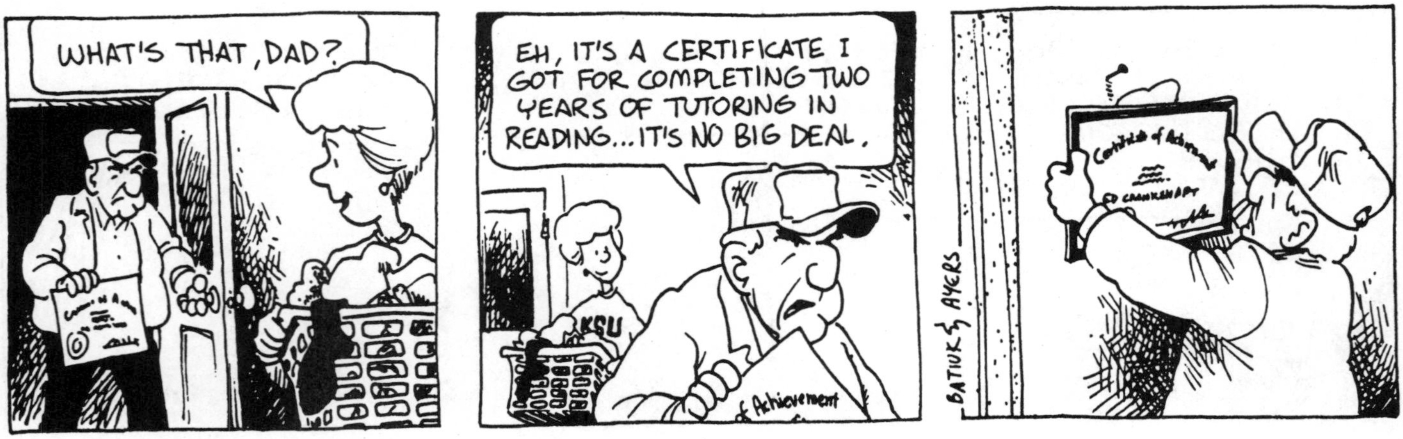
WHAT'S THAT, DAD?
EH, IT'S A CERTIFICATE I GOT FOR COMPLETING TWO YEARS OF TUTORING IN READING... IT'S NO BIG DEAL.
KSU
of Achievement
BATIUK & AYERS

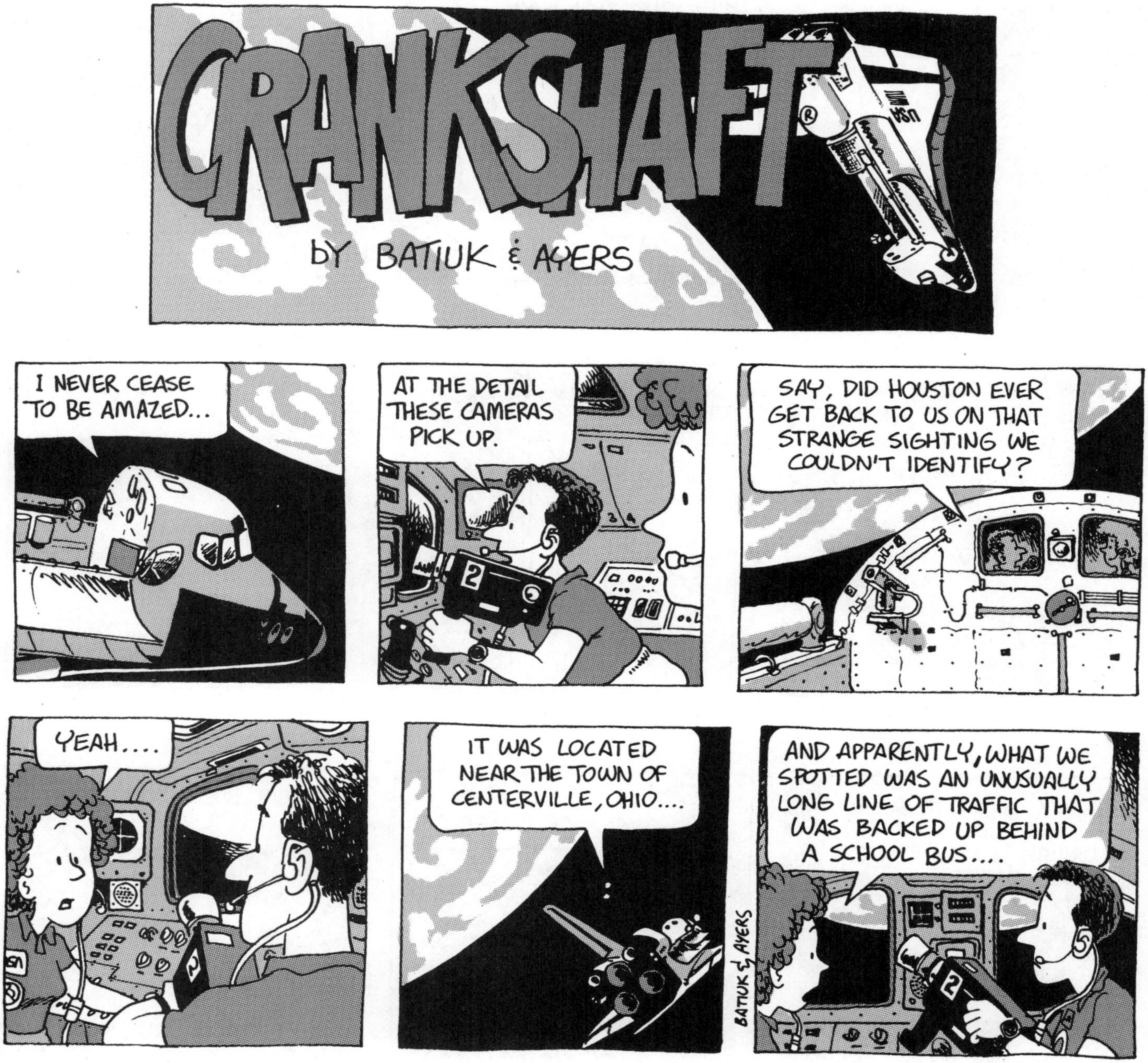
CRANKSHAFT
by BATIUK & AYERS
I NEVER CEASE TO BE AMAZED...
AT THE DETAIL THESE CAMERAS PICK UP.
SAY, DID HOUSTON EVER GET BACK TO US ON THAT STRANGE SIGHTING WE COULDN'T IDENTIFY?
YEAH....
IT WAS LOCATED NEAR THE TOWN OF CENTERVILLE, OHIO....
AND APPARENTLY, WHAT WE SPOTTED WAS AN UNUSUALLY LONG LINE OF TRAFFIC THAT WAS BACKED UP BEHIND A SCHOOL BUS....
BATIUK & AYERS

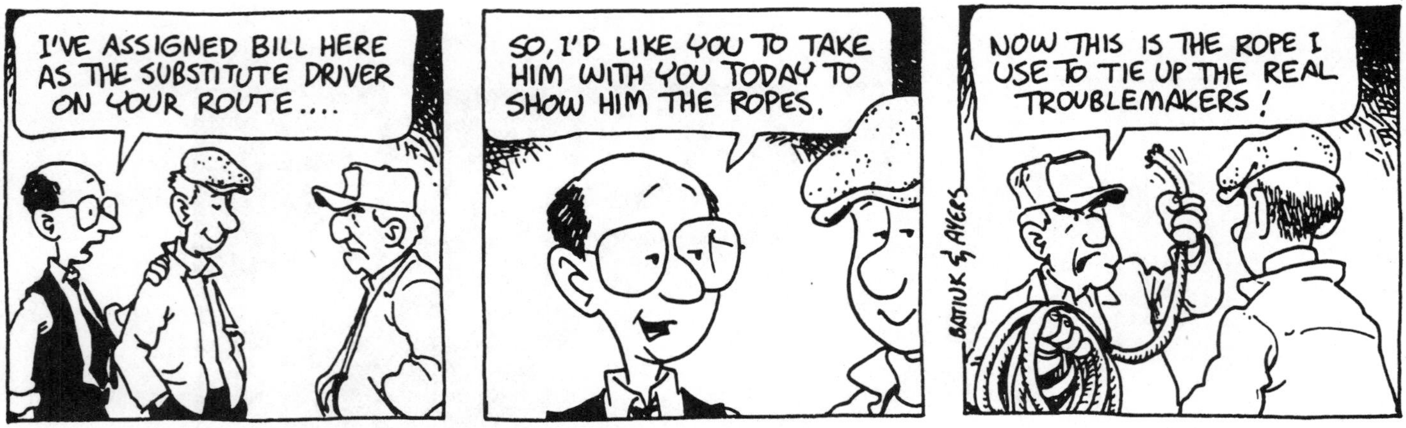
I'VE ASSIGNED BILL HERE AS THE SUBSTITUTE DRIVER ON YOUR ROUTE....
SO, I'D LIKE YOU TO TAKE HIM WITH YOU TODAY TO SHOW HIM THE ROPES.
NOW THIS IS THE ROPE I USE TO TIE UP THE REAL TROUBLEMAKERS!
BATIUK & AYERS

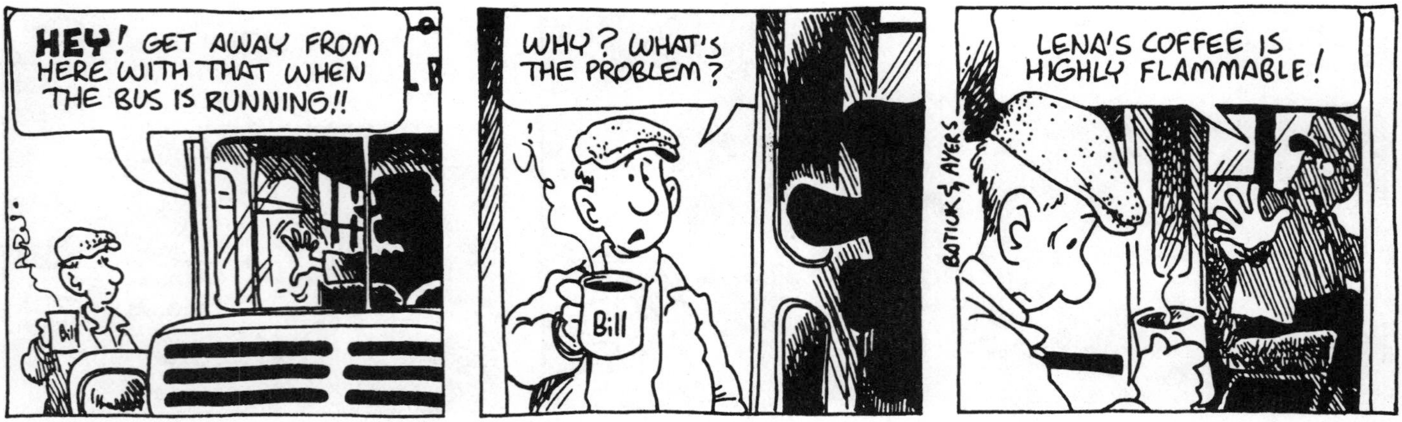
HEY! GET AWAY FROM HERE WITH THAT WHEN THE BUS IS RUNNING!!
Bill
WHY? WHAT'S THE PROBLEM?
Bill
LENA'S COFFEE IS HIGHLY FLAMMABLE!
BATIUK & AYERS

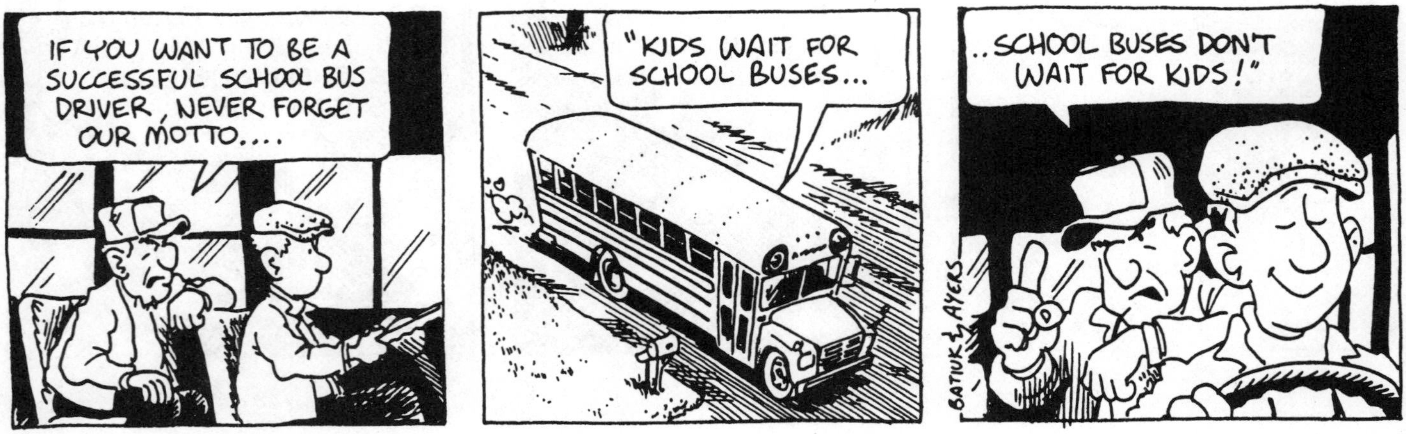
IF YOU WANT TO BE A SUCCESSFUL SCHOOL BUS DRIVER, NEVER FORGET OUR MOTTO....
"KIDS WAIT FOR SCHOOL BUSES...
..SCHOOL BUSES DON'T WAIT FOR KIDS!"
BATIUK & AYERS

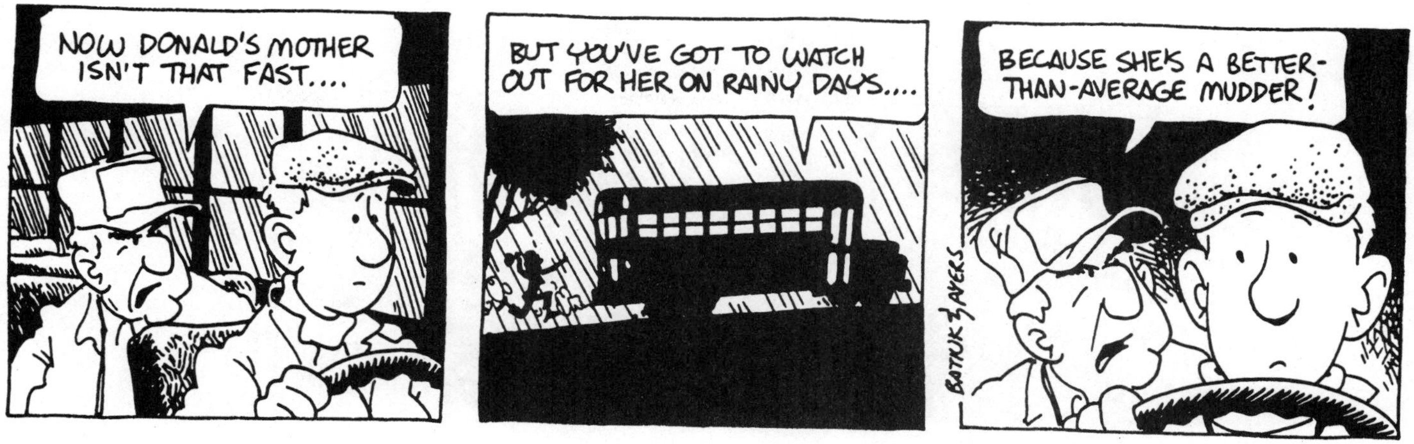
NOW DONALD'S MOTHER ISN'T THAT FAST....
BUT YOU'VE GOT TO WATCH OUT FOR HER ON RAINY DAYS....
BATIUK & AYERS
BECAUSE SHE'S A BETTER-THAN-AVERAGE MUDDER!

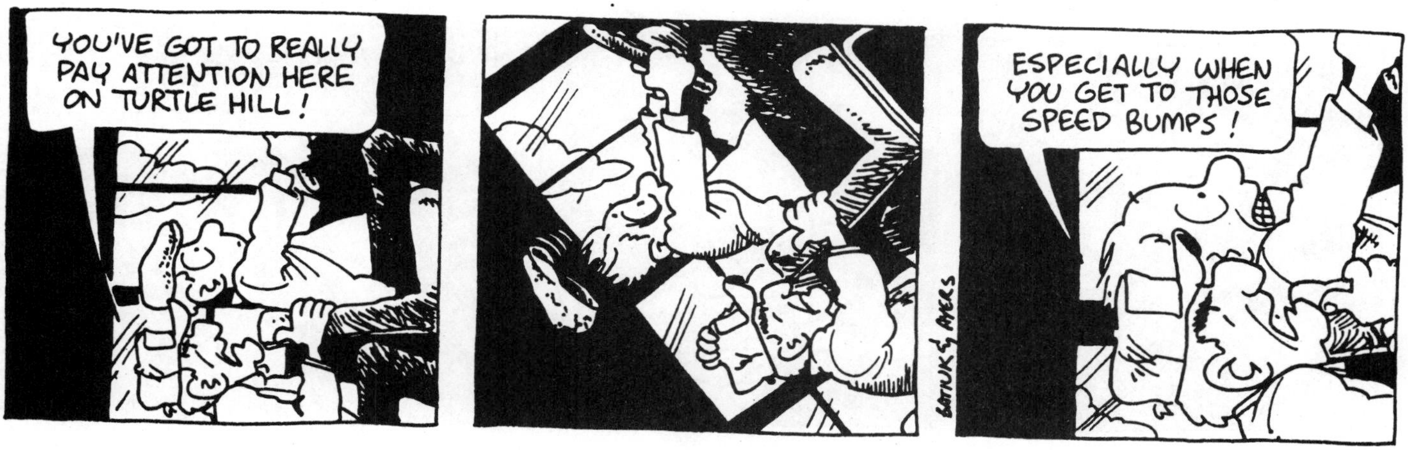
YOU'VE GOT TO REALLY PAY ATTENTION HERE ON TURTLE HILL!
BATIUK & AYERS
ESPECIALLY WHEN YOU GET TO THOSE SPEED BUMPS!

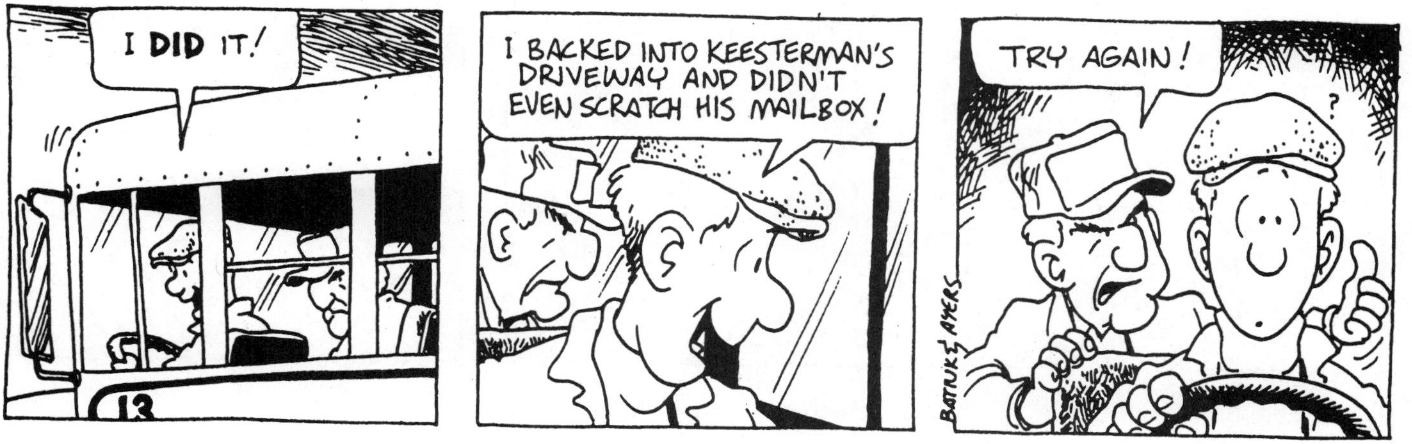
I DID IT!
13
I BACKED INTO KEESTERMAN'S DRIVEWAY AND DIDN'T EVEN SCRATCH HIS MAILBOX!
BATIUK & AYERS
TRY AGAIN!
?

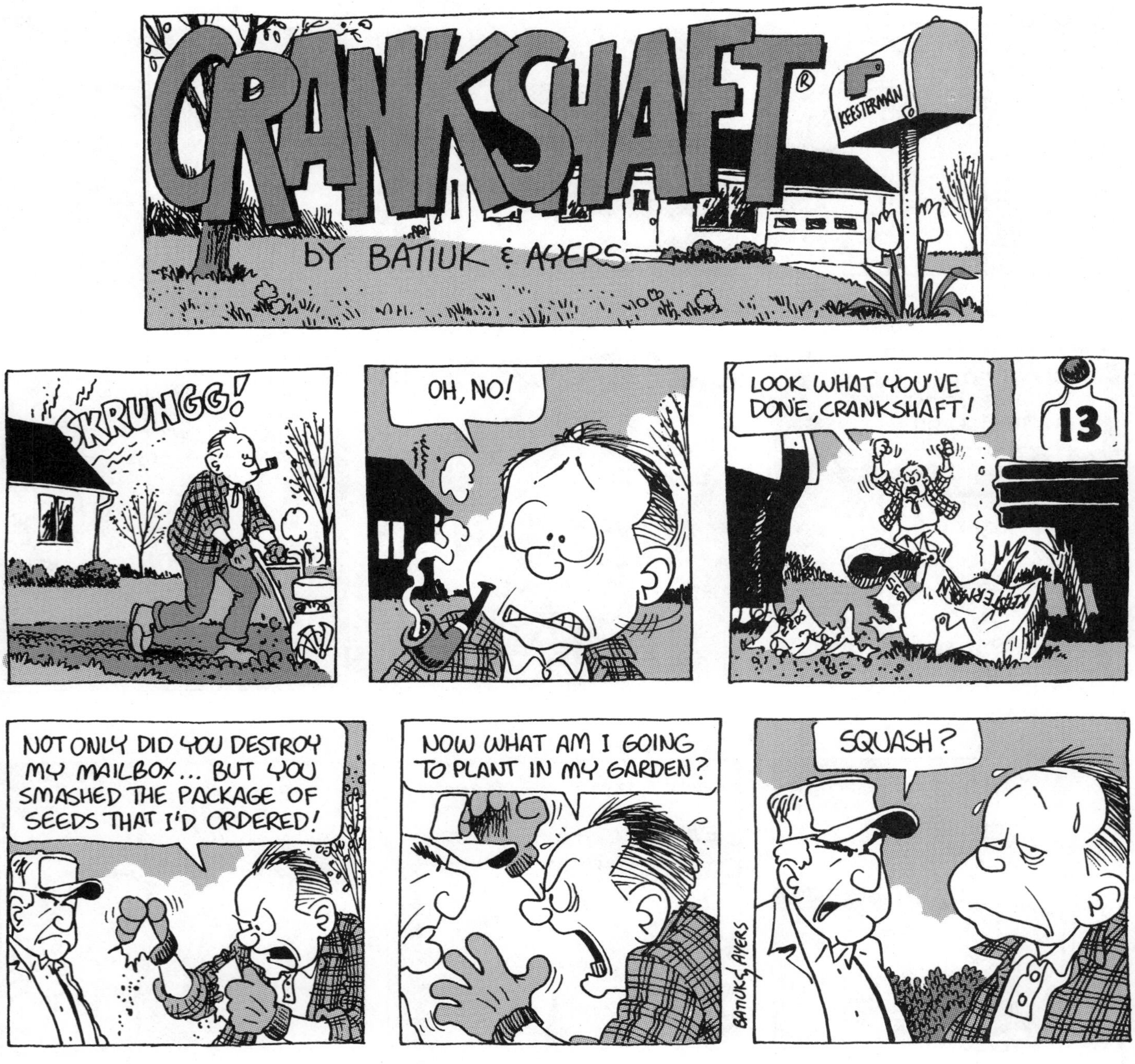
CRANKSHAFT®
KEESTERMAN
BY BATIUK & AYERS
SKRUNGG!
OH, NO!
LOOK WHAT YOU'VE DONE, CRANKSHAFT!
13
KEESTERMAN
NOT ONLY DID YOU DESTROY MY MAILBOX... BUT YOU SMASHED THE PACKAGE OF SEEDS THAT I'D ORDERED!
NOW WHAT AM I GOING TO PLANT IN MY GARDEN?
BATIUK & AYERS
SQUASH?

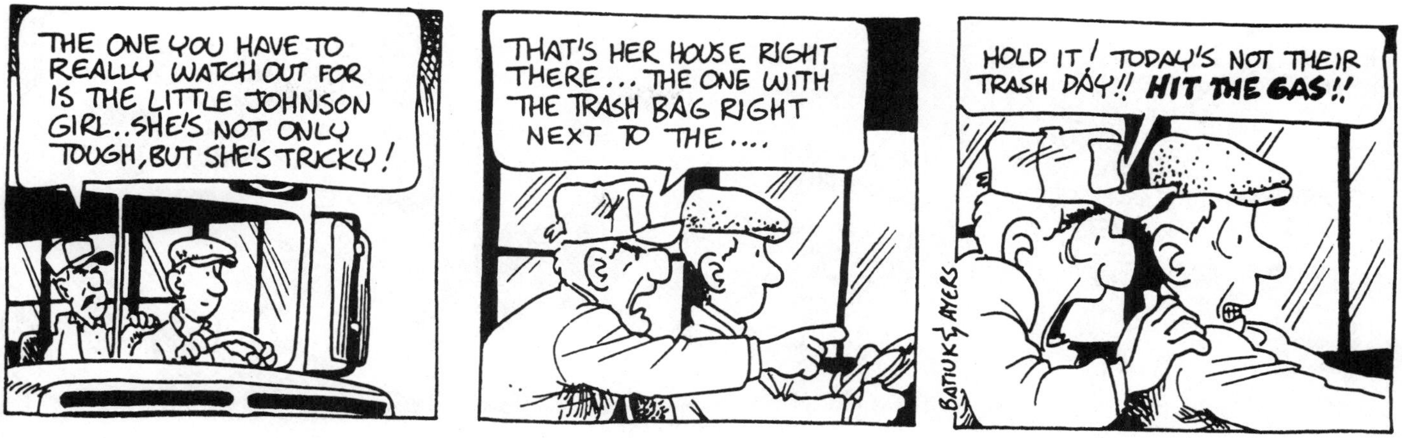
THE ONE YOU HAVE TO REALLY WATCH OUT FOR IS THE LITTLE JOHNSON GIRL..SHE'S NOT ONLY TOUGH, BUT SHE'S TRICKY!
THAT'S HER HOUSE RIGHT THERE... THE ONE WITH THE TRASH BAG RIGHT NEXT TO THE....
HOLD IT! TODAY'S NOT THEIR TRASH DAY!! **HIT THE GAS!!**
BATIUK & AYERS

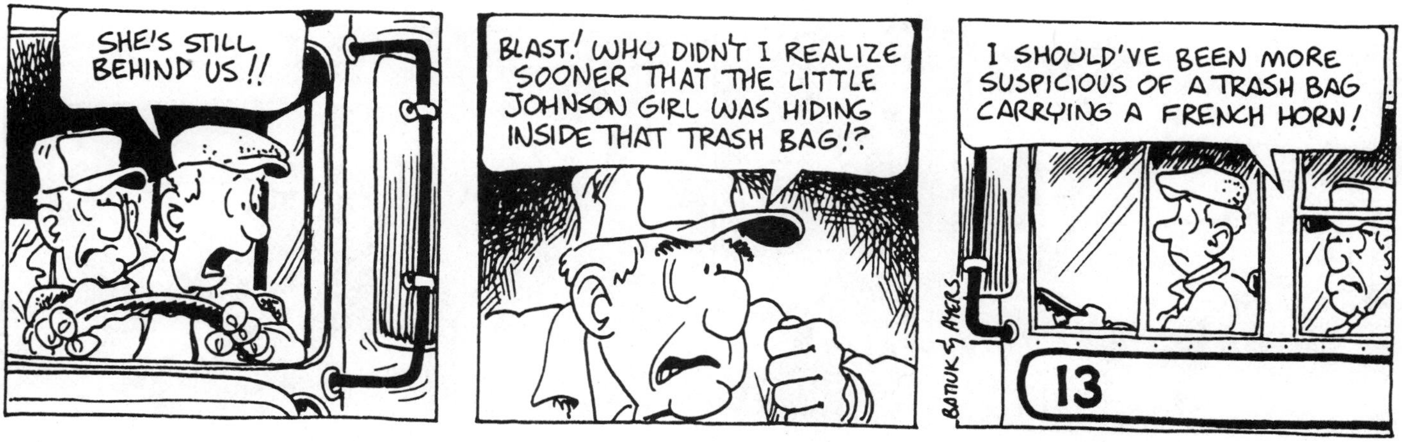
SHE'S STILL BEHIND US!!
BLAST! WHY DIDN'T I REALIZE SOONER THAT THE LITTLE JOHNSON GIRL WAS HIDING INSIDE THAT TRASH BAG!?
I SHOULD'VE BEEN MORE SUSPICIOUS OF A TRASH BAG CARRYING A FRENCH HORN!
13
BATIUK & AYERS

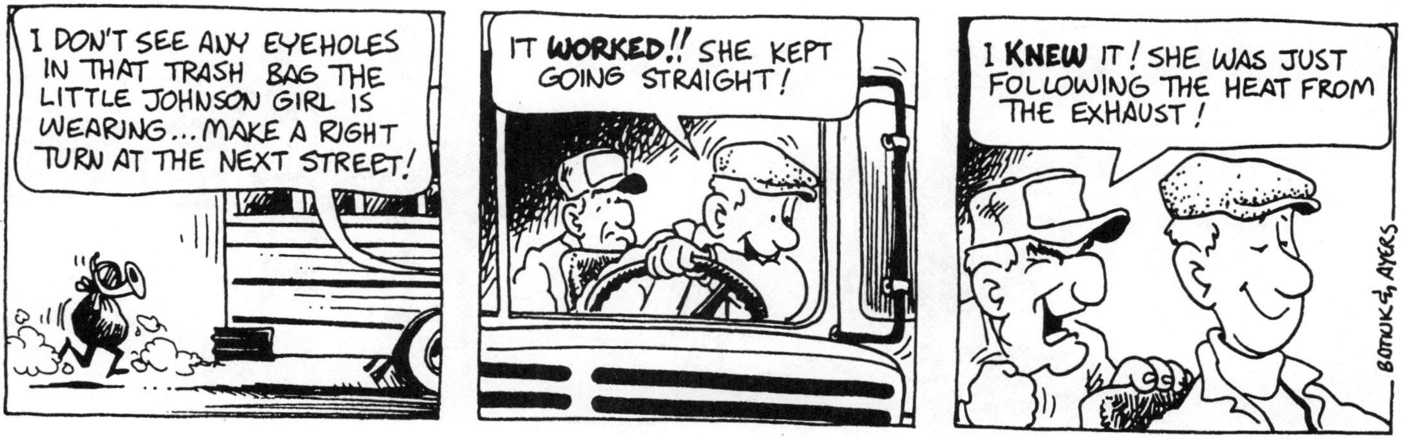
I DON'T SEE ANY EYEHOLES IN THAT TRASH BAG THE LITTLE JOHNSON GIRL IS WEARING... MAKE A RIGHT TURN AT THE NEXT STREET!
IT **WORKED!!** SHE KEPT GOING STRAIGHT!
I **KNEW** IT! SHE WAS JUST FOLLOWING THE HEAT FROM THE EXHAUST!
BATIUK & AYERS

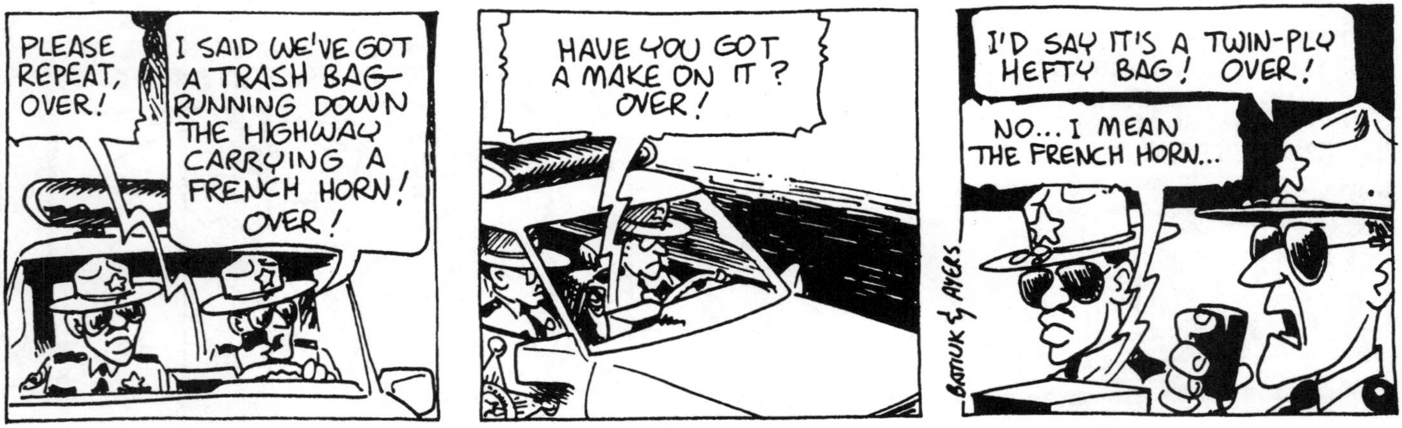
PLEASE REPEAT, OVER!
I SAID WE'VE GOT A TRASH BAG RUNNING DOWN THE HIGHWAY CARRYING A FRENCH HORN! OVER!
HAVE YOU GOT A MAKE ON IT? OVER!
I'D SAY IT'S A TWIN-PLY HEFTY BAG! OVER!
NO... I MEAN THE FRENCH HORN...
BATIUK & AYERS

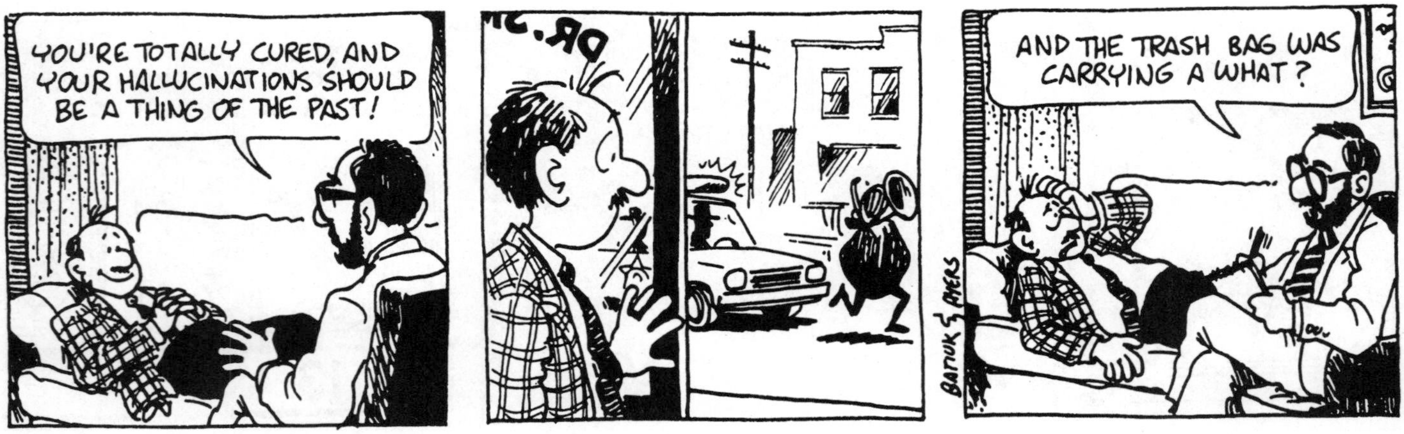
YOU'RE TOTALLY CURED, AND YOUR HALLUCINATIONS SHOULD BE A THING OF THE PAST!
AND THE TRASH BAG WAS CARRYING A WHAT?
BATIUK & AYERS

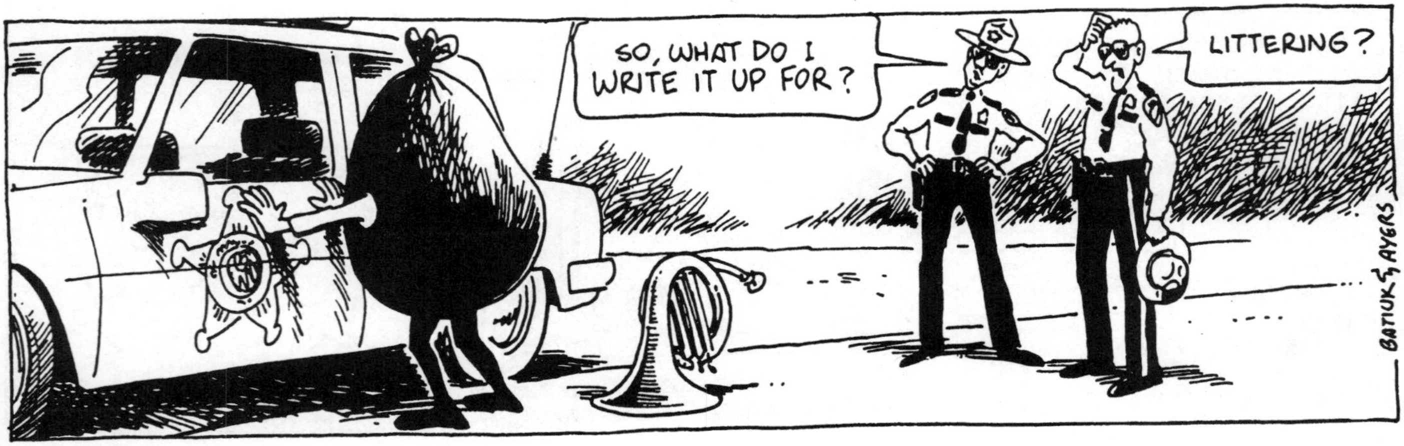
SO, WHAT DO I WRITE IT UP FOR?
LITTERING?
BATIUK & AYERS

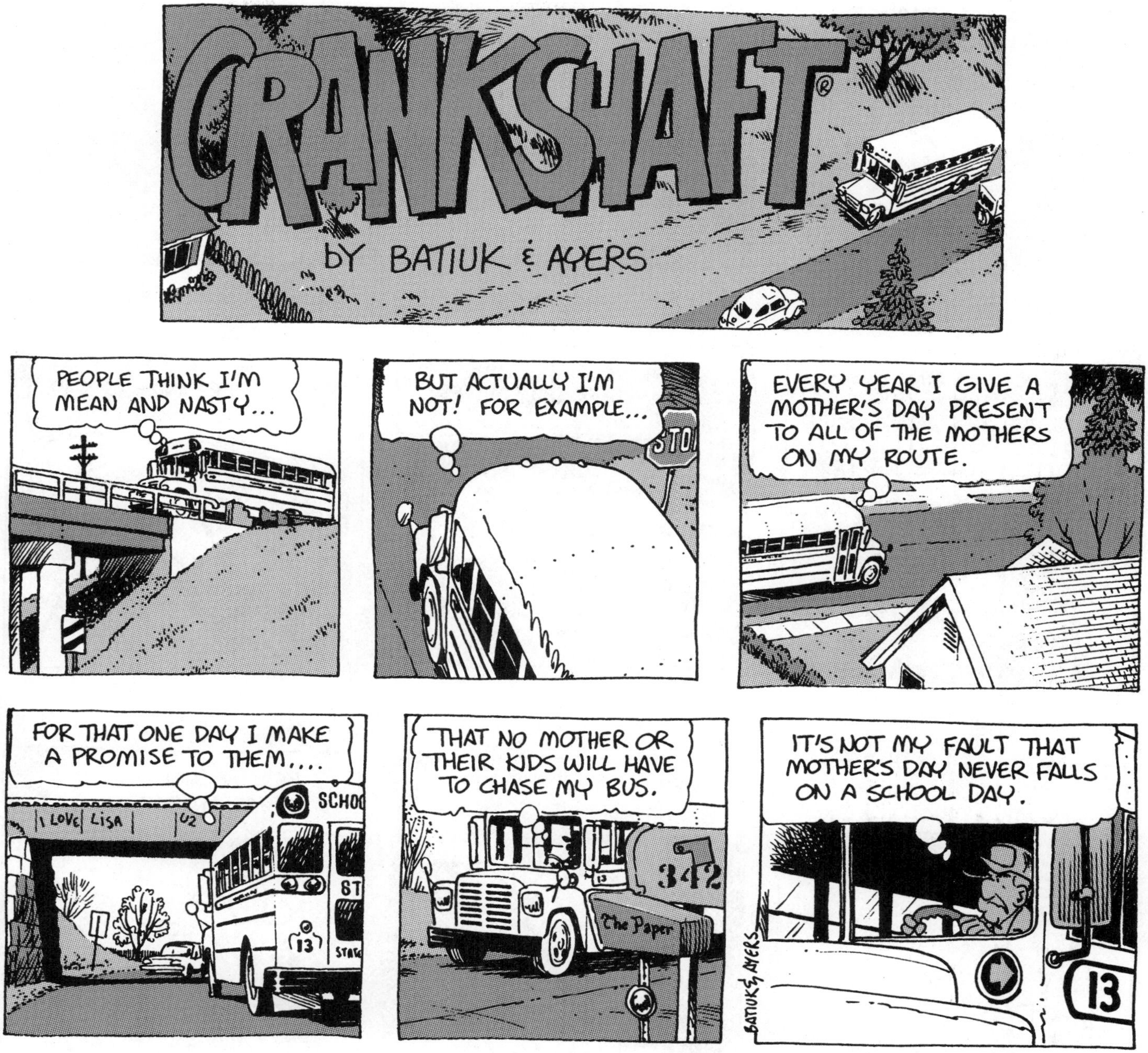
CRANKSHAFT®
BY BATIUK & AYERS
PEOPLE THINK I'M MEAN AND NASTY...
BUT ACTUALLY I'M NOT! FOR EXAMPLE...
STOP
EVERY YEAR I GIVE A MOTHER'S DAY PRESENT TO ALL OF THE MOTHERS ON MY ROUTE.
FOR THAT ONE DAY I MAKE A PROMISE TO THEM....
I LOVE LISA
U2
SCHOO
13
THAT NO MOTHER OR THEIR KIDS WILL HAVE TO CHASE MY BUS.
342
The Paper
IT'S NOT MY FAULT THAT MOTHER'S DAY NEVER FALLS ON A SCHOOL DAY.
BATIUK & AYERS
13

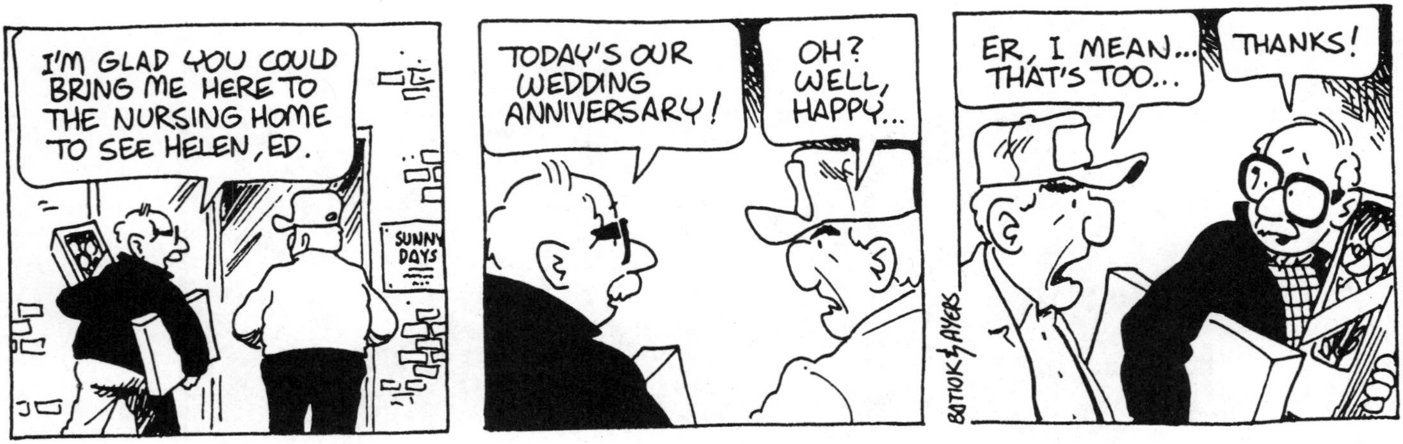
I'M GLAD YOU COULD BRING ME HERE TO THE NURSING HOME TO SEE HELEN, ED.
SUNNY DAYS
TODAY'S OUR WEDDING ANNIVERSARY!
OH? WELL, HAPPY...
ER, I MEAN... THAT'S TOO...
THANKS!
BATIUK & AYERS

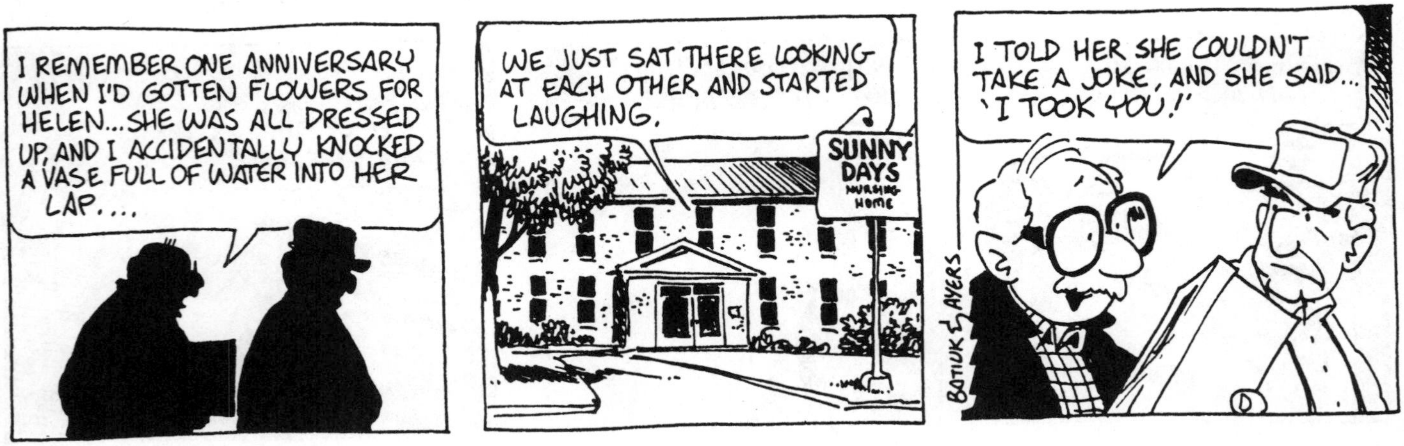
I REMEMBER ONE ANNIVERSARY WHEN I'D GOTTEN FLOWERS FOR HELEN...SHE WAS ALL DRESSED UP, AND I ACCIDENTALLY KNOCKED A VASE FULL OF WATER INTO HER LAP....
WE JUST SAT THERE LOOKING AT EACH OTHER AND STARTED LAUGHING.
SUNNY DAYS NURSING HOME
I TOLD HER SHE COULDN'T TAKE A JOKE, AND SHE SAID... 'I TOOK YOU!'
BATIUK & AYERS

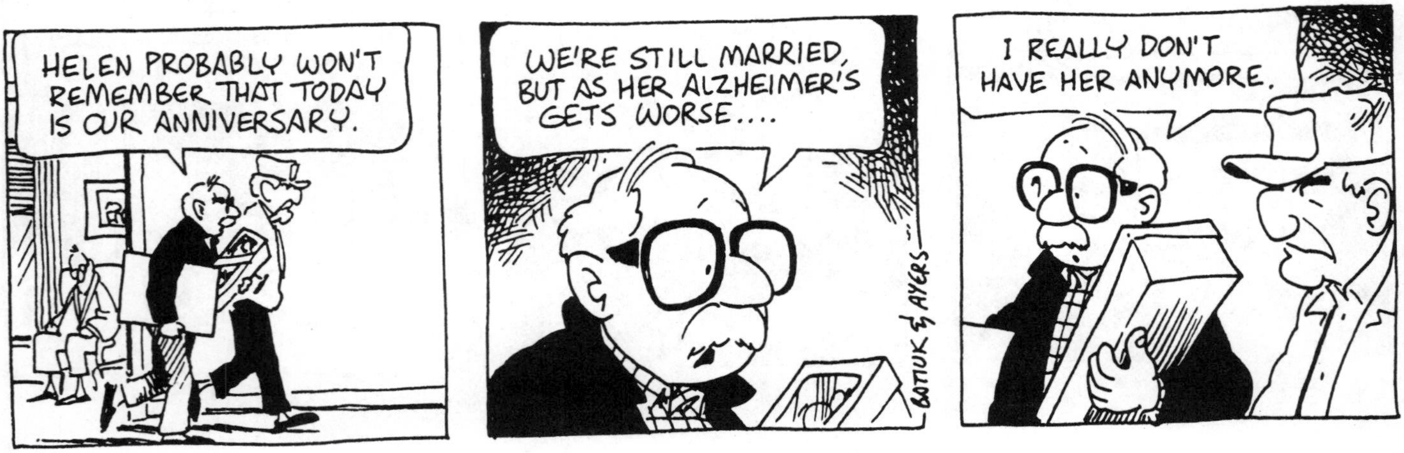
HELEN PROBABLY WON'T REMEMBER THAT TODAY IS OUR ANNIVERSARY.
WE'RE STILL MARRIED, BUT AS HER ALZHEIMER'S GETS WORSE....
BATIUK & AYERS
I REALLY DON'T HAVE HER ANYMORE.

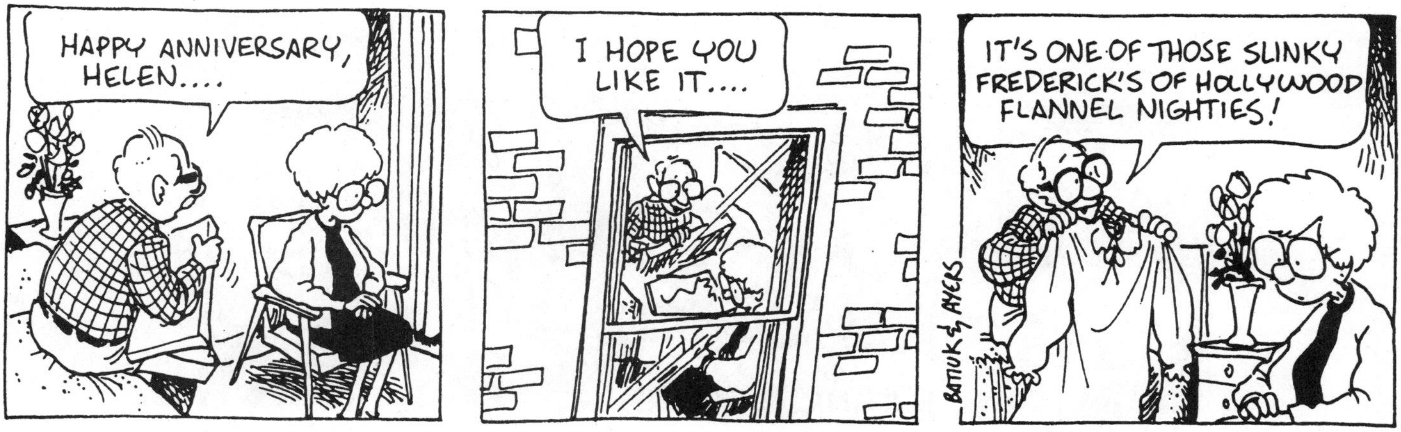
HAPPY ANNIVERSARY, HELEN....
I HOPE YOU LIKE IT....
IT'S ONE OF THOSE SLINKY FREDERICK'S OF HOLLYWOOD FLANNEL NIGHTIES!
BATIUK & AYERS

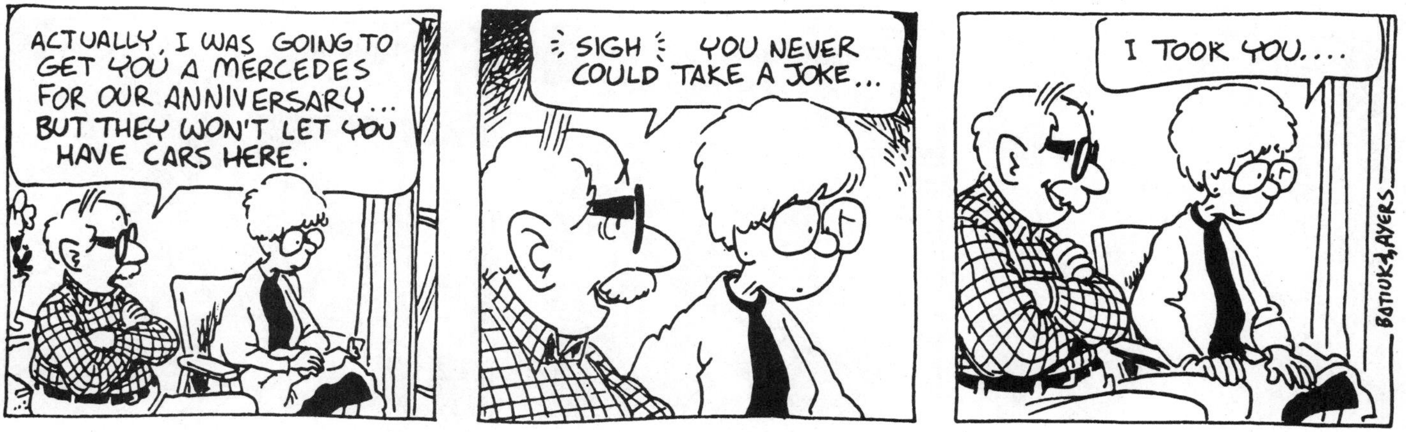
ACTUALLY, I WAS GOING TO GET YOU A MERCEDES FOR OUR ANNIVERSARY... BUT THEY WON'T LET YOU HAVE CARS HERE.
SIGH
YOU NEVER COULD TAKE A JOKE...
I TOOK YOU....
BATIUK & AYERS

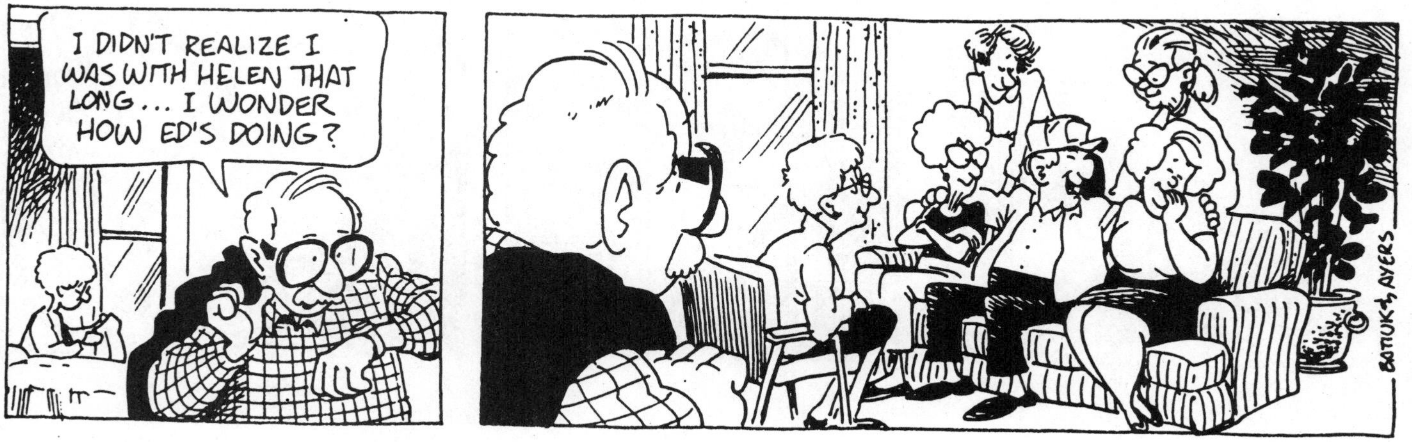
I DIDN'T REALIZE I WAS WITH HELEN THAT LONG... I WONDER HOW ED'S DOING?
BATIUK & AYERS

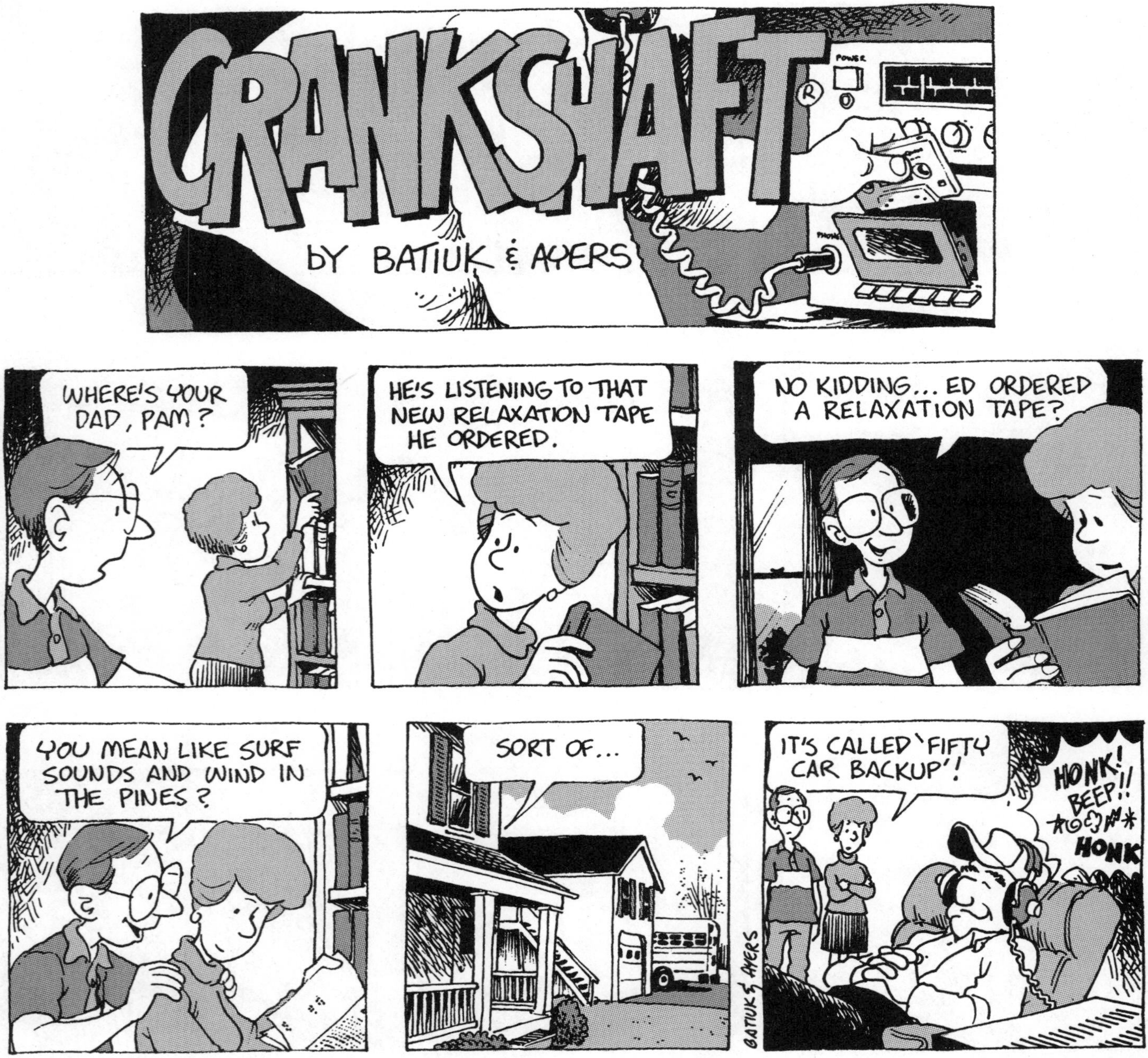
CRANKSHAFT
BY BATIUK & AYERS
WHERE'S YOUR DAD, PAM?
HE'S LISTENING TO THAT NEW RELAXATION TAPE HE ORDERED.
NO KIDDING... ED ORDERED A RELAXATION TAPE?
YOU MEAN LIKE SURF SOUNDS AND WIND IN THE PINES?
SORT OF...
BATIUK & AYERS
IT'S CALLED 'FIFTY CAR BACKUP'!
HONK! BEEP!!
HONK

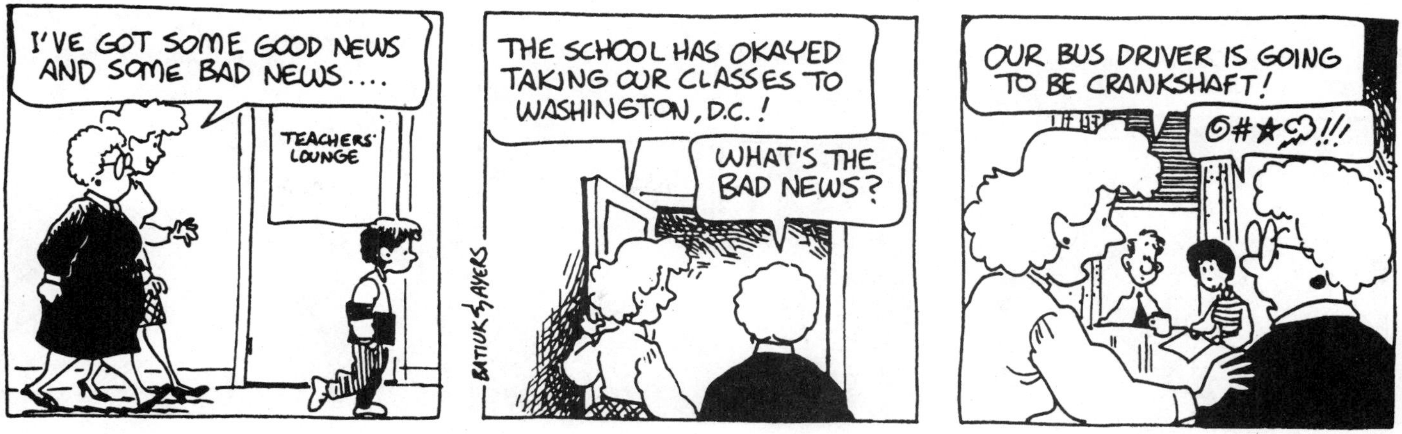
I'VE GOT SOME GOOD NEWS AND SOME BAD NEWS....
TEACHERS' LOUNGE
THE SCHOOL HAS OKAYED TAKING OUR CLASSES TO WASHINGTON, D.C.!
WHAT'S THE BAD NEWS?
OUR BUS DRIVER IS GOING TO BE CRANKSHAFT!

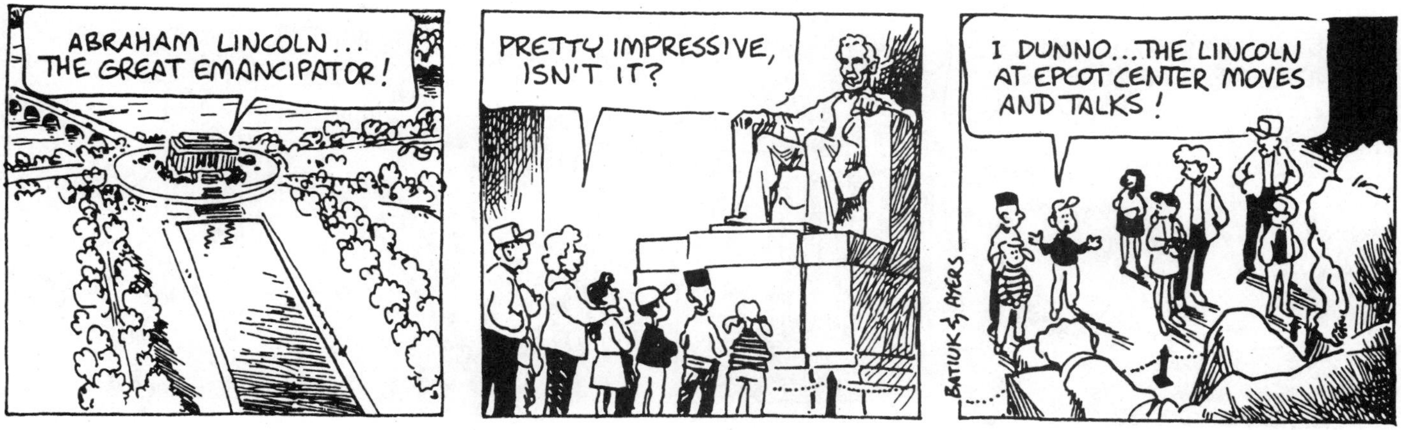
ABRAHAM LINCOLN... THE GREAT EMANCIPATOR!
PRETTY IMPRESSIVE, ISN'T IT?
I DUNNO... THE LINCOLN AT EPCOT CENTER MOVES AND TALKS!

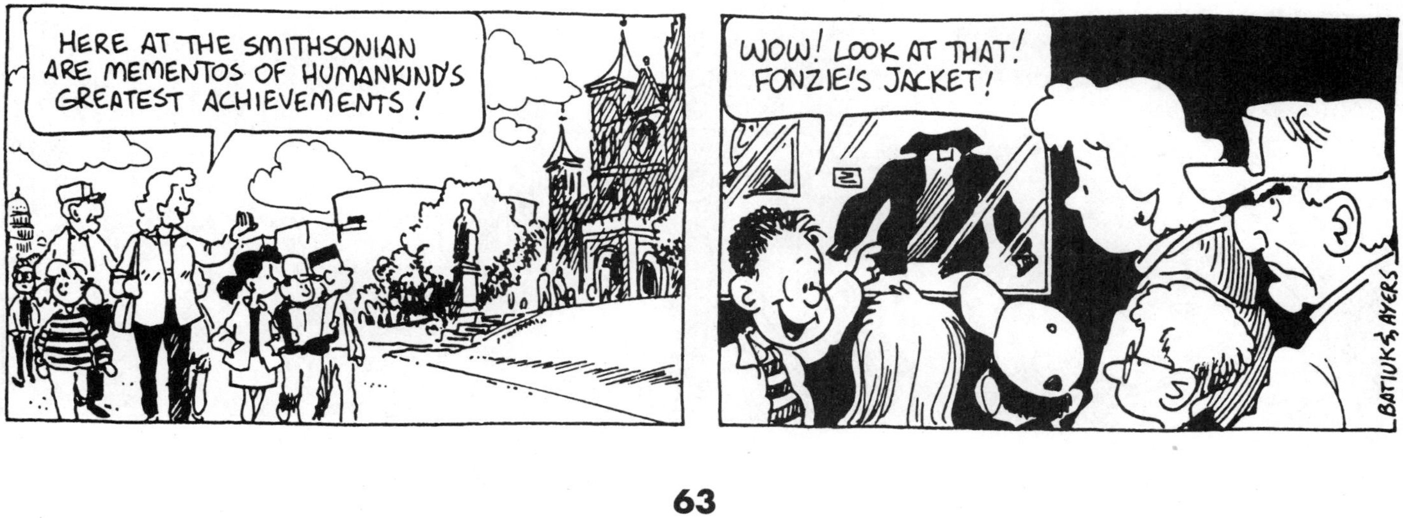
HERE AT THE SMITHSONIAN ARE MEMENTOS OF HUMANKIND'S GREATEST ACHIEVEMENTS!
WOW! LOOK AT THAT! FONZIE'S JACKET!

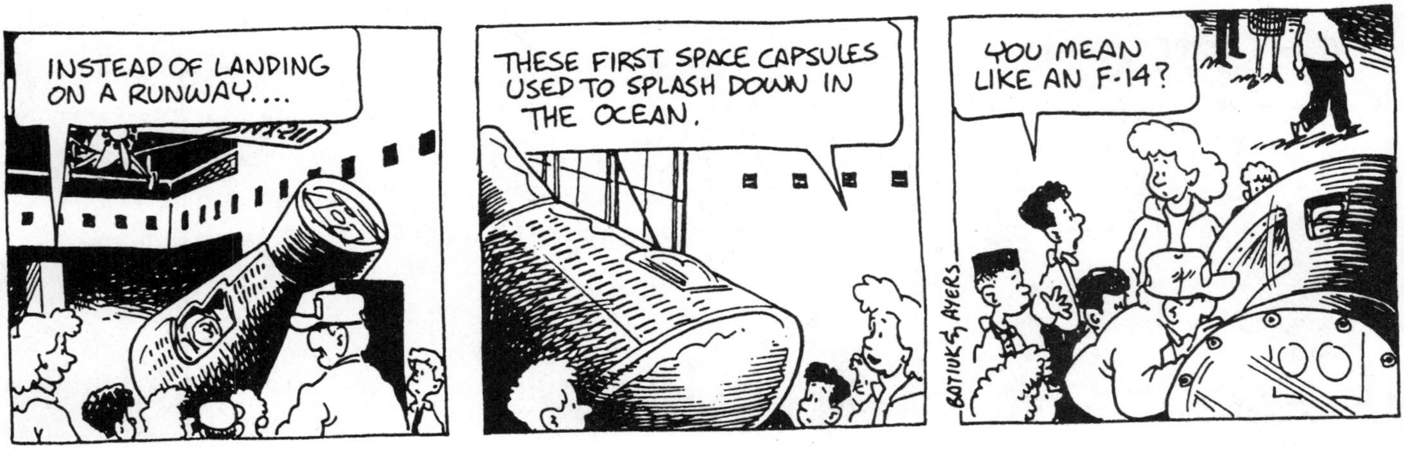
INSTEAD OF LANDING ON A RUNWAY....
THESE FIRST SPACE CAPSULES USED TO SPLASH DOWN IN THE OCEAN.
YOU MEAN LIKE AN F-14?
BATIUK & AYERS

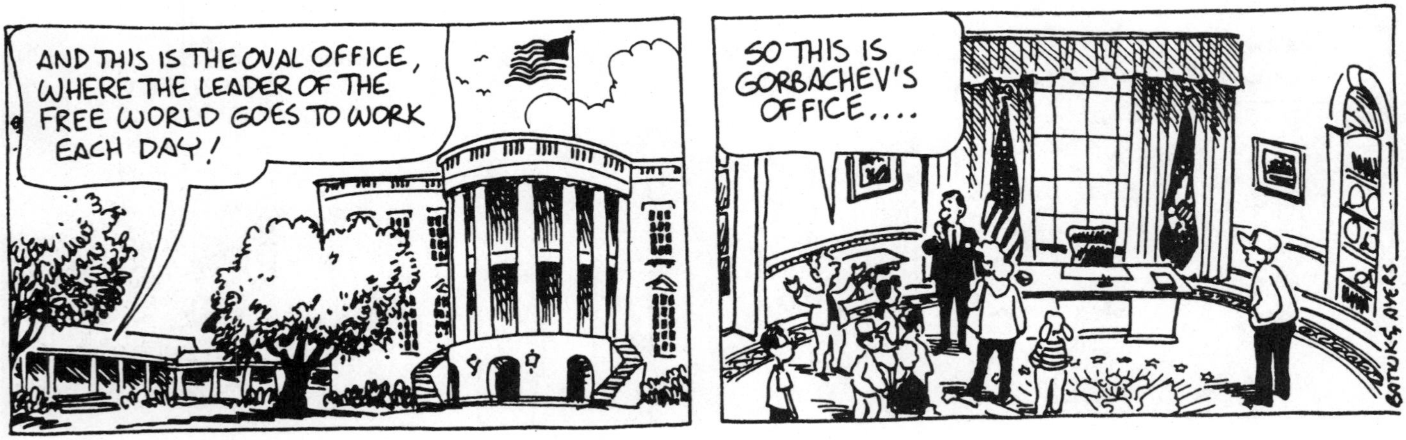
AND THIS IS THE OVAL OFFICE, WHERE THE LEADER OF THE FREE WORLD GOES TO WORK EACH DAY!
SO THIS IS GORBACHEV'S OFFICE....
BATIUK & AYERS

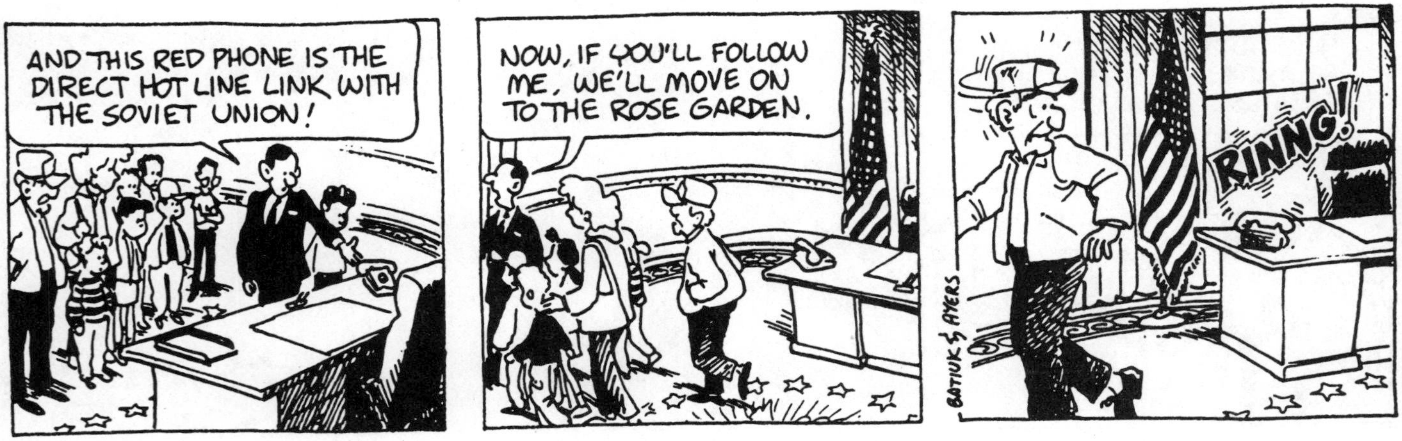
AND THIS RED PHONE IS THE DIRECT HOT LINE LINK WITH THE SOVIET UNION!
NOW, IF YOU'LL FOLLOW ME, WE'LL MOVE ON TO THE ROSE GARDEN.
BATIUK & AYERS
RINNG!

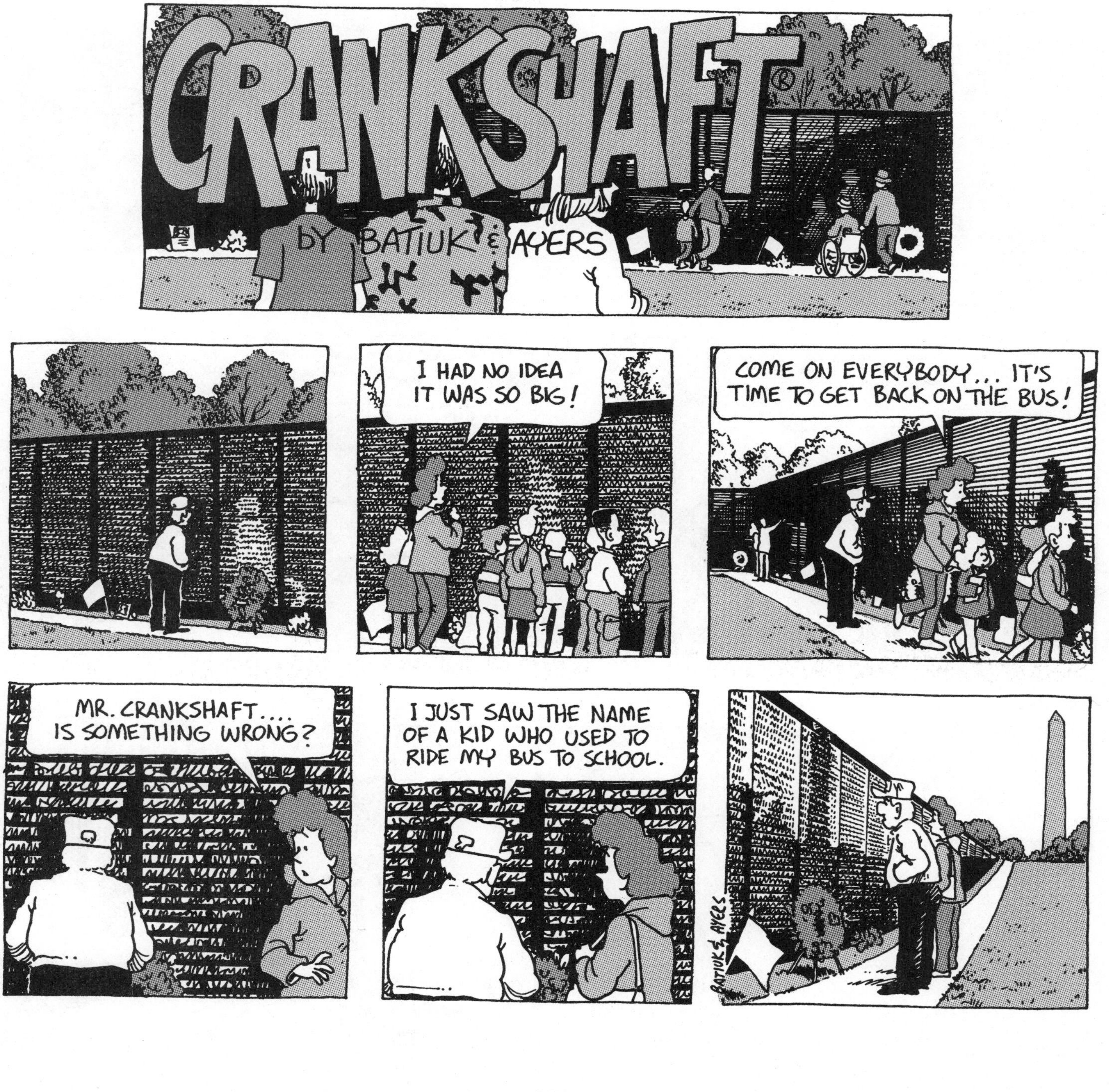
CRANKSHAFT®
BY BATIUK & AYERS
I HAD NO IDEA IT WAS SO BIG!
COME ON EVERYBODY... IT'S TIME TO GET BACK ON THE BUS!
MR. CRANKSHAFT.... IS SOMETHING WRONG?
I JUST SAW THE NAME OF A KID WHO USED TO RIDE MY BUS TO SCHOOL.
BATIUK & AYERS

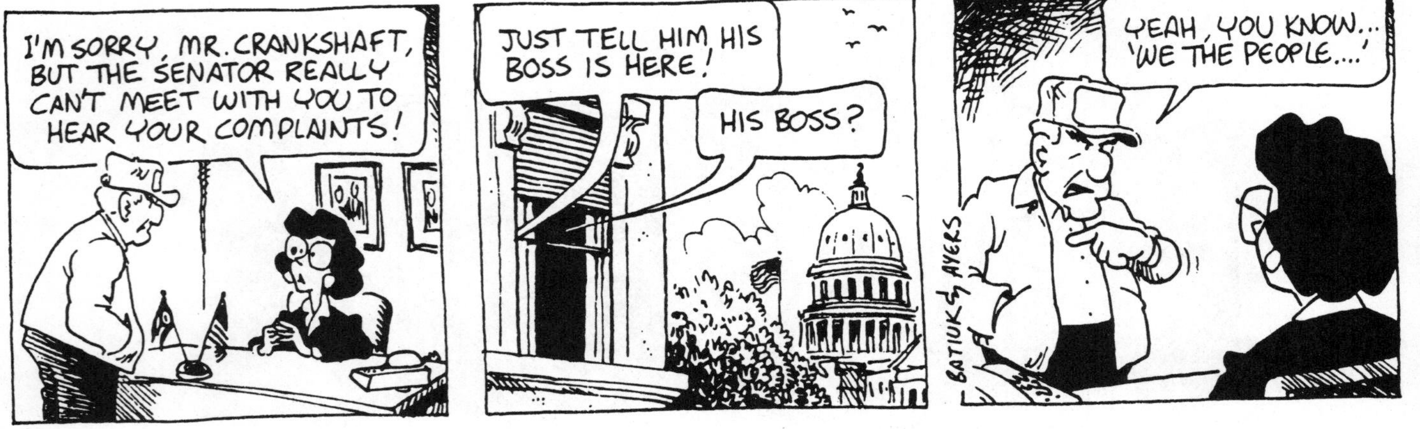
I'M SORRY, MR. CRANKSHAFT, BUT THE SENATOR REALLY CAN'T MEET WITH YOU TO HEAR YOUR COMPLAINTS!
JUST TELL HIM HIS BOSS IS HERE!
HIS BOSS?
YEAH, YOU KNOW... 'WE THE PEOPLE....'
BATIUK & AYERS

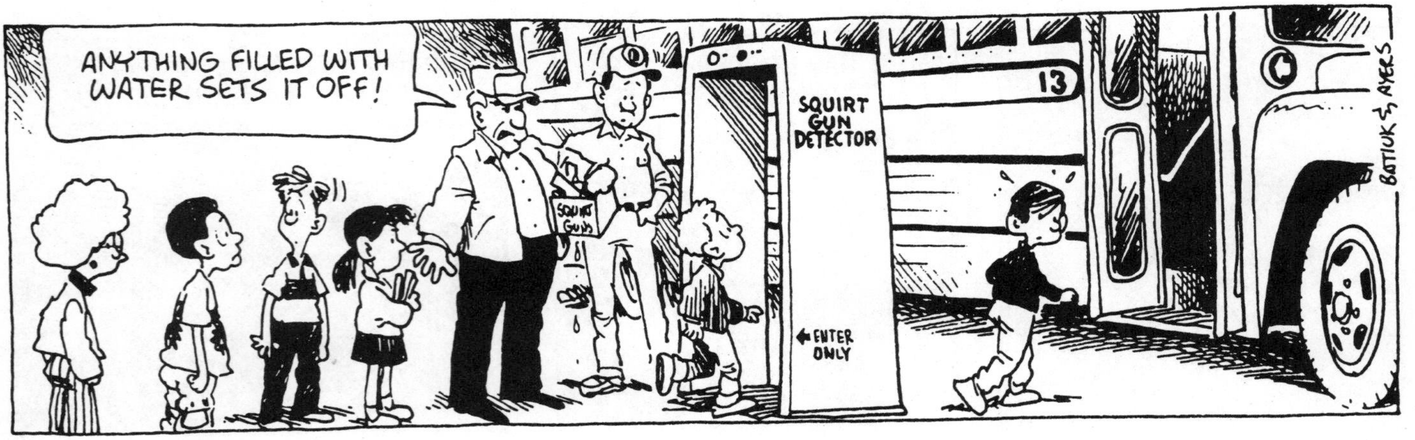
ANYTHING FILLED WITH WATER SETS IT OFF!
SQUIRT GUNS
SQUIRT GUN DETECTOR
ENTER ONLY
13
BATIUK & AYERS

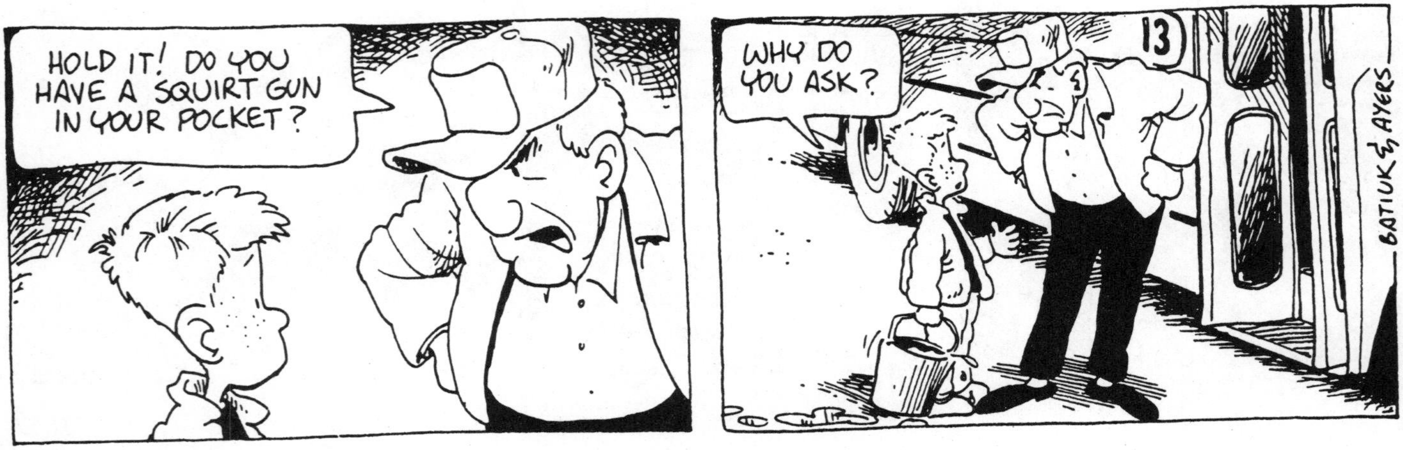
HOLD IT! DO YOU HAVE A SQUIRT GUN IN YOUR POCKET?
WHY DO YOU ASK?
13
BATIUK & AYERS

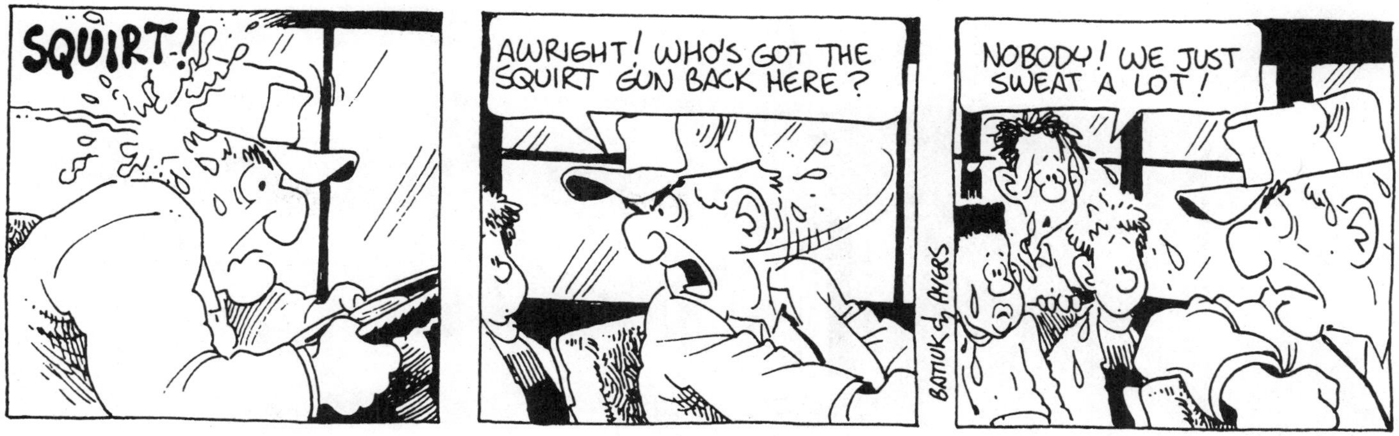
SQUIRT!
AWRIGHT! WHO'S GOT THE SQUIRT GUN BACK HERE?
NOBODY! WE JUST SWEAT A LOT!
BATIUK & AYERS

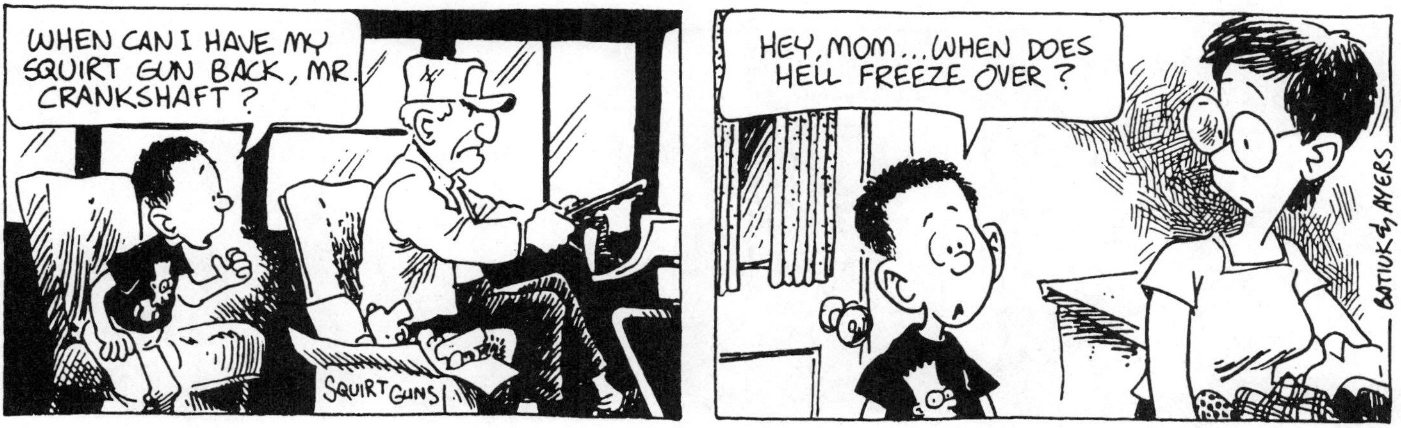
WHEN CAN I HAVE MY SQUIRT GUN BACK, MR. CRANKSHAFT?
SQUIRT GUNS
HEY, MOM... WHEN DOES HELL FREEZE OVER?
BATIUK & AYERS

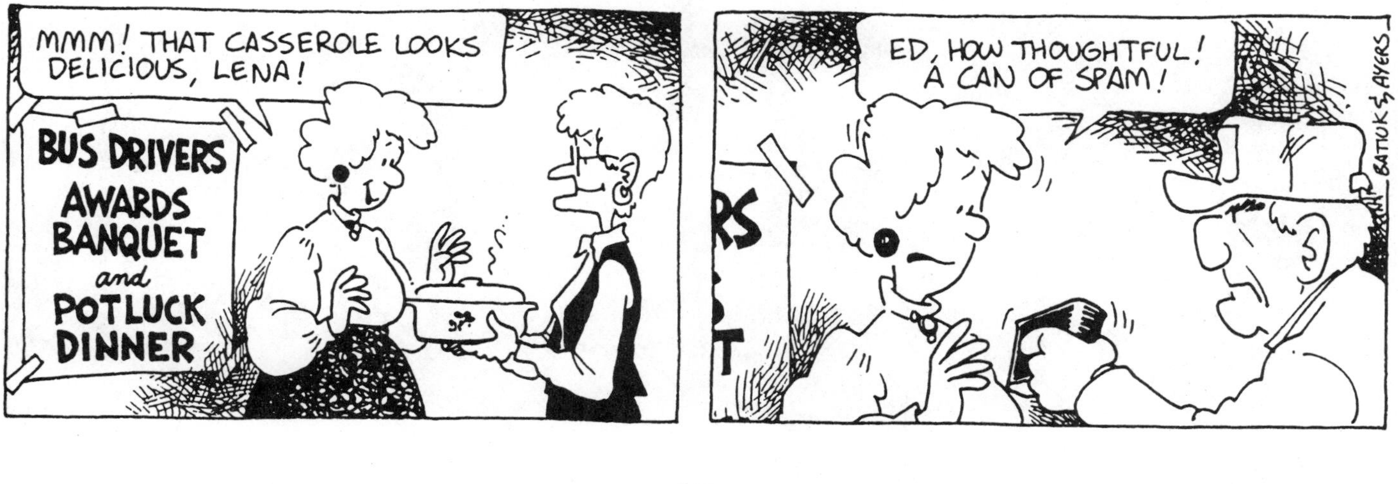
MMM! THAT CASSEROLE LOOKS DELICIOUS, LENA!
BUS DRIVERS AWARDS BANQUET and POTLUCK DINNER
ED, HOW THOUGHTFUL! A CAN OF SPAM!
BATIUK & AYERS

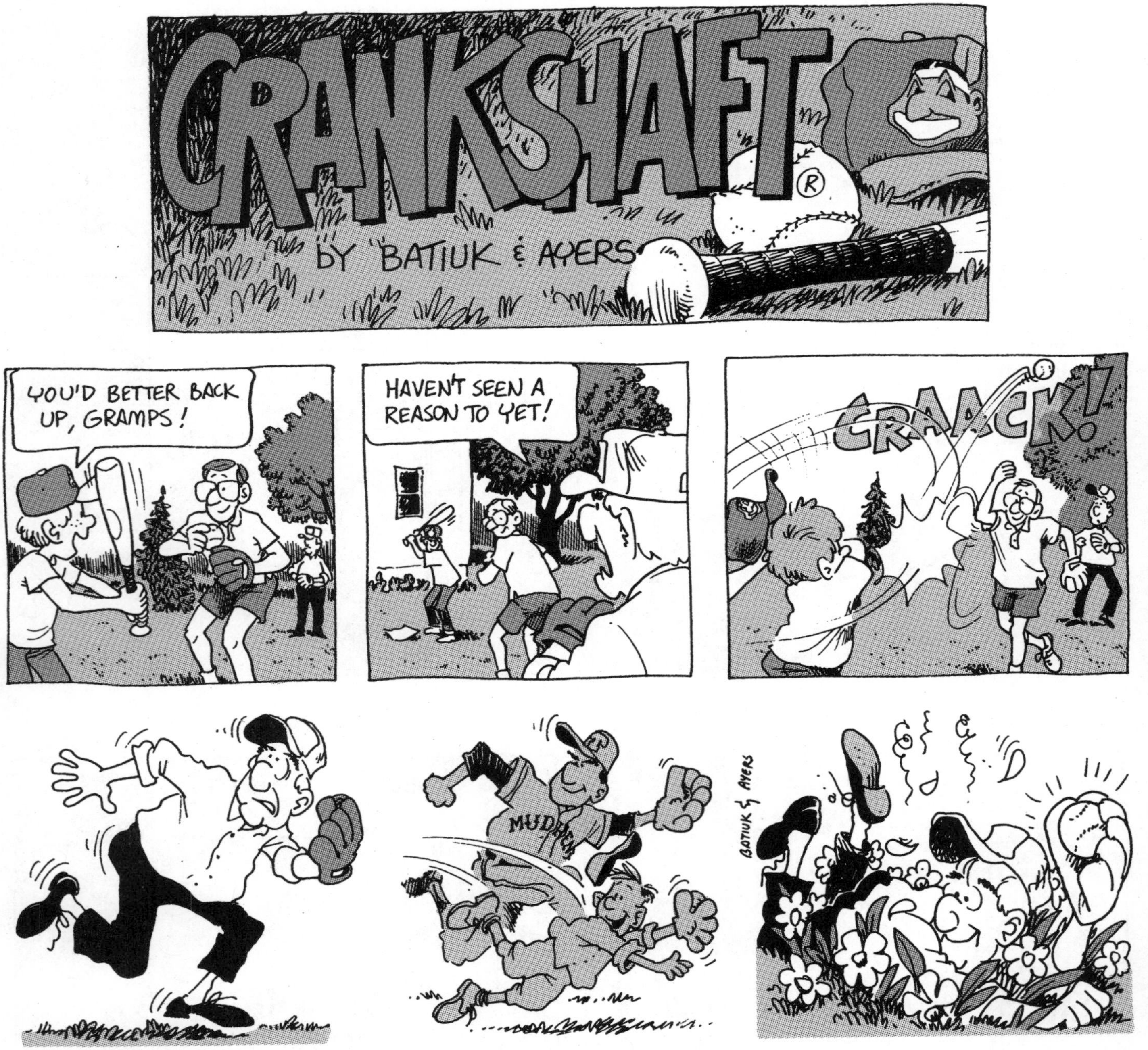
CRANKSHAFT ®
BY BATIUK & AYERS
YOU'D BETTER BACK UP, GRAMPS!
HAVEN'T SEEN A REASON TO YET!
CRAAACK!
BATIUK & AYERS

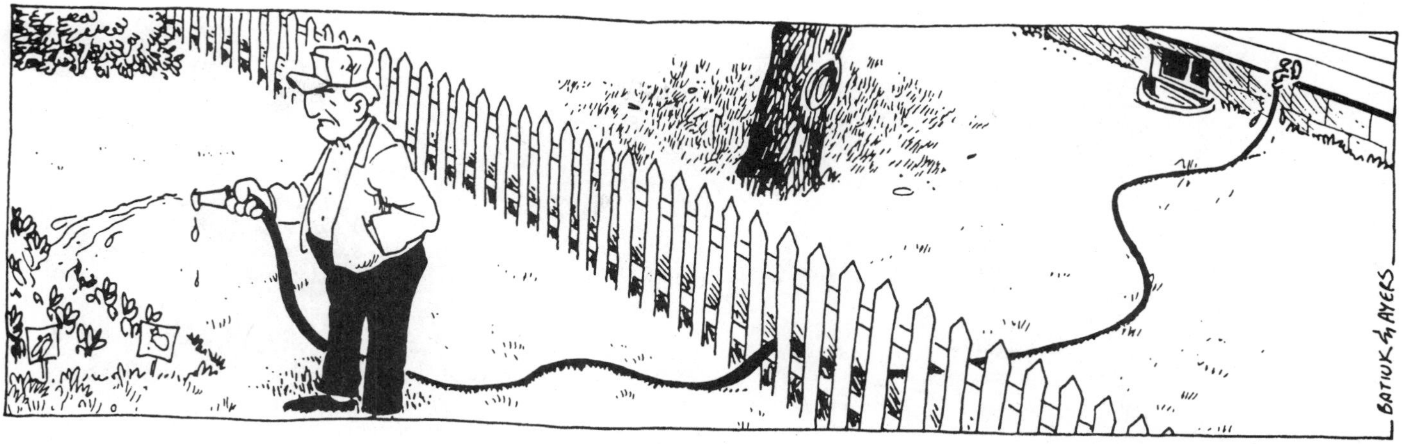
BATIUK & AYERS

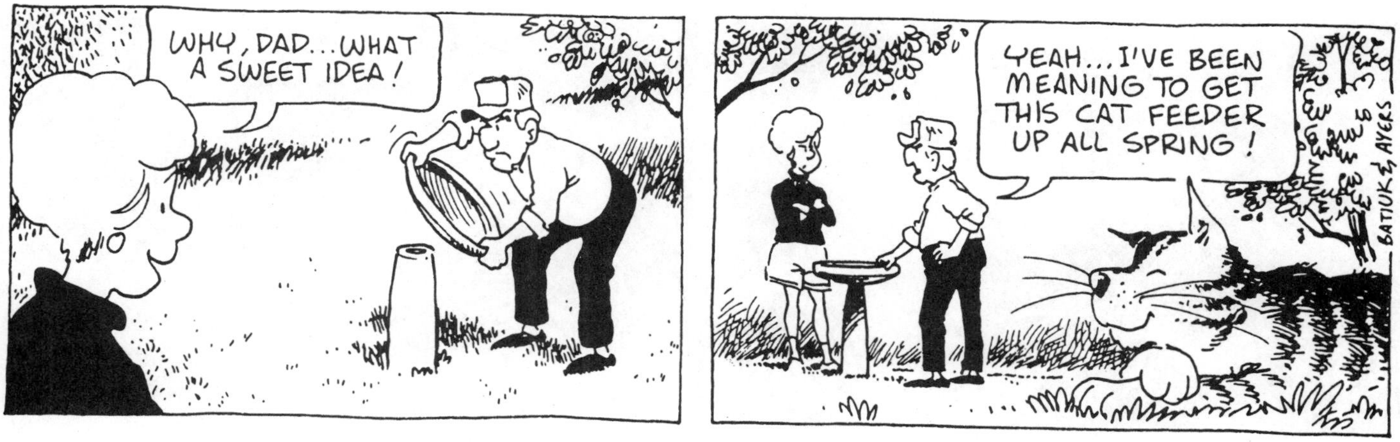
WHY, DAD...WHAT A SWEET IDEA!
YEAH... I'VE BEEN MEANING TO GET THIS CAT FEEDER UP ALL SPRING!
BATIUK & AYERS

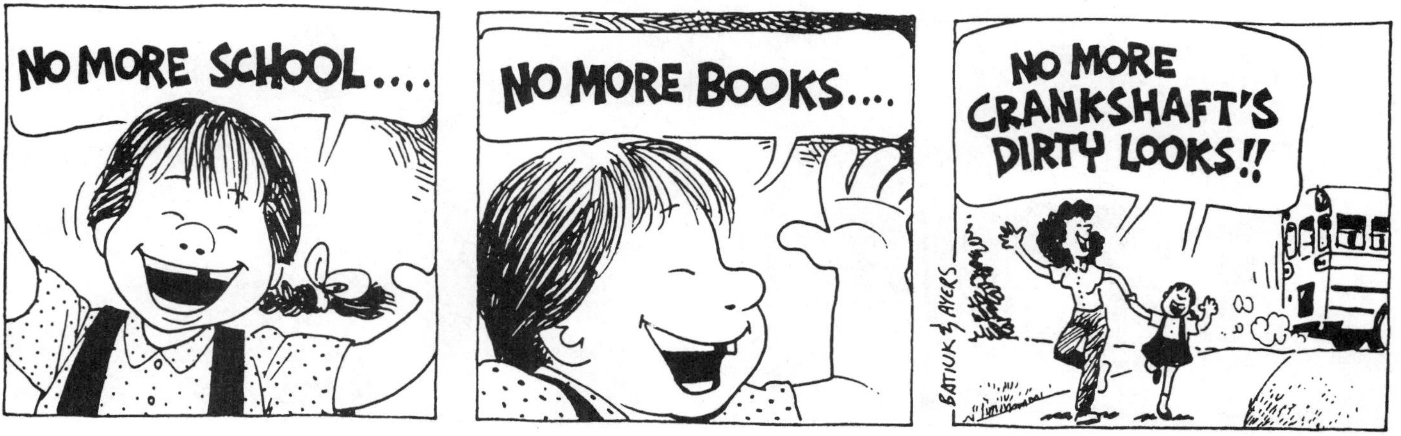
NO MORE SCHOOL....
NO MORE BOOKS....
NO MORE CRANKSHAFT'S DIRTY LOOKS!!
BATIUK & AYERS

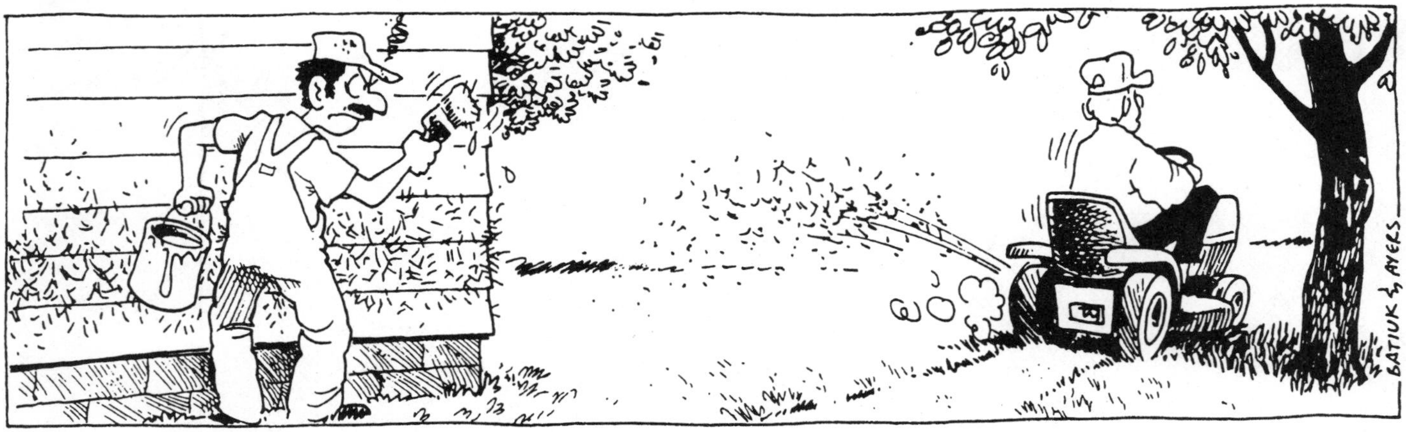
BATIUK & AYERS

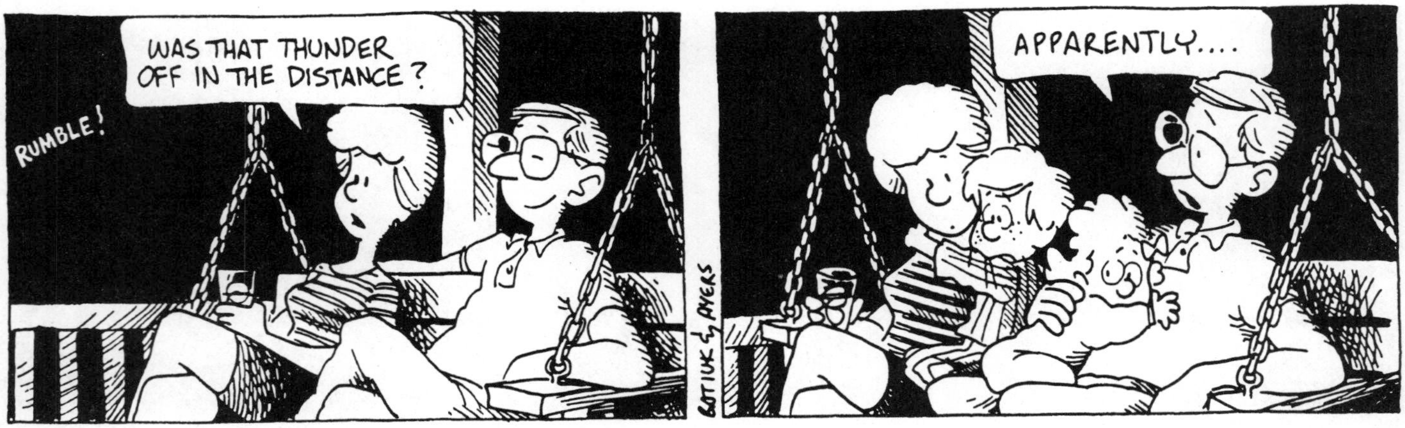
RUMBLE!
WAS THAT THUNDER OFF IN THE DISTANCE?
BATIUK & AYERS
APPARENTLY....

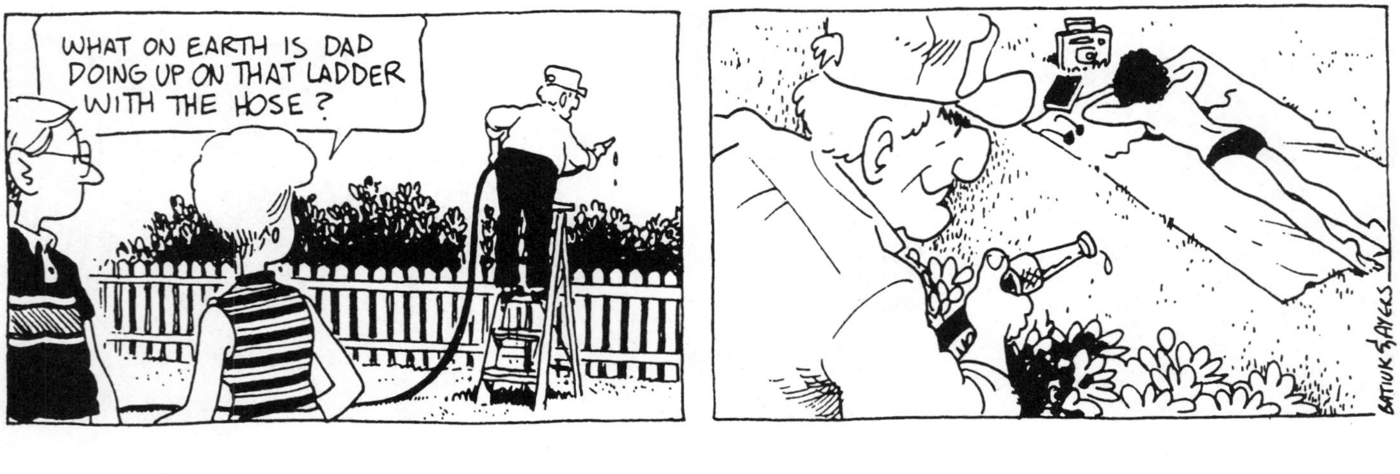
WHAT ON EARTH IS DAD DOING UP ON THAT LADDER WITH THE HOSE?
BATIUK & AYERS

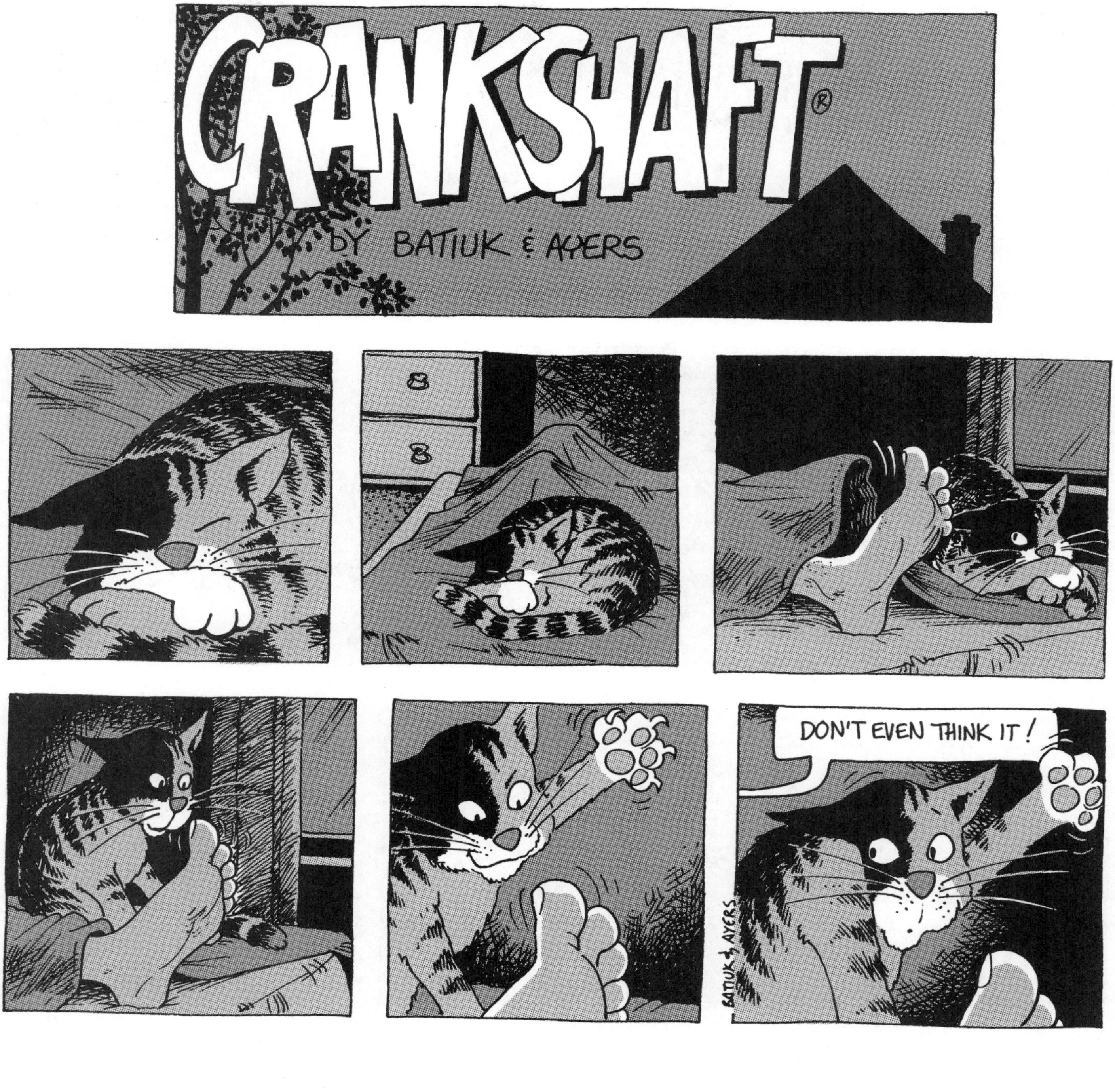
CRANKSHAFT®
BY BATIUK & AYERS
DON'T EVEN THINK IT!
BATIUK & AYERS

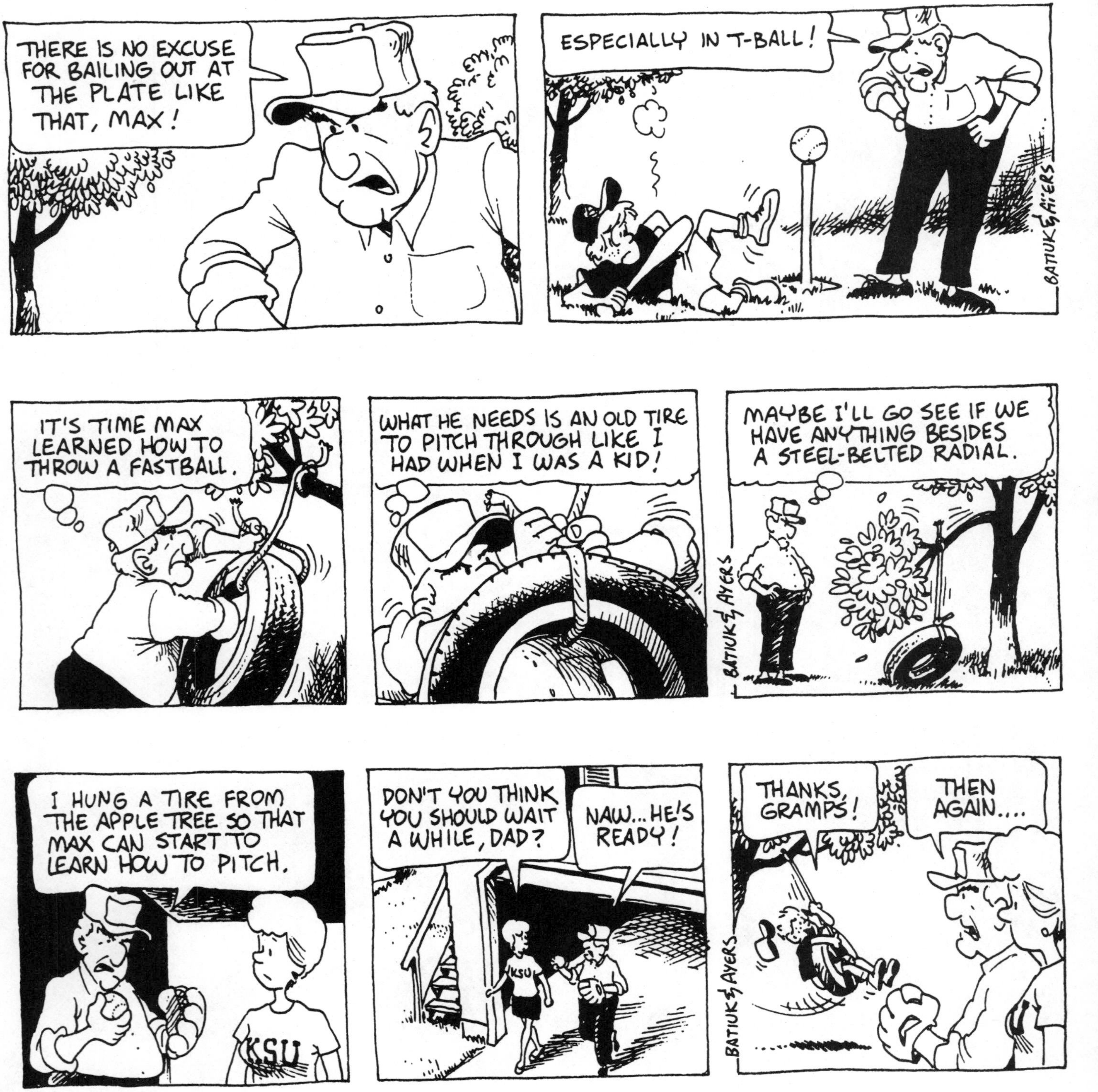
THERE IS NO EXCUSE FOR BAILING OUT AT THE PLATE LIKE THAT, MAX!
ESPECIALLY IN T-BALL!
BATIUK & AYERS
IT'S TIME MAX LEARNED HOW TO THROW A FASTBALL.
WHAT HE NEEDS IS AN OLD TIRE TO PITCH THROUGH LIKE I HAD WHEN I WAS A KID!
MAYBE I'LL GO SEE IF WE HAVE ANYTHING BESIDES A STEEL-BELTED RADIAL.
BATIUK & AYERS
I HUNG A TIRE FROM THE APPLE TREE SO THAT MAX CAN START TO LEARN HOW TO PITCH.
KSU
DON'T YOU THINK YOU SHOULD WAIT A WHILE, DAD?
NAW... HE'S READY!
KSU
THANKS, GRAMPS!
THEN AGAIN....
BATIUK & AYERS

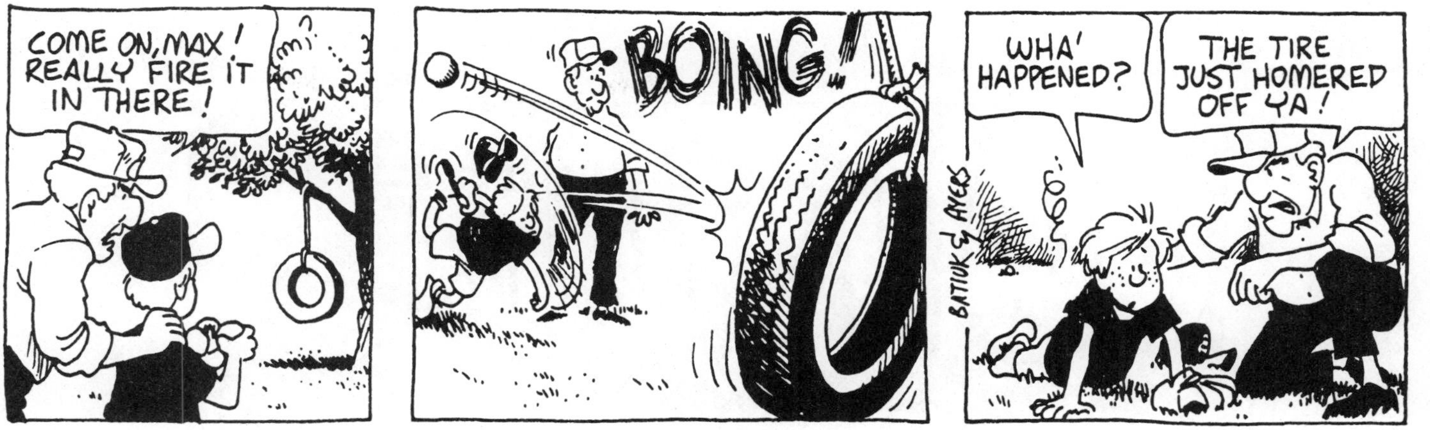
COME ON, MAX! REALLY FIRE IT IN THERE!
BOING!
WHA' HAPPENED?
THE TIRE JUST HOMERED OFF YA!
BATIUK & AYERS

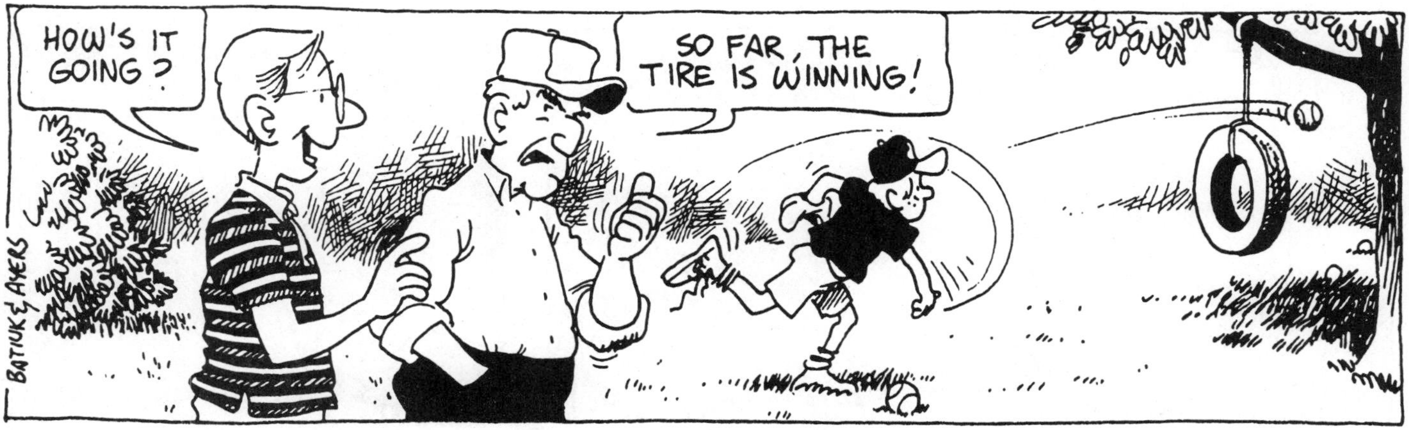
HOW'S IT GOING?
SO FAR, THE TIRE IS WINNING!
BATIUK & AYERS

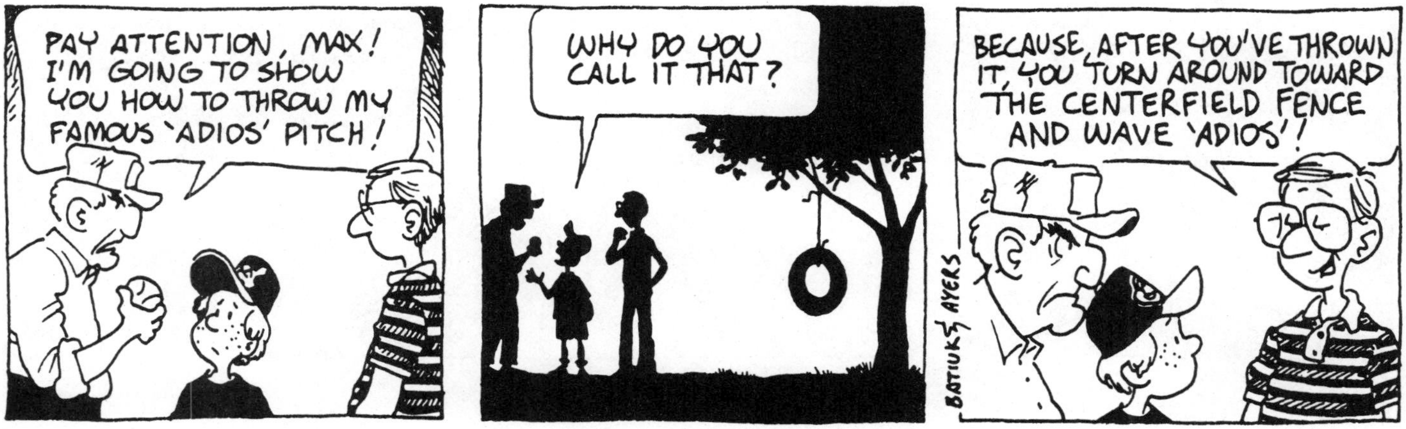
PAY ATTENTION, MAX! I'M GOING TO SHOW YOU HOW TO THROW MY FAMOUS 'ADIOS' PITCH!
WHY DO YOU CALL IT THAT?
BECAUSE, AFTER YOU'VE THROWN IT, YOU TURN AROUND TOWARD THE CENTERFIELD FENCE AND WAVE 'ADIOS'!
BATIUK & AYERS

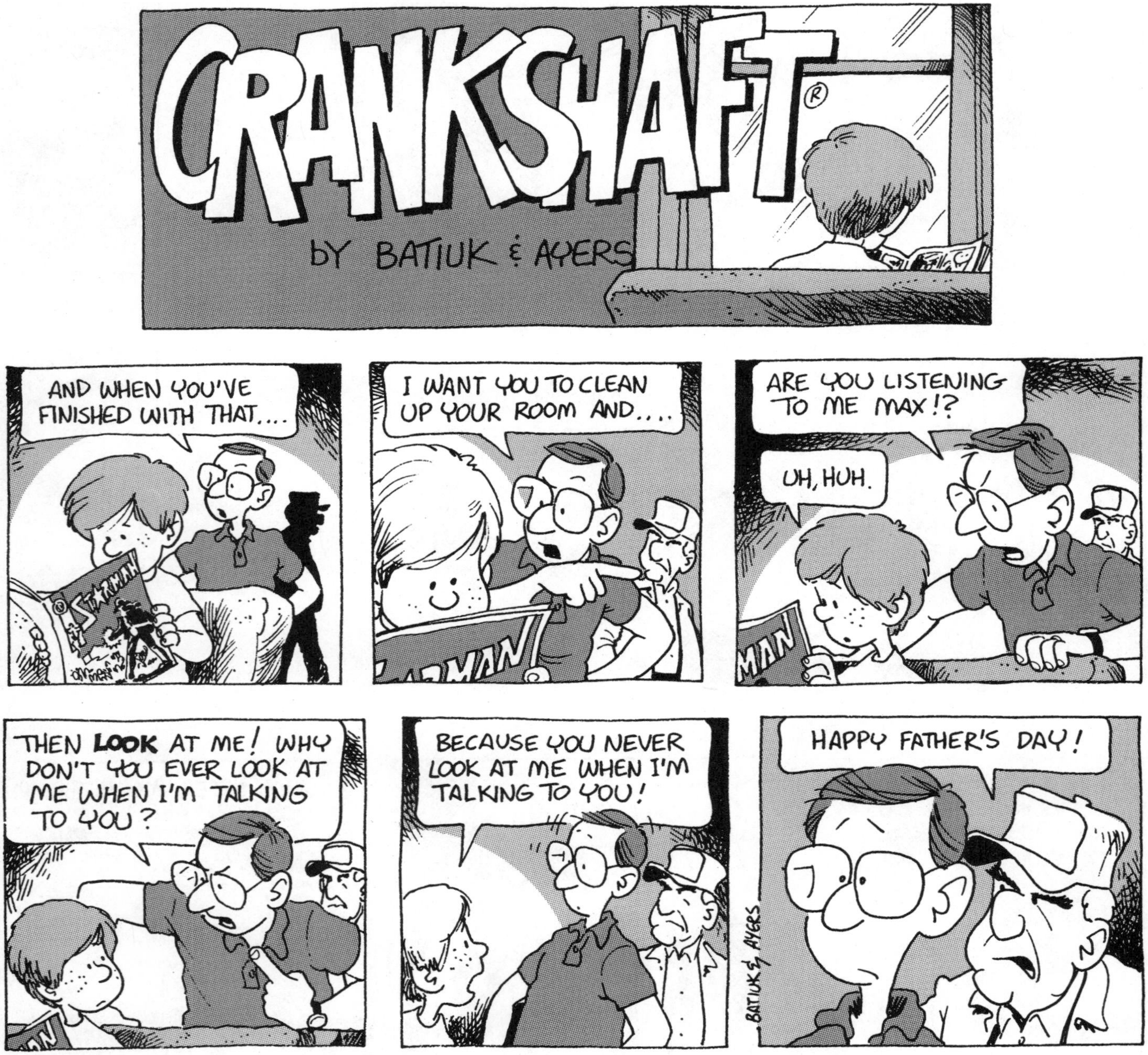
CRANKSHAFT®
BY BATIUK & AYERS
AND WHEN YOU'VE FINISHED WITH THAT....
I WANT YOU TO CLEAN UP YOUR ROOM AND....
ARE YOU LISTENING TO ME MAX!?
UH, HUH.
THEN **LOOK** AT ME! WHY DON'T YOU EVER LOOK AT ME WHEN I'M TALKING TO YOU?
BECAUSE YOU NEVER LOOK AT ME WHEN I'M TALKING TO YOU!
BATIUK & AYERS
HAPPY FATHER'S DAY!

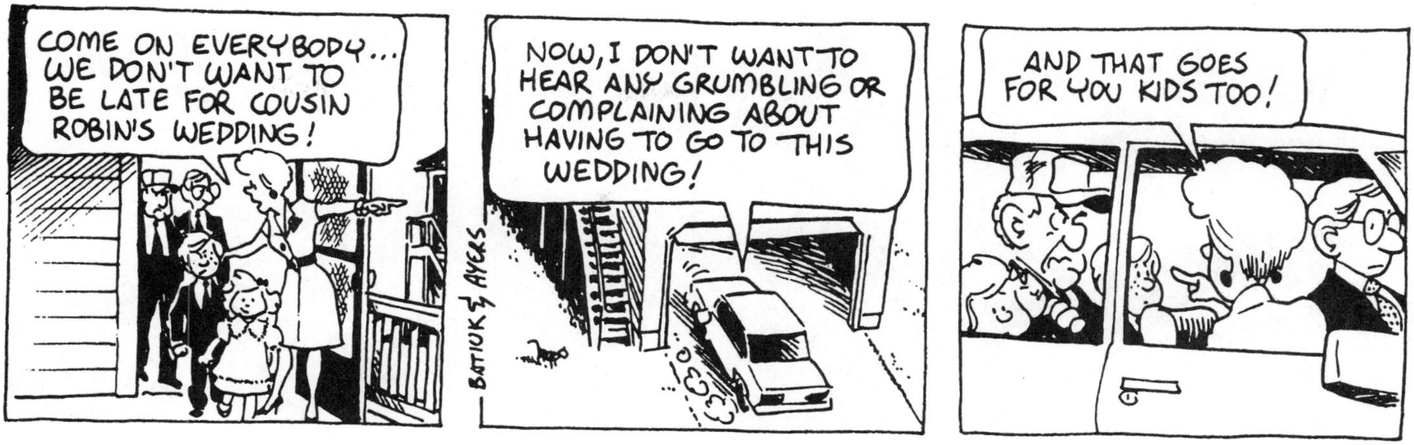
COME ON EVERYBODY... WE DON'T WANT TO BE LATE FOR COUSIN ROBIN'S WEDDING!
BATIUK & AYERS
NOW, I DON'T WANT TO HEAR ANY GRUMBLING OR COMPLAINING ABOUT HAVING TO GO TO THIS WEDDING!
AND THAT GOES FOR YOU KIDS TOO!

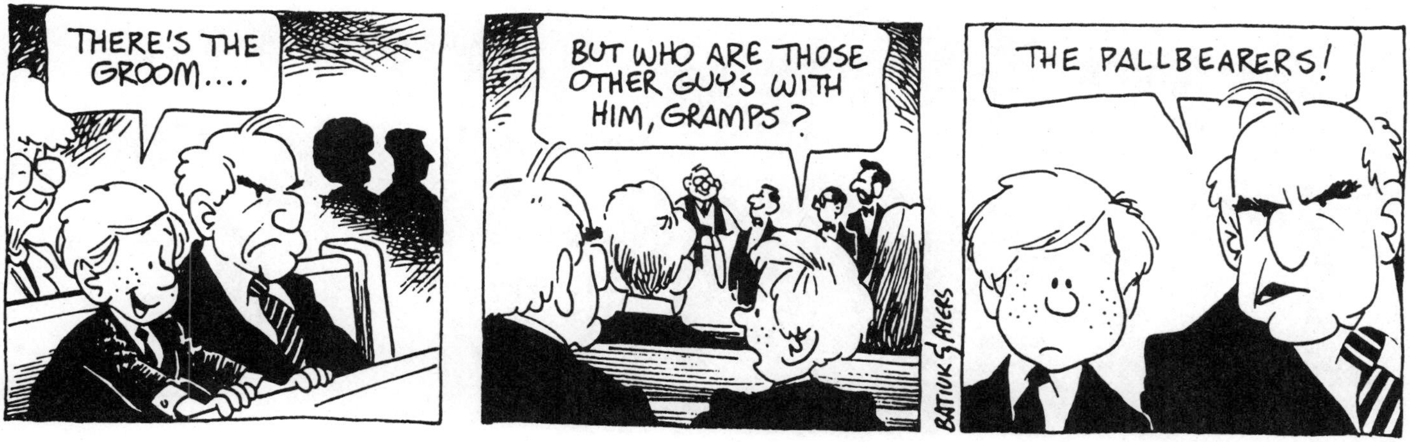
THERE'S THE GROOM....
BUT WHO ARE THOSE OTHER GUYS WITH HIM, GRAMPS?
BATIUK & AYERS
THE PALLBEARERS!

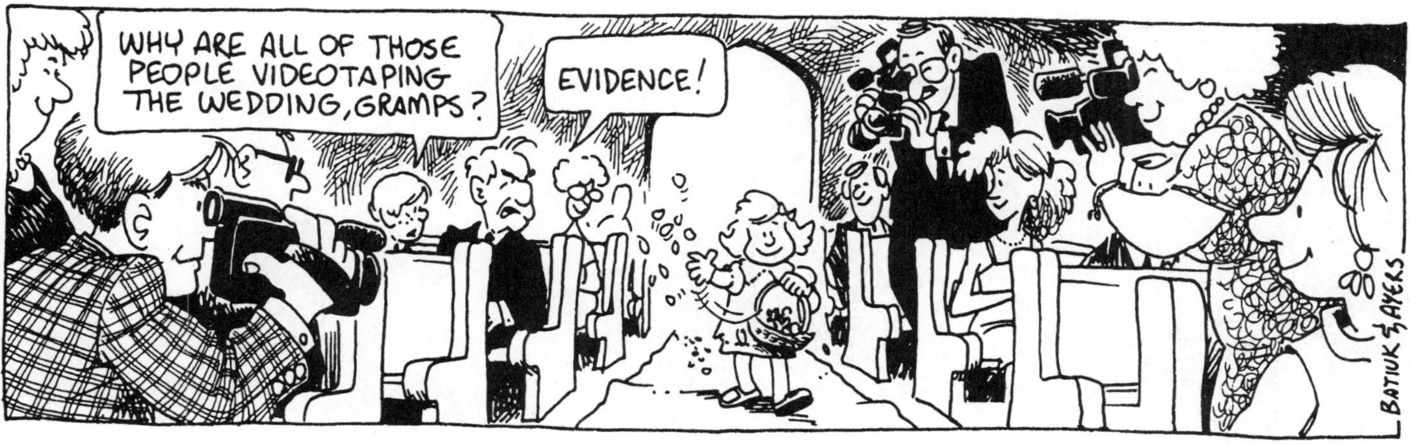
WHY ARE ALL OF THOSE PEOPLE VIDEOTAPING THE WEDDING, GRAMPS?
EVIDENCE!
BATIUK & AYERS

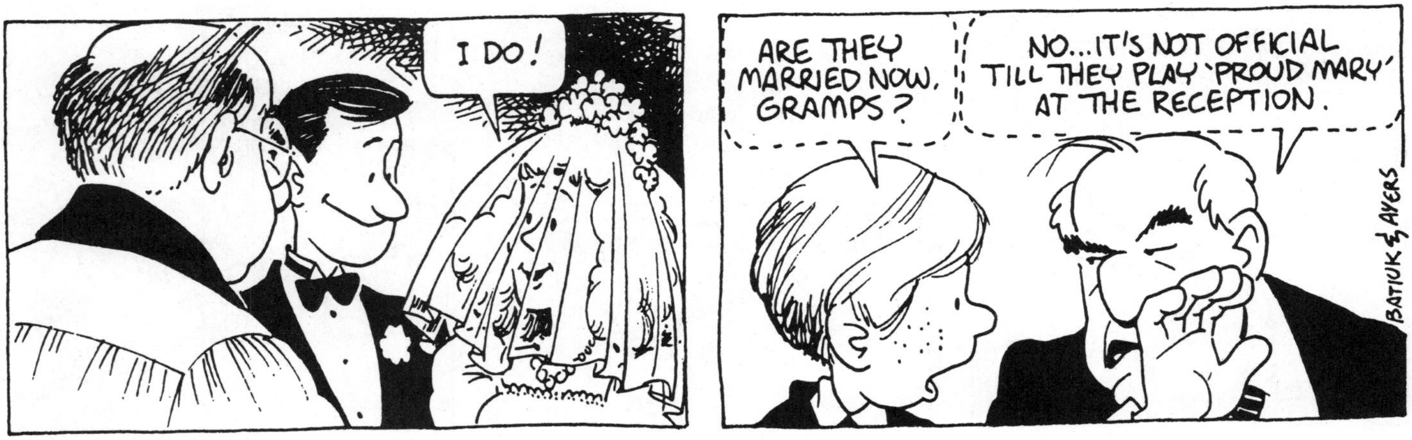
I DO!
ARE THEY MARRIED NOW, GRAMPS?
NO...IT'S NOT OFFICIAL TILL THEY PLAY 'PROUD MARY' AT THE RECEPTION.
BATIUK & AYERS

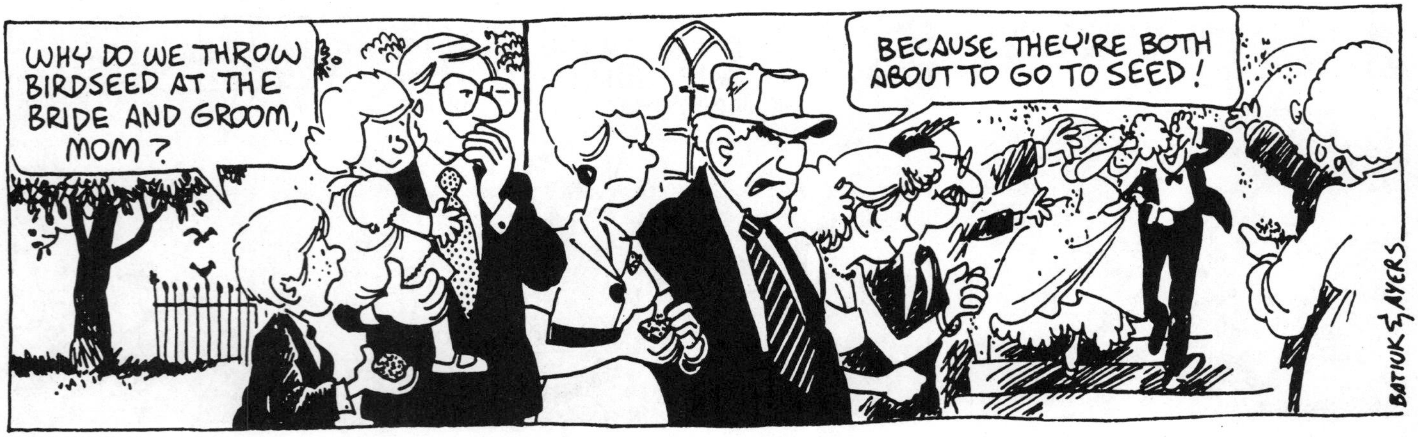
WHY DO WE THROW BIRDSEED AT THE BRIDE AND GROOM, MOM?
BECAUSE THEY'RE BOTH ABOUT TO GO TO SEED!
BATIUK & AYERS

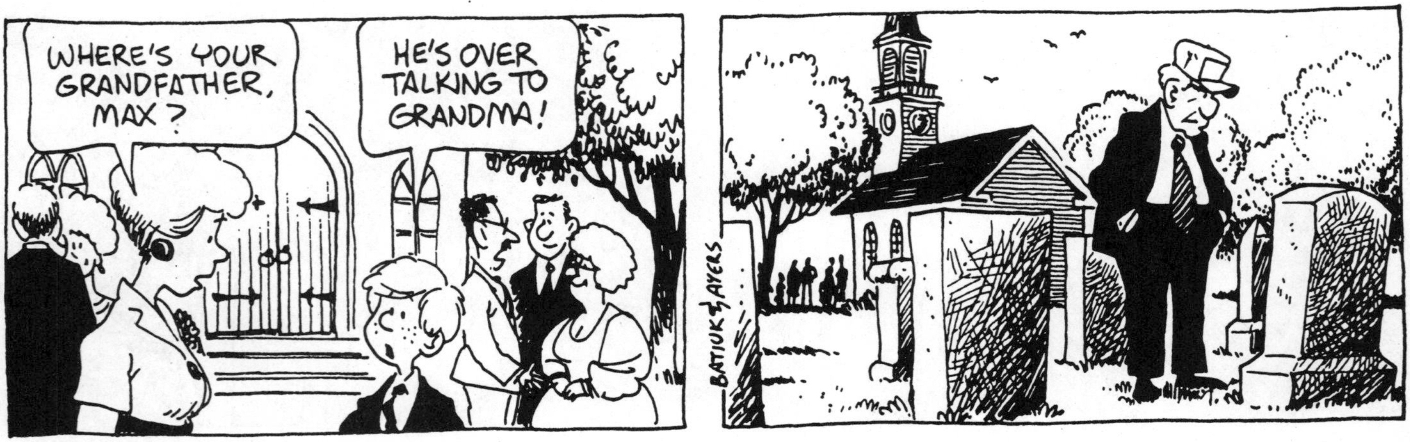
WHERE'S YOUR GRANDFATHER, MAX?
HE'S OVER TALKING TO GRANDMA!
BATIUK & AYERS

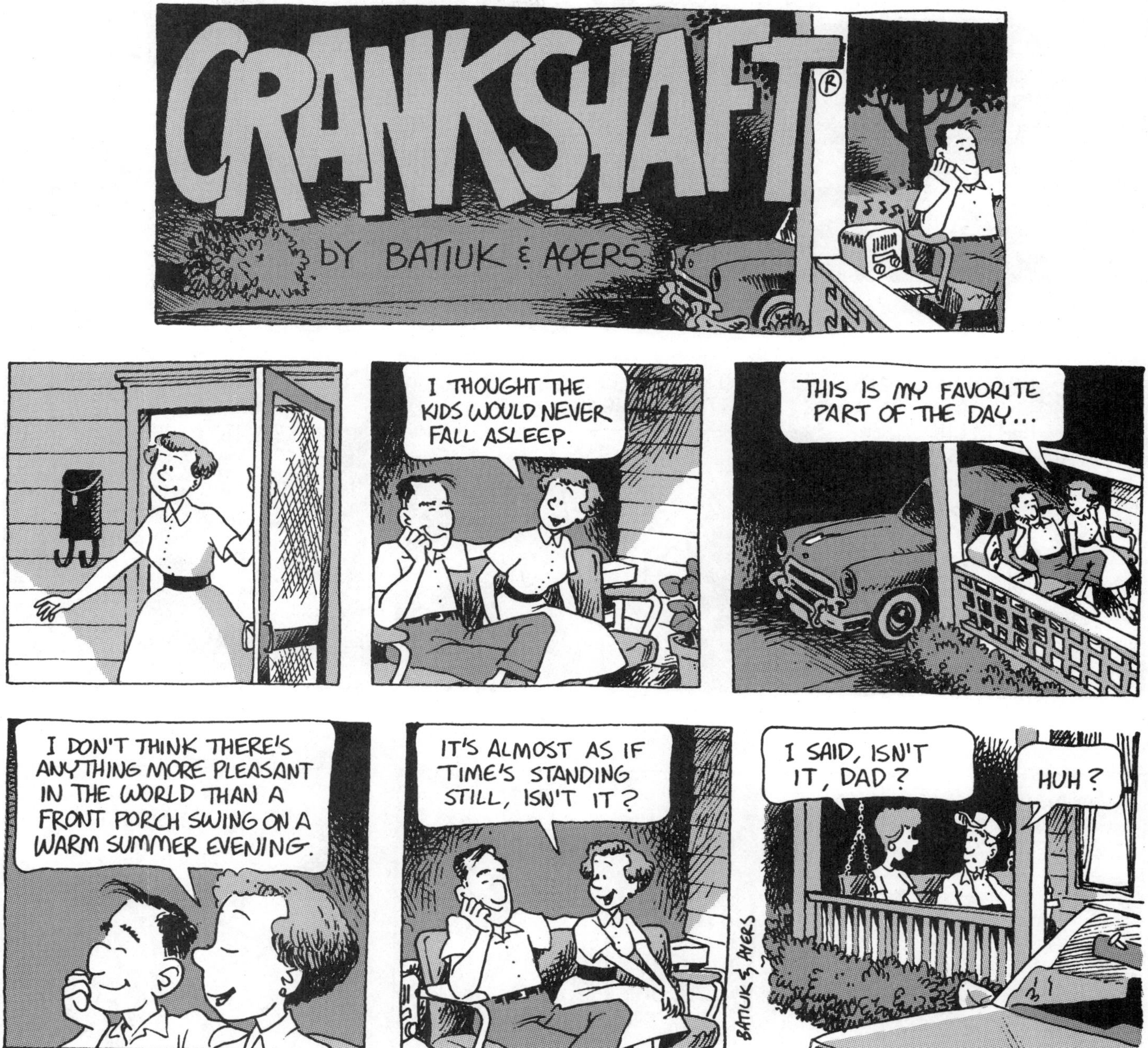
CRANKSHAFT®
BY BATIUK & AYERS
I THOUGHT THE KIDS WOULD NEVER FALL ASLEEP.
THIS IS MY FAVORITE PART OF THE DAY...
I DON'T THINK THERE'S ANYTHING MORE PLEASANT IN THE WORLD THAN A FRONT PORCH SWING ON A WARM SUMMER EVENING.
IT'S ALMOST AS IF TIME'S STANDING STILL, ISN'T IT?
BATIUK & AYERS
I SAID, ISN'T IT, DAD?
HUH?

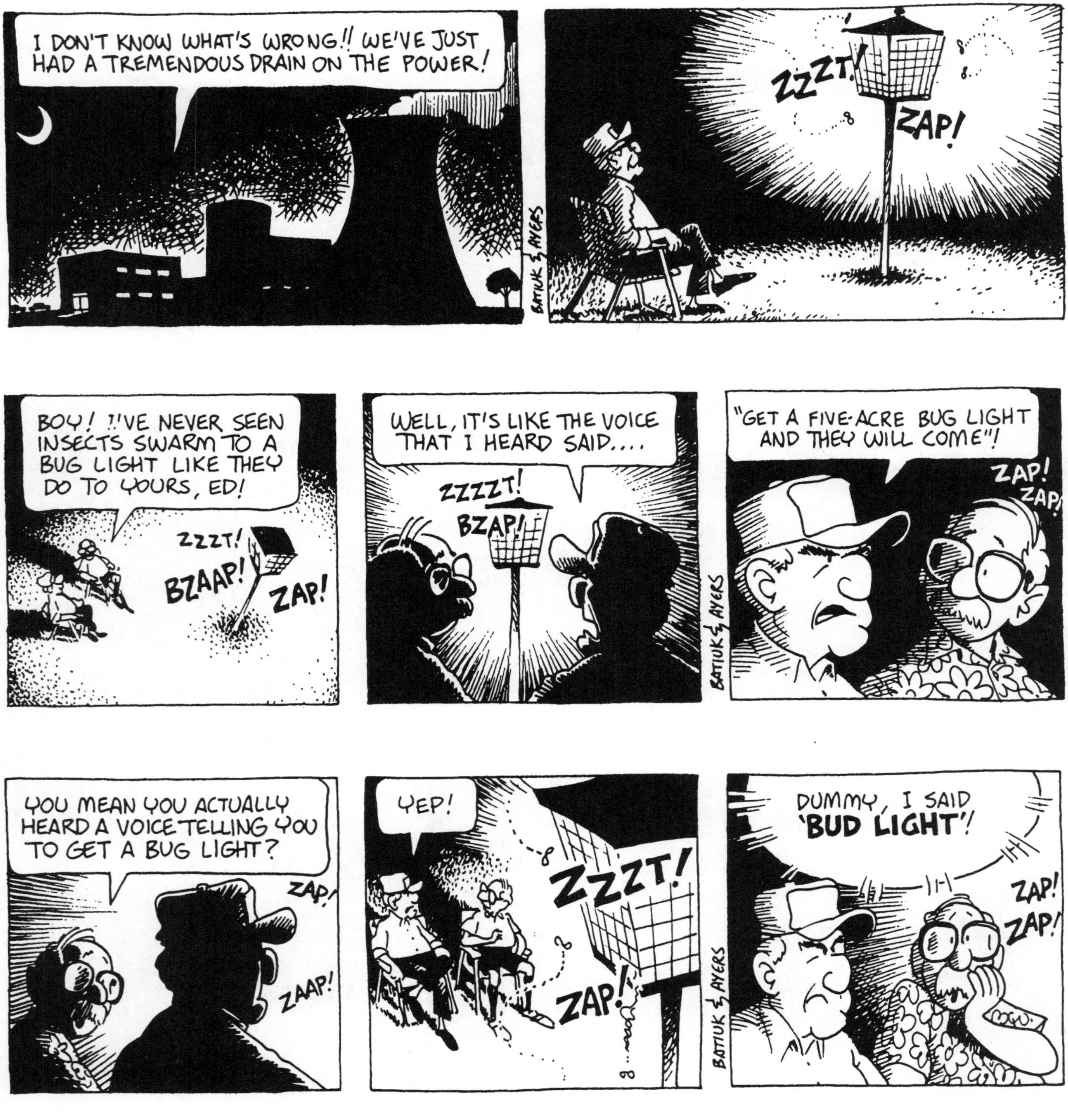
I DON'T KNOW WHAT'S WRONG!! WE'VE JUST HAD A TREMENDOUS DRAIN ON THE POWER!
BATIUK & AYERS
ZZZT!
ZAP!
BOY! I'VE NEVER SEEN INSECTS SWARM TO A BUG LIGHT LIKE THEY DO TO YOURS, ED!
ZZZT!
BZAAP!
ZAP!
WELL, IT'S LIKE THE VOICE THAT I HEARD SAID....
ZZZZT!
BZAP!
BATIUK & AYERS
"GET A FIVE-ACRE BUG LIGHT AND THEY WILL COME"!
ZAP!
ZAP!
YOU MEAN YOU ACTUALLY HEARD A VOICE TELLING YOU TO GET A BUG LIGHT?
ZAP!
ZAAP!
YEP!
ZZZT!
ZAP!
BATIUK & AYERS
DUMMY, I SAID 'BUD LIGHT'!
ZAP!
ZAP!

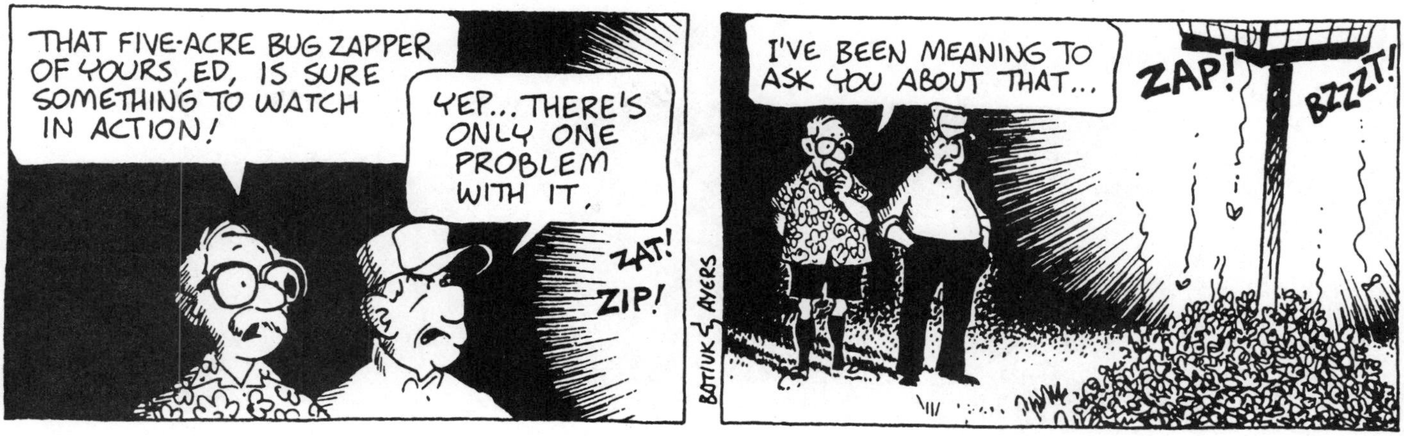
THAT FIVE-ACRE BUG ZAPPER OF YOURS, ED, IS SURE SOMETHING TO WATCH IN ACTION!
YEP... THERE'S ONLY ONE PROBLEM WITH IT.
ZAT!
ZIP!
BATIUK & AYERS
I'VE BEEN MEANING TO ASK YOU ABOUT THAT...
ZAP!
BZZZT!

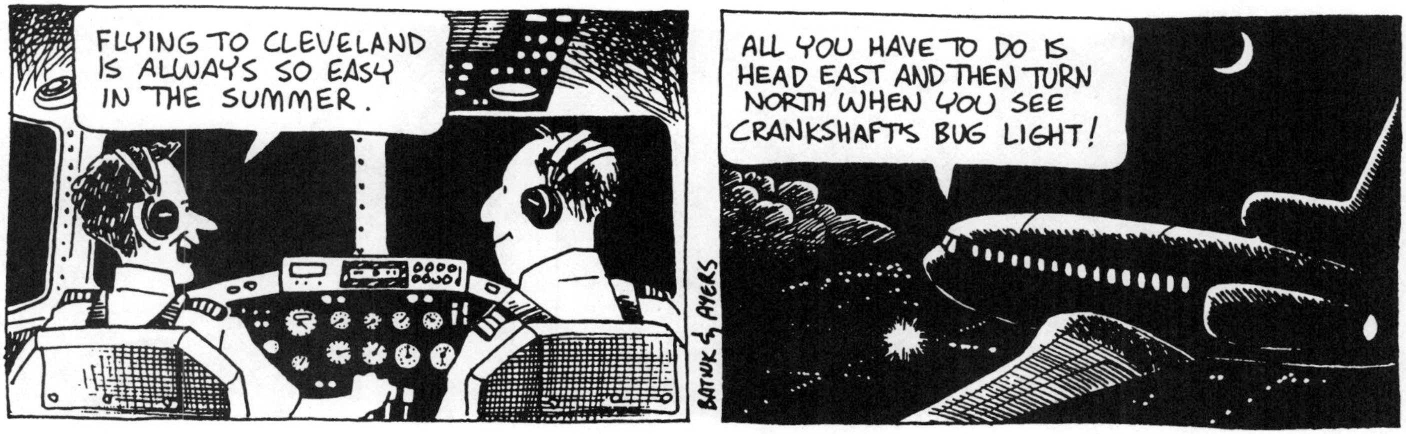
FLYING TO CLEVELAND IS ALWAYS SO EASY IN THE SUMMER.
BATIUK & AYERS
ALL YOU HAVE TO DO IS HEAD EAST AND THEN TURN NORTH WHEN YOU SEE CRANKSHAFT'S BUG LIGHT!

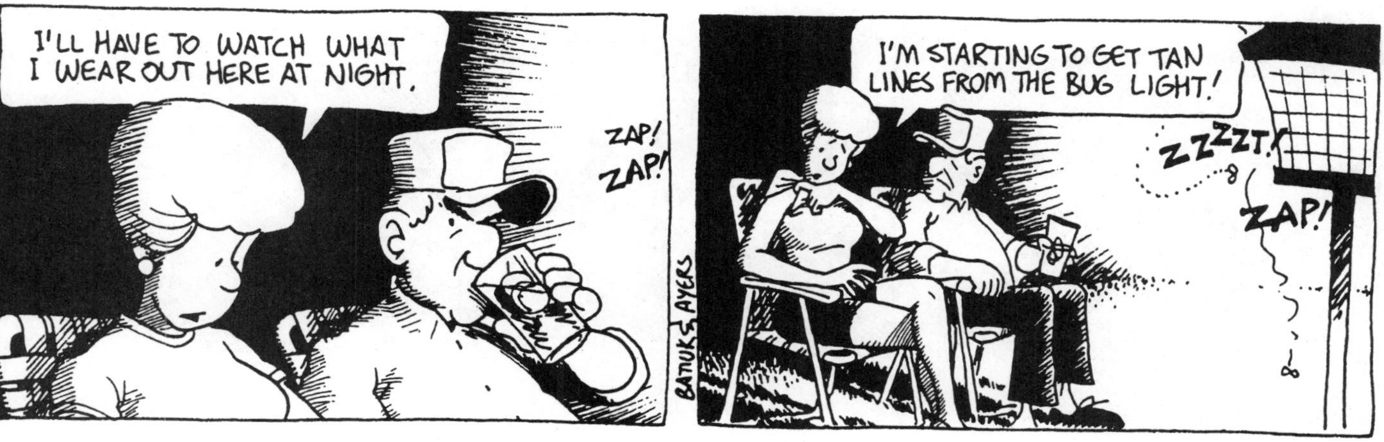
I'LL HAVE TO WATCH WHAT I WEAR OUT HERE AT NIGHT.
ZAP!
ZAP!
BATIUK & AYERS
I'M STARTING TO GET TAN LINES FROM THE BUG LIGHT!
ZZZZT!
ZAP!

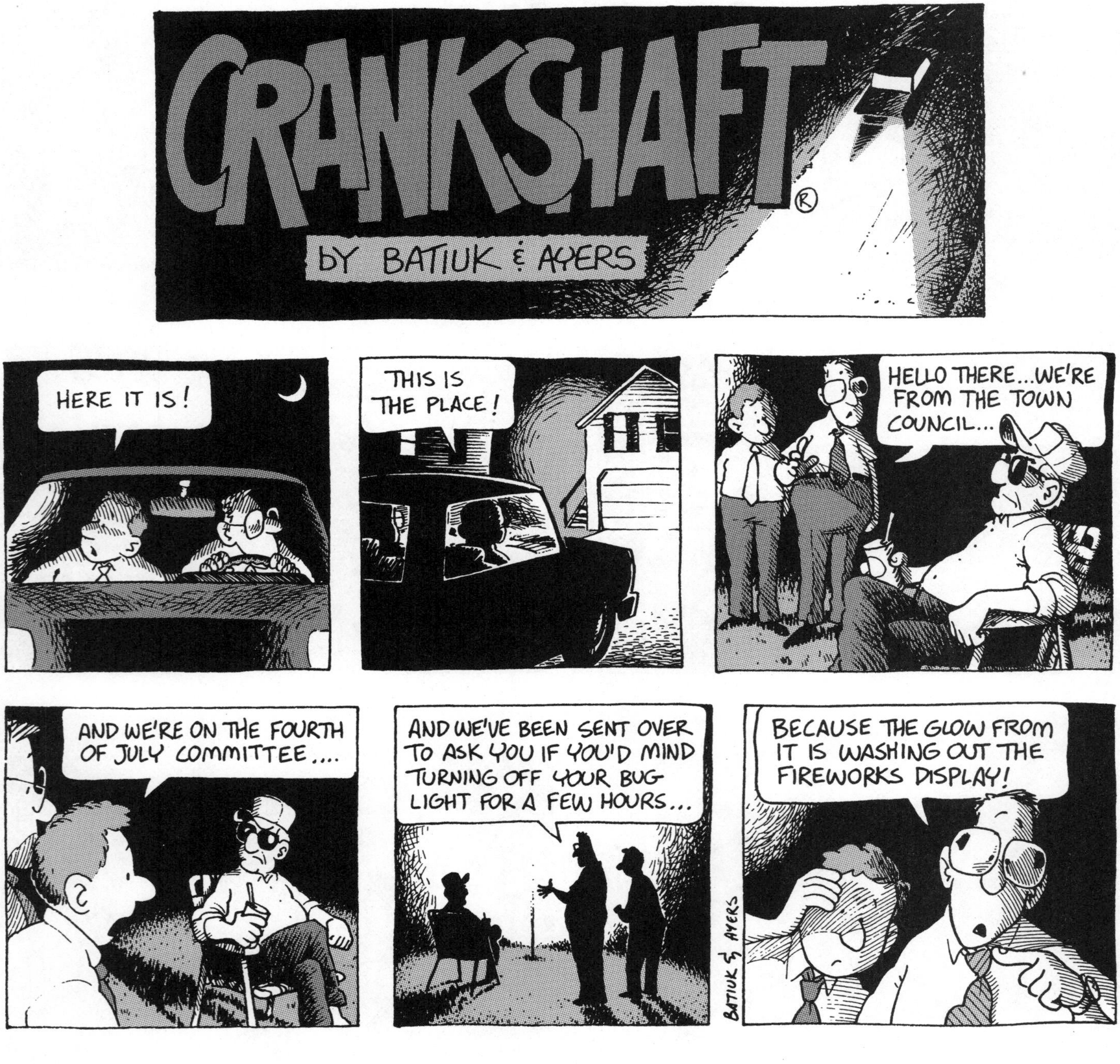
CRANKSHAFT®
BY BATIUK & AYERS
HERE IT IS!
THIS IS THE PLACE!
HELLO THERE...WE'RE FROM THE TOWN COUNCIL...
AND WE'RE ON THE FOURTH OF JULY COMMITTEE....
AND WE'VE BEEN SENT OVER TO ASK YOU IF YOU'D MIND TURNING OFF YOUR BUG LIGHT FOR A FEW HOURS...
BATIUK & AYERS
BECAUSE THE GLOW FROM IT IS WASHING OUT THE FIREWORKS DISPLAY!

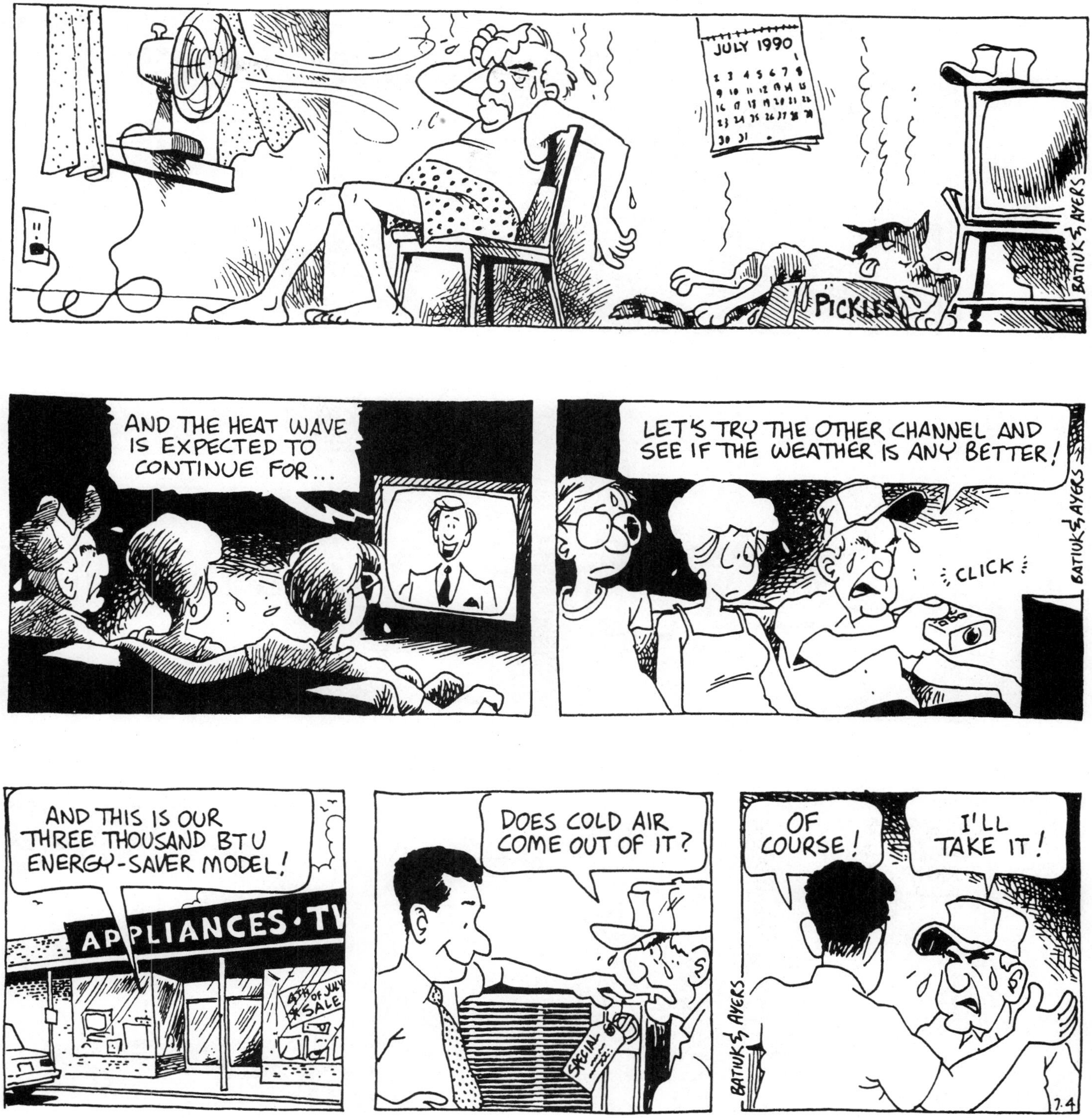
JULY 1990
PICKLES
AND THE HEAT WAVE IS EXPECTED TO CONTINUE FOR...
LET'S TRY THE OTHER CHANNEL AND SEE IF THE WEATHER IS ANY BETTER!
CLICK
AND THIS IS OUR THREE THOUSAND BTU ENERGY-SAVER MODEL!
APPLIANCES · TV
4TH OF JULY SALE
DOES COLD AIR COME OUT OF IT?
SPECIAL
OF COURSE!
I'LL TAKE IT!
7-4

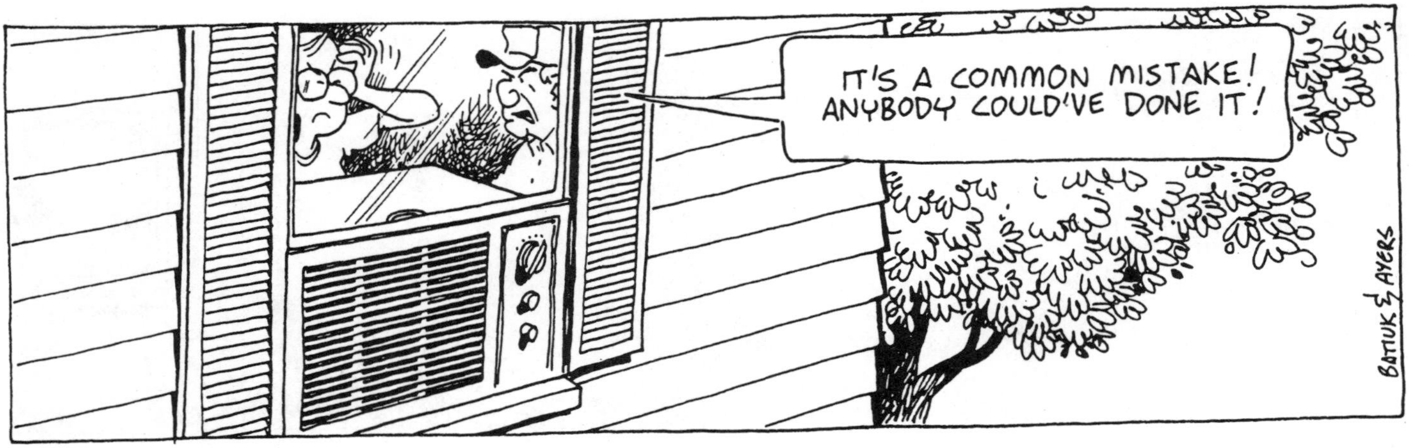
IT'S A COMMON MISTAKE! ANYBODY COULD'VE DONE IT!
BATIUK & AYERS

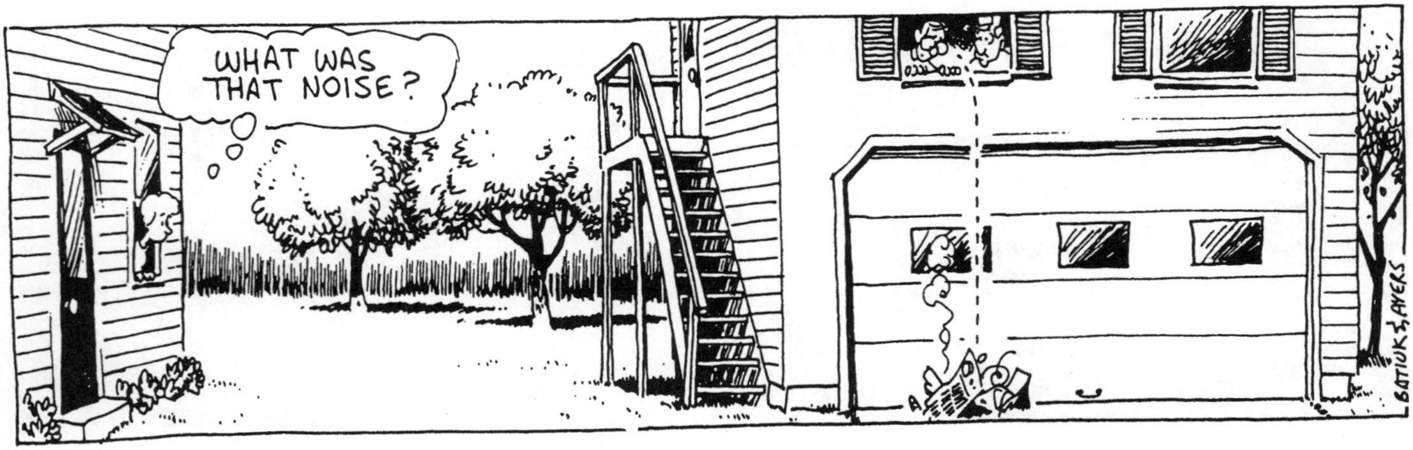
WHAT WAS THAT NOISE?
BATIUK & AYERS

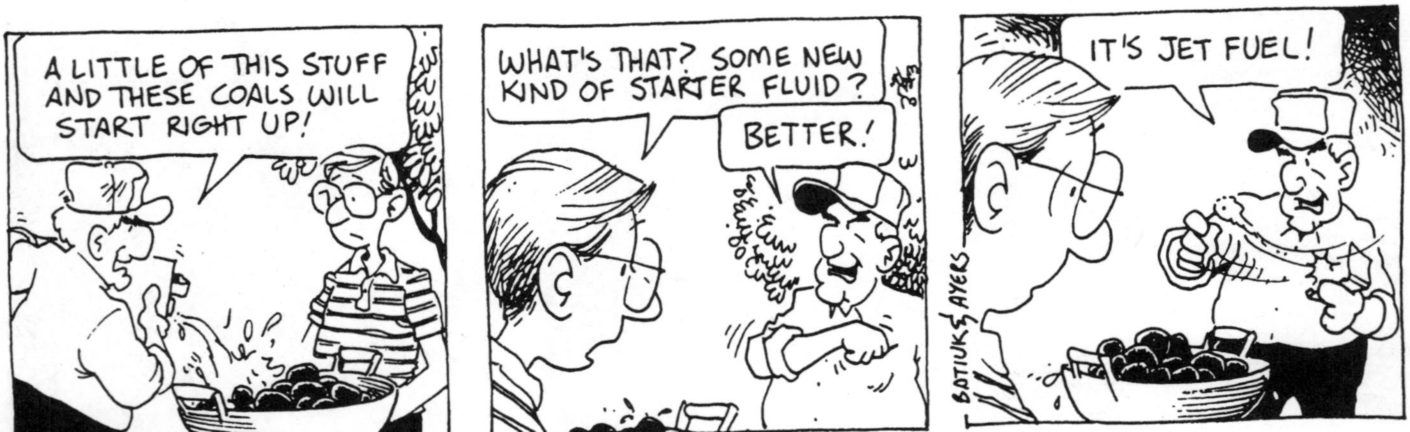
A LITTLE OF THIS STUFF AND THESE COALS WILL START RIGHT UP!
WHAT'S THAT? SOME NEW KIND OF STARTER FLUID?
BETTER!
IT'S JET FUEL!
BATIUK & AYERS

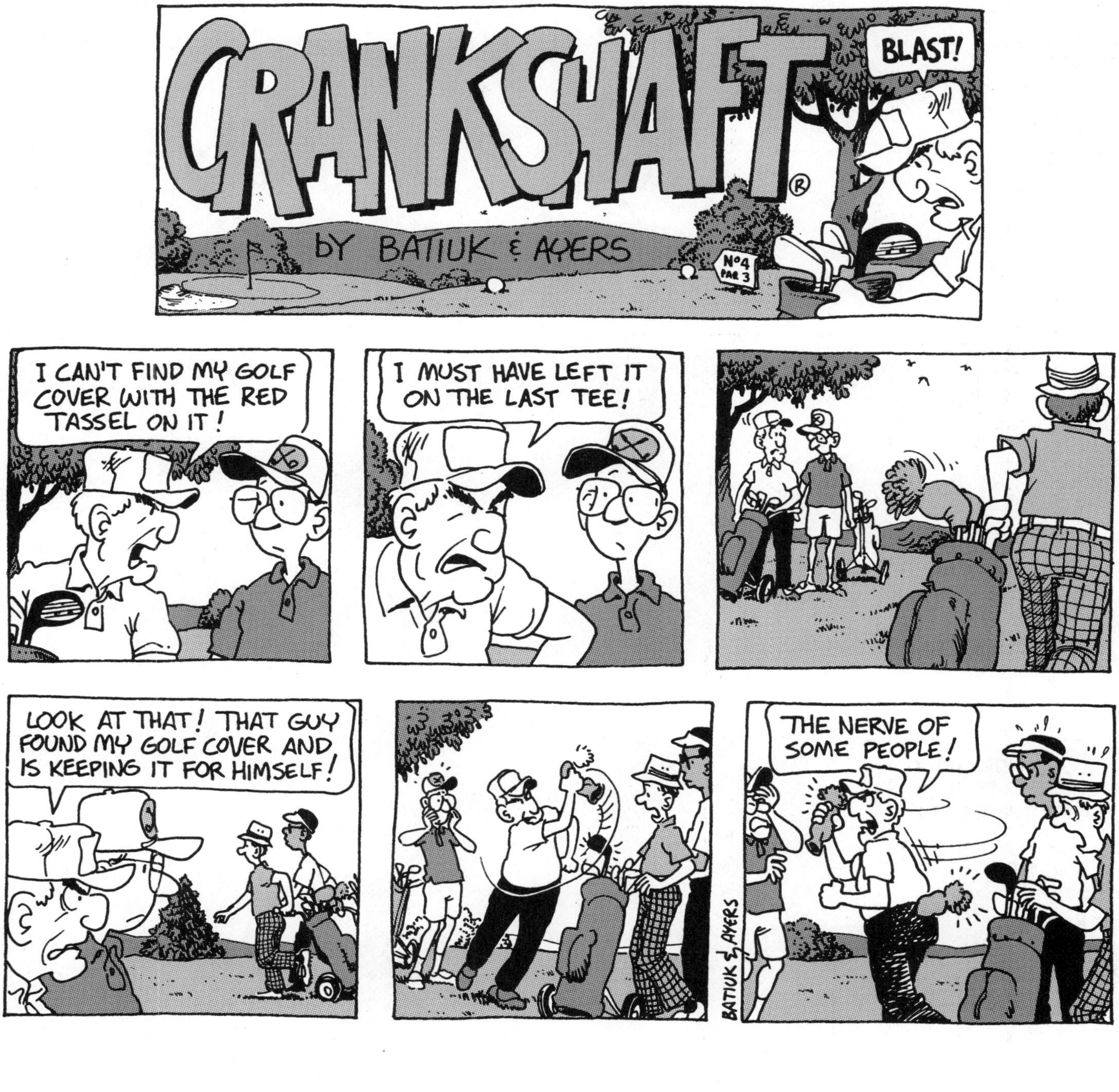
CRANKSHAFT®
BY BATIUK & AYERS
BLAST!
Nº4 PAR 3
I CAN'T FIND MY GOLF COVER WITH THE RED TASSEL ON IT!
I MUST HAVE LEFT IT ON THE LAST TEE!
LOOK AT THAT! THAT GUY FOUND MY GOLF COVER AND IS KEEPING IT FOR HIMSELF!
BATIUK & AYERS
THE NERVE OF SOME PEOPLE!

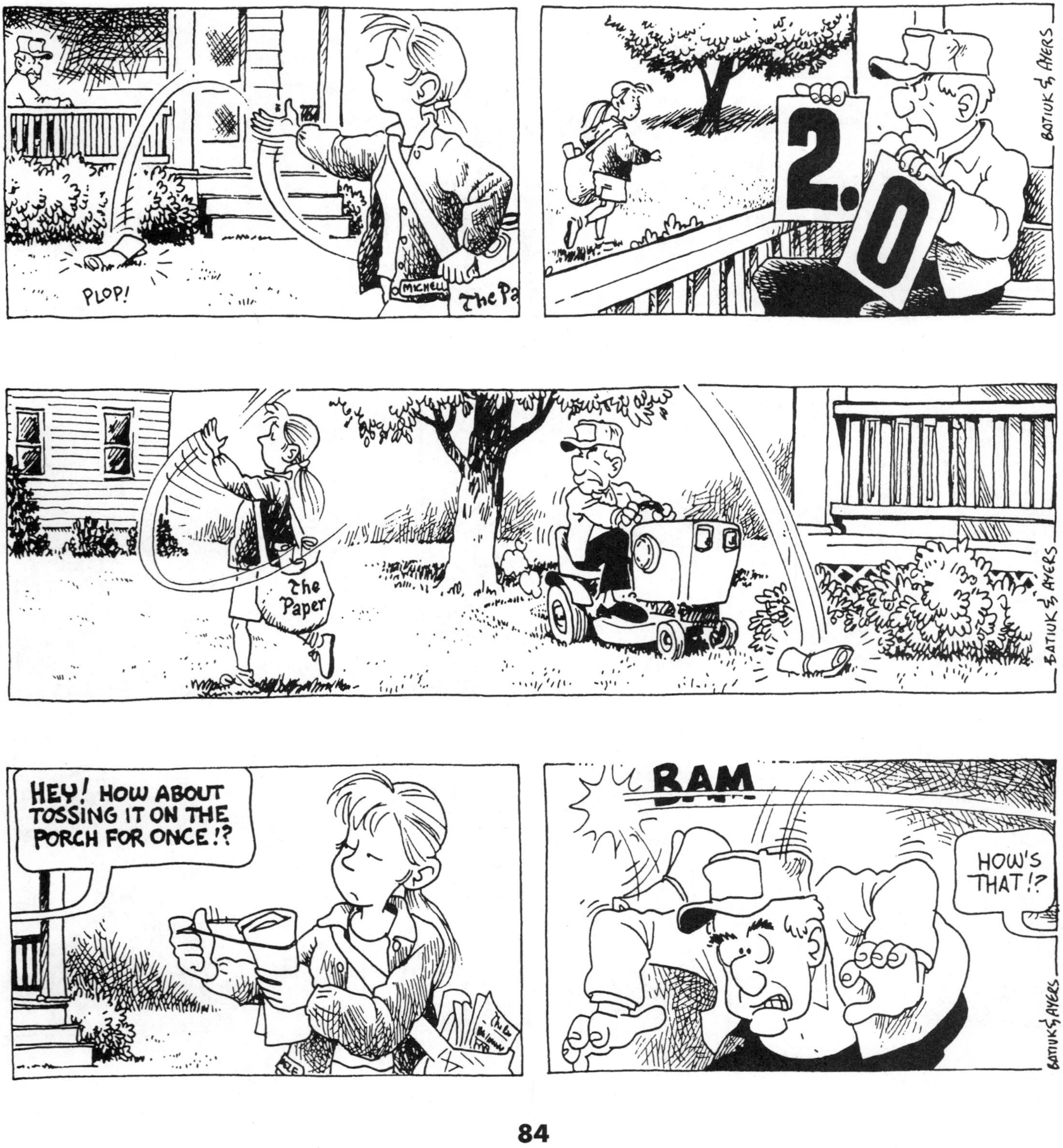
PLOP!
MICHELL
The Pa
BATIUK & AYERS
2.0
The Paper
BATIUK & AYERS
HEY! HOW ABOUT TOSSING IT ON THE PORCH FOR ONCE!?
BAM
HOW'S THAT!?
BATIUK & AYERS

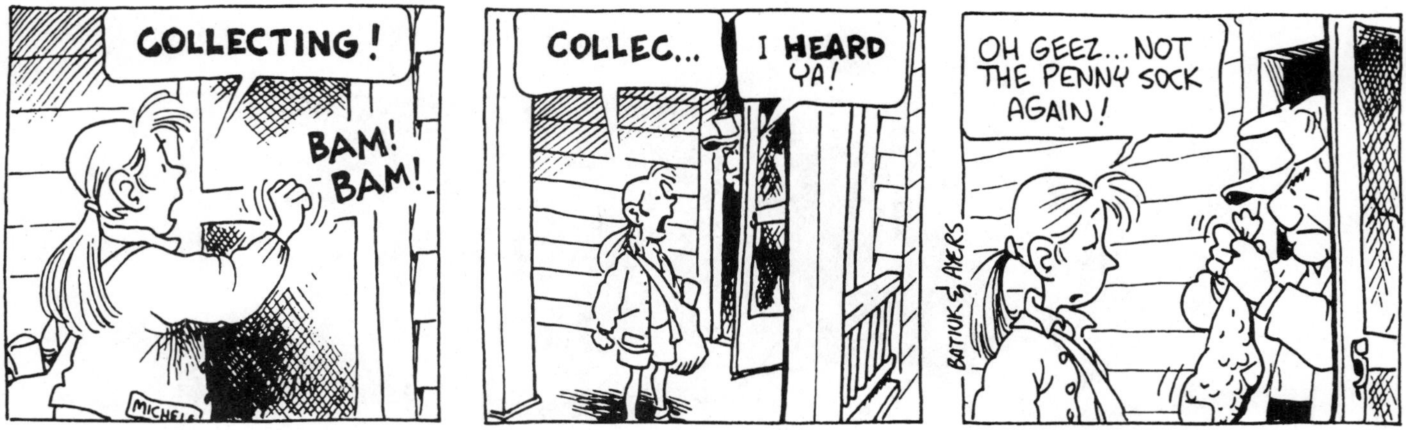
COLLECTING!
BAM! BAM!
COLLEC...
I HEARD YA!
OH GEEZ... NOT THE PENNY SOCK AGAIN!
BATIUK & AYERS

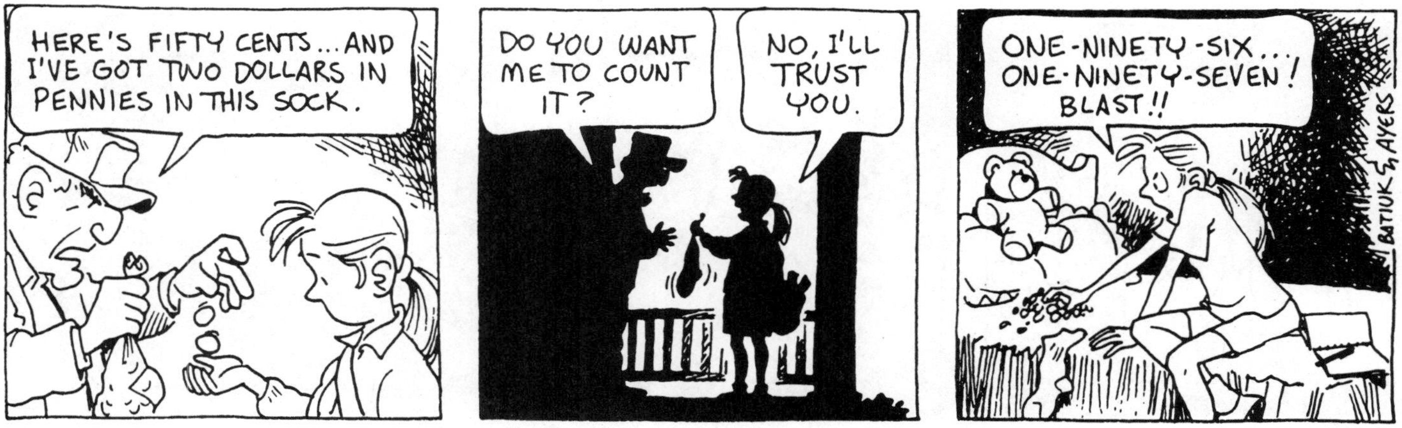
HERE'S FIFTY CENTS... AND I'VE GOT TWO DOLLARS IN PENNIES IN THIS SOCK.
DO YOU WANT ME TO COUNT IT?
NO, I'LL TRUST YOU.
ONE-NINETY-SIX... ONE-NINETY-SEVEN! BLAST!!
BATIUK & AYERS

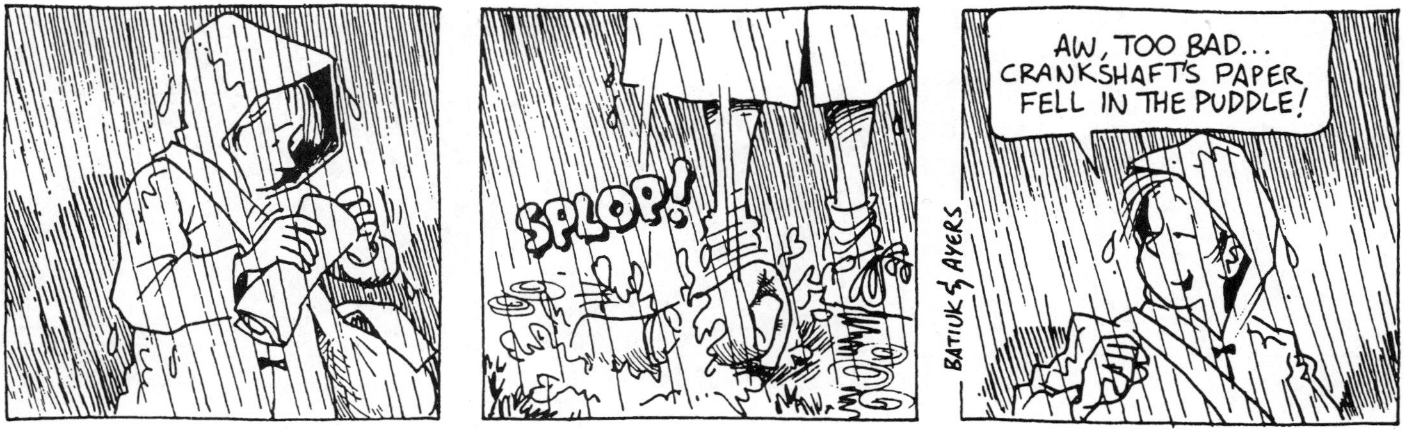
SPLOP!
BATIUK & AYERS
AW, TOO BAD... CRANKSHAFT'S PAPER FELL IN THE PUDDLE!

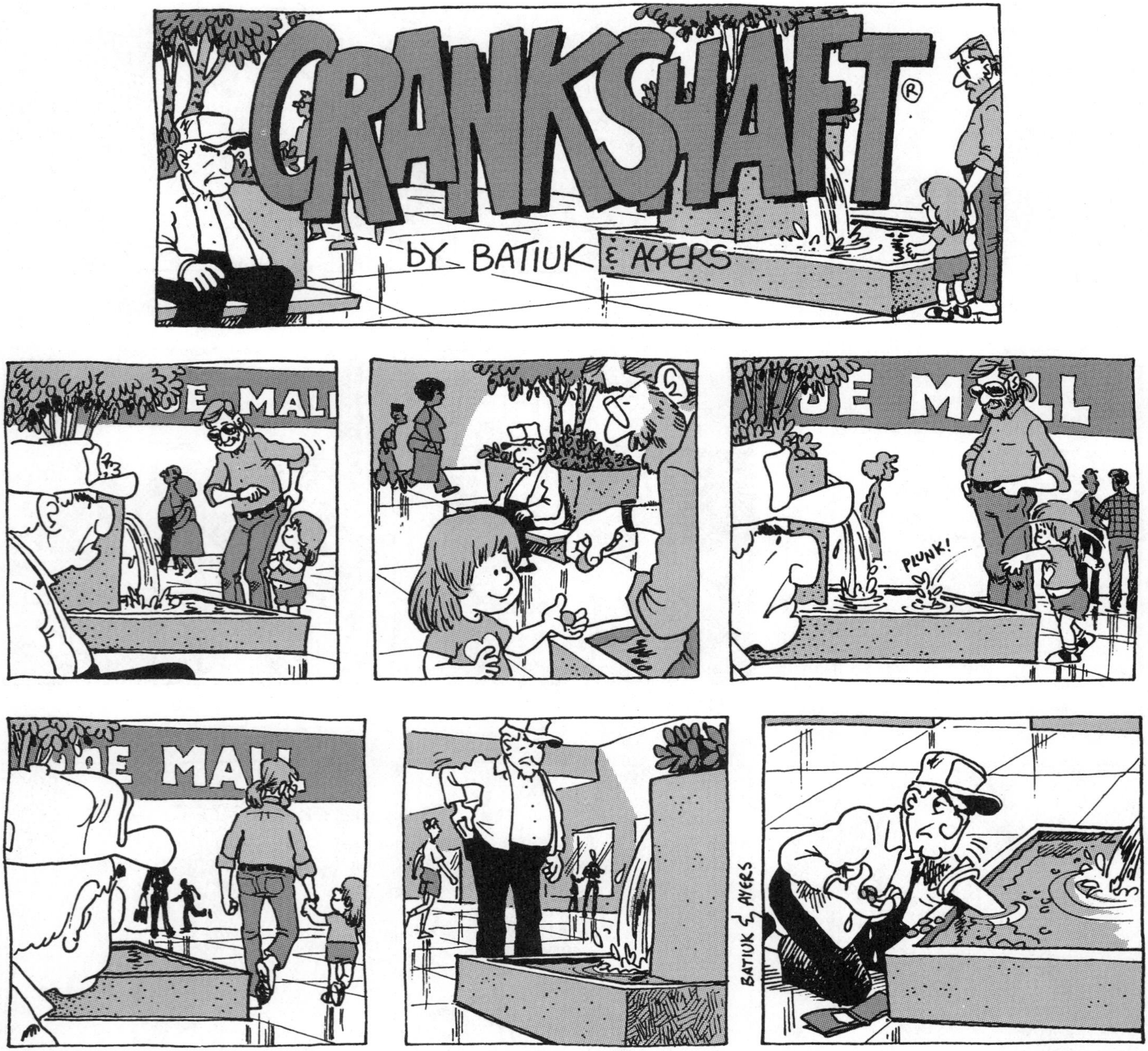
CRANKSHAFT
BY BATIUK & AYERS
MALL
PLUNK!
MALL
BATIUK & AYERS

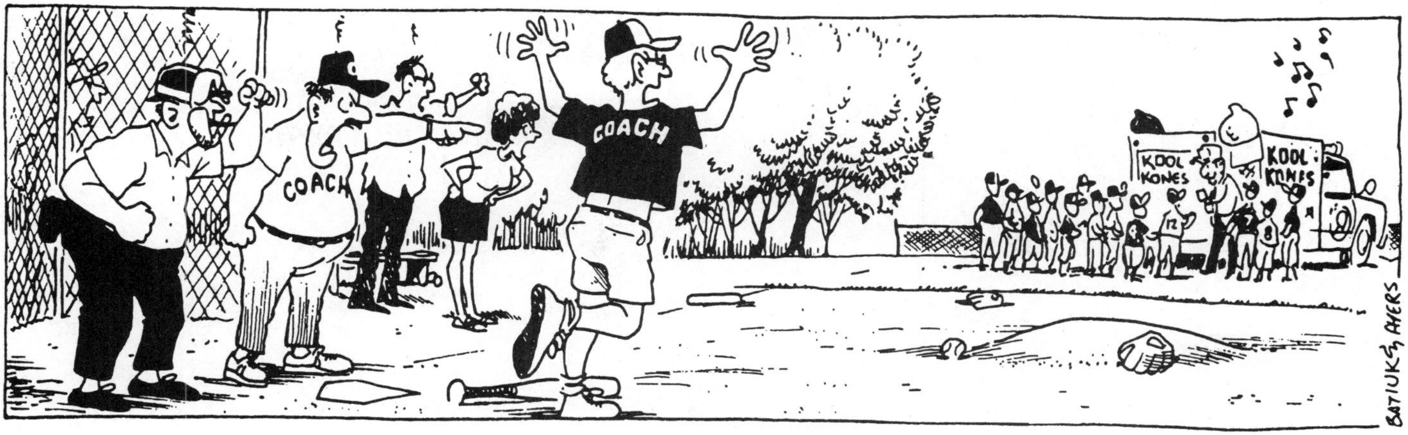
COACH
COACH
COACH
KOOL KONES
KOOL KONES
BATIUK & AYERS

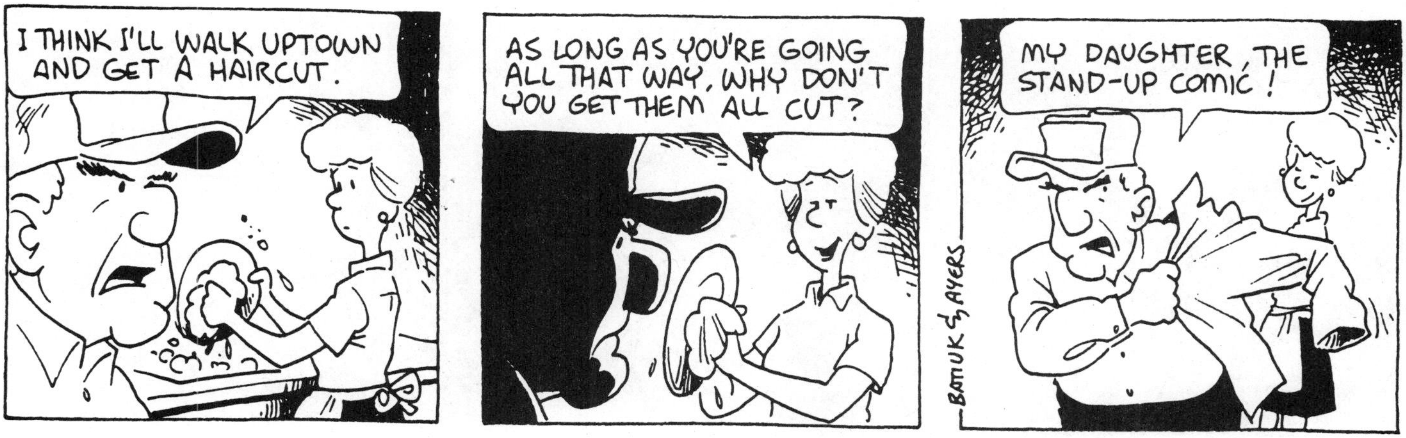
I THINK I'LL WALK UPTOWN AND GET A HAIRCUT.
AS LONG AS YOU'RE GOING ALL THAT WAY, WHY DON'T YOU GET THEM ALL CUT?
MY DAUGHTER, THE STAND-UP COMIC!
BATIUK & AYERS

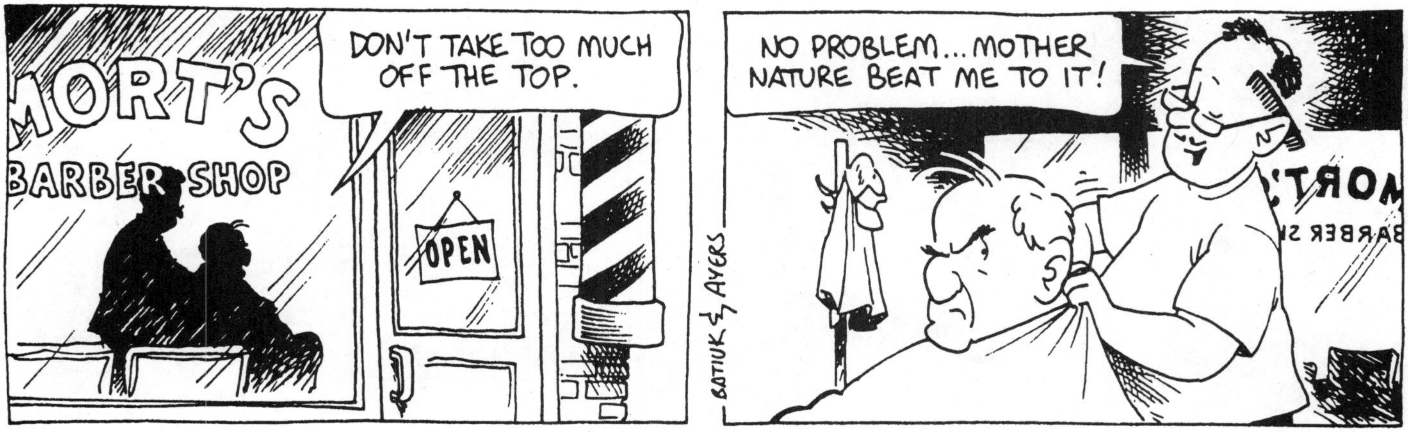
MORT'S
BARBER SHOP
DON'T TAKE TOO MUCH OFF THE TOP.
OPEN
NO PROBLEM... MOTHER NATURE BEAT ME TO IT!
BATIUK & AYERS

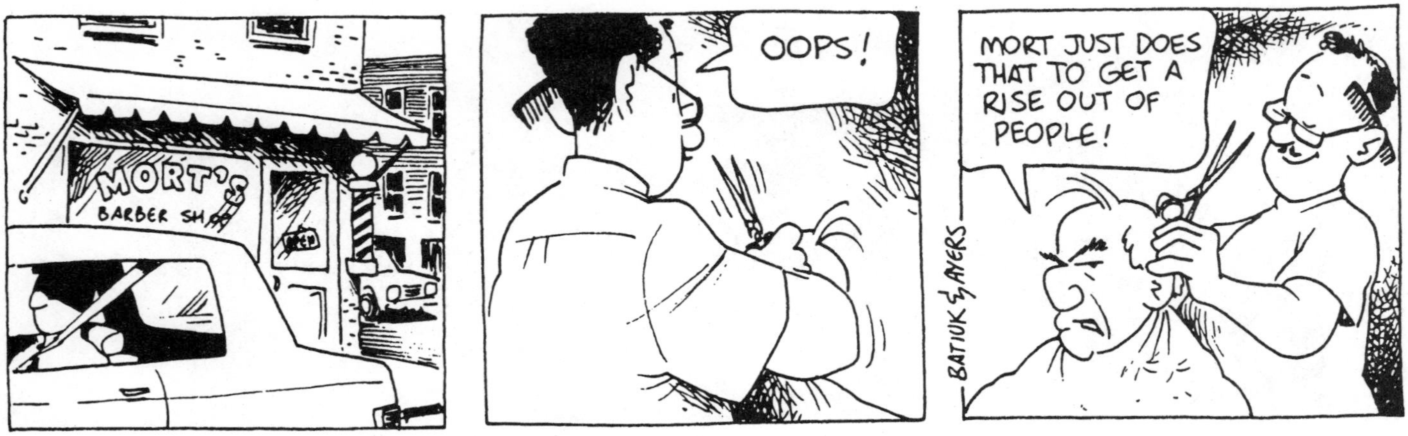
MORT'S
BARBER SH
OOPS!
MORT JUST DOES THAT TO GET A RISE OUT OF PEOPLE!
BATIUK & AYERS

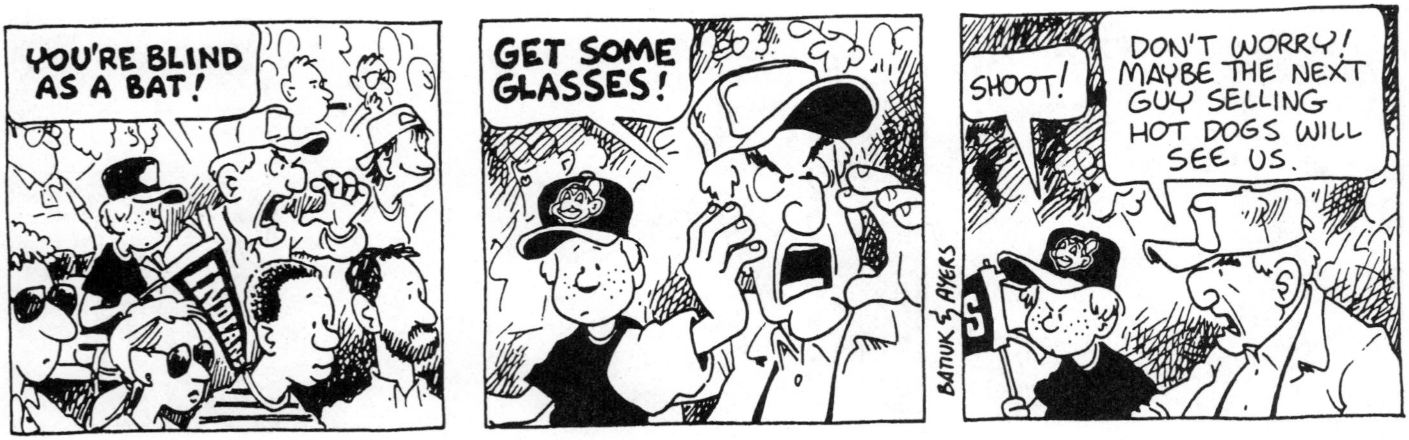
YOU'RE BLIND AS A BAT!
GET SOME GLASSES!
SHOOT!
DON'T WORRY! MAYBE THE NEXT GUY SELLING HOT DOGS WILL SEE US.
BATIUK & AYERS

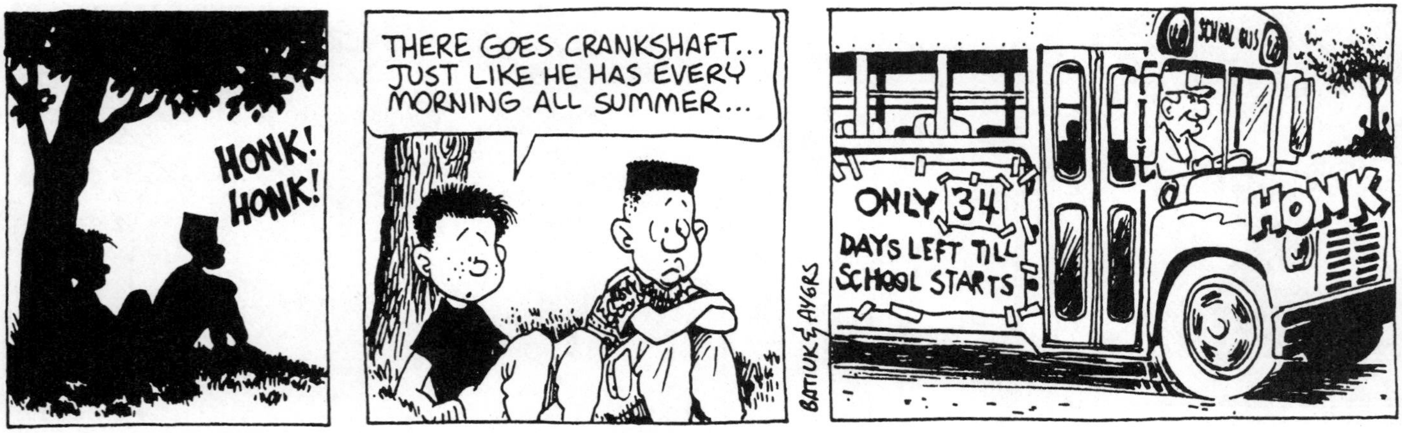
HONK! HONK!
THERE GOES CRANKSHAFT... JUST LIKE HE HAS EVERY MORNING ALL SUMMER...
BATIUK & AYERS
ONLY 34 DAYS LEFT TILL SCHOOL STARTS
HONK

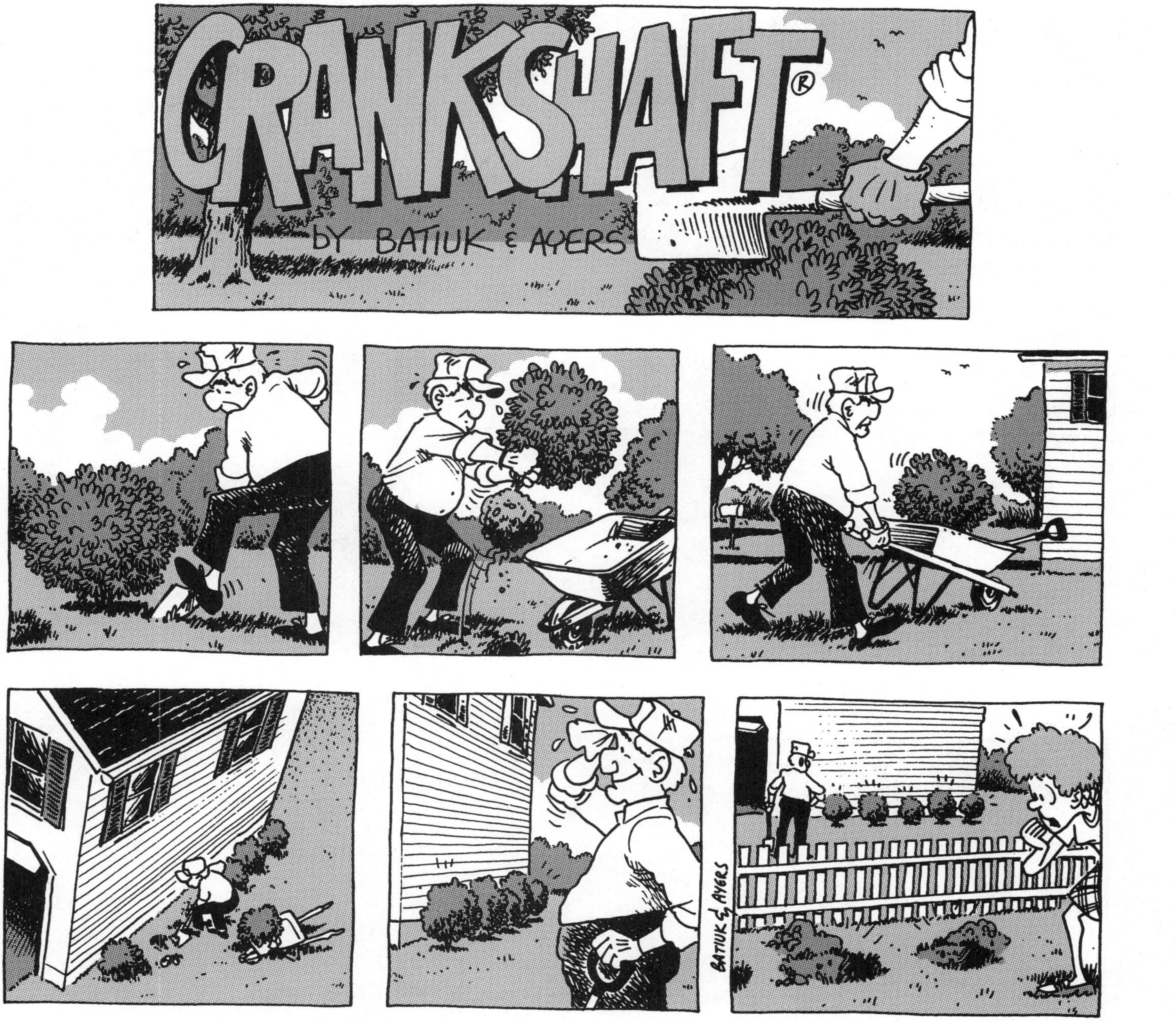
CRANKSHAFT®
BY BATIUK & AYERS
BATIUK & AYERS

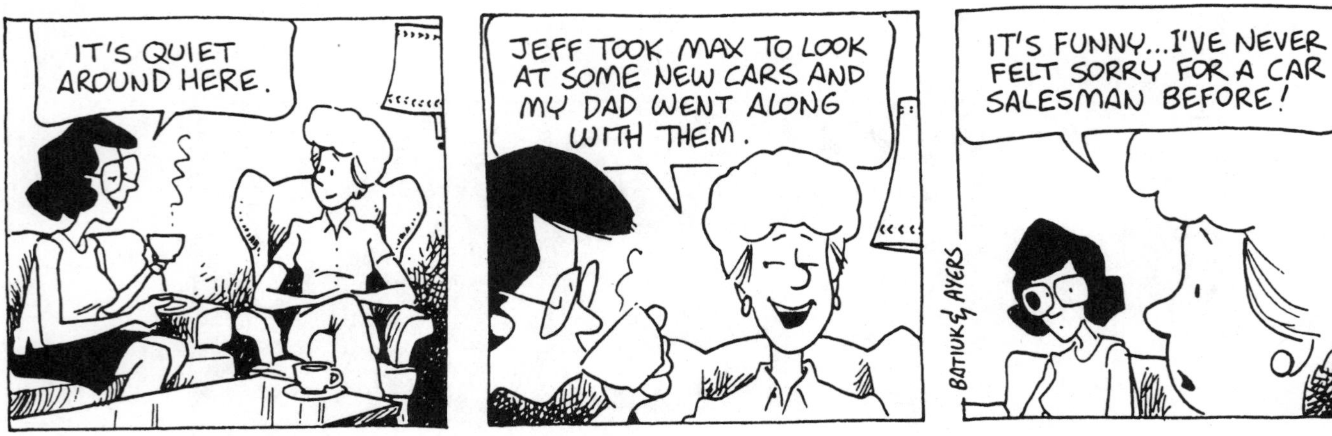
IT'S QUIET AROUND HERE.
JEFF TOOK MAX TO LOOK AT SOME NEW CARS AND MY DAD WENT ALONG WITH THEM.
IT'S FUNNY...I'VE NEVER FELT SORRY FOR A CAR SALESMAN BEFORE!
BATIUK & AYERS

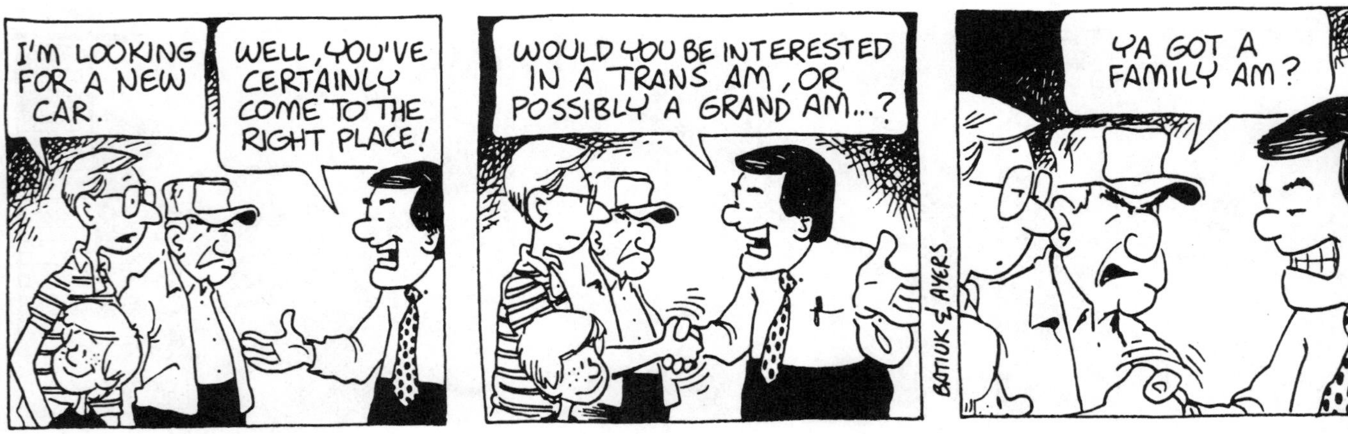
I'M LOOKING FOR A NEW CAR.
WELL, YOU'VE CERTAINLY COME TO THE RIGHT PLACE!
WOULD YOU BE INTERESTED IN A TRANS AM, OR POSSIBLY A GRAND AM...?
YA GOT A FAMILY AM?
BATIUK & AYERS

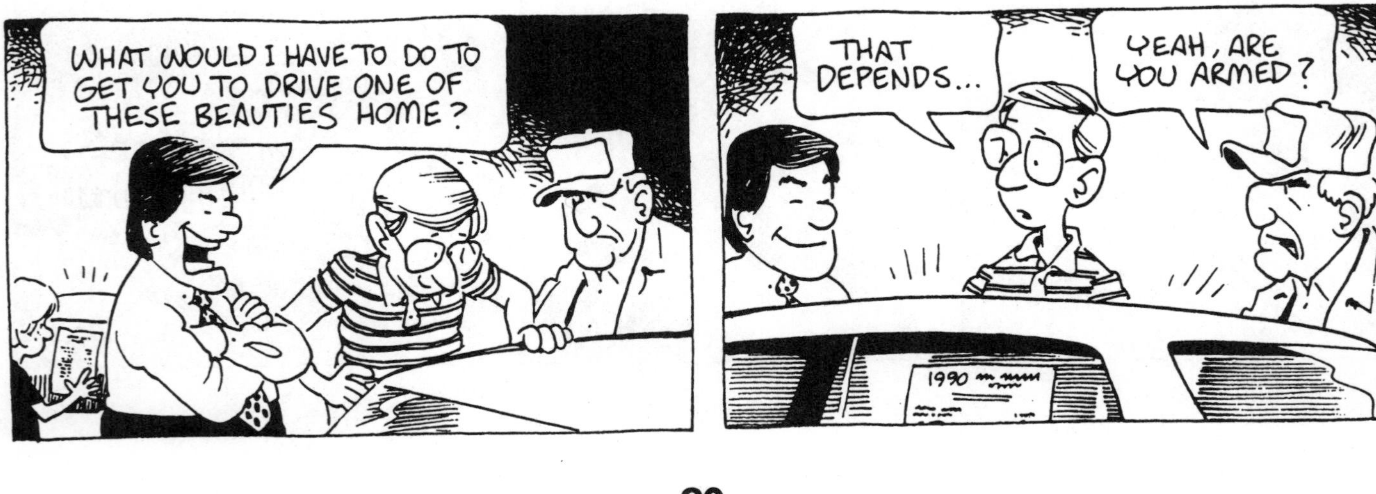
WHAT WOULD I HAVE TO DO TO GET YOU TO DRIVE ONE OF THESE BEAUTIES HOME?
THAT DEPENDS...
YEAH, ARE YOU ARMED?
1990
BATIUK & AYERS

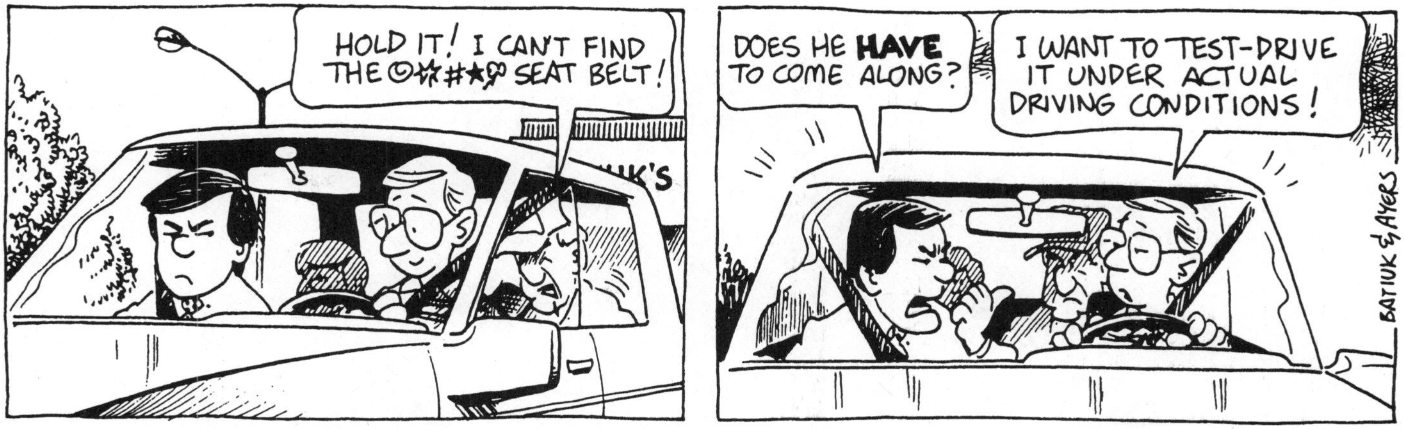
HOLD IT! I CAN'T FIND THE ☺✫#★♡ SEAT BELT!
DOES HE **HAVE** TO COME ALONG?
I WANT TO TEST-DRIVE IT UNDER ACTUAL DRIVING CONDITIONS!
BATIUK & AYERS

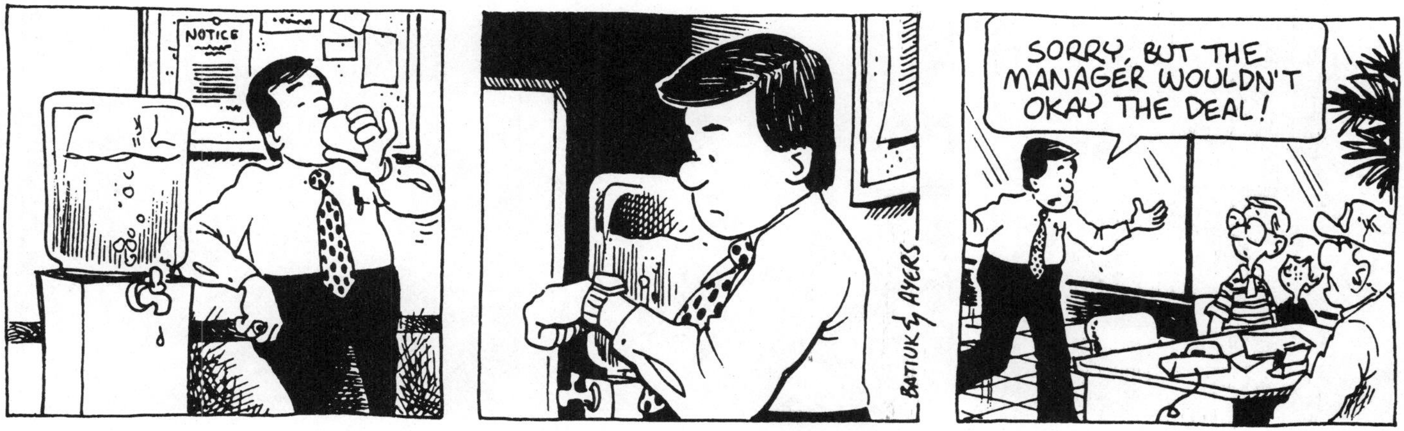
NOTICE
BATIUK & AYERS
SORRY, BUT THE MANAGER WOULDN'T OKAY THE DEAL!

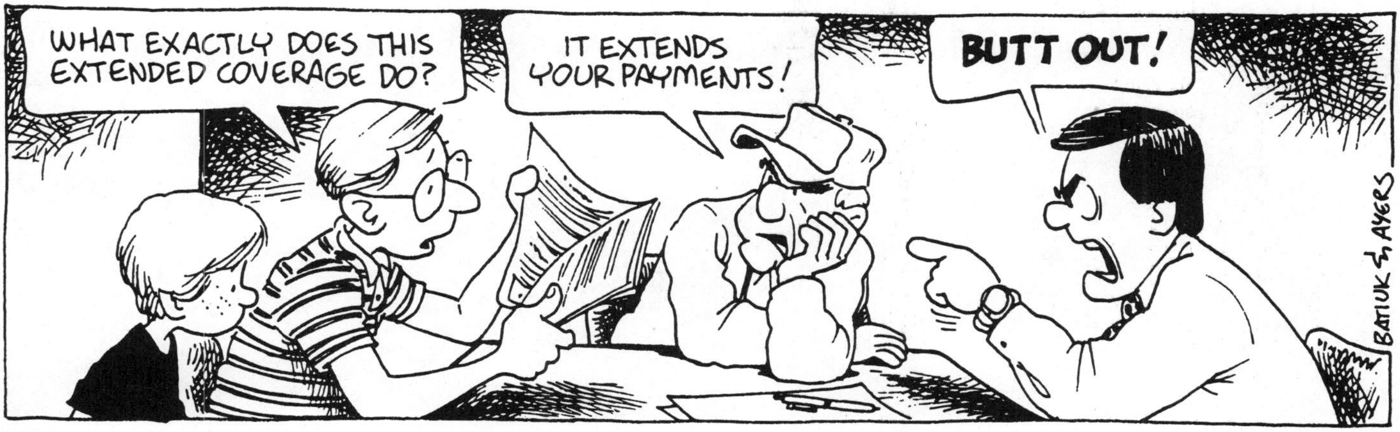
WHAT EXACTLY DOES THIS EXTENDED COVERAGE DO?
IT EXTENDS YOUR PAYMENTS!
BUTT OUT!
BATIUK & AYERS

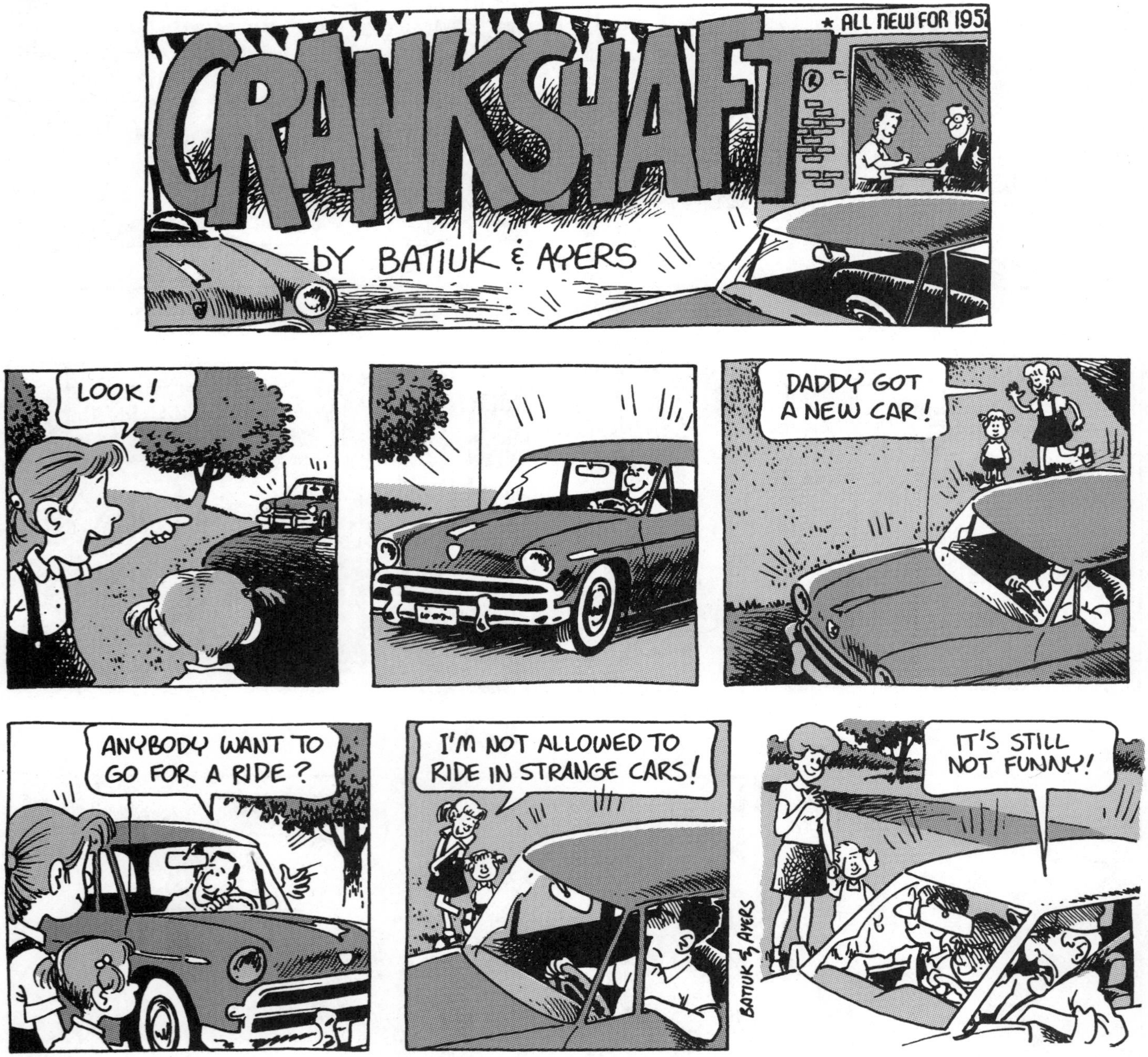

CRANKSHAFT®
★ ALL NEW FOR 195
BY BATIUK & AYERS
LOOK!
DADDY GOT A NEW CAR!
ANYBODY WANT TO GO FOR A RIDE?
I'M NOT ALLOWED TO RIDE IN STRANGE CARS!
BATIUK & AYERS
IT'S STILL NOT FUNNY!

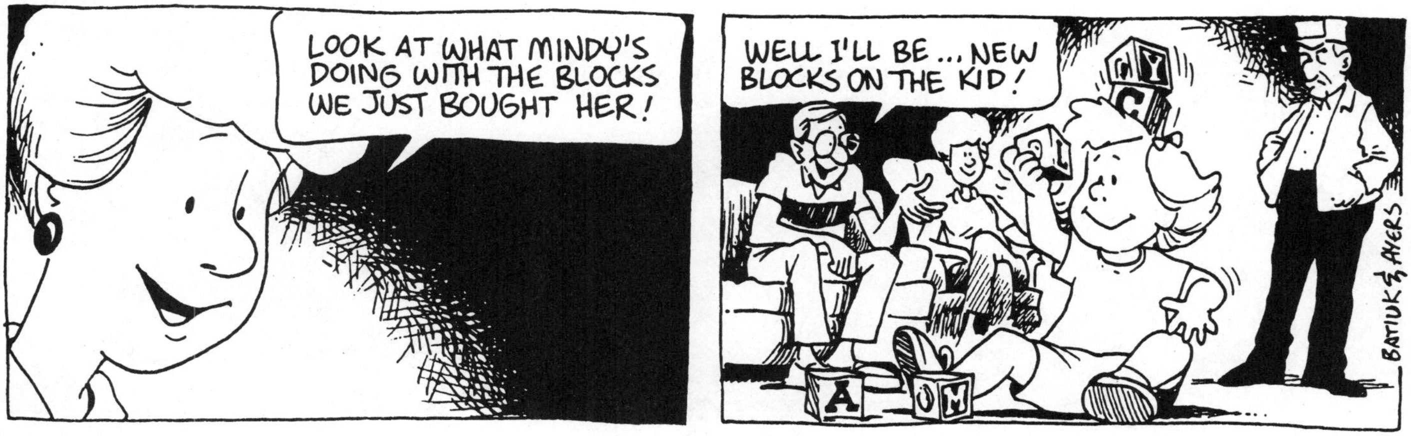
LOOK AT WHAT MINDY'S DOING WITH THE BLOCKS WE JUST BOUGHT HER!
WELL I'LL BE ... NEW BLOCKS ON THE KID!
BATIUK & AYERS

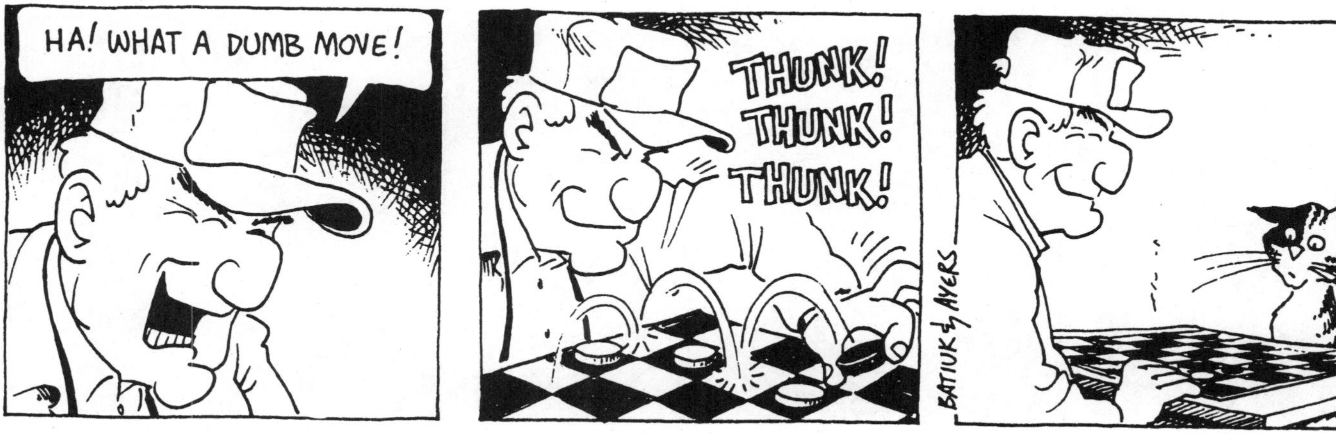
HA! WHAT A DUMB MOVE!
THUNK! THUNK! THUNK!
BATIUK & AYERS

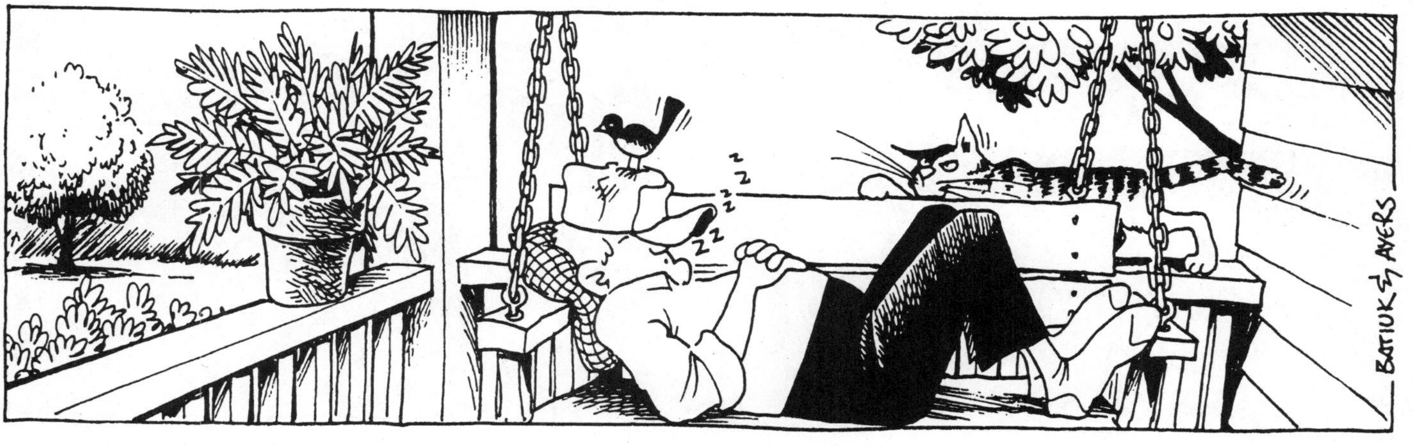
BATIUK & AYERS

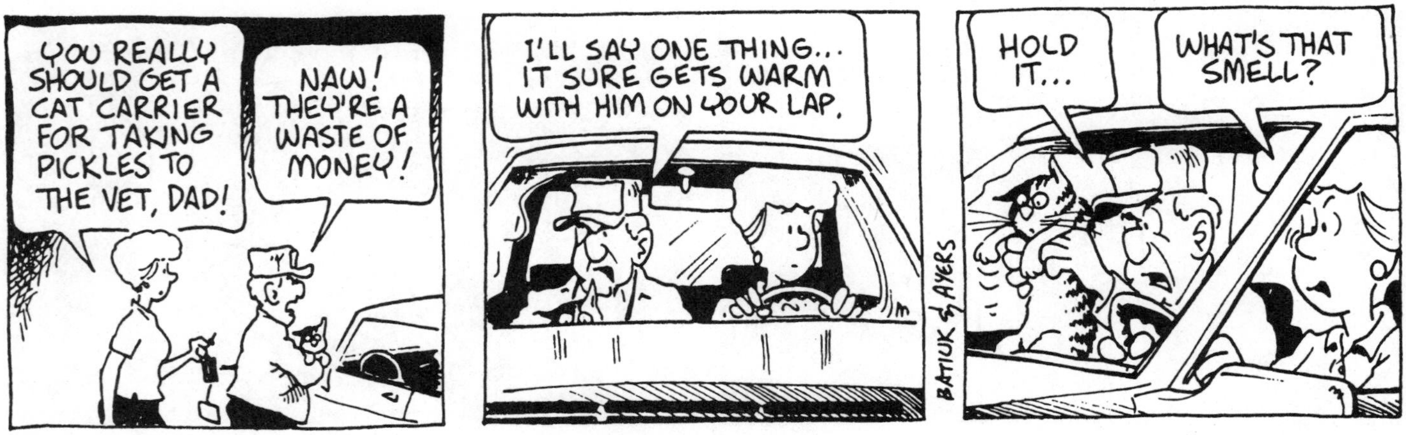
YOU REALLY SHOULD GET A CAT CARRIER FOR TAKING PICKLES TO THE VET, DAD!
NAW! THEY'RE A WASTE OF MONEY!
I'LL SAY ONE THING... IT SURE GETS WARM WITH HIM ON YOUR LAP.
HOLD IT...
WHAT'S THAT SMELL?
BATIUK & AYERS

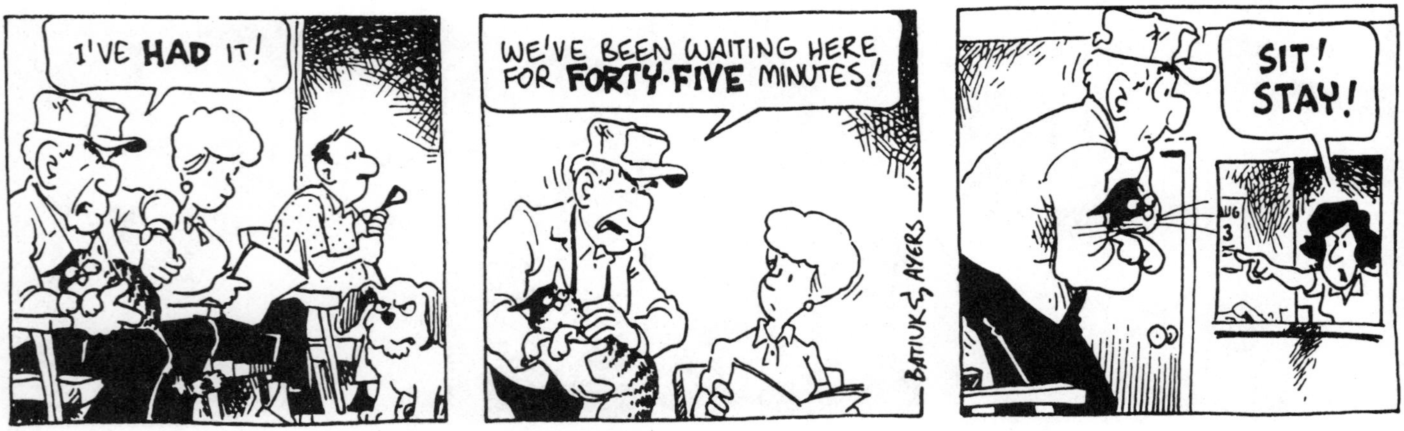
I'VE **HAD** IT!
WE'VE BEEN WAITING HERE FOR **FORTY-FIVE** MINUTES!
BATIUK & AYERS
SIT! STAY!

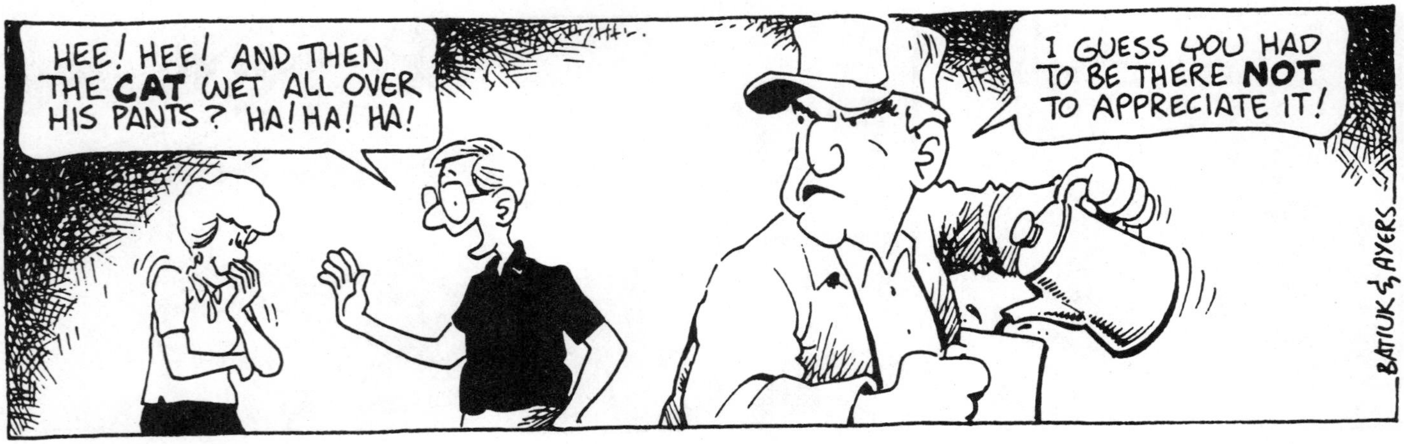
HEE! HEE! AND THEN THE **CAT** WET ALL OVER HIS PANTS? HA! HA! HA!
I GUESS YOU HAD TO BE THERE **NOT** TO APPRECIATE IT!
BATIUK & AYERS

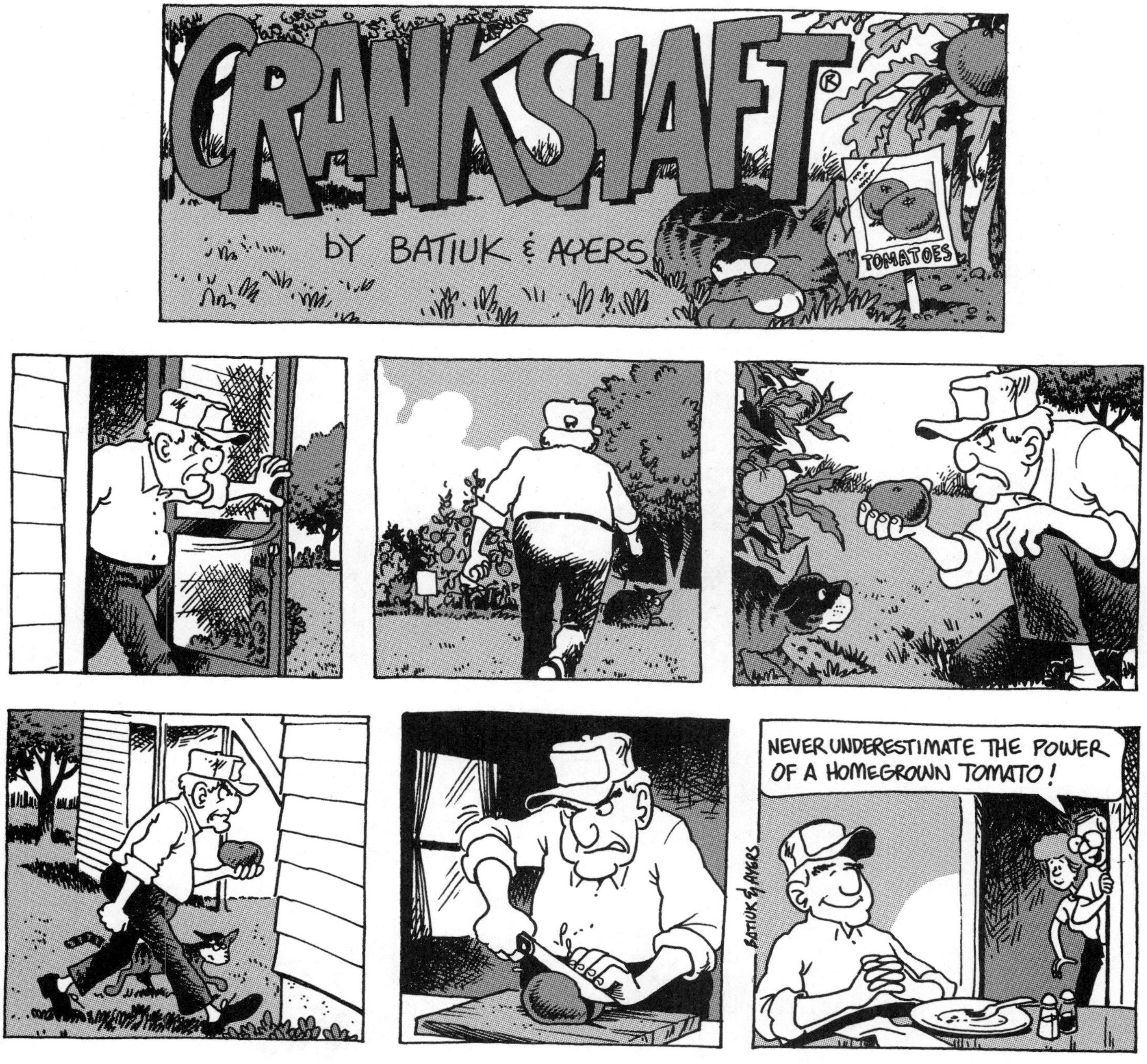
CRANKSHAFT®
BY BATIUK & AYERS
TOMATOES
BATIUK & AYERS
NEVER UNDERESTIMATE THE POWER OF A HOMEGROWN TOMATO!

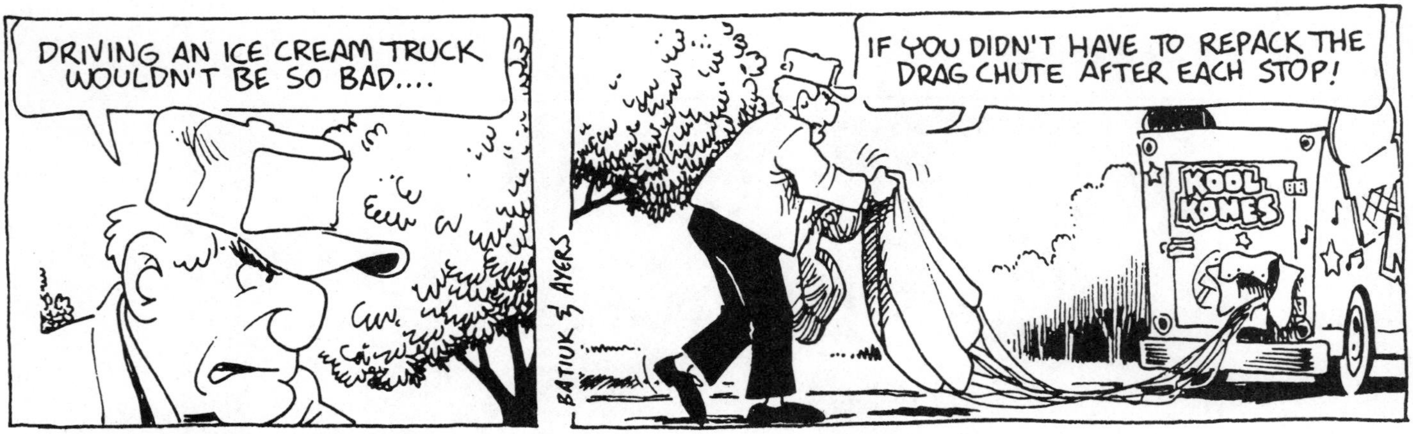
DRIVING AN ICE CREAM TRUCK WOULDN'T BE SO BAD....
IF YOU DIDN'T HAVE TO REPACK THE DRAG CHUTE AFTER EACH STOP!
KOOL KONES
BATIUK & AYERS

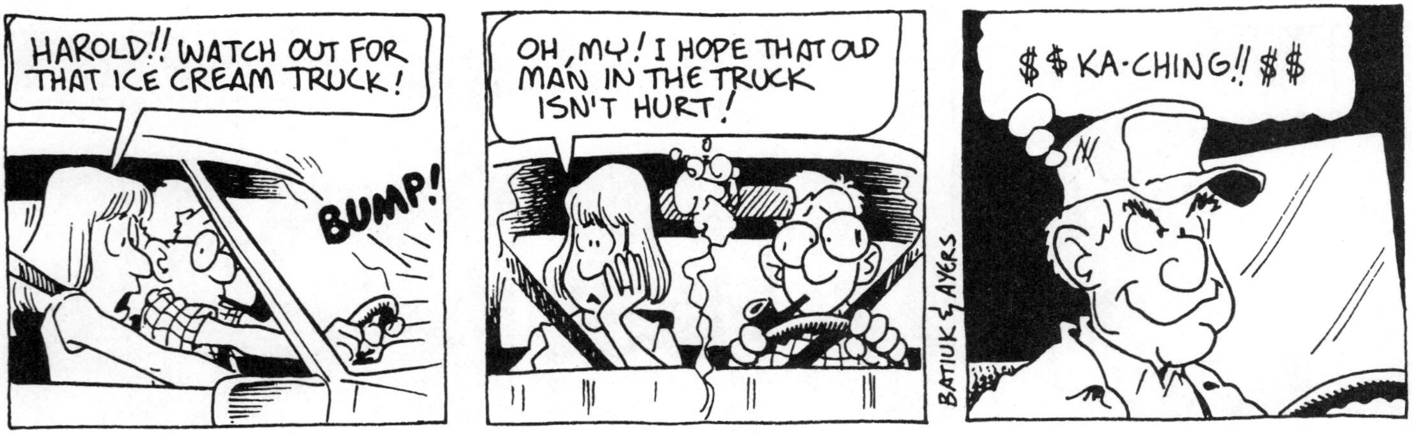
HAROLD!! WATCH OUT FOR THAT ICE CREAM TRUCK!
BUMP!
OH, MY! I HOPE THAT OLD MAN IN THE TRUCK ISN'T HURT!
$ $ KA-CHING!! $ $
BATIUK & AYERS

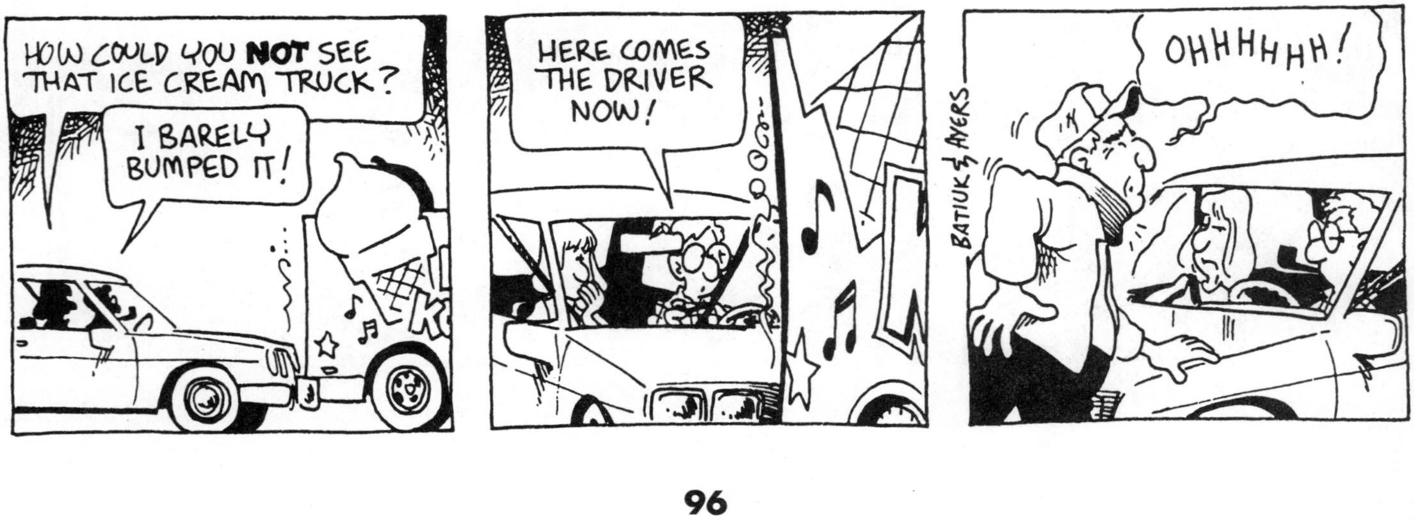
HOW COULD YOU **NOT** SEE THAT ICE CREAM TRUCK?
I BARELY BUMPED IT!
HERE COMES THE DRIVER NOW!
OHHHHHH!
BATIUK & AYERS

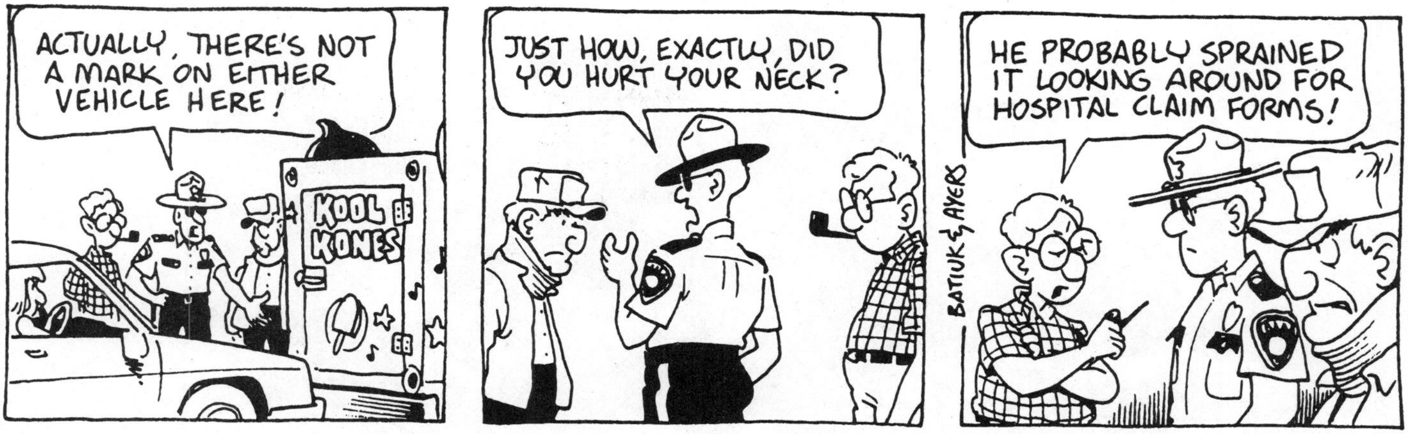
ACTUALLY, THERE'S NOT A MARK ON EITHER VEHICLE HERE!
KOOL KONES
JUST HOW, EXACTLY, DID YOU HURT YOUR NECK?
BATIUK & AYERS
HE PROBABLY SPRAINED IT LOOKING AROUND FOR HOSPITAL CLAIM FORMS!

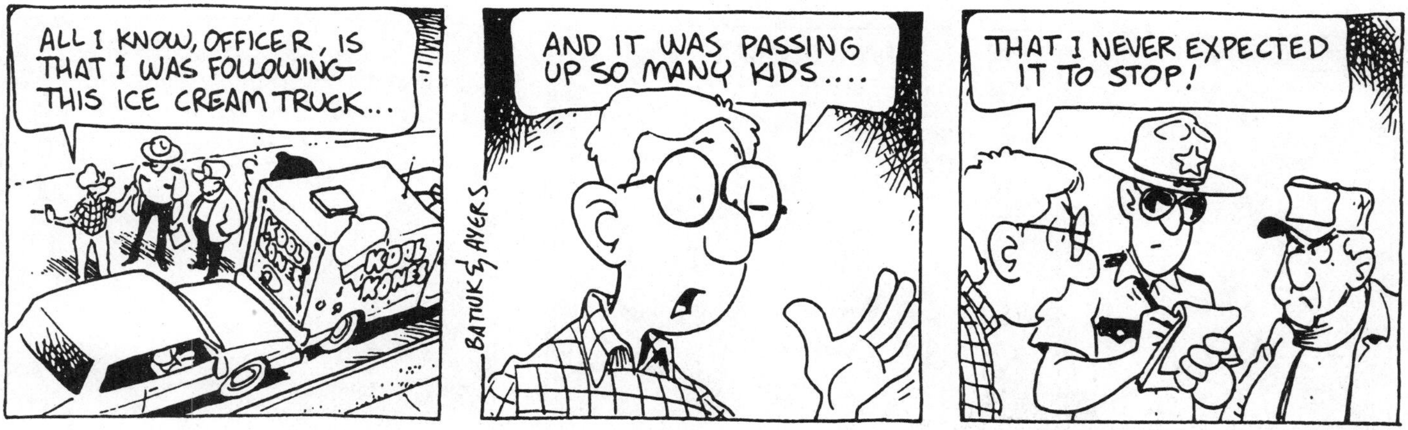
ALL I KNOW, OFFICER, IS THAT I WAS FOLLOWING THIS ICE CREAM TRUCK...
KOOL KONES
BATIUK & AYERS
AND IT WAS PASSING UP SO MANY KIDS....
THAT I NEVER EXPECTED IT TO STOP!

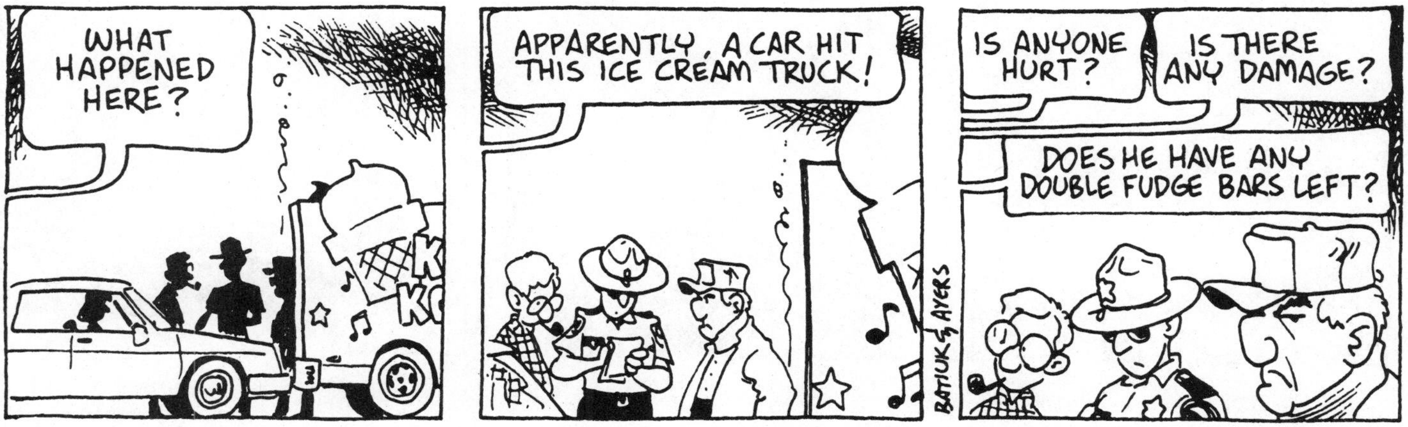
WHAT HAPPENED HERE?
APPARENTLY, A CAR HIT THIS ICE CREAM TRUCK!
BATIUK & AYERS
IS ANYONE HURT?
IS THERE ANY DAMAGE?
DOES HE HAVE ANY DOUBLE FUDGE BARS LEFT?

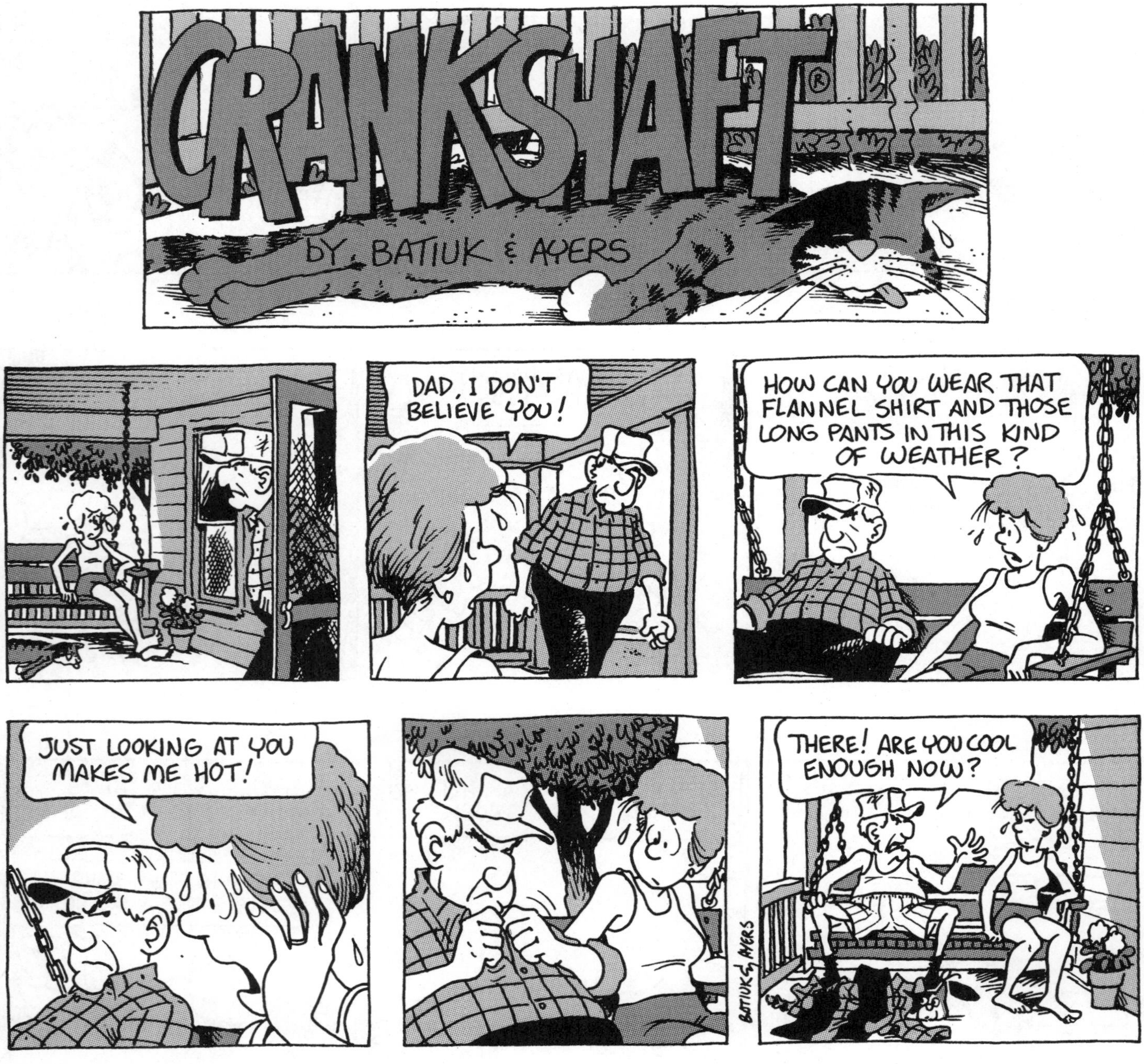
CRANKSHAFT®
BY BATIUK & AYERS
DAD, I DON'T BELIEVE YOU!
HOW CAN YOU WEAR THAT FLANNEL SHIRT AND THOSE LONG PANTS IN THIS KIND OF WEATHER?
JUST LOOKING AT YOU MAKES ME HOT!
BATIUK & AYERS
THERE! ARE YOU COOL ENOUGH NOW?

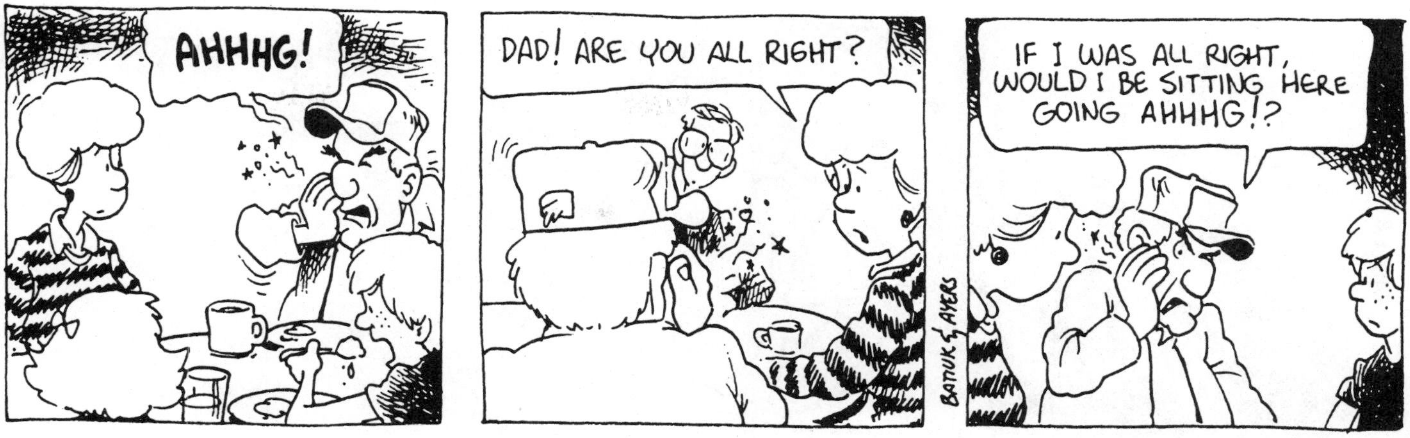
AHHHG!
DAD! ARE YOU ALL RIGHT?
IF I WAS ALL RIGHT, WOULD I BE SITTING HERE GOING AHHHG!?
BATIUK & AYERS

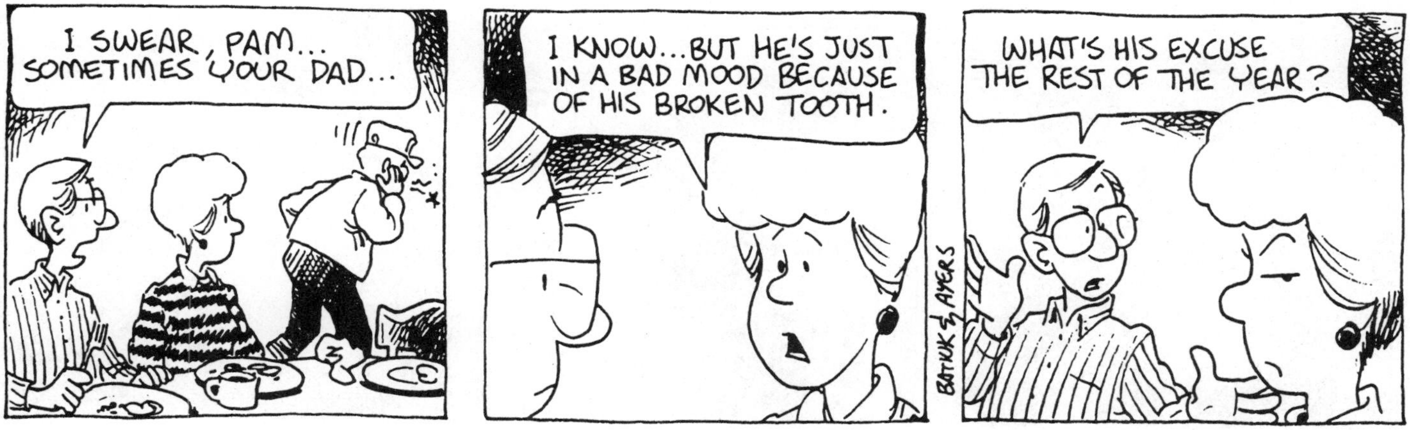
I SWEAR, PAM... SOMETIMES YOUR DAD...
I KNOW...BUT HE'S JUST IN A BAD MOOD BECAUSE OF HIS BROKEN TOOTH.
WHAT'S HIS EXCUSE THE REST OF THE YEAR?
BATIUK & AYERS

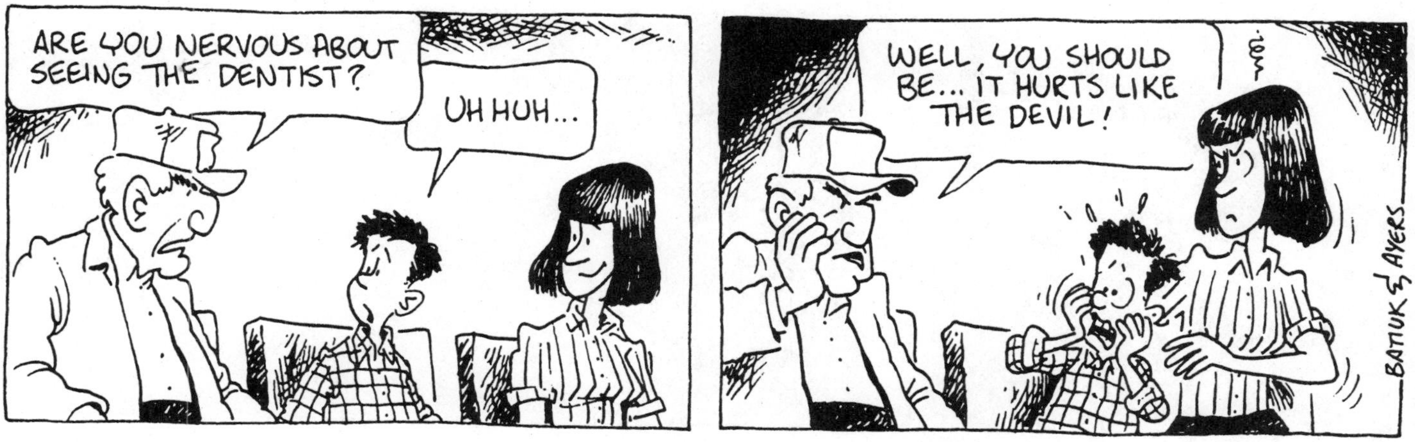
ARE YOU NERVOUS ABOUT SEEING THE DENTIST?
UH HUH...
WELL, YOU SHOULD BE... IT HURTS LIKE THE DEVIL!
BATIUK & AYERS

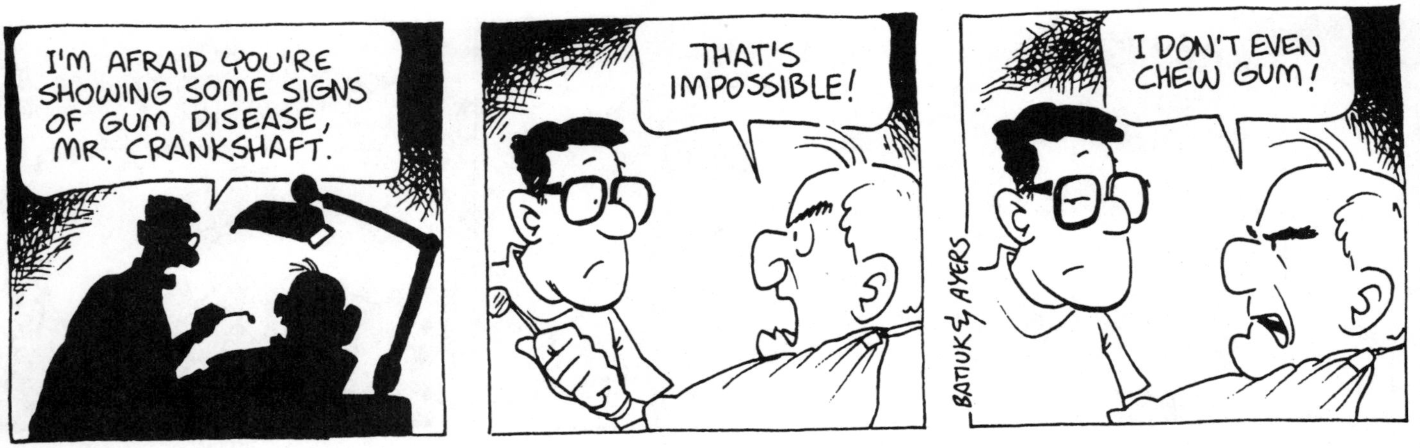
I'M AFRAID YOU'RE SHOWING SOME SIGNS OF GUM DISEASE, MR. CRANKSHAFT.
THAT'S IMPOSSIBLE!
I DON'T EVEN CHEW GUM!
BATIUK & AYERS

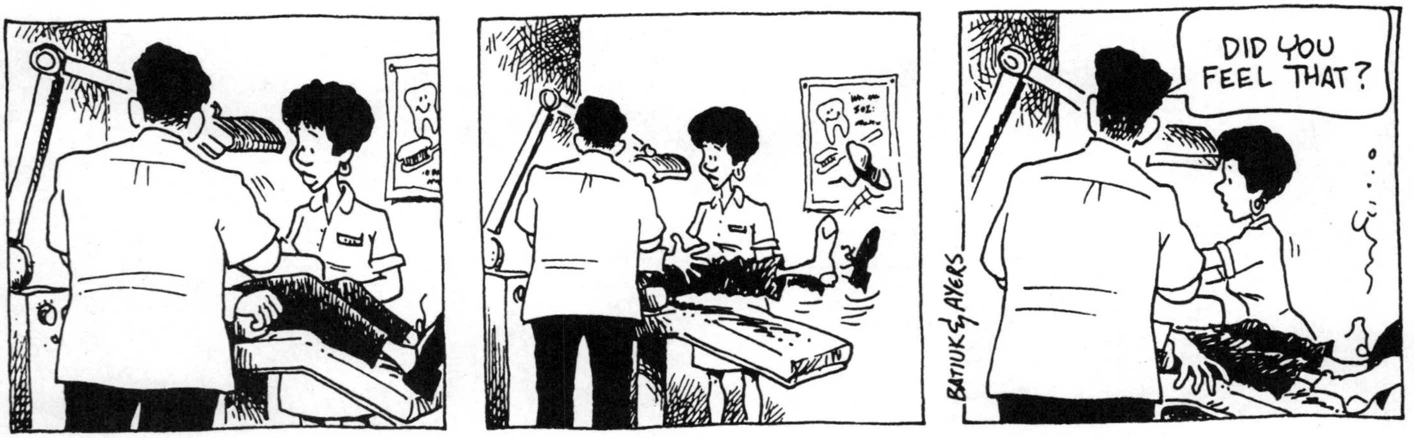
DID YOU FEEL THAT?
BATIUK & AYERS

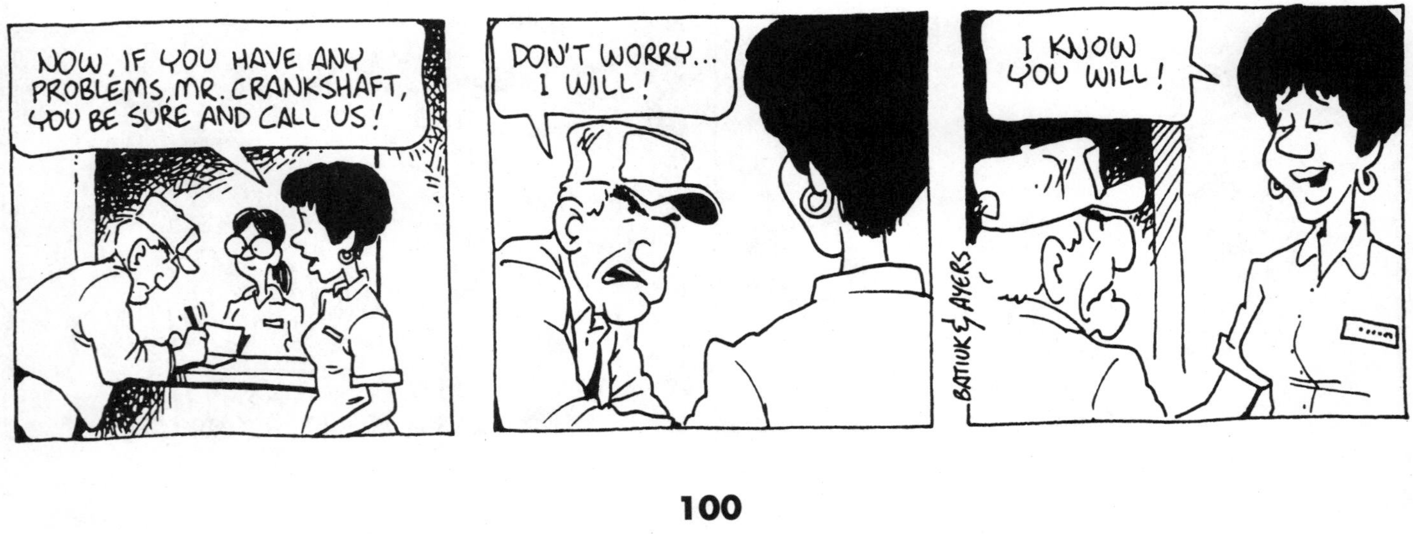
NOW, IF YOU HAVE ANY PROBLEMS, MR. CRANKSHAFT, YOU BE SURE AND CALL US!
DON'T WORRY... I WILL!
I KNOW YOU WILL!
BATIUK & AYERS

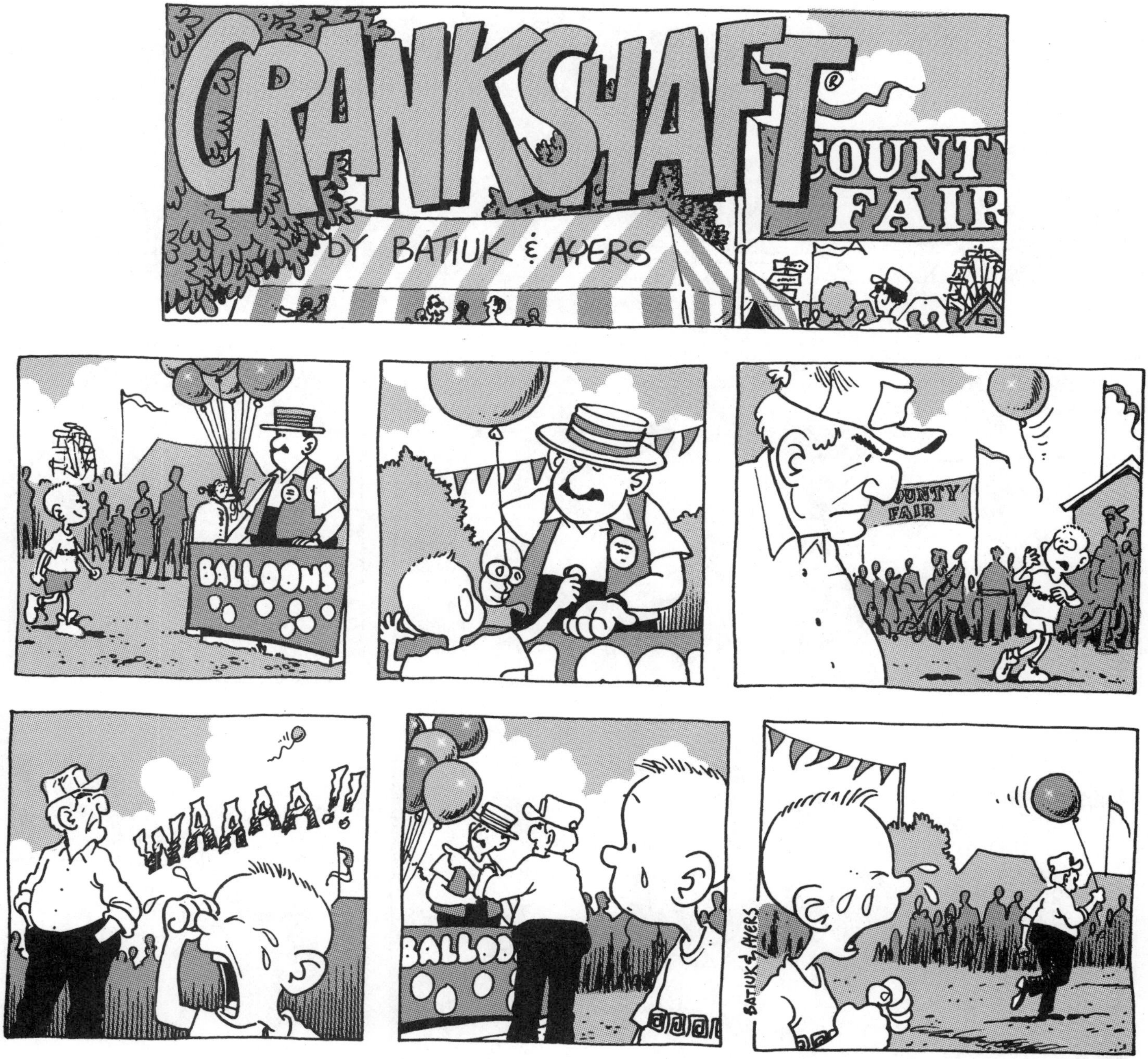
CRANKSHAFT®
BY BATIUK & AYERS
COUNTY FAIR
BALLOONS
COUNTY FAIR
WAAAAA!!
BATIUK & AYERS

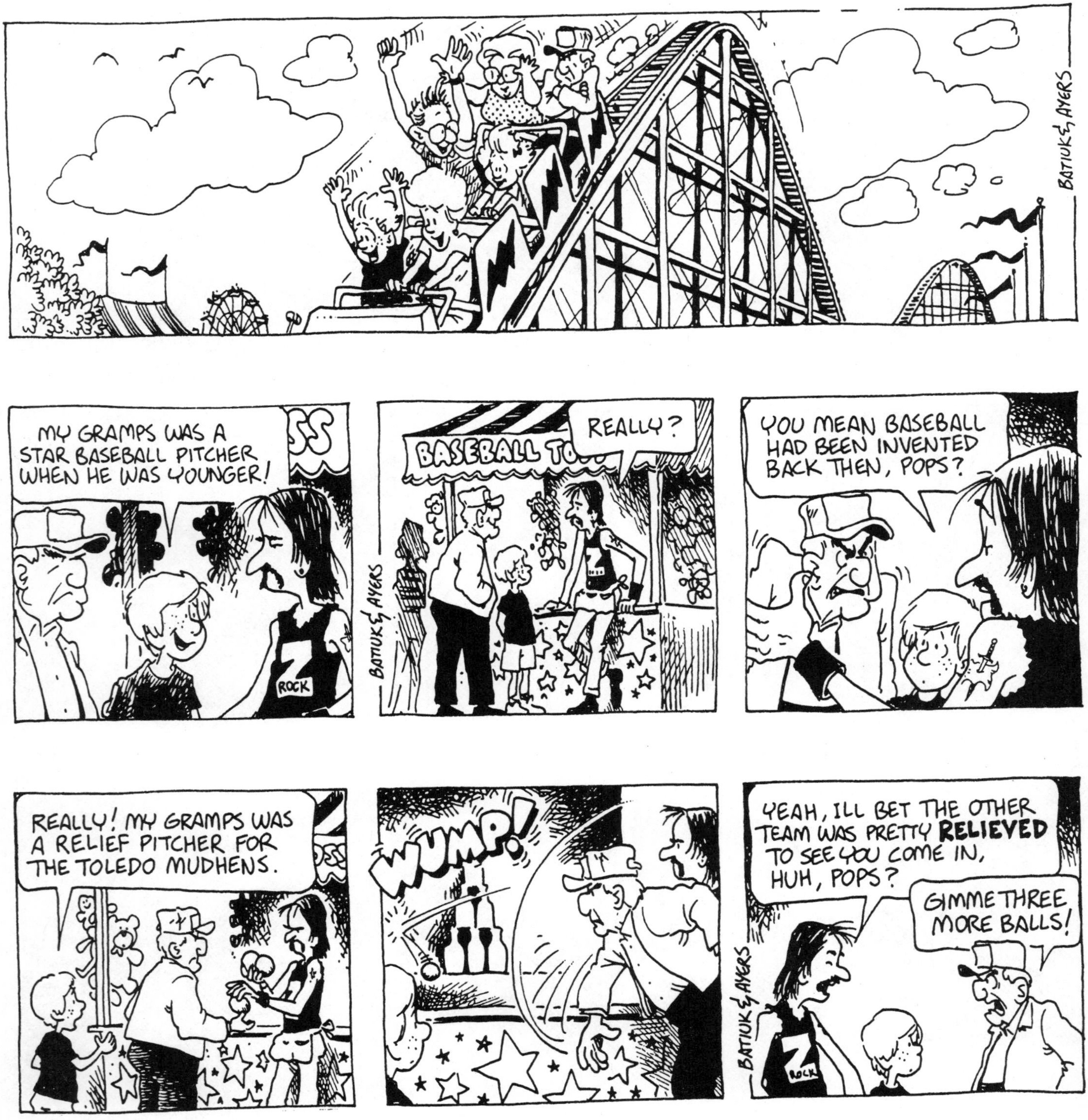
BATIUK & AYERS
MY GRAMPS WAS A STAR BASEBALL PITCHER WHEN HE WAS YOUNGER!
ROCK
BASEBALL TO
REALLY?
BATIUK & AYERS
YOU MEAN BASEBALL HAD BEEN INVENTED BACK THEN, POPS?
REALLY! MY GRAMPS WAS A RELIEF PITCHER FOR THE TOLEDO MUDHENS.
WUMP!
YEAH, ILL BET THE OTHER TEAM WAS PRETTY **RELIEVED** TO SEE YOU COME IN, HUH, POPS?
GIMME THREE MORE BALLS!
BATIUK & AYERS
ROCK

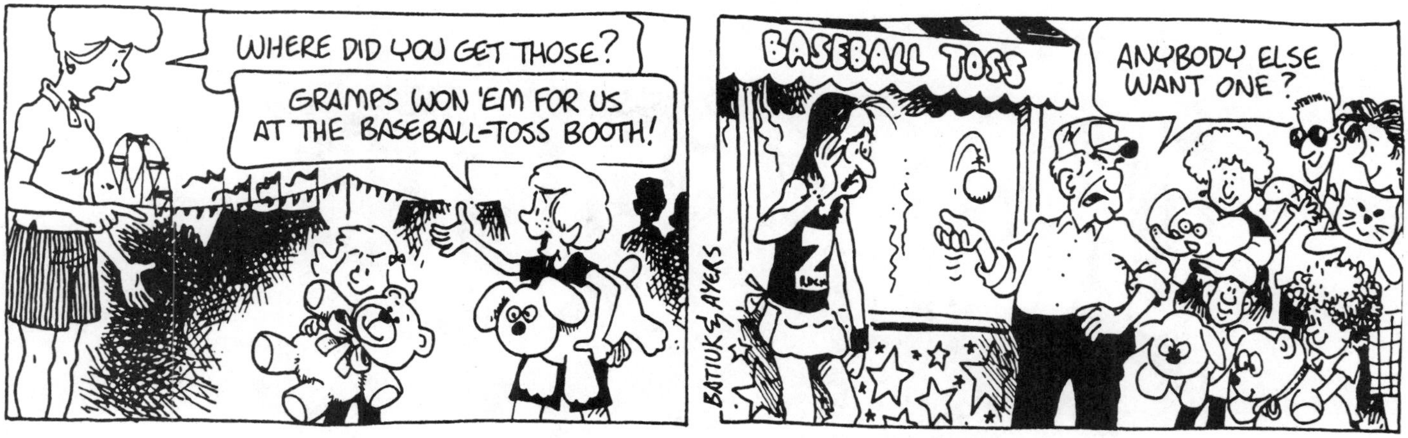
WHERE DID YOU GET THOSE?
GRAMPS WON 'EM FOR US AT THE BASEBALL-TOSS BOOTH!
BATIUK & AYERS
BASEBALL TOSS
ANYBODY ELSE WANT ONE?

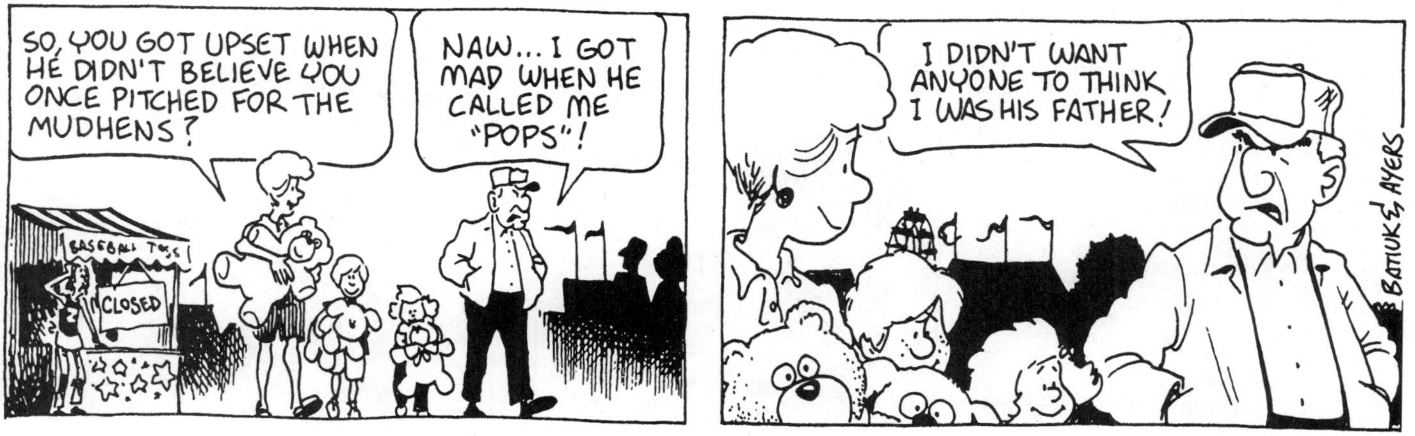
SO, YOU GOT UPSET WHEN HE DIDN'T BELIEVE YOU ONCE PITCHED FOR THE MUDHENS?
NAW... I GOT MAD WHEN HE CALLED ME "POPS"!
BASEBALL TOSS
CLOSED
I DIDN'T WANT ANYONE TO THINK I WAS HIS FATHER!
BATIUK & AYERS

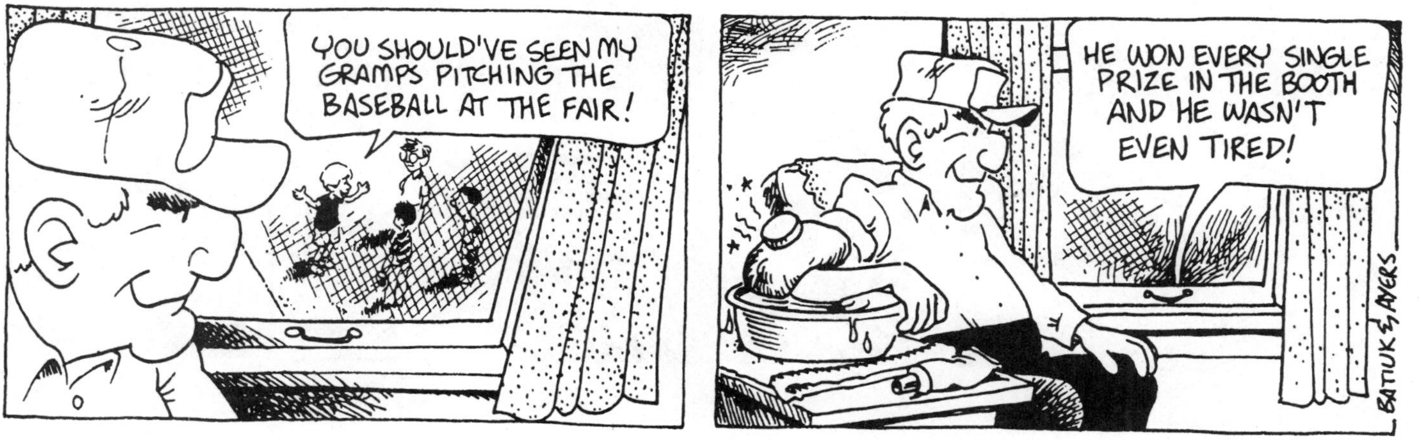
YOU SHOULD'VE SEEN MY GRAMPS PITCHING THE BASEBALL AT THE FAIR!
HE WON EVERY SINGLE PRIZE IN THE BOOTH AND HE WASN'T EVEN TIRED!
BATIUK & AYERS

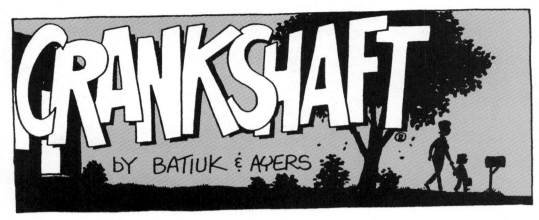

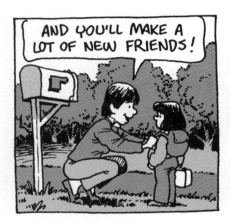

CRANKSHAFT
BY BATIUK & AYERS
AND YOU'LL MAKE A LOT OF NEW FRIENDS!
SCHOOL'S GOING TO BE A LOT OF FUN!
I CAN'T BELIEVE SHE'S ACTUALLY ABOUT TO LEAVE FOR HER FIRST DAY OF SCHOOL!
A WHOLE NEW AND EXCITING WORLD OF EXPERIENCES IS ABOUT TO UNFOLD FOR HER!
GET ON!
BATIUK & AYERS
MEANWHILE.... BACK IN REALITY...
13
SLAM!

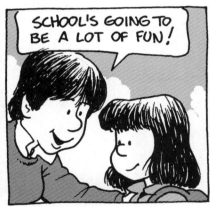

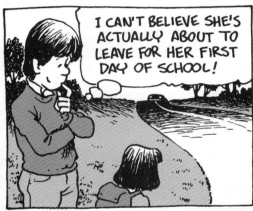

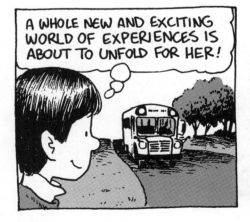

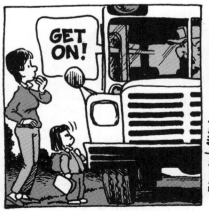

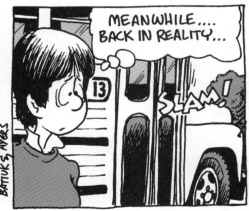

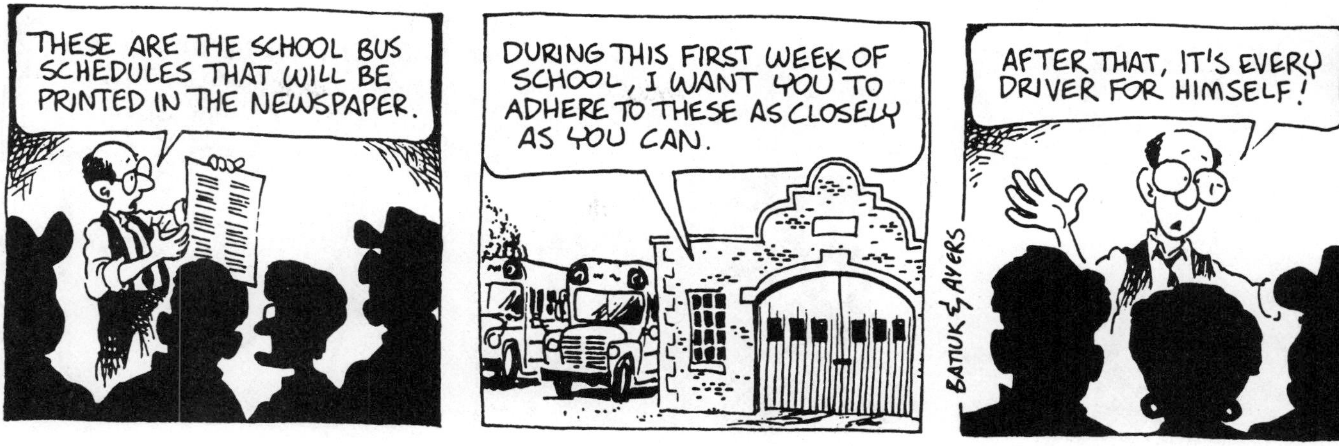
THESE ARE THE SCHOOL BUS SCHEDULES THAT WILL BE PRINTED IN THE NEWSPAPER.
DURING THIS FIRST WEEK OF SCHOOL, I WANT YOU TO ADHERE TO THESE AS CLOSELY AS YOU CAN.
AFTER THAT, IT'S EVERY DRIVER FOR HIMSELF!
BATIUK & AYERS

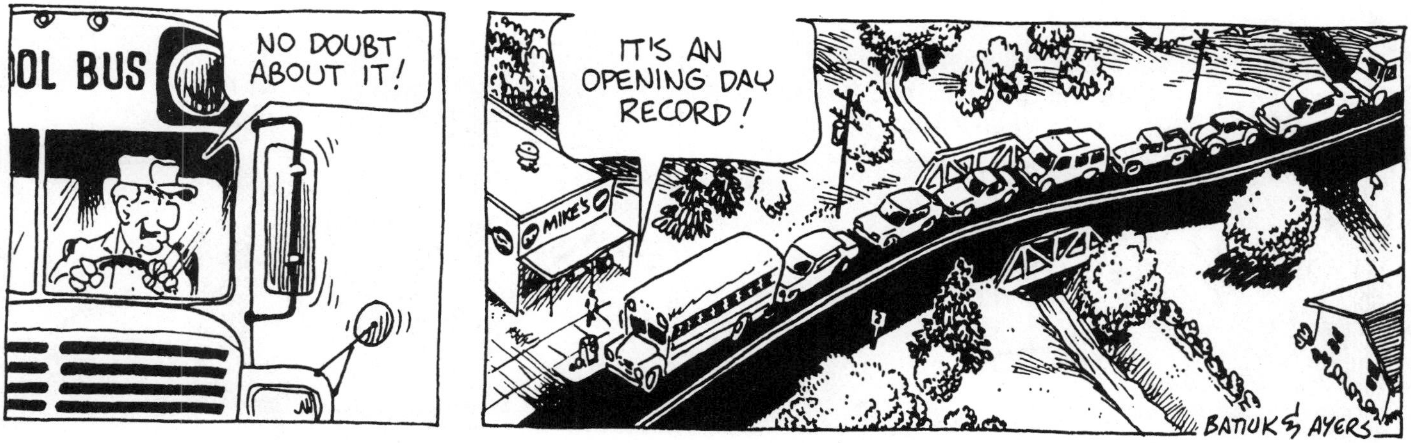
OOL BUS
NO DOUBT ABOUT IT!
IT'S AN OPENING DAY RECORD!
MIKE'S
BATIUK & AYERS

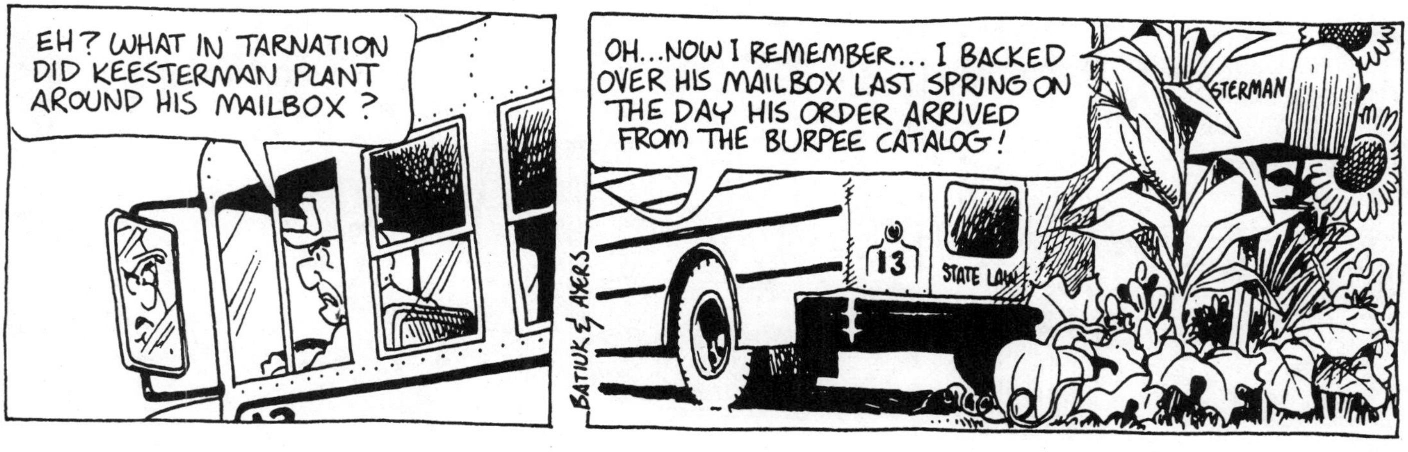
EH? WHAT IN TARNATION DID KEESTERMAN PLANT AROUND HIS MAILBOX?
OH...NOW I REMEMBER... I BACKED OVER HIS MAILBOX LAST SPRING ON THE DAY HIS ORDER ARRIVED FROM THE BURPEE CATALOG!
STERMAN
13
STATE LAW
BATIUK & AYERS

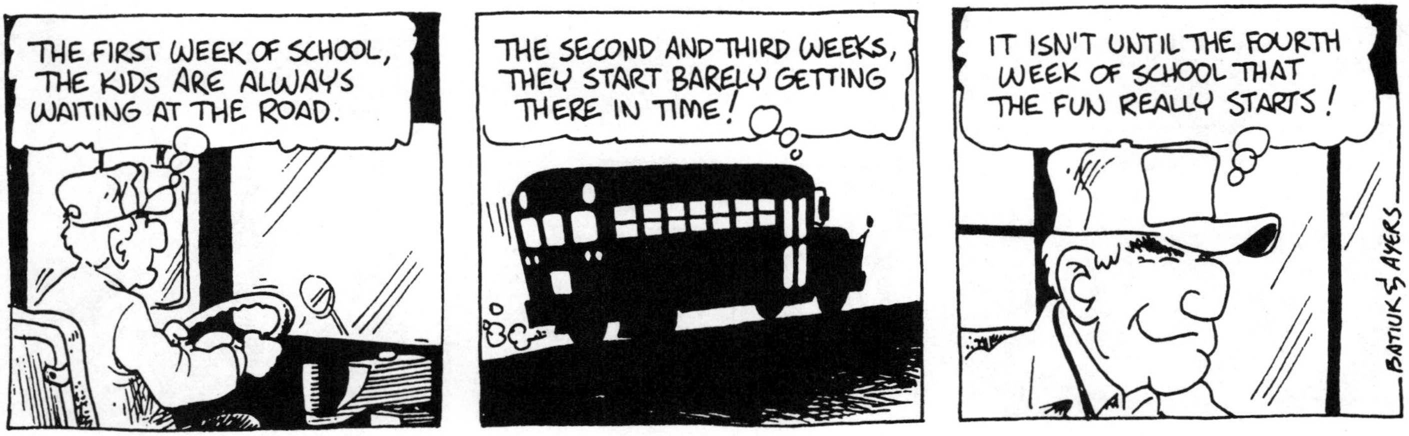
THE FIRST WEEK OF SCHOOL, THE KIDS ARE ALWAYS WAITING AT THE ROAD.
THE SECOND AND THIRD WEEKS, THEY START BARELY GETTING THERE IN TIME!
IT ISN'T UNTIL THE FOURTH WEEK OF SCHOOL THAT THE FUN REALLY STARTS!
BATIUK & AYERS

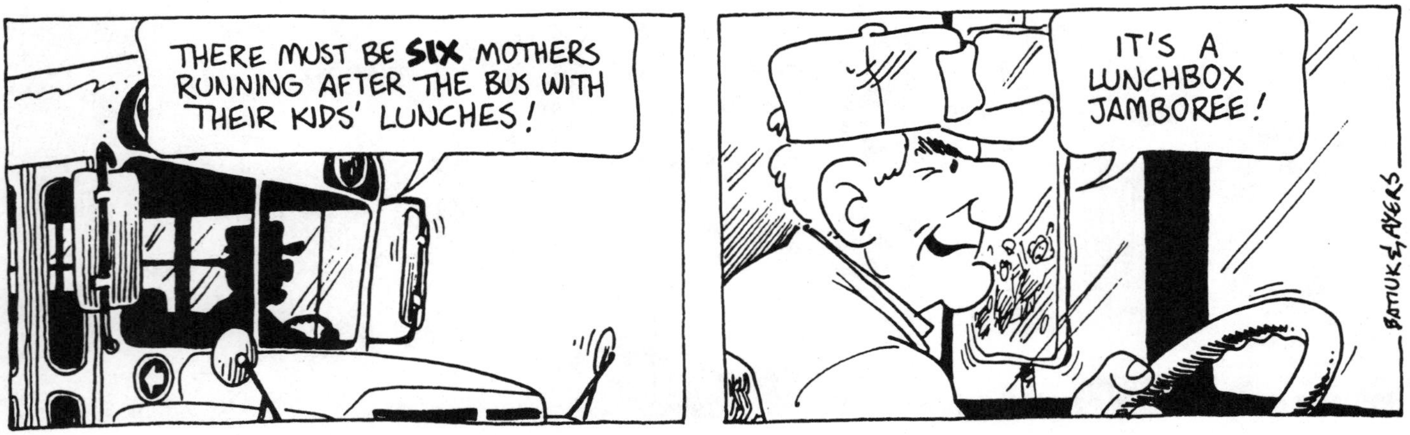
THERE MUST BE SIX MOTHERS RUNNING AFTER THE BUS WITH THEIR KIDS' LUNCHES!
IT'S A LUNCHBOX JAMBOREE!
BATIUK & AYERS

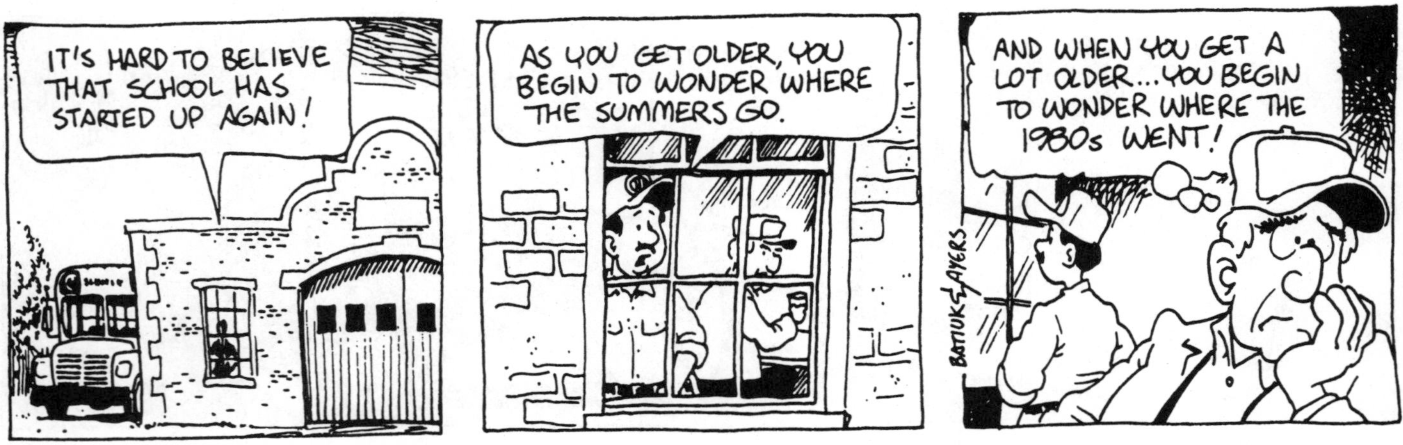
IT'S HARD TO BELIEVE THAT SCHOOL HAS STARTED UP AGAIN!
AS YOU GET OLDER, YOU BEGIN TO WONDER WHERE THE SUMMERS GO.
AND WHEN YOU GET A LOT OLDER... YOU BEGIN TO WONDER WHERE THE 1980s WENT!
BATIUK & AYERS

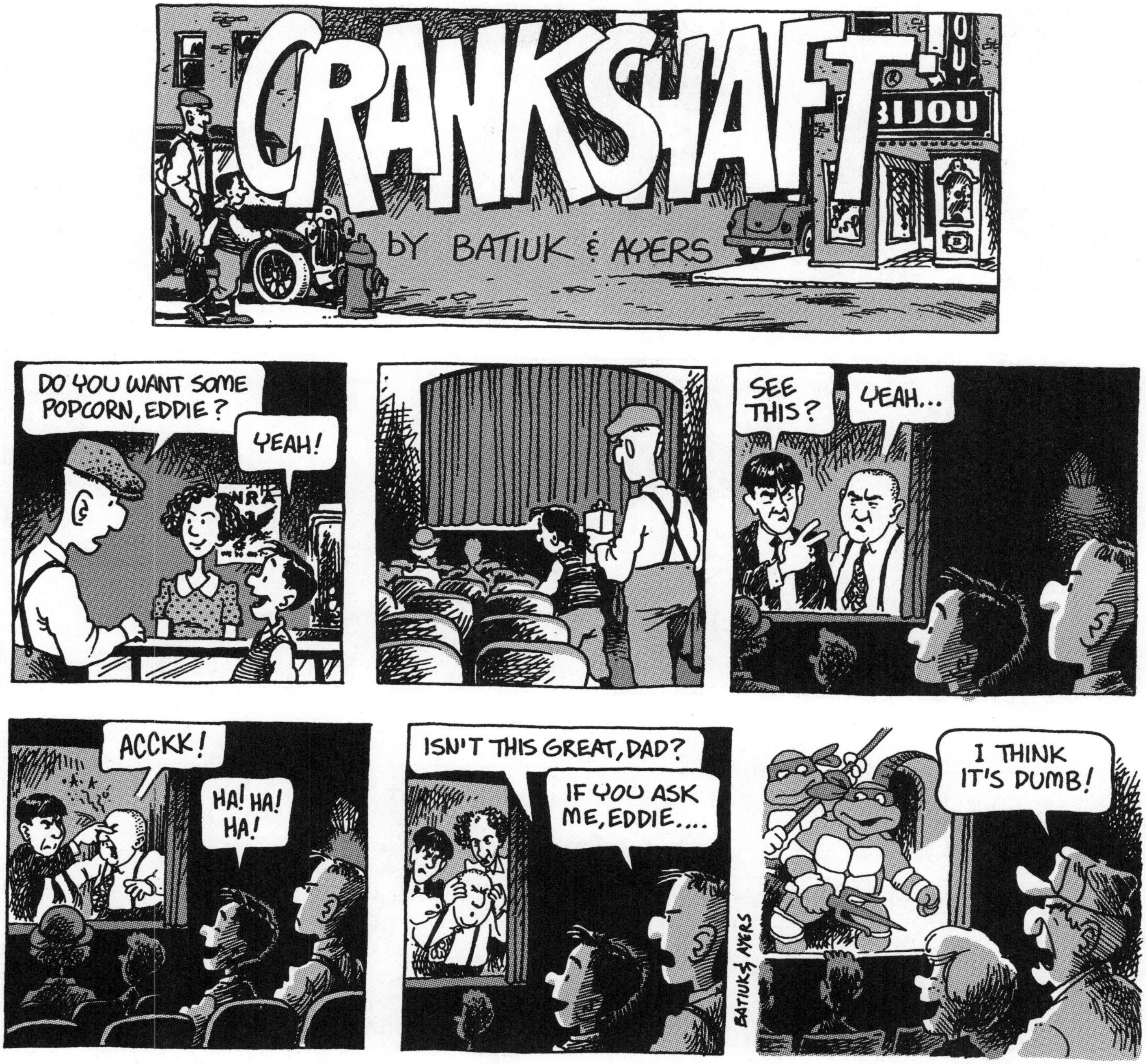
CRANKSHAFT
BY BATIUK & AYERS
BIJOU
DO YOU WANT SOME POPCORN, EDDIE?
YEAH!
NRA
SEE THIS?
YEAH...
ACCKK!
HA! HA! HA!
ISN'T THIS GREAT, DAD?
IF YOU ASK ME, EDDIE....
BATIUK & AYERS
I THINK IT'S DUMB!

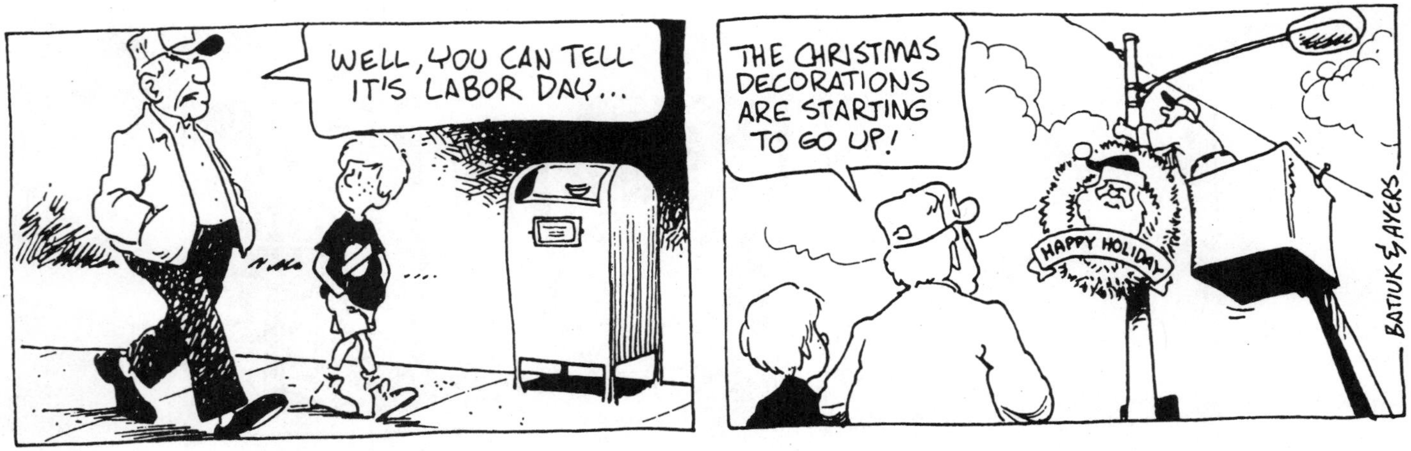
WELL, YOU CAN TELL IT'S LABOR DAY...
THE CHRISTMAS DECORATIONS ARE STARTING TO GO UP!
HAPPY HOLIDAY
BATIUK & AYERS

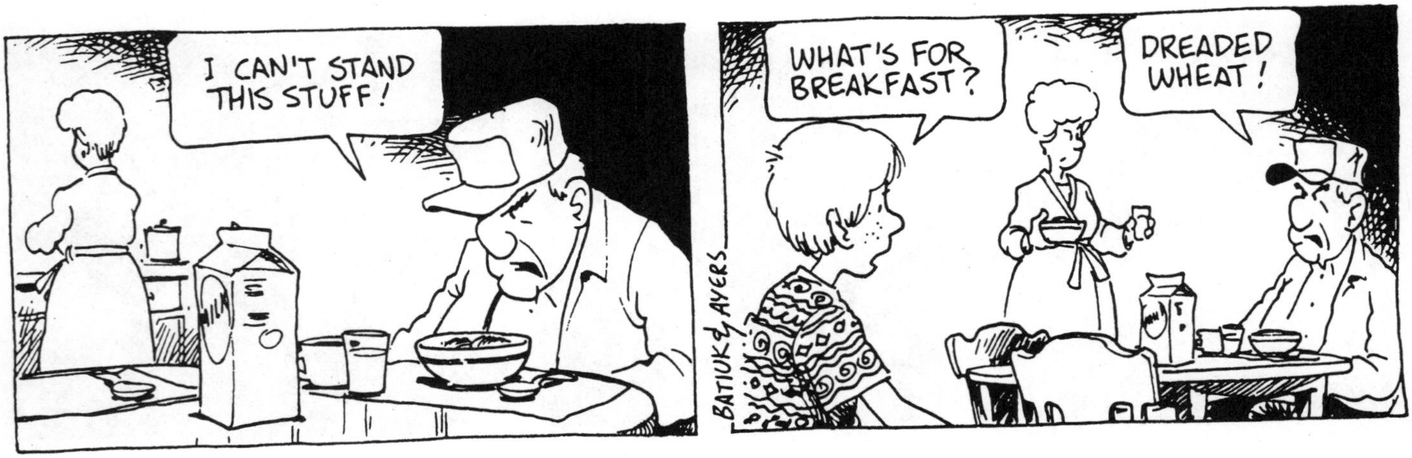
I CAN'T STAND THIS STUFF!
BATIUK & AYERS
WHAT'S FOR BREAKFAST?
DREADED WHEAT!

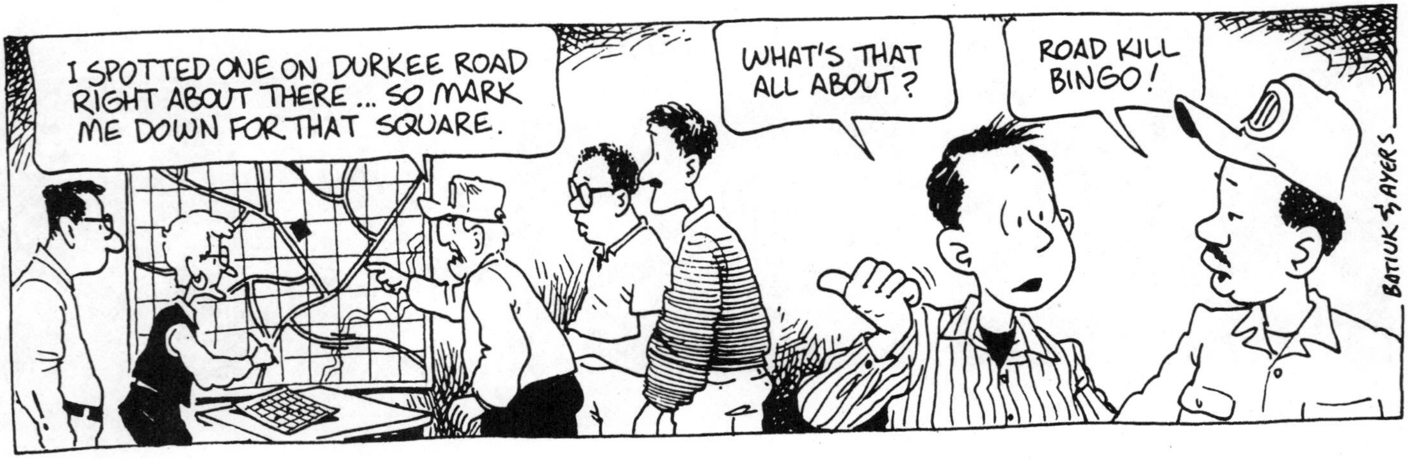
I SPOTTED ONE ON DURKEE ROAD RIGHT ABOUT THERE... SO MARK ME DOWN FOR THAT SQUARE.
WHAT'S THAT ALL ABOUT?
ROAD KILL BINGO!
BATIUK & AYERS

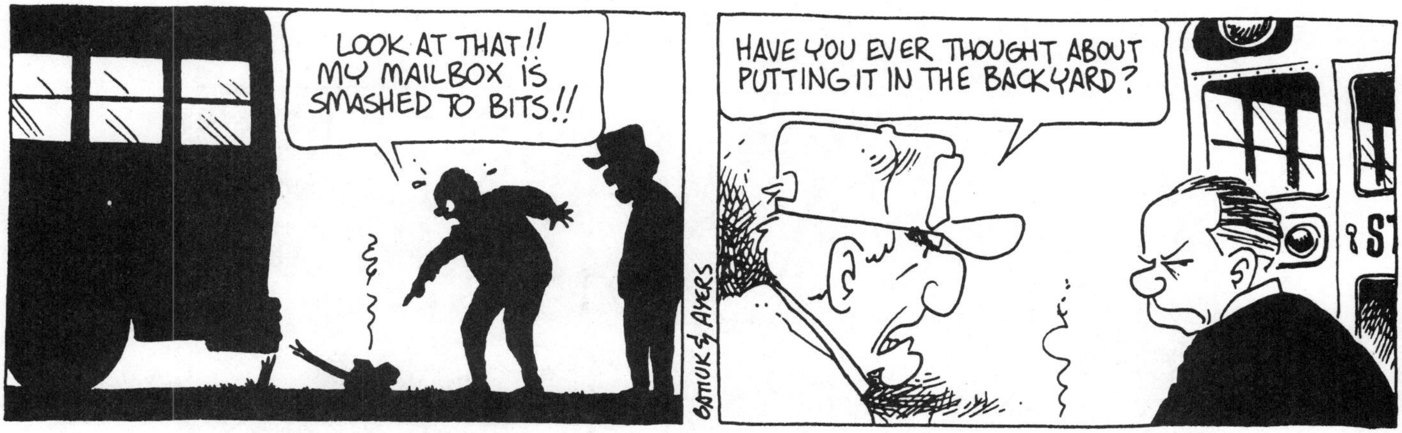
LOOK AT THAT!! MY MAILBOX IS SMASHED TO BITS!!
HAVE YOU EVER THOUGHT ABOUT PUTTING IT IN THE BACKYARD?
BATIUK & AYERS

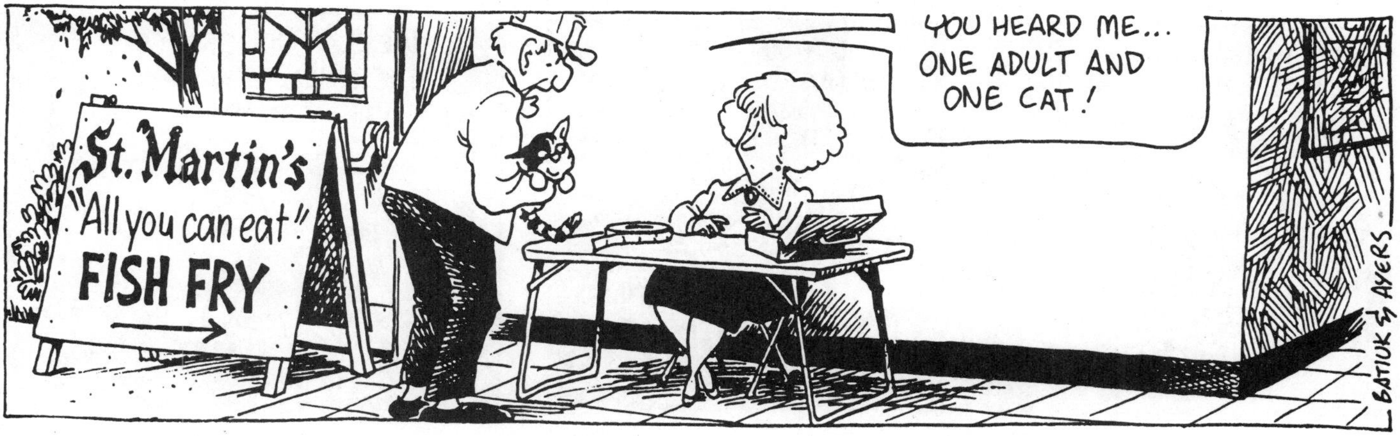
St. Martin's
"All you can eat"
FISH FRY
YOU HEARD ME... ONE ADULT AND ONE CAT!
BATIUK & AYERS

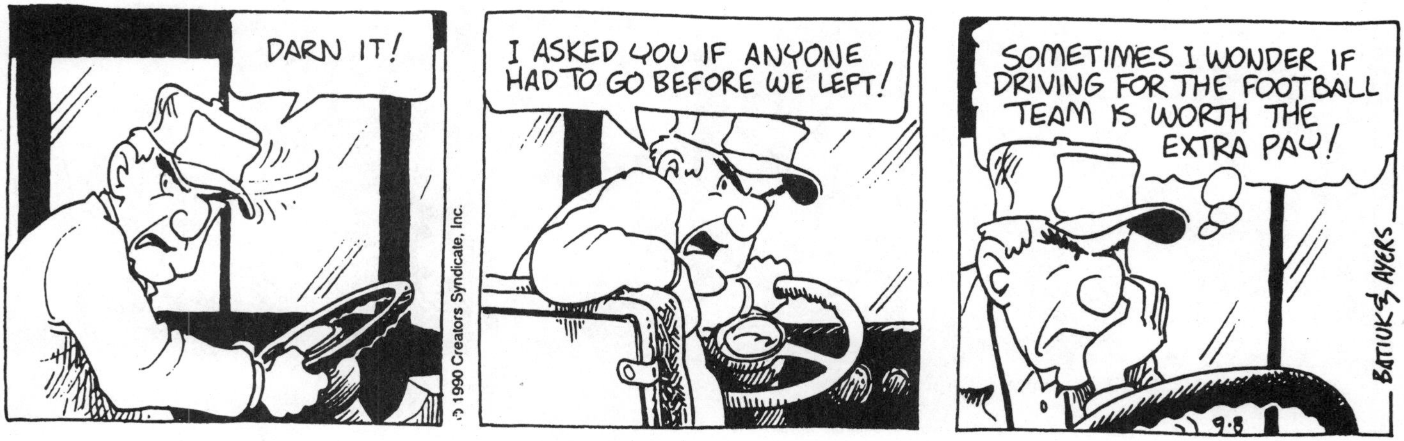
DARN IT!
I ASKED YOU IF ANYONE HAD TO GO BEFORE WE LEFT!
SOMETIMES I WONDER IF DRIVING FOR THE FOOTBALL TEAM IS WORTH THE EXTRA PAY!
BATIUK & AYERS
9-8

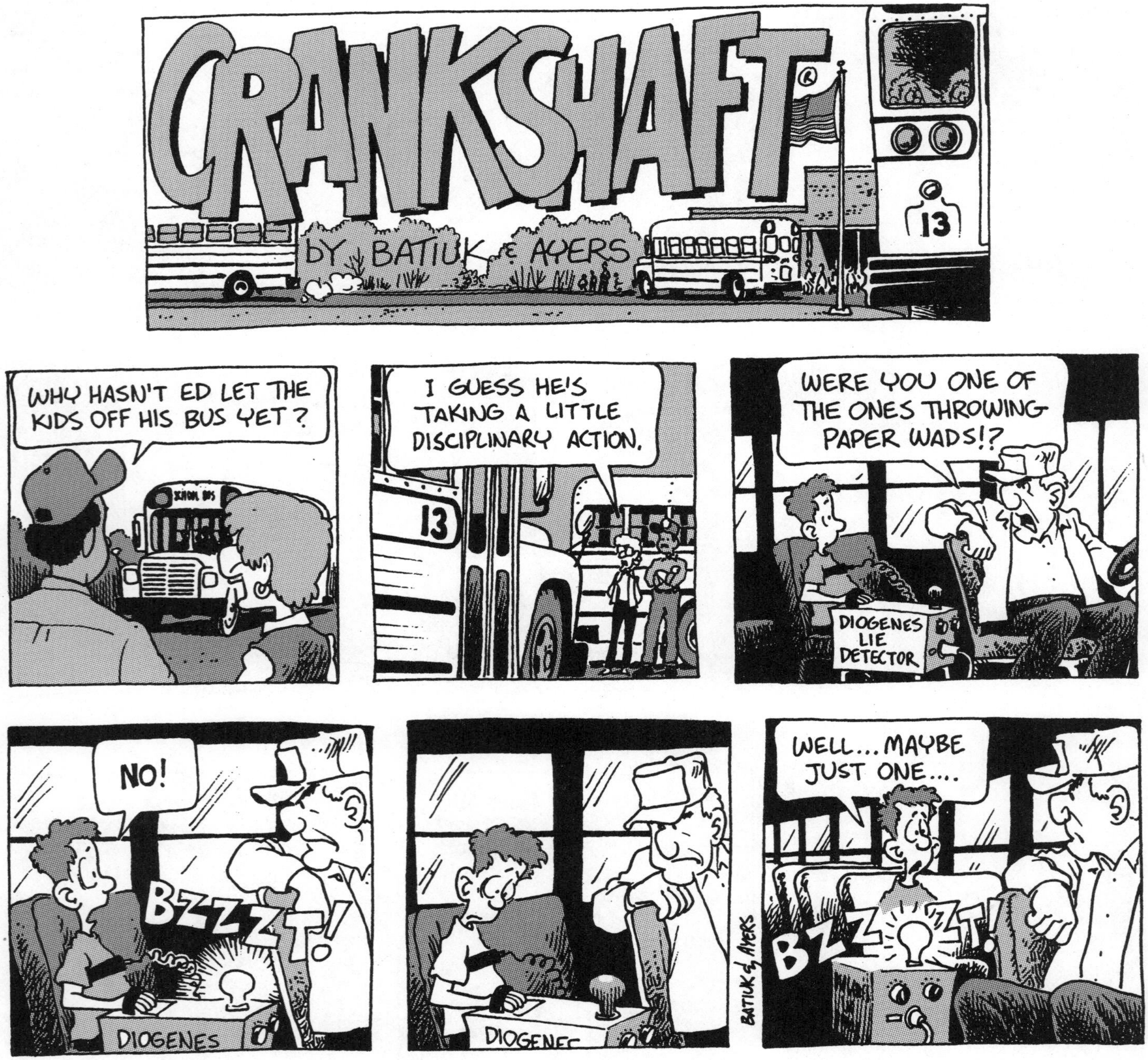
CRANKSHAFT®
BY BATIUK & AYERS
13
WHY HASN'T ED LET THE KIDS OFF HIS BUS YET?
SCHOOL BUS
I GUESS HE'S TAKING A LITTLE DISCIPLINARY ACTION.
13
WERE YOU ONE OF THE ONES THROWING PAPER WADS!?
DIOGENES LIE DETECTOR
NO!
BZZZZT!
DIOGENES
DIOGENES
BATIUK & AYERS
WELL... MAYBE JUST ONE....
BZZ ZZT!

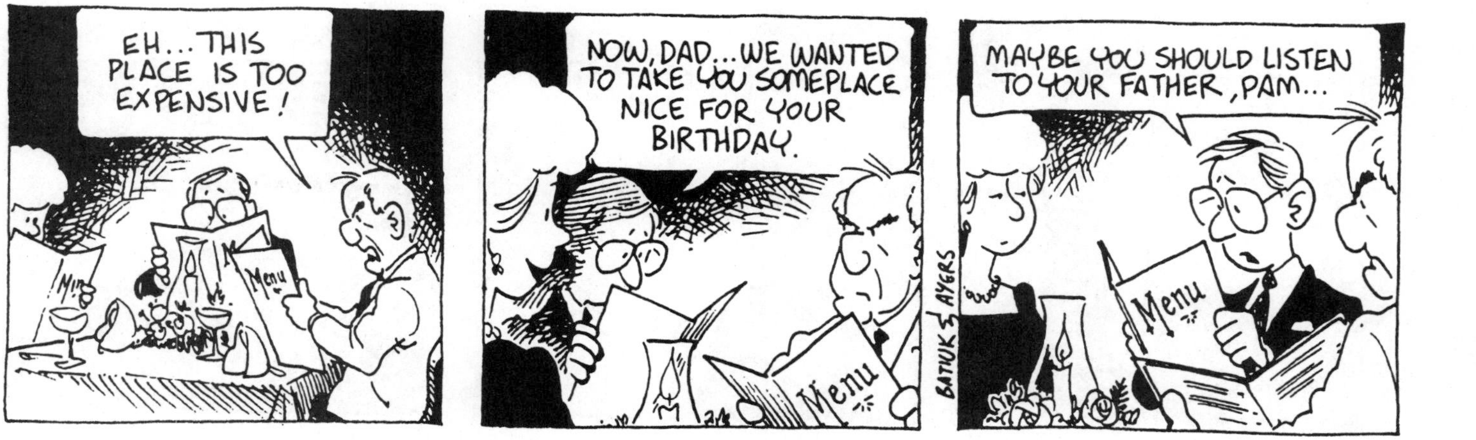
EH... THIS PLACE IS TOO EXPENSIVE!
NOW, DAD... WE WANTED TO TAKE YOU SOMEPLACE NICE FOR YOUR BIRTHDAY.
MAYBE YOU SHOULD LISTEN TO YOUR FATHER, PAM...
Menu
BATIUK & AYERS

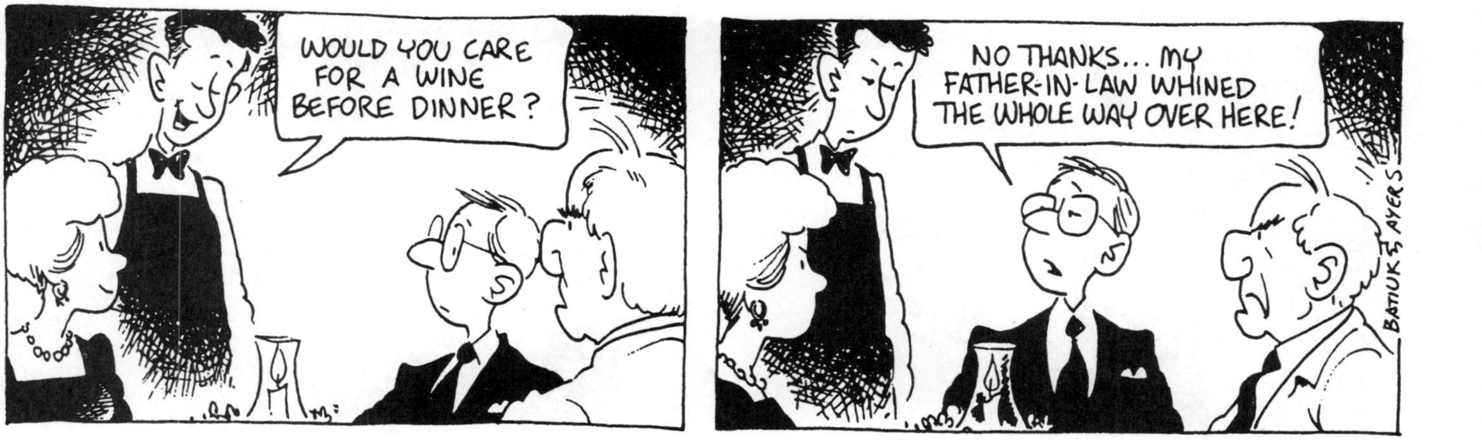
WOULD YOU CARE FOR A WINE BEFORE DINNER?
NO THANKS... MY FATHER-IN-LAW WHINED THE WHOLE WAY OVER HERE!
BATIUK & AYERS

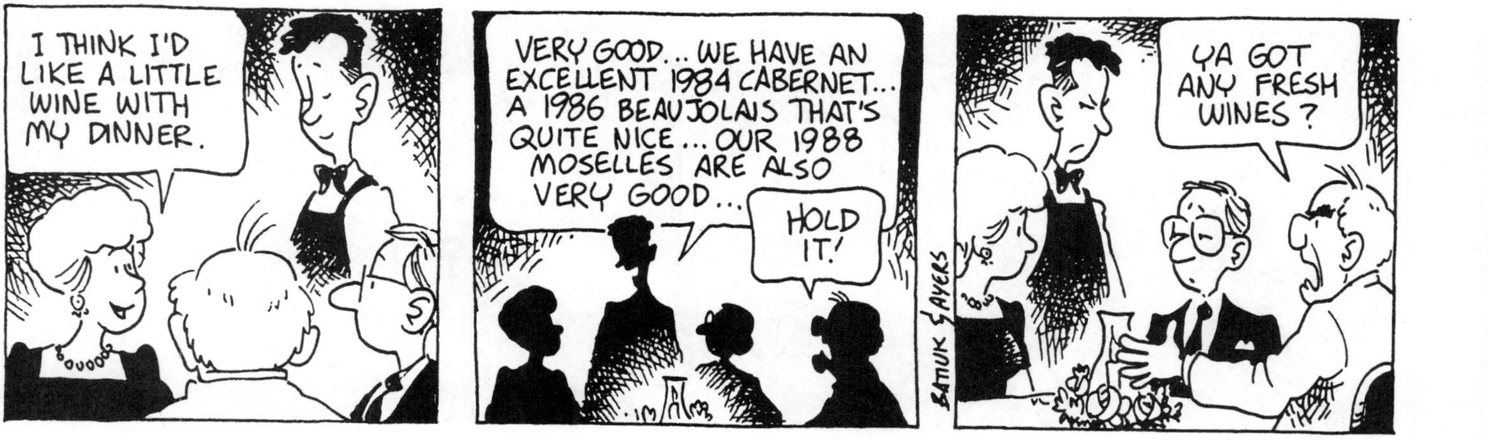
I THINK I'D LIKE A LITTLE WINE WITH MY DINNER.
VERY GOOD... WE HAVE AN EXCELLENT 1984 CABERNET... A 1986 BEAUJOLAIS THAT'S QUITE NICE... OUR 1988 MOSELLES ARE ALSO VERY GOOD...
HOLD IT!
YA GOT ANY FRESH WINES?
BATIUK & AYERS

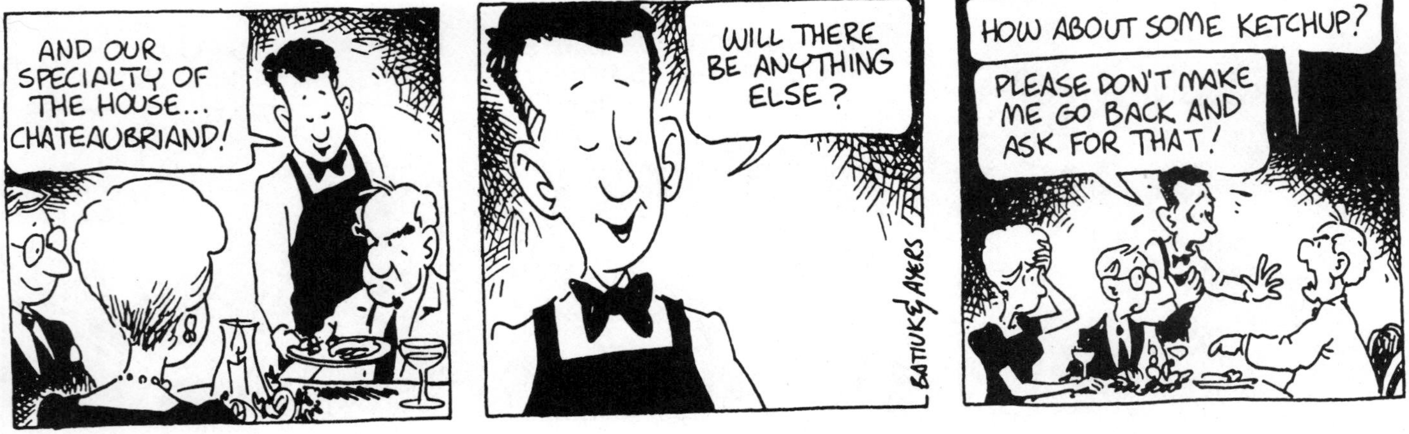
AND OUR SPECIALTY OF THE HOUSE... CHATEAUBRIAND!
WILL THERE BE ANYTHING ELSE?
BATIUK & AYERS
HOW ABOUT SOME KETCHUP?
PLEASE DON'T MAKE ME GO BACK AND ASK FOR THAT!

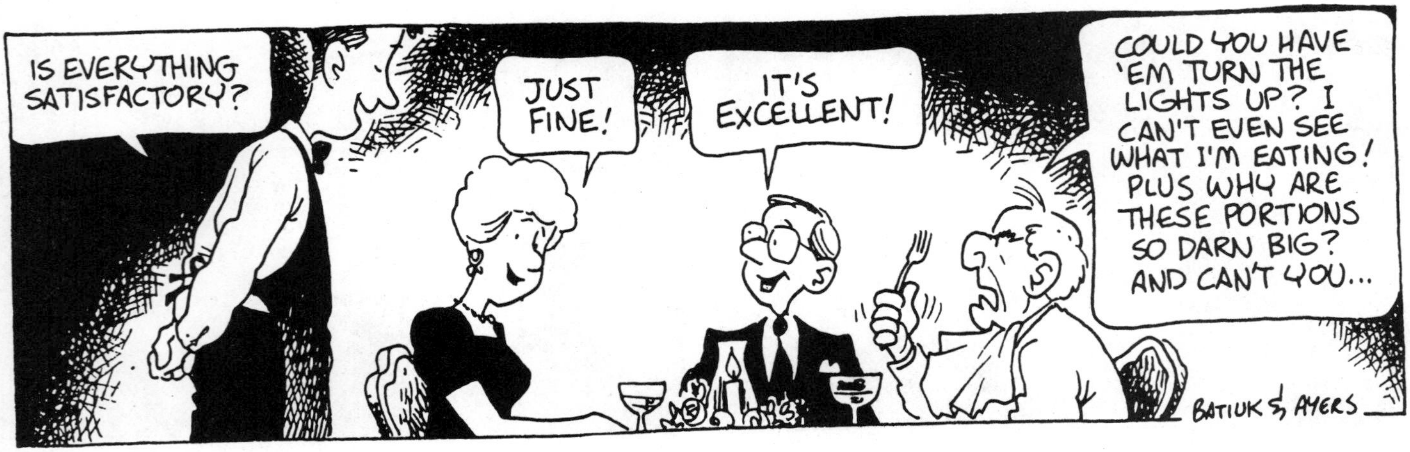
IS EVERYTHING SATISFACTORY?
JUST FINE!
IT'S EXCELLENT!
COULD YOU HAVE 'EM TURN THE LIGHTS UP? I CAN'T EVEN SEE WHAT I'M EATING! PLUS WHY ARE THESE PORTIONS SO DARN BIG? AND CAN'T YOU...
BATIUK & AYERS

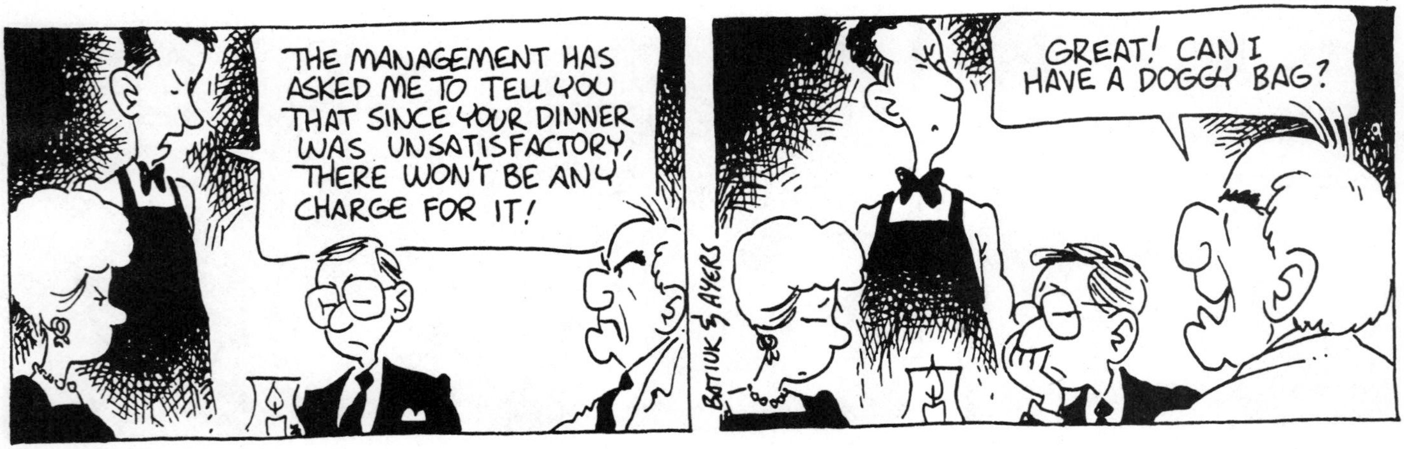
THE MANAGEMENT HAS ASKED ME TO TELL YOU THAT SINCE YOUR DINNER WAS UNSATISFACTORY, THERE WON'T BE ANY CHARGE FOR IT!
BATIUK & AYERS
GREAT! CAN I HAVE A DOGGY BAG?

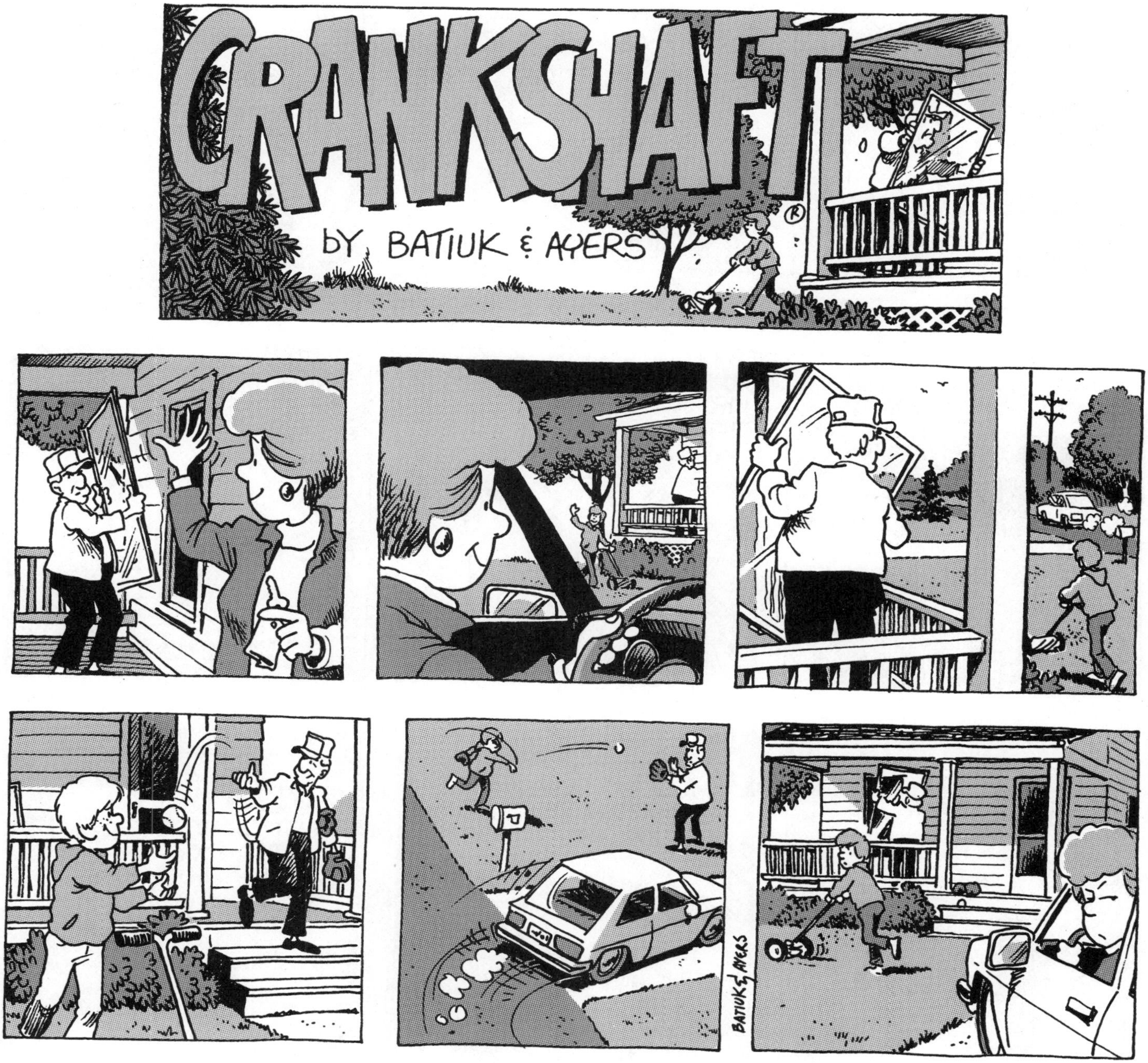
CRANKSHAFT
BY BATIUK & AYERS
BATIUK & AYERS

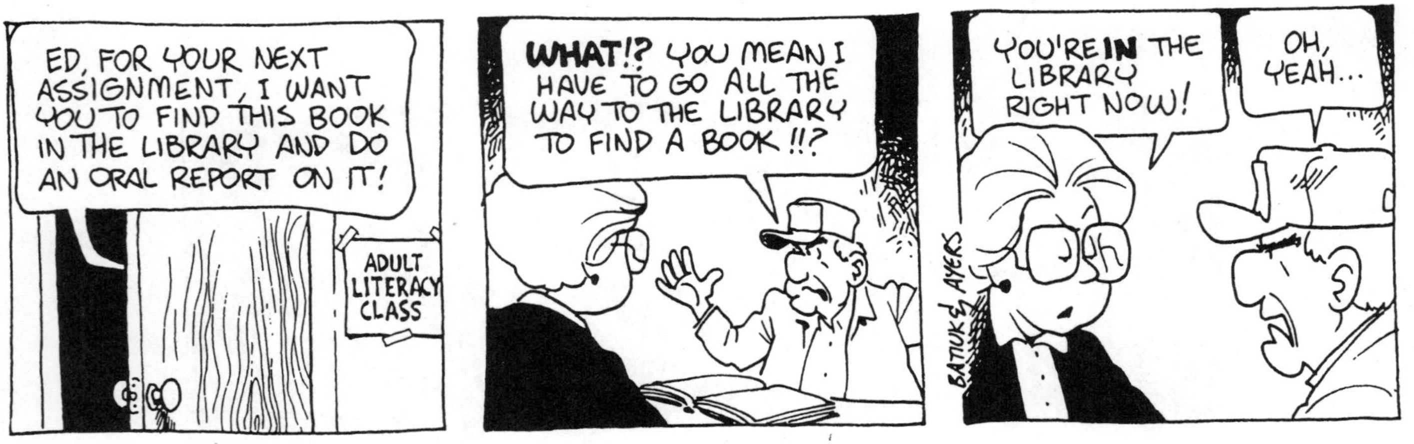
ED, FOR YOUR NEXT ASSIGNMENT, I WANT YOU TO FIND THIS BOOK IN THE LIBRARY AND DO AN ORAL REPORT ON IT!
ADULT LITERACY CLASS
WHAT!? YOU MEAN I HAVE TO GO ALL THE WAY TO THE LIBRARY TO FIND A BOOK!!?
BATIUK & AYERS
YOU'RE **IN** THE LIBRARY RIGHT NOW!
OH, YEAH...

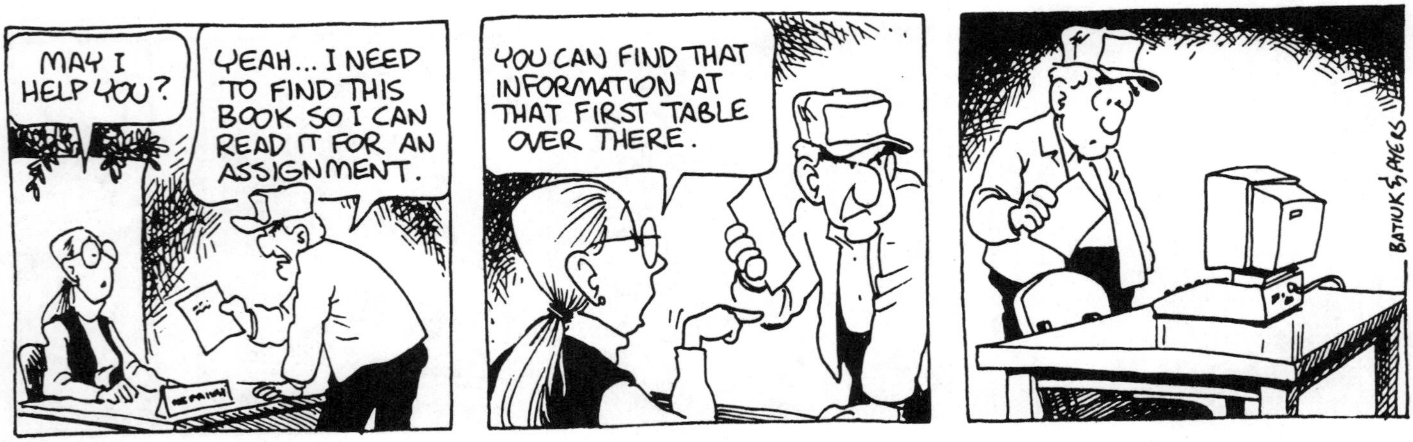
MAY I HELP YOU?
YEAH... I NEED TO FIND THIS BOOK SO I CAN READ IT FOR AN ASSIGNMENT.
YOU CAN FIND THAT INFORMATION AT THAT FIRST TABLE OVER THERE.
BATIUK & AYERS

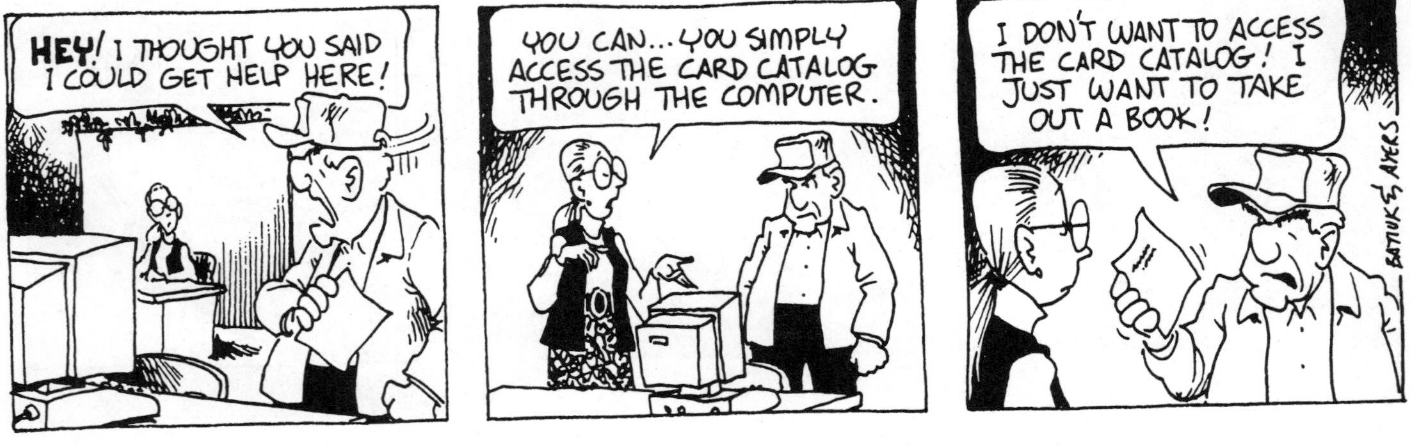
HEY! I THOUGHT YOU SAID I COULD GET HELP HERE!
YOU CAN... YOU SIMPLY ACCESS THE CARD CATALOG THROUGH THE COMPUTER.
I DON'T WANT TO ACCESS THE CARD CATALOG! I JUST WANT TO TAKE OUT A BOOK!
BATIUK & AYERS

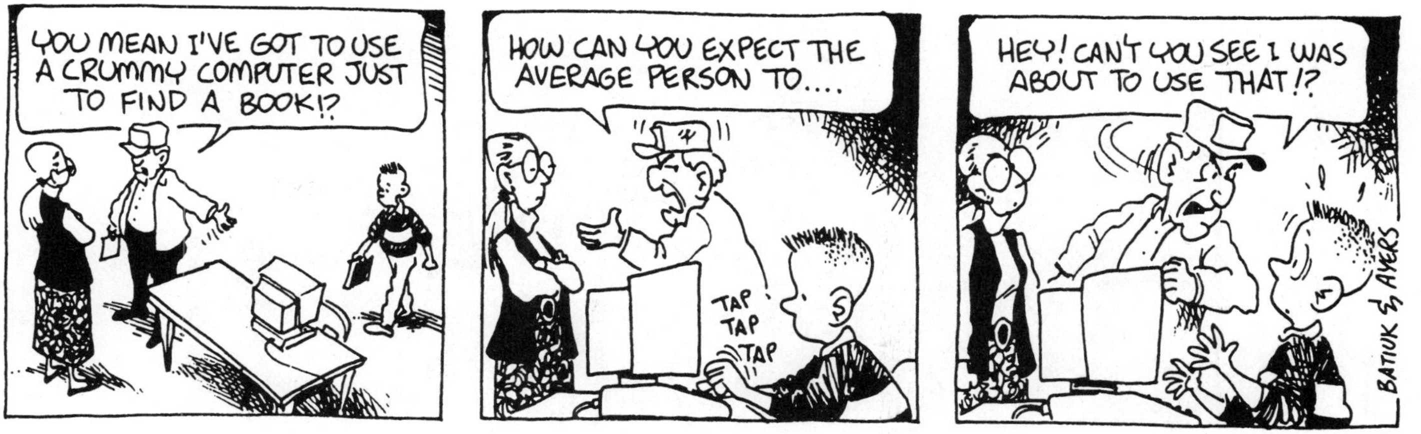
YOU MEAN I'VE GOT TO USE A CRUMMY COMPUTER JUST TO FIND A BOOK!?
HOW CAN YOU EXPECT THE AVERAGE PERSON TO....
TAP TAP TAP
HEY! CAN'T YOU SEE I WAS ABOUT TO USE THAT!?
BATIUK & AYERS

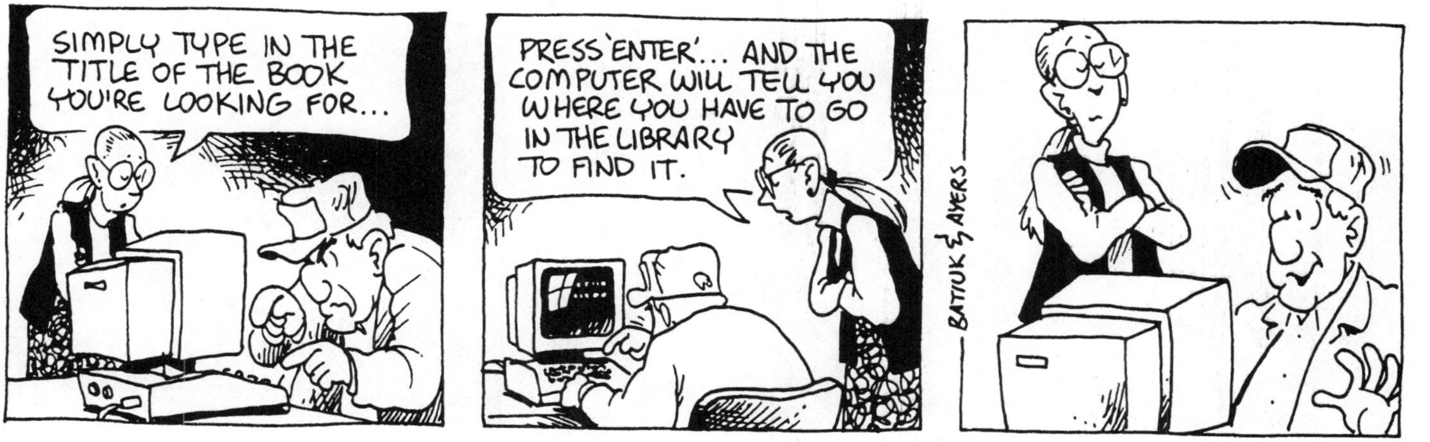
SIMPLY TYPE IN THE TITLE OF THE BOOK YOU'RE LOOKING FOR...
PRESS 'ENTER'... AND THE COMPUTER WILL TELL YOU WHERE YOU HAVE TO GO IN THE LIBRARY TO FIND IT.
BATIUK & AYERS

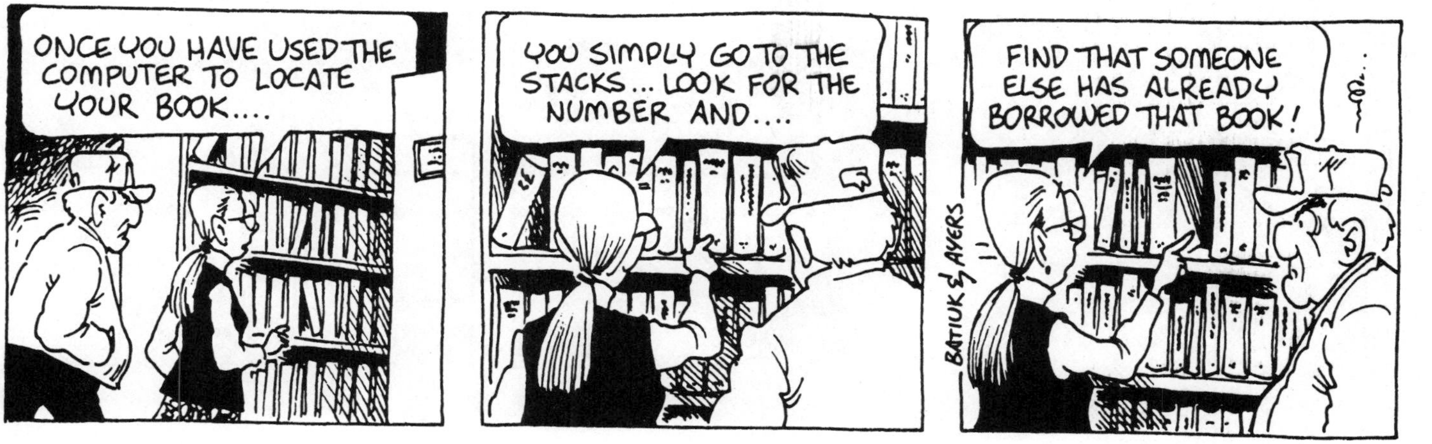
ONCE YOU HAVE USED THE COMPUTER TO LOCATE YOUR BOOK....
YOU SIMPLY GO TO THE STACKS... LOOK FOR THE NUMBER AND....
FIND THAT SOMEONE ELSE HAS ALREADY BORROWED THAT BOOK!
BATIUK & AYERS

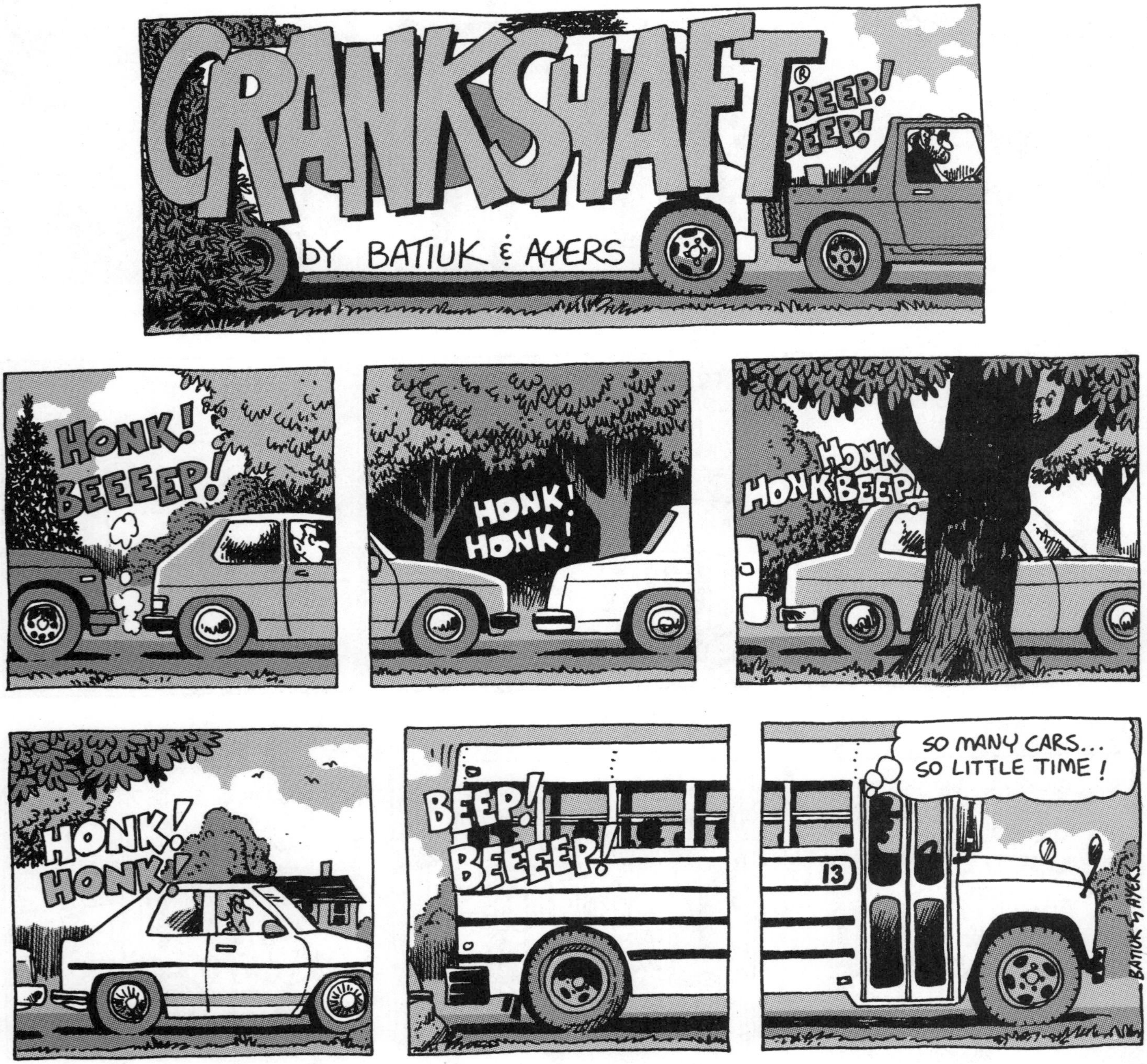
CRANKSHAFT®
BY BATIUK & AYERS
BEEP! BEEP!
HONK! BEEEEP!
HONK! HONK!
HONK HONK BEEP!
HONK! HONK!
BEEP! BEEEEP!
13
SO MANY CARS... SO LITTLE TIME!
BATIUK & AYERS

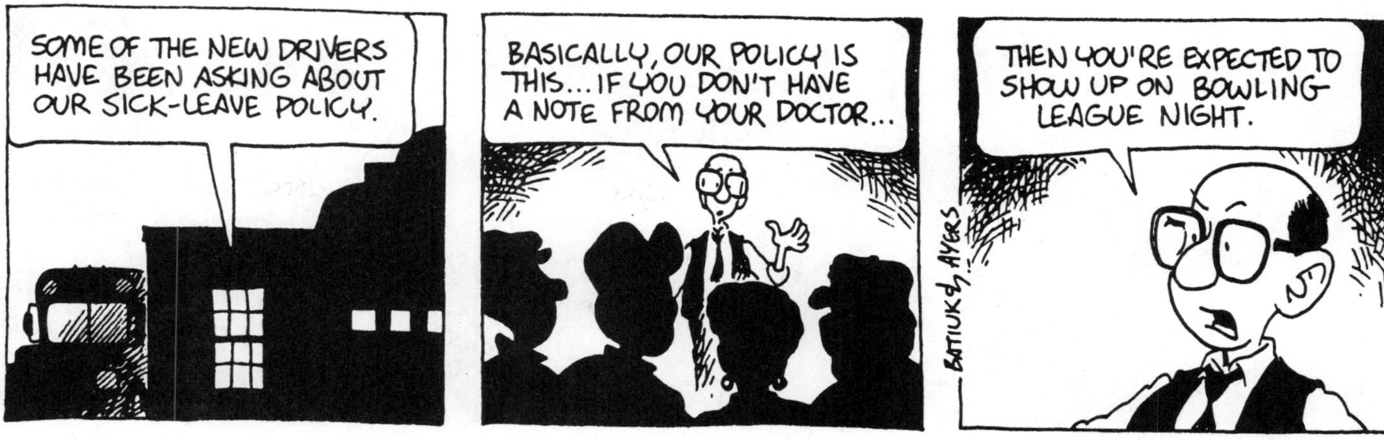
SOME OF THE NEW DRIVERS HAVE BEEN ASKING ABOUT OUR SICK-LEAVE POLICY.
BASICALLY, OUR POLICY IS THIS... IF YOU DON'T HAVE A NOTE FROM YOUR DOCTOR...
THEN YOU'RE EXPECTED TO SHOW UP ON BOWLING LEAGUE NIGHT.
BATIUK & AYERS

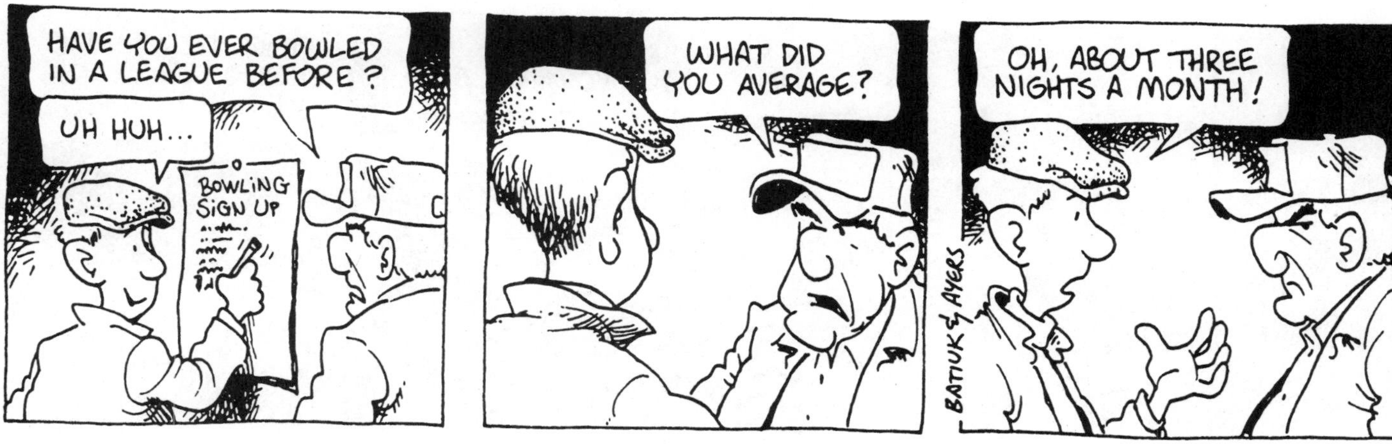
HAVE YOU EVER BOWLED IN A LEAGUE BEFORE?
UH HUH...
BOWLING SIGN UP
WHAT DID YOU AVERAGE?
OH, ABOUT THREE NIGHTS A MONTH!
BATIUK & AYERS

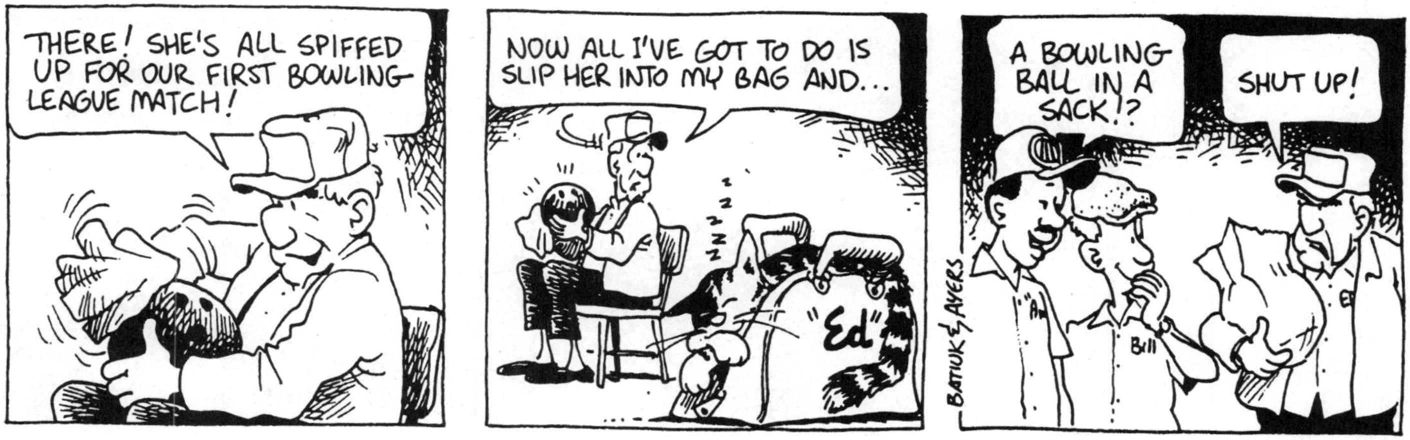
THERE! SHE'S ALL SPIFFED UP FOR OUR FIRST BOWLING LEAGUE MATCH!
NOW ALL I'VE GOT TO DO IS SLIP HER INTO MY BAG AND...
"Ed"
A BOWLING BALL IN A SACK!?
SHUT UP!
Bill
BATIUK & AYERS

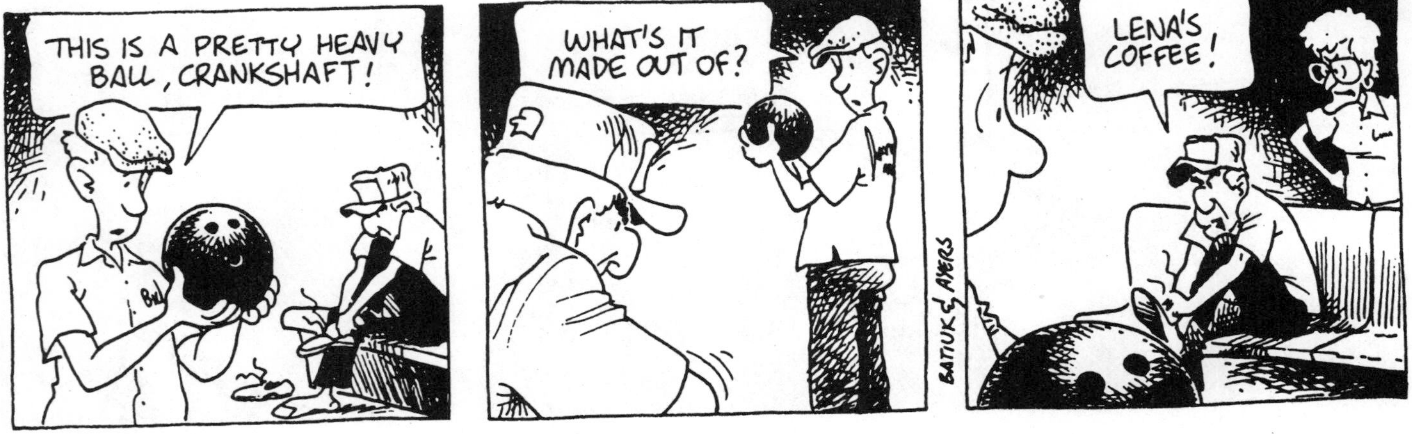
THIS IS A PRETTY HEAVY BALL, CRANKSHAFT!
WHAT'S IT MADE OUT OF?
LENA'S COFFEE!
BATIUK & AYERS

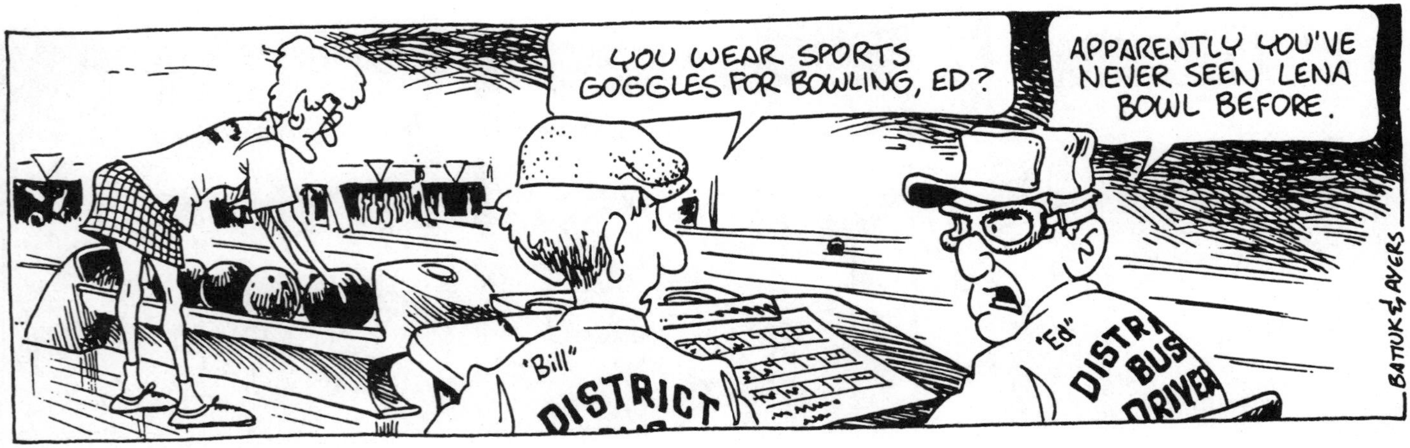
YOU WEAR SPORTS GOGGLES FOR BOWLING, ED?
APPARENTLY YOU'VE NEVER SEEN LENA BOWL BEFORE.
"Bill"
DISTRICT
"Ed"
BATIUK & AYERS

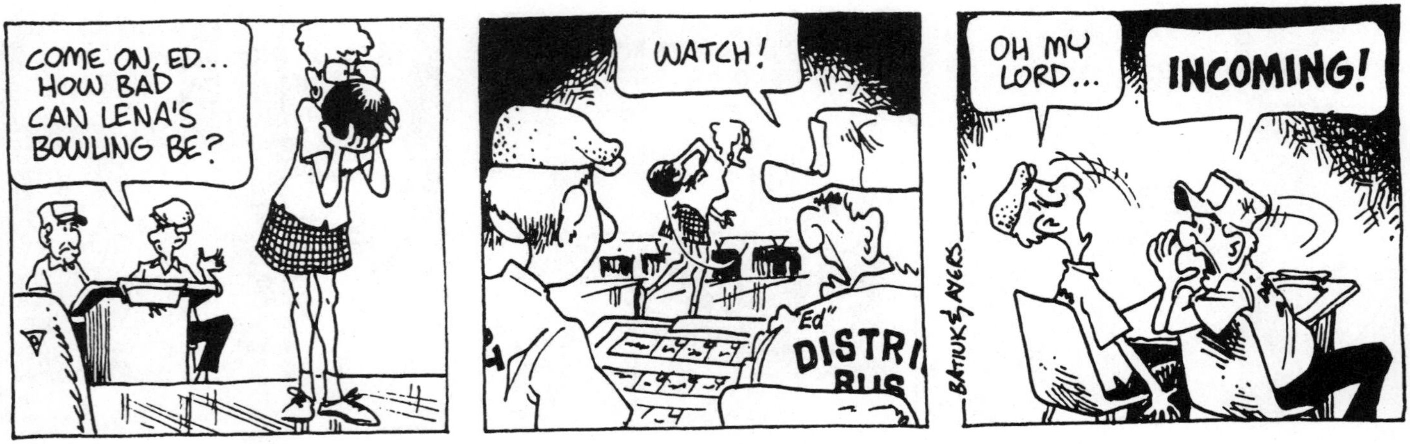
COME ON, ED... HOW BAD CAN LENA'S BOWLING BE?
WATCH!
"Ed"
DISTRI
OH MY LORD...
INCOMING!
BATIUK & AYERS

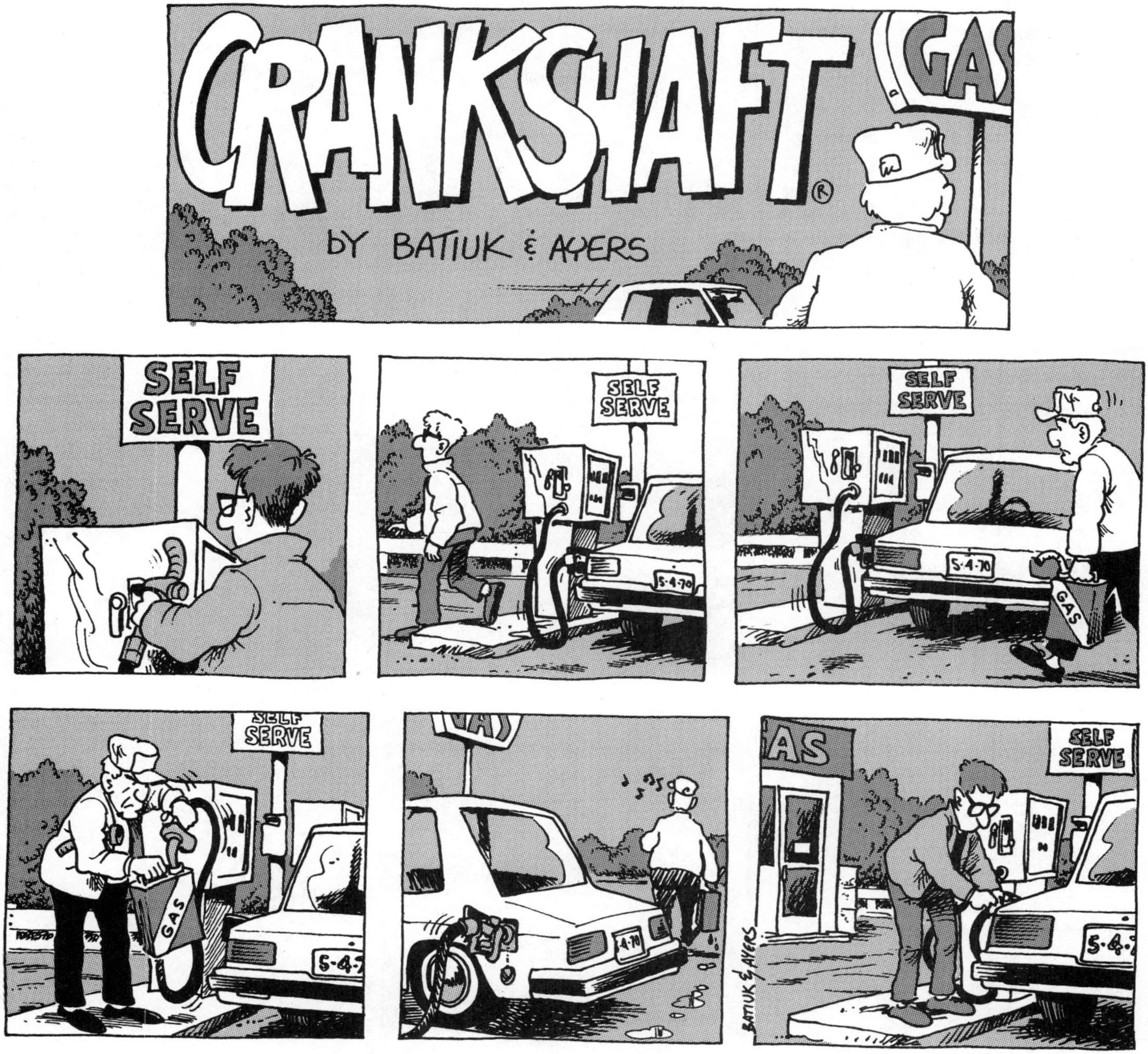
CRANKSHAFT®
BY BATIUK & AYERS
GAS
SELF SERVE
SELF SERVE
SELF SERVE
GAS
SELF SERVE
GAS
GAS
SELF SERVE
BATIUK & AYERS

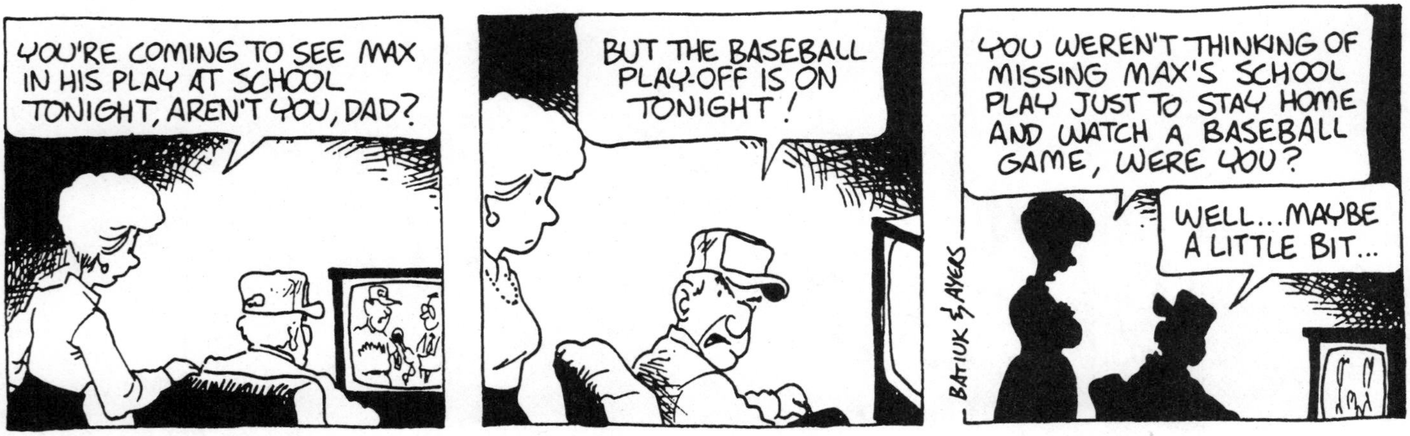
YOU'RE COMING TO SEE MAX IN HIS PLAY AT SCHOOL TONIGHT, AREN'T YOU, DAD?
BUT THE BASEBALL PLAY-OFF IS ON TONIGHT!
YOU WEREN'T THINKING OF MISSING MAX'S SCHOOL PLAY JUST TO STAY HOME AND WATCH A BASEBALL GAME, WERE YOU?
WELL... MAYBE A LITTLE BIT...
BATIUK & AYERS

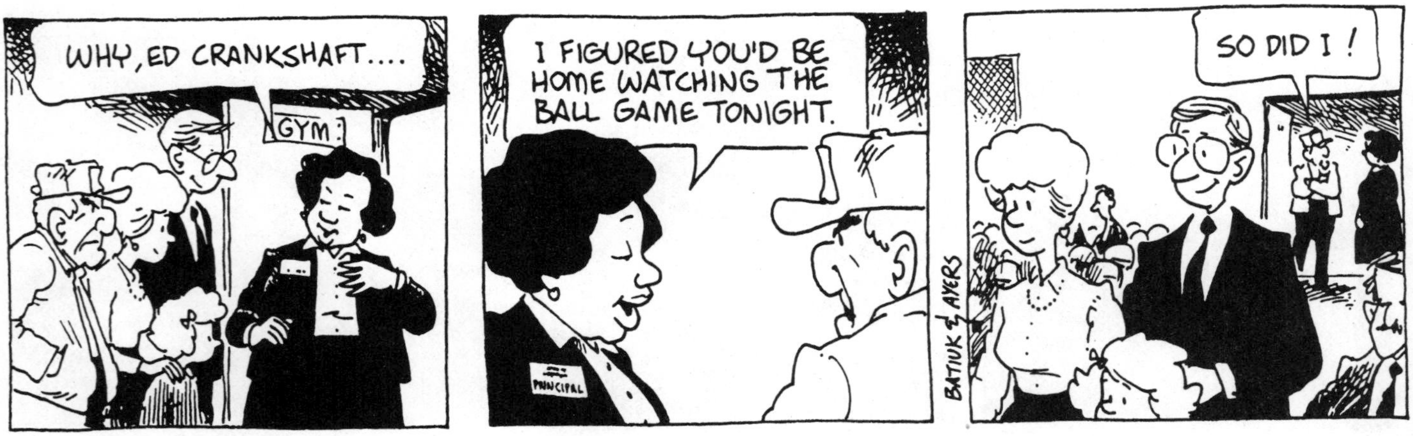
WHY, ED CRANKSHAFT....
GYM
I FIGURED YOU'D BE HOME WATCHING THE BALL GAME TONIGHT.
PRINCIPAL
SO DID I!
BATIUK & AYERS

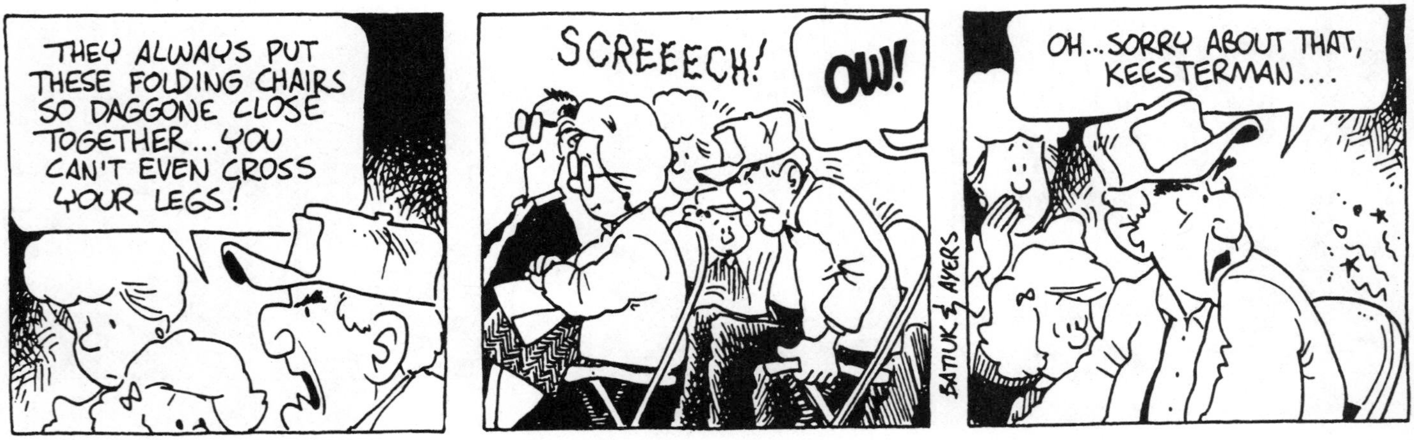
THEY ALWAYS PUT THESE FOLDING CHAIRS SO DAGGONE CLOSE TOGETHER... YOU CAN'T EVEN CROSS YOUR LEGS!
SCREEECH!
OW!
OH... SORRY ABOUT THAT, KEESTERMAN....
BATIUK & AYERS

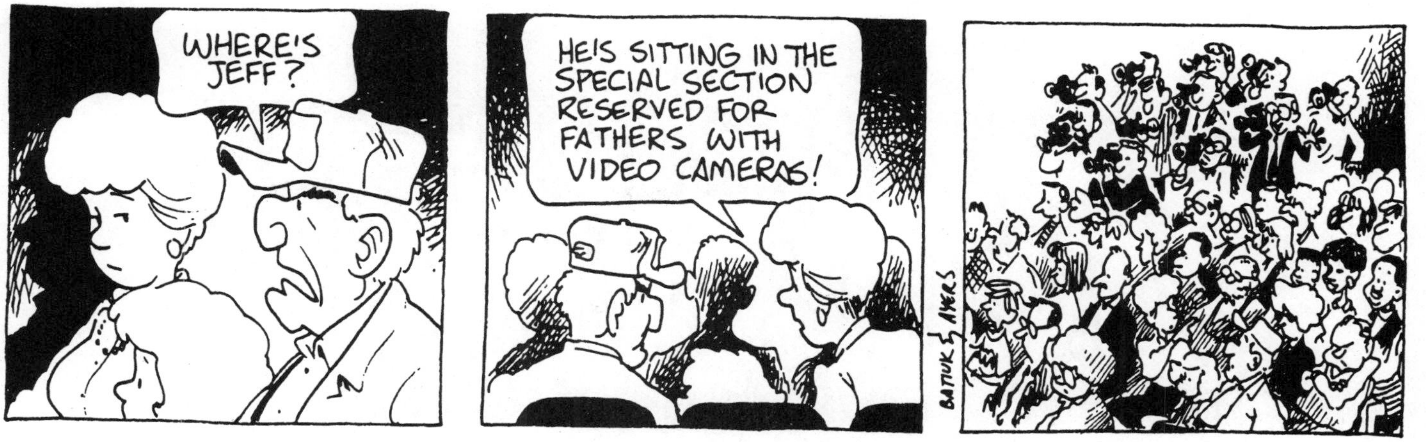
WHERE'S JEFF?
HE'S SITTING IN THE SPECIAL SECTION RESERVED FOR FATHERS WITH VIDEO CAMERAS!
BATIUK & AYERS

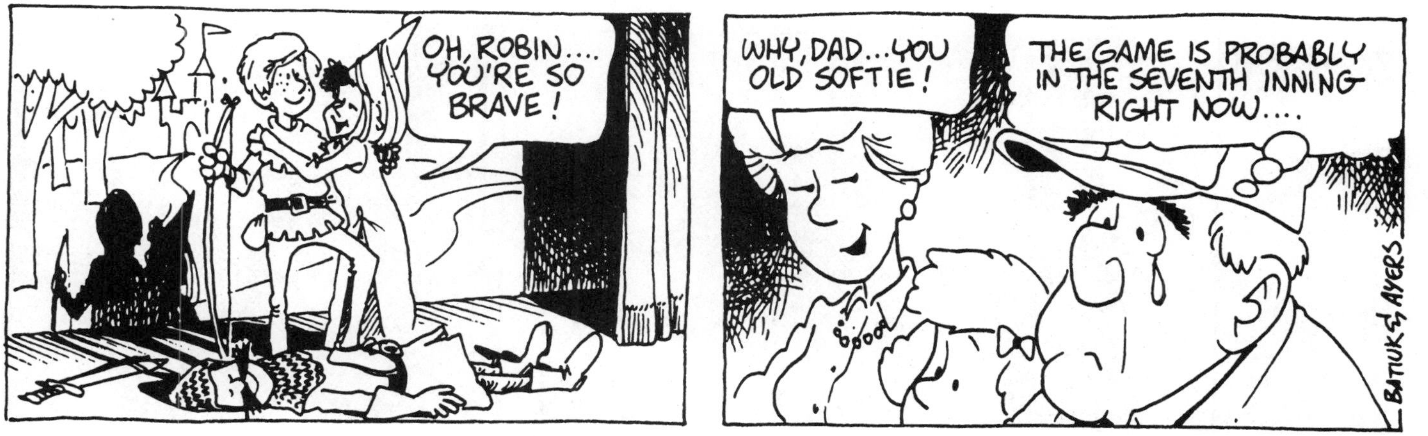
OH, ROBIN.... YOU'RE SO BRAVE!
WHY, DAD...YOU OLD SOFTIE!
THE GAME IS PROBABLY IN THE SEVENTH INNING RIGHT NOW....
BATIUK & AYERS

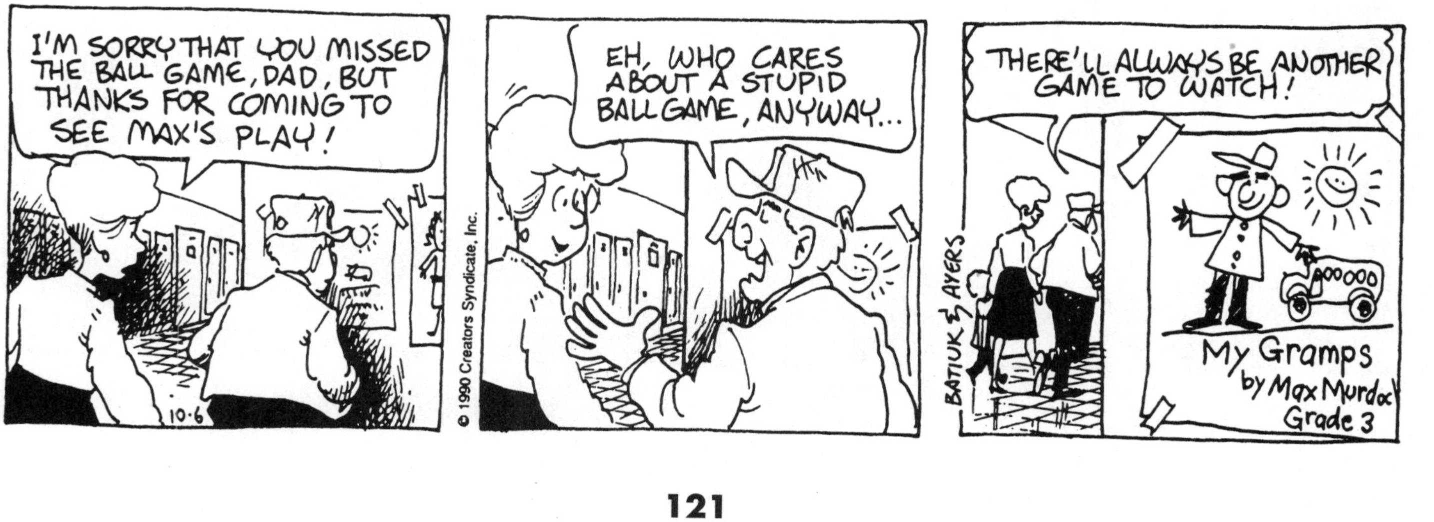
I'M SORRY THAT YOU MISSED THE BALL GAME, DAD, BUT THANKS FOR COMING TO SEE MAX'S PLAY!
10-6
© 1990 Creators Syndicate, Inc.
EH, WHO CARES ABOUT A STUPID BALL GAME, ANYWAY...
THERE'LL ALWAYS BE ANOTHER GAME TO WATCH!
BATIUK & AYERS
My Gramps
by Max Murdoc
Grade 3

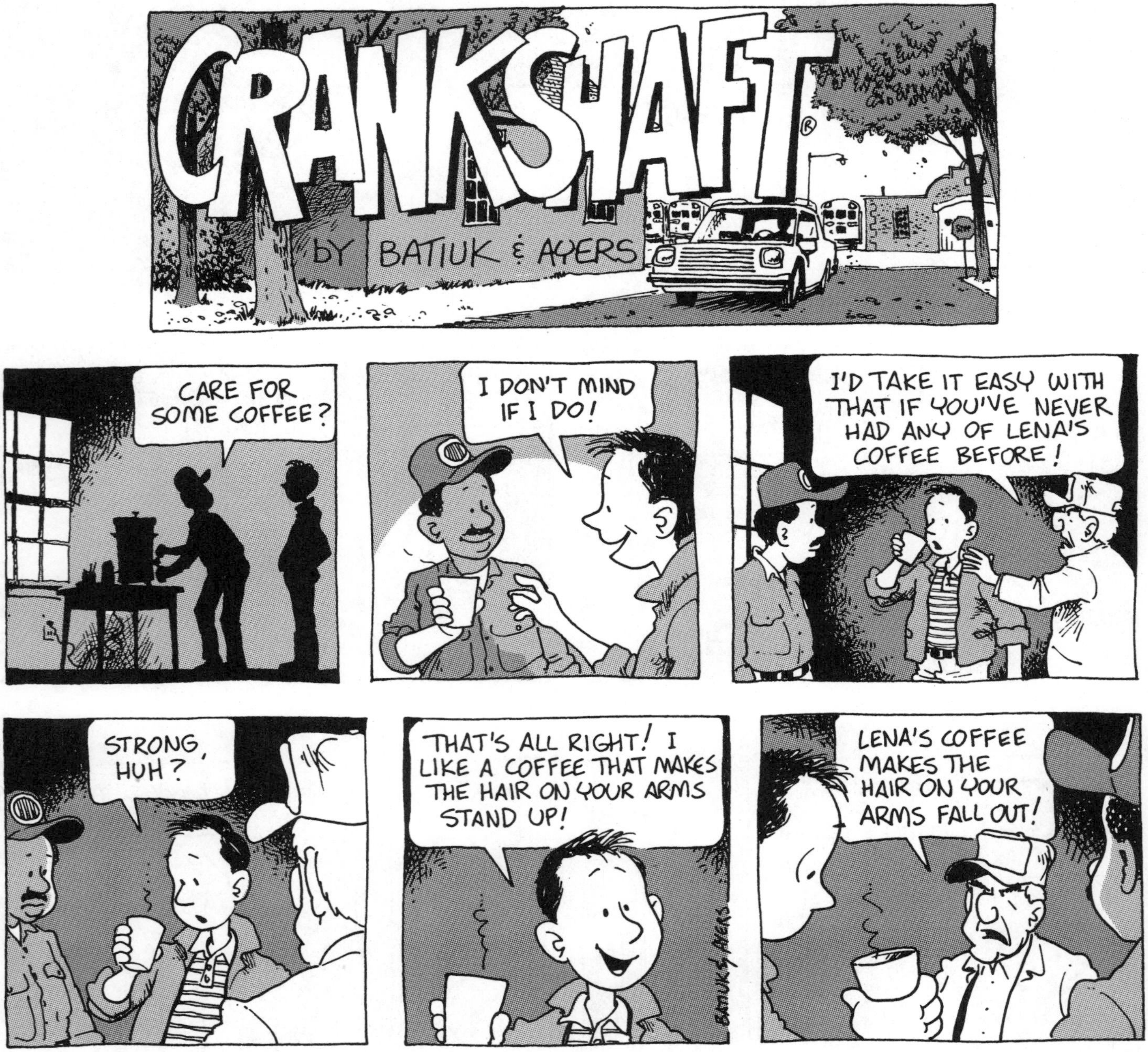
CRANKSHAFT
BY BATIUK & AYERS
CARE FOR SOME COFFEE?
I DON'T MIND IF I DO!
I'D TAKE IT EASY WITH THAT IF YOU'VE NEVER HAD ANY OF LENA'S COFFEE BEFORE!
STRONG, HUH?
THAT'S ALL RIGHT! I LIKE A COFFEE THAT MAKES THE HAIR ON YOUR ARMS STAND UP!
BATIUK & AYERS
LENA'S COFFEE MAKES THE HAIR ON YOUR ARMS FALL OUT!

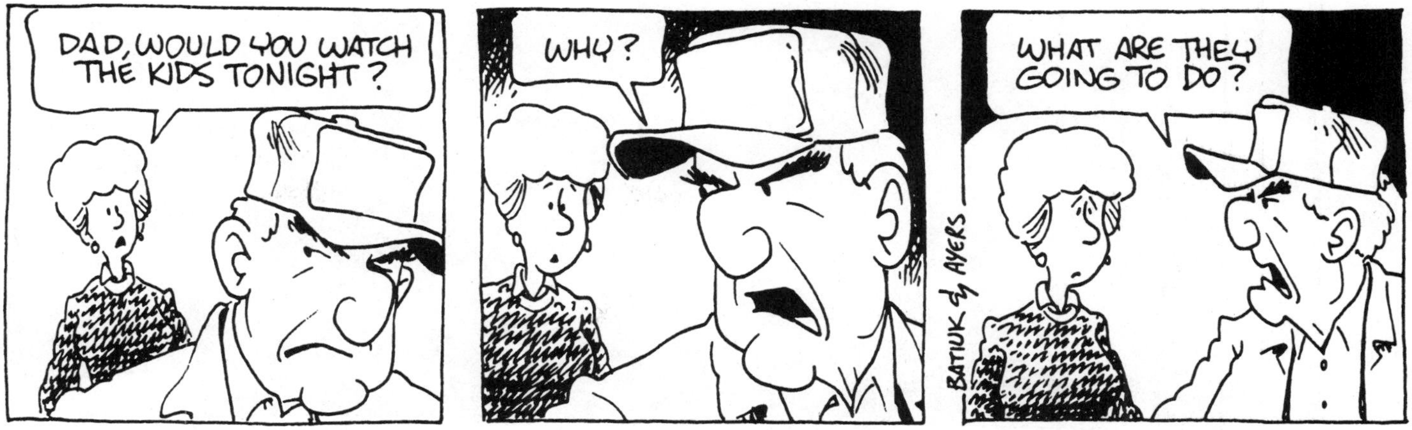
DAD, WOULD YOU WATCH THE KIDS TONIGHT?
WHY?
WHAT ARE THEY GOING TO DO?
BATIUK & AYERS

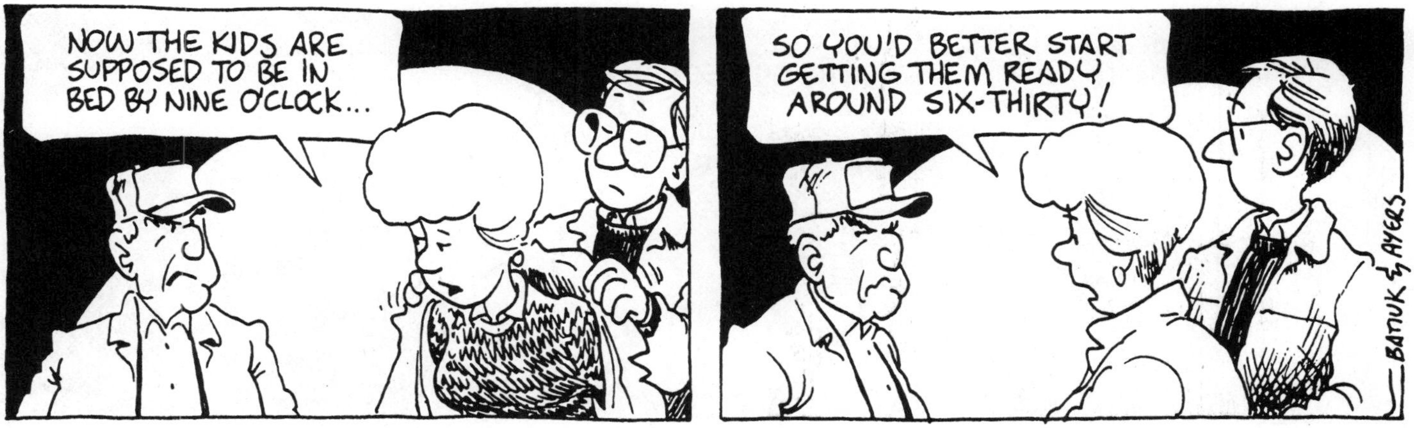
NOW THE KIDS ARE SUPPOSED TO BE IN BED BY NINE O'CLOCK...
SO YOU'D BETTER START GETTING THEM READY AROUND SIX-THIRTY!
BATIUK & AYERS

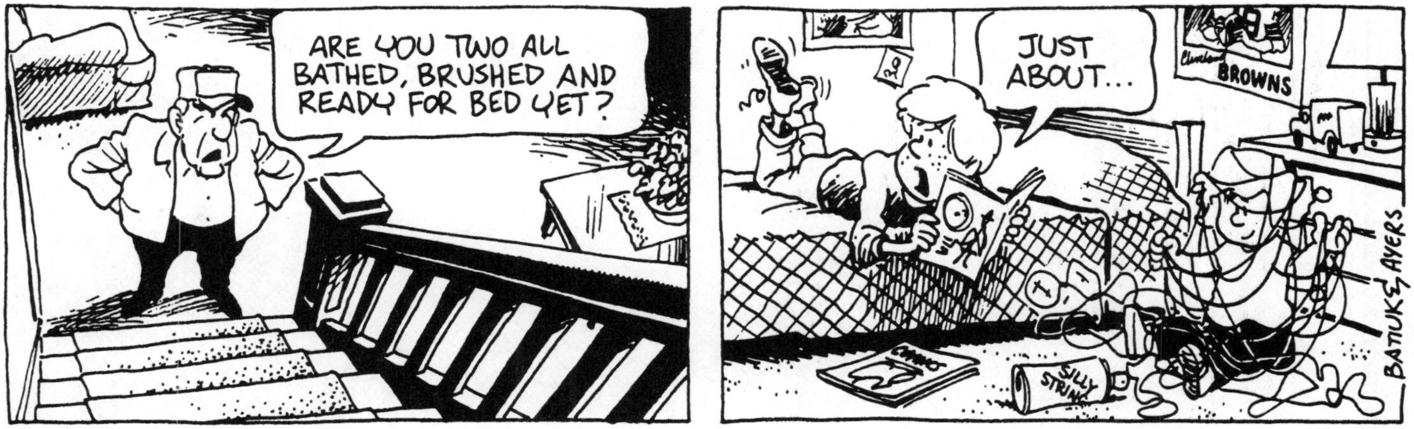
ARE YOU TWO ALL BATHED, BRUSHED AND READY FOR BED YET?
JUST ABOUT...
BROWNS
SILLY STRING
BATIUK & AYERS

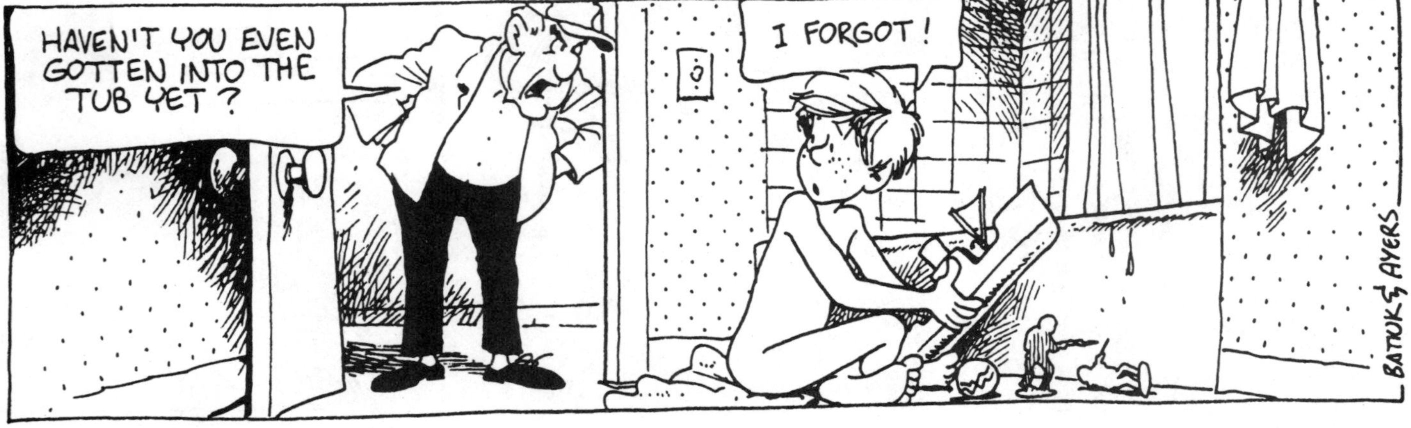
HAVEN'T YOU EVEN GOTTEN INTO THE TUB YET ?
I FORGOT !
BATIUK & AYERS

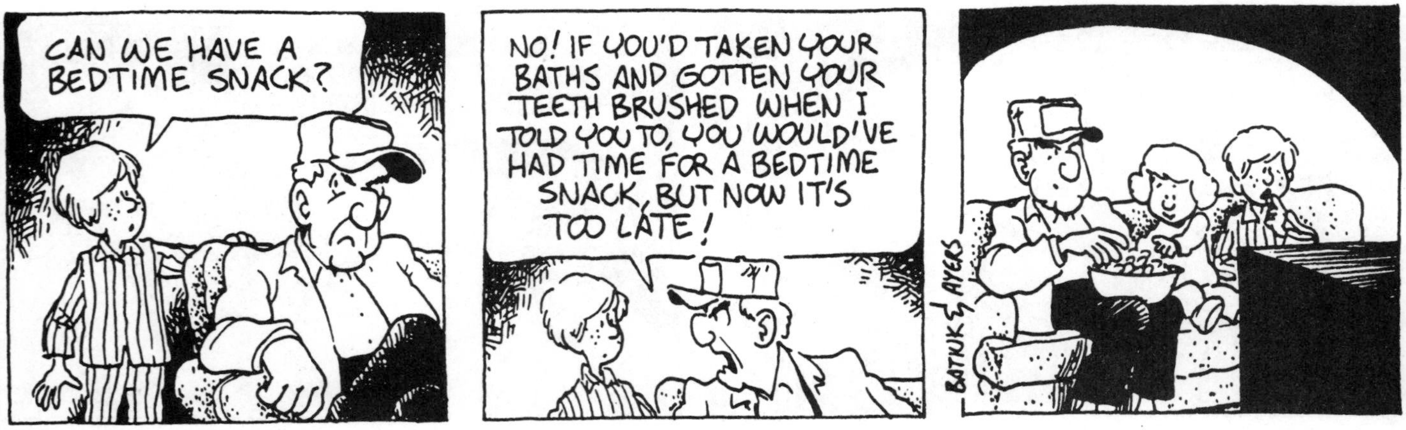
CAN WE HAVE A BEDTIME SNACK?
NO! IF YOU'D TAKEN YOUR BATHS AND GOTTEN YOUR TEETH BRUSHED WHEN I TOLD YOU TO, YOU WOULD'VE HAD TIME FOR A BEDTIME SNACK, BUT NOW IT'S TOO LATE !
BATIUK & AYERS

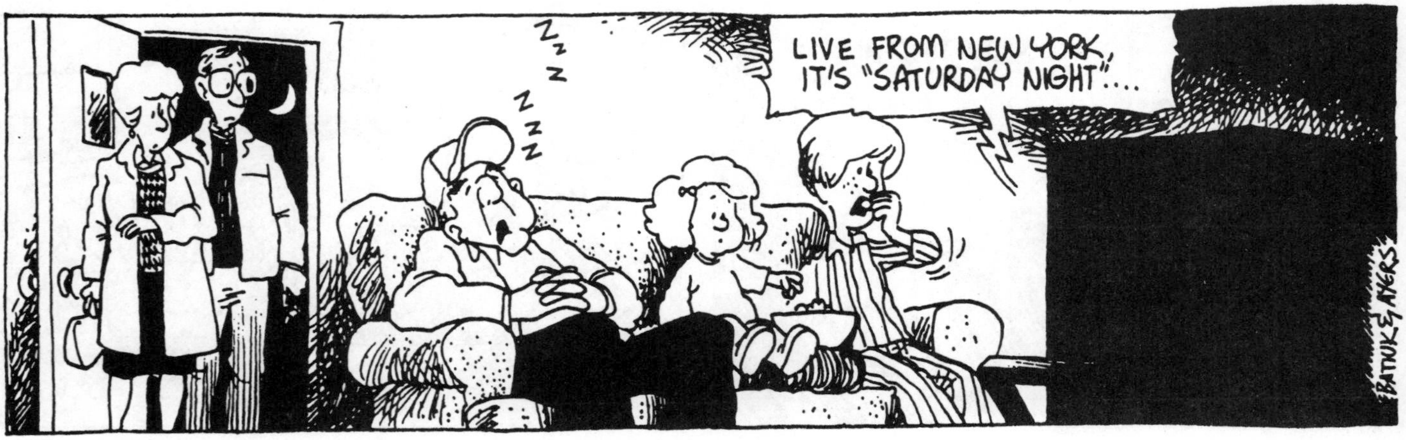
Z Z Z
Z Z Z
LIVE FROM NEW YORK, IT'S "SATURDAY NIGHT"....
BATIUK & AYERS

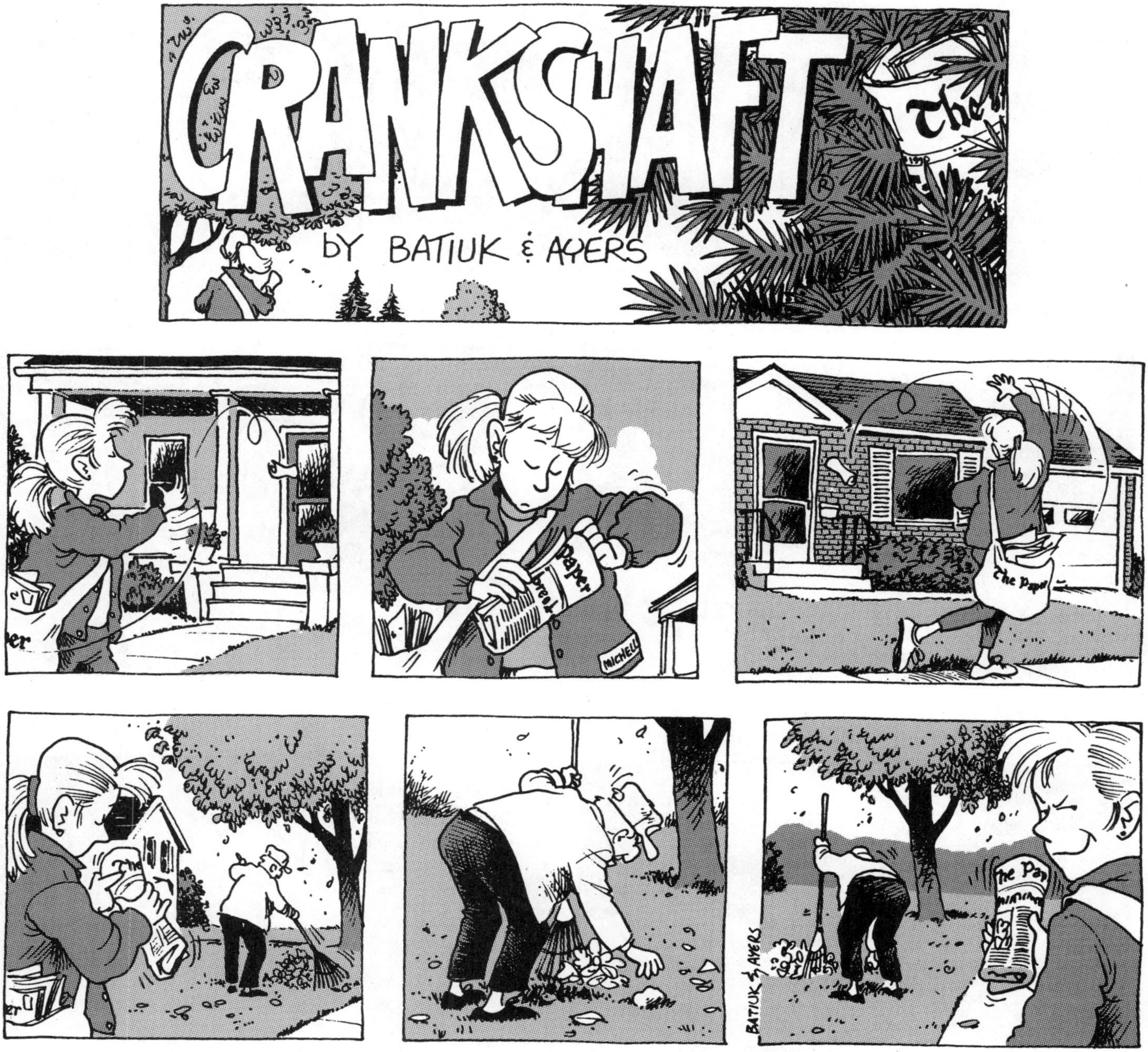
CRANKSHAFT
BY BATIUK & AYERS
The Paper
MICHELLE
BATIUK & AYERS

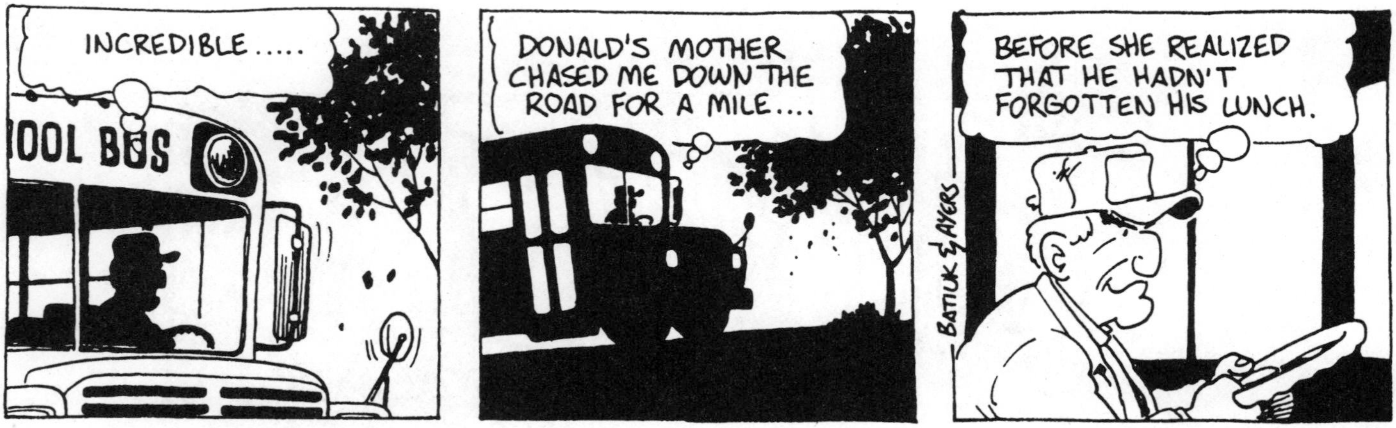
INCREDIBLE.....
DONALD'S MOTHER CHASED ME DOWN THE ROAD FOR A MILE....
BEFORE SHE REALIZED THAT HE HADN'T FORGOTTEN HIS LUNCH.
BATIUK & AYERS

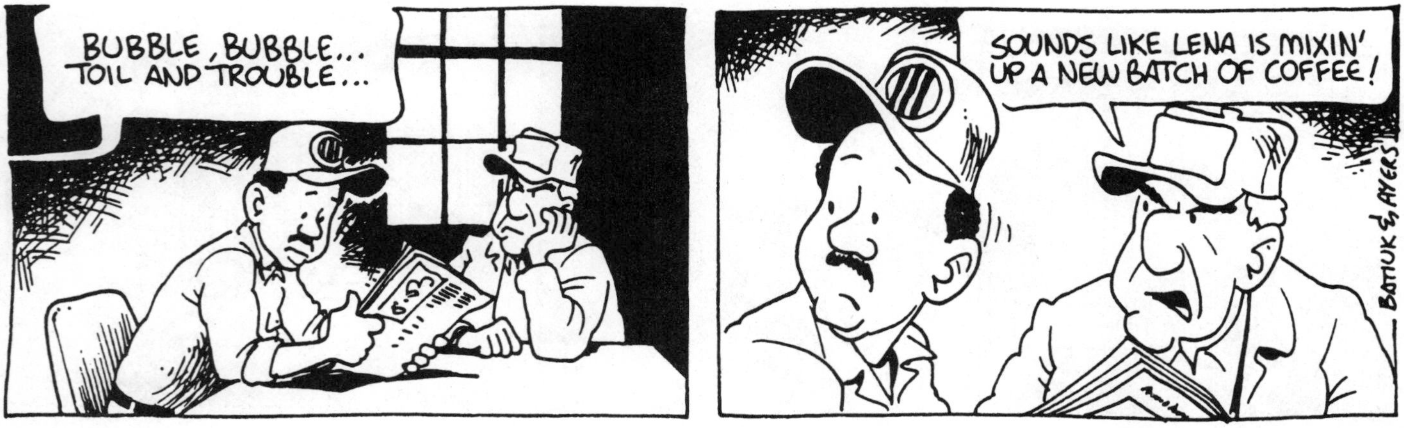
BUBBLE, BUBBLE... TOIL AND TROUBLE...
SOUNDS LIKE LENA IS MIXIN' UP A NEW BATCH OF COFFEE!
BATIUK & AYERS

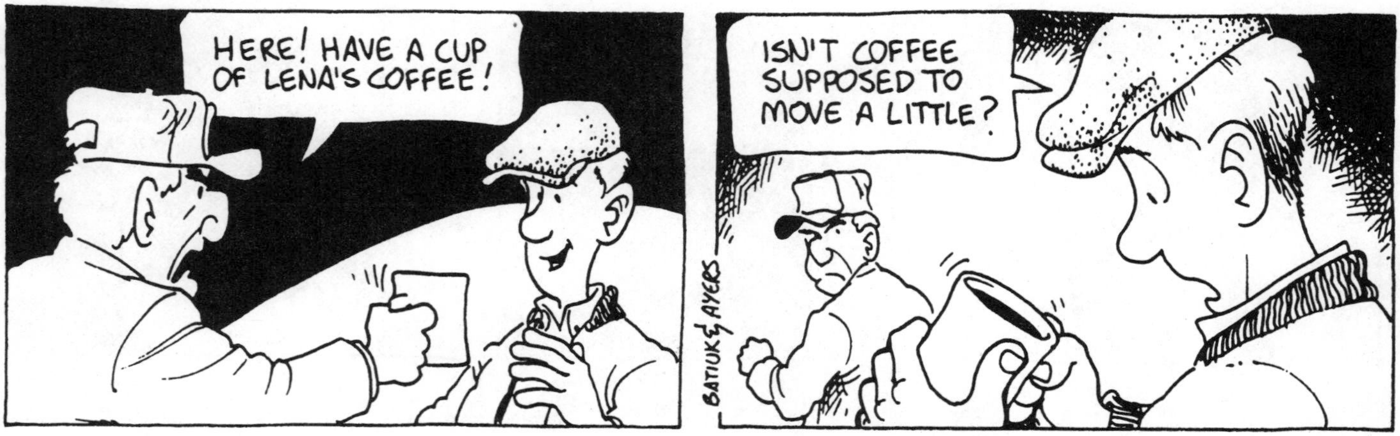
HERE! HAVE A CUP OF LENA'S COFFEE!
BATIUK & AYERS
ISN'T COFFEE SUPPOSED TO MOVE A LITTLE?

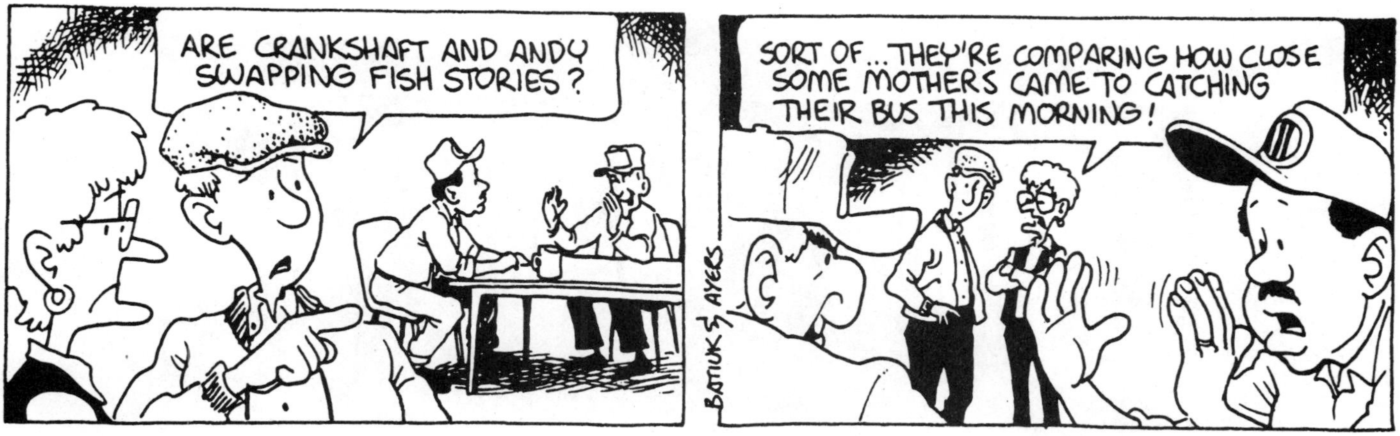
ARE CRANKSHAFT AND ANDY SWAPPING FISH STORIES?
BATIUK & AYERS
SORT OF... THEY'RE COMPARING HOW CLOSE SOME MOTHERS CAME TO CATCHING THEIR BUS THIS MORNING!

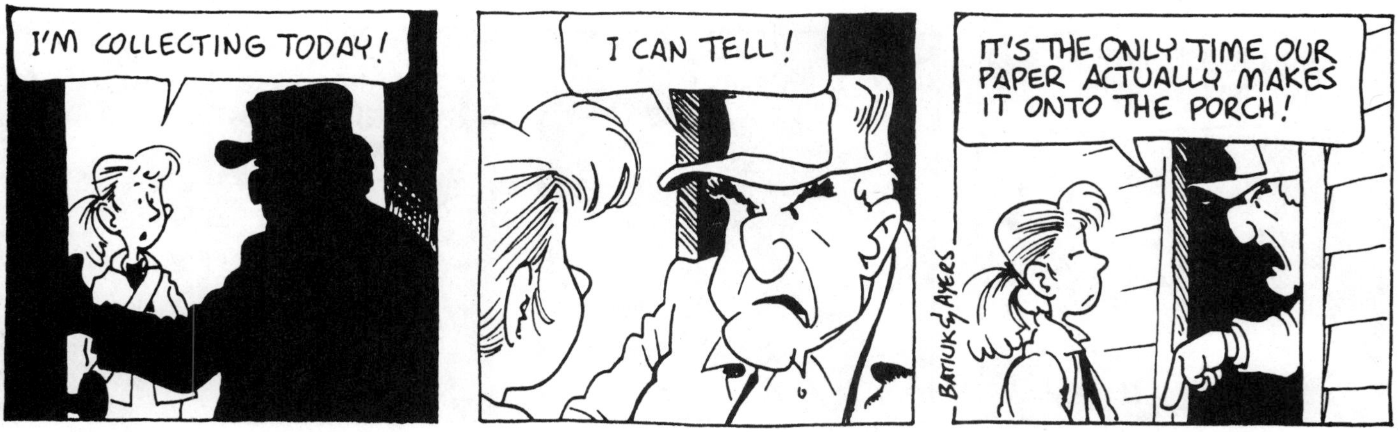
I'M COLLECTING TODAY!
I CAN TELL!
BATIUK & AYERS
IT'S THE ONLY TIME OUR PAPER ACTUALLY MAKES IT ONTO THE PORCH!

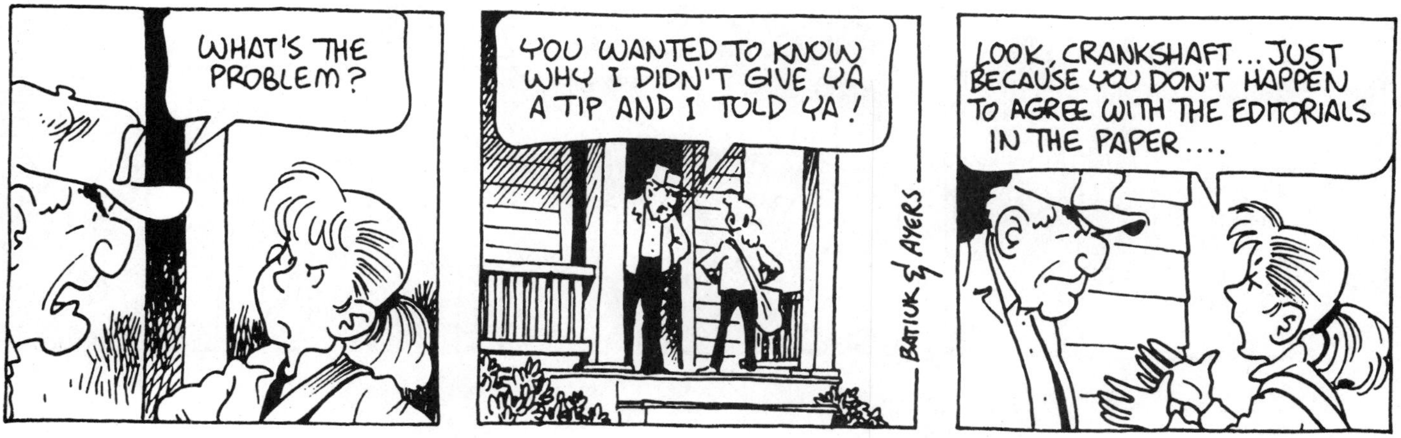
WHAT'S THE PROBLEM?
YOU WANTED TO KNOW WHY I DIDN'T GIVE YA A TIP AND I TOLD YA!
BATIUK & AYERS
LOOK, CRANKSHAFT... JUST BECAUSE YOU DON'T HAPPEN TO AGREE WITH THE EDITORIALS IN THE PAPER....

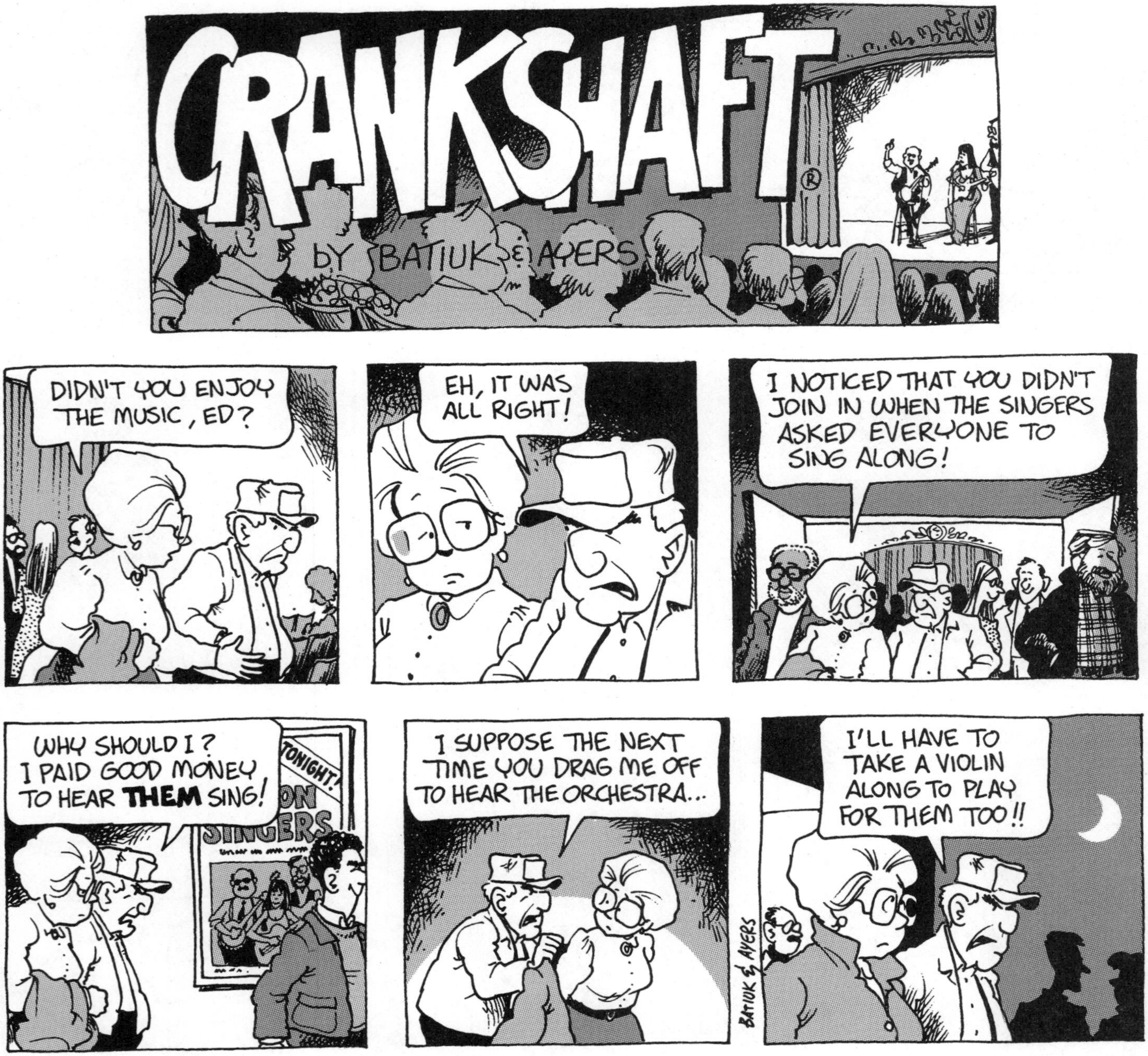
CRANKSHAFT
BY BATIUK & AYERS
DIDN'T YOU ENJOY THE MUSIC, ED?
EH, IT WAS ALL RIGHT!
I NOTICED THAT YOU DIDN'T JOIN IN WHEN THE SINGERS ASKED EVERYONE TO SING ALONG!
WHY SHOULD I? I PAID GOOD MONEY TO HEAR **THEM** SING!
TONIGHT!
SINGERS
I SUPPOSE THE NEXT TIME YOU DRAG ME OFF TO HEAR THE ORCHESTRA...
I'LL HAVE TO TAKE A VIOLIN ALONG TO PLAY FOR THEM TOO!!
BATIUK & AYERS